MARTY FELDMAN

The Biography of a Comedy Legend

ROBERT ROSS

TITAN BOOKS

"I have a Holy Trinity, which is Buster Keaton the Father, Stan Laurel the Son and Harpo Marx the Holy Ghost."

For Lauretta and Barry,
Marty's other halves.

CONTENTS

Acknowledgements

"Just before they made me, they broke the mould."

A salute to the inspirational comedy of Marty Feldman has been a pet project of mine for several years, so firstly many thanks to Adam Newell at Titan Books for sharing my passion for the subject. I am eternally grateful to the late Barry Took. After my first book was published in 1996 I got to know Barry well, meeting up at countless screenings, signings, Broadcasting House assignments and memorial services. These always ended with a pint or two in the nearest public house and, unless otherwise stated, Barry's memories come from those impromptu chats. I am also greatly indebted to Marty's friends, and fellow performers and writers Dick Clement OBE, Bernard Cribbins OBE, Barry Cryer OBE, Vera Day, Harry Fowler MBE, Ray Galton OBE, Derek Griffiths, Bill Harman, Terry Jones, Denis King, Ian La Frenais OBE, Warren Mitchell, Bill Oddie OBE, Michael Palin CBE, Alan Simpson OBE, Alan Spencer, Graham Stark, Sheila Steafel, Brian Trenchard-Smith, David Weddle, Ronnie Wolfe, Rose Wolfe and Nicholas Young for insightful memories and encouraging words. A very special thank you goes to Tim Brooke-Taylor OBE, who not only shared his many Marty stories but also made the initial connection with Tony Hobbs. Tony's preservation of the interview tapes conducted by his late father, Jack Hobbs, has proved invaluable. A writer, editor and jazz pianist, Jack Hobbs and Marty were kindred spirits of the Soho jazz spots and drinking clubs. As a result "The Marty

Tapes" are both relaxed and candid; as Marty says, "It's all very rambly. Just things that happened." If no source is given, Marty's comments come from these. I am hugely indebted to Marty's sister Pamela Franklin and his niece Suzannah Galland who provided me with wonderful memories and insights. Telephone conversations with them both have been hilarious, informative and heart-warming. They have also sifted through the family archive and provided some truly unique photographs for the book. Their support has been totally invaluable. I also thank Jeff Walden at the BBC Written Archives and Sarah Currant at the British Film Institute Library who was particularly enthused during many googly-eyed sessions. I gratefully acknowledge the kind permission of General Media Communications, Inc., a subsidiary of FriendFinder Networks, for the quotations from 'The *Penthouse* interview – Marty Feldman' by Richard Kleiner, published in the October, 1980 US Edition of *Penthouse* magazine. Many thanks to Larry Sutter for arranging this. Thanks to Sharon Gosling for her *Battlestar Galactica* connections. I thank those stalwart people Alan Coles, Henry Holland, Melanie Clark, Paul Cole, Dick Fiddy, Andrew Pixley and Bob Golding for being supportive. Love and thanks to Abby (Normal) Naylor. And lastly to my Mum, Eileen, who is invariably the first person to read anything I write. Thank you!

Prologue

"Good Lord Boyet, my beauty, though but mean,
Needs not the painted flourish of your praise:
Beauty is bought by judgement of the eye,
Not utter'd by base sale of chapmen's tongues"
William Shakespeare

"It doesn't bother me how they describe me. I'm me and that's it. I have to admit my face helps me in my work as a comedian. It used to worry me a bit when I was seventeen or eighteen, when I was trying to pull the birds. But now I don't worry any more."

Today if you mention the name Marty Feldman to even the most ardent of comedy fans, the chances are you will get one of two responses. Either an affectionate chuckle at those lop-sided eyes of his as he gallantly crusades through psychedelic sixties countryside, usually with a golf club firmly gripped in his hand; or, more likely, an affectionate chuckle at those lop-sided eyes of his as he channels old-school vaudeville within a vintage Universal horror setting, with a cry of "What hump?", or one of a dozen or so other deliciously quotable lines from Mel Brooks' *Young Frankenstein*.

For *Young Frankenstein* remains the most celebrated and accessible example of Marty's work: an international, block-busting comedy success that made him a Hollywood favourite at the age of forty.

"Marty was saddled with this title of clown," says his friend Bill Oddie.

"It was almost as if God had given him the make up and the costume: 'We'll have these googly eyes and the Harpo Marx hair and the slightly odd accent – a bit of cockney, a bit of Jewish. The slightly crooked nose. And you were made to play hunchbacks and other comedy weirdoes. There you go, son.' It was like this was the way he was delivered to the world. Like a clown in kit form."[1]

Marty was painfully conscious that his features shaped his life: "I have always been idiosyncratic and something of an aberration," he said. "I've always been treated as a freak anyway, and in a sense I am. I've always felt like an alien who never belonged anywhere: just a temporary member of the human race."[2]

But for Marty, despite the international success of *Young Frankenstein*, life didn't begin at forty. Although he had reached fulfilment as a film star and his future in Hollywood looked guaranteed, never again was he as relaxed, creative, popular or just plain likeable on screen. Bitter clashes with studio executives and an endearing refusal to compromise his integrity saw his most personal projects scuppered by corporate politics. Almost as soon as he tasted fame in America he began missing the "hungry" years in England. But not in that glorious, all-conquering winter of 1974.

Marty had made it. This was the pinnacle he had worked so hard to achieve. "I'm driven," he said. "The impulsion is from behind me. I go where that takes me and it takes me to some strange places!" As the California sunshine shone and the palm trees swayed, an endless line of media interviewers clamoured for his thoughts on the film industry and life in general; not that Hollywood was that interested in life in general. Still, throughout it all, Marty doggedly retained his Englishness. Talking to the *Daily Express* Hollywood reporter, Ivor Davis, Marty sported his prized Chelsea football shirt – once worn by Charlie Cooke circa 1970[3] – and his favourite pair of blue jeans. He had upped sticks from Hampstead to Hollywood simply to be where the film industry was but, typically, he didn't feel at home in either place. He was "a martian – like most comics."[4] Even his dream destination of Hollywood was an empty sham. His home in the Beverly Hills was rented and rumours of a nod from the

Academy for his iconic performance as Igor came to nought. He wasn't even nominated.[5]

Still, he was in Hollywood and that wasn't all bad. It was a long way from the thankless slog around British variety theatres as part of Morris, Marty and Mitch. In 1974 he was more likely to be spotted at the Hollywood Bowl than the Chiswick Empire. His friends and colleagues were the likes of Dean Martin, Orson Welles and Groucho Marx rather than bottom of the bill variety turns.

But Marty retained his affection for his early days. That far-off time when a combined passion for jazz and silent comedy propelled him through a myriad of dead-end jobs and half-realised ambitions. He was most content in his favourite London haunt, Ronnie Scott's jazz club, or as Tim Brooke-Taylor says: "Marty would be at his happiest in a Paris café, smoking and talking about the latest French film or obscure jazz artist."[6]

As he sipped fruity-flavoured alcohol and mapped out his first big solo Hollywood project, Marty could look back on a twenty-year long stint of writing comedy. Throughout the 1950s he had written solid situation comedy and radio variety for the big names of the day. He had brought fresh blood to ITV's flagship show *The Army Game* and put words into the wooden mouth of Peter Brough's badly behaved ventriloquist dummy Archie Andrews.

Family-geared entertainment for the masses, but with Marty's jet-black comic imagination in the mix, a deceptively mild show could conceal sharp barbs of satire and surrealism. This taste for, in effect, bucking the trend of British comedy found its longest-lasting and most potent home in BBC Radio's *Round the Horne*. One of the four cornerstones of radio humour, the show was a Trojan horse of smut, satire and silliness. The English Sunday lunchtime was never quite the same again.

But Marty was nobody's fool. He knew that success in England meant very little to the majority of his American audience. Indeed, success as a scriptwriter didn't mean all that much to audiences in England either. Rather than being famous for over a decade, he was simply known; and then only by a relatively select few. He was known as the most inventive, prolific and speediest scriptwriter in the business. His sharp mind and world-weariness captured within those scripts of his. An off-kilter squint at life wrapped in cosy familiarity.

In America, the lengthy list of writers on a television show would whiz past your eyes so fast no one was known except the star of the show. Woody Allen and Neil Simon may have been slaving away behind the scenes but Sid Caesar was the national treasure. It was only when Marty went out on a limb and in front of the cameras that audiences sat up and took notice. Only when colour was added to the mix would American stations begin to bring Marty's outlandish blend of slapstick and surrealism to an even wider audience. Every decade or so America would pick up an English performer and embrace him. They would almost always become a sideshow freak. The English comic tempted over from his homeland to sit in captivity in Hollywood and entertain studio bosses with their funny accent and outmoded good manners. In effect it was America poking him with a stick and making him dance. However, Marty was only going to dance to his own tune.

It was an approach to comedy that Marty had firmly established during a fairly short period at the BBC. Pied Piper-like, he had a choice collection of writers and stooges who trailed after him wherever he wanted them to go. With his affable charm, softly spoken determination and keen perfectionism he found his niche on British television. Here was a performer unique in every sense of the word. His face was instantly recognisable, his comedy was deeply rooted in the past while continually taking huge strides into the future, and he was a star personality and performer who retained his dignity and humility.

In the late 1960s it was the coolest thing in the world to be English. Marty was at the epicentre of fashion, art, music and politics. He was a satirical hippie with mad hair, mad eyes and a heart full of justice for his fellow man. He was a guru for the comedy children of the revolution.

Michael Palin recalls "being in awe of Marty. He seemed so wise and assured at what he was doing."[7] Marty was perfectly suited to the surreal here and now of London in the late 1960s. He could wear a Flower Power T-shirt or a floral tie and make it look as "in" and "groovy" as John Lennon could. *At Last the 1948 Show*, the pioneering TV sketch series that made his name, may have been the immediate jump-lead to *Monty Python's Flying Circus* and *The Goodies* but it was Marty and Marty alone who was propelled to almost instant solo stardom.

His name was big enough to put into the title of a television hit. Indeed, his finest work with the BBC was enjoyed under the simple, ego-pleasing title of *Marty*. Skilfully and lovingly combining the visual dexterity of Buster Keaton with the insane babble of Spike Milligan, Marty became a national figure of some clout and importance. More than just a comedian, he was a symbol for the swinging sixties movement of expression and self-censorship. As much a part of the in-crowd as Keith Richards, David Hockney and Terence Stamp, Marty would wear the latest fashion, support the latest campaign and comment on the latest world events.

He gave evidence for the defence at the *Oz* magazine decency trial at the Old Bailey and even recorded his own hit album of comedy songs. It was hardly *Abbey Road*, but still! Marty was the hip comedian. One of the beautiful people.

He could even charm the hard-bitten press. "What really amazed me about Marty," wrote Lynn Barber of *Petticoat*, "was how soft-centred he is. His 'malicious dwarf' image on telly makes him seem hard and unsentimental, but when he talks he reveals his inner warmth. Unlike some showbiz people who utter a lot of heart-warming gush on stage, but would really boot their grandmother downstairs at the drop of a five pound contract – Marty's sincerity is the genuine article."

In some ways it must have seemed a lifetime away as Marty sat discussing his Igor character in *Young Frankenstein*. The classic television he had produced during the late 1960s and early 1970s was still vibrant and fresh in the States. Indeed, he would often recreate vintage material for American television variety spots. But in England he was already being thought of as yesterday's man. The British audiences loved success, of course, but weren't that keen on huge, American-sized success. There was always that danger that he would make a name for himself in Hollywood and never come back. As Marty's own big film projects later crashed and burned and his presence on English television came to a grinding halt, the major insecurities started to emerge. For a performer who lived on his nerves, this was disastrous for Marty. He was the personification of the neurotic, tortured artist. "Comedy performing, or for me anyway, is a kind of neurosis which I exploit," he said. "You plagiarise your inadequacies, your hang ups, and you make comic capital out of them."[8]

But success on British television had just been a stepping-stone to success in American films. This wasn't an arrogant attitude on Marty's part, it was simply what he wanted. Or, as regular writing partner Barry Took noted, "what he thought he wanted. It was Marty's dream to be making his own starring vehicles in Hollywood. He thought it would be just like the Golden Age of his heroes like Buster Keaton, Harold Lloyd and Laurel and Hardy. But of course it wasn't. Hollywood in the 1970s was far, far different from what it had been fifty years earlier. It had always been a business but when Marty was making his films the business aspect was all-consuming. Keaton worked bloody hard but he had fun on set. One got the impression that Marty's Hollywood experience was a pretty depressing one."[9]

Throughout the wild eighteen months that saw him burn brightest in Britain, Marty had become the most talked about and influential comedian in the country. His family life was his rock and his artistic passion was comedy. As long as there was room for jazz and cigarettes as well he was a very contented man indeed. His ego, though bloated by success, was never completely inflated.

In America, a few remnants of colour television insanity from Hollywood and a much-loved and influential turn for Mel Brooks wasn't enough to sustain him. His subsequent collaborations with Gene Wilder and Mel Brooks would never equal the razor-sharp, freewheeling, unbridled joy of *Young Frankenstein*. His own writing and directing projects would turn into a living hell.

But that winter of 1974 must have been wonderful. An international star in a major box-office hit, Marty was fit, funny and forty. If the sun could have slowly sunk in the west and the end credits had rolled there and then, it would have been the perfect Hollywood ending. But, alas, that doesn't happen: particularly not in Hollywood.

Chapter One

"Money can't buy poverty."

Ever since Marty Feldman's face became public property in the swinging sixties, a thousand and one journalists have started interviews and appraisals with a pondering on that strange, pop-eyed child from London's East Ham. Even when Marty was casting his directorial debut, *The Last Remake of Beau Geste*, and required a junior version of himself, he embraced the myth and tracked down a pop-eyed youth.[1]

In actual fact, when Marty first appeared, pink and soft and kicking and screaming, on 8th July 1934 he was a perfectly ordinary baby; angelic almost. He would pull interviewers' legs and convince them that he was adorable. "As a child, I was really quite beautiful – sort of a male Shirley Temple."[2] "A sort of Gothic Shirley Temple. A Jewish Shirley Temple."[3] Looking at baby photographs of Marty you can see his point. Certainly the ringlets were in the right place. "I didn't always look like this," he would protest. "My mother tells me I was a very pretty baby with a little snub nose."[4] Even so, he would often later readily dismiss 1934 as "a bad year, nothing else happened."

Martin Alan Feldman was a product of an honest East End upbringing. A melting pot of cultures and attitudes that instilled in him the value of money, the pain of not having much of it and the heart-pounding thrill of a colourful, cosmopolitan lifestyle. But from the very outset there was something of the outsider about him.

Marty's Jewish emigrant parents had gratefully settled in London's Canning Town after journeying from their native Kiev in the Ukrainian Soviet Socialist Republic. "It's a very stunted family tree," he said. "It only goes back one generation. Even now I'm not too sure of it. But they were just peasants. I'd liked to have found someone spectacular in my past. I'd like to find one lovely idiot. I'd like a homicidal maniac as an ancestor. I wish I were related to Jack the Ripper. We can't trace our madness back. The royal family know they're mad, they're lucky. How lovely to know you've been potty. Authentic lunatics. I like lunatics. I hate eccentrics. My grandfather on my father's side aspired to be an artist, he re-touched photographs and called himself a painter but before that they were boring peasants, so I have to generate my own lunacy." The past was meaningless to Marty: "A horse with blinkers on can't see what's going on either side, he can just see where he's going. I can't even see where I'm going. I can just see where I am!" Although at least he felt wanted. At first, at least. "My father and mother married when they were both sixteen and I came along when they were twenty-one," he explained. "They had five years to think about it, so they obviously knew what they were doing when they produced me."[5]

He would always display a charming, lyrical delight in his lot. He could fall into despair, anger or a heady mixture of both but, as a rule, his view on life was always positive: "When I was about two years old, I was *so* handsome," he would say.[6]

Marty was an optimist, a gentle man and a cheerful Artful Dodger. He certainly needed to be. His childhood was a poor but happy one in which material things weren't really that important. A family could get by simply by being a family. "I never suffered from poverty," Marty remembered, "although our environment was far from affluent." However, like Charlie Chaplin, Marty's poor beginnings would stay with him throughout his life. Fame was important, fortune even more so, for Marty had experience of being at the bottom of the heap and he wasn't planning on going back there. Still, if his parents could survive a Russian winter they could certainly survive the East End on a budget. Even when their family was extended to include a new, bouncing baby sister for Marty, namely Pamela, at the end of 1940. "He was a lovely brother," she remembers. "There was nearly seven years difference between us so he could always get his own way with me. He would hold me over the banisters at home if I didn't do what he wanted! I would spend time with my friends around Golders Green and he would pop down to make fun of us. He was madcap, even then."[7]

"My parents were poor," Marty said. "They were always slipping out of digs because they couldn't pay the rent. But you never think you are poor when you are a kid. No one ever says there is nothing for you to eat tonight. You just don't know that your folks haven't eaten."[8]

Marty lived through it happily, simply because he didn't know or expect anything better. Years later, surrounded by the wealth that Hollywood had given him, Marty could be more damning of his humble upbringing: "It's comparable to the East Bronx in New York or New York's Lower East Side of thirty-five years ago," he reflected. "The Jews who got on a boat and left Russia or Poland ended up either in the East End of London or in New York. It was a matter of which boat got out first."[9]

In actual fact, the full extent of Marty's poverty-stricken childhood fully depends on which account you believe. During his most successful period in Hollywood Marty himself endorsed the fact that his anxiety "likely derives from a Dickensian youth in London's East End, the son of a Russian immigrant."[10] Writing shortly after Marty's death, Barry Took remembered the facts slightly differently. "Marty was born to a moderately well-to-do Jewish family in London's East End."

Marty certainly had an affinity with New York. Particularly the jazz tradition. "I've been fiddling with music ever since the age of four," he said. "Music informs everything that I do. I'm audibly orientated."

Although life in Canning Town in the 1930s was scarcely comparable to the Bowery, it certainly stimulated him audibly. Unfortunately, the sounds were going to get much louder. Death and destruction was just around the corner for hard-bitten Londoners. When the war in Europe erupted in the autumn of 1939 the conflict might as well have been on another planet, but by 1940 the 'phoney war' was over and the East End was a prime target. The narrow streets and bustling marketplaces that had become Marty's playground were now a "waste-land". Barry Took asserted that: "When he was six years old the war came and Feldman senior departed for the RAF, and Marty and his younger sister, Pamela, were left in the sole charge of their deep-voiced, super-competent mother."[11] In fact, it was soon after his father's departure that the young Marty was evacuated to live with a family near Nottingham. Along with millions of other threatened Londoners, he discovered a new, fresh, open-air life in the countryside. Peace and quiet replaced the drone of bombers and the yell of street-vendors. Muddy ditches and haylofts replaced craters and shelters as the setting for his play. "I used to put on a one-man show for the local kids," he remembered. "Chasing a butterfly and falling over, doing whatever I felt like. It made them laugh." The experience would change his life. For the first time he actually realised where his food was coming from. A salt beef sandwich in the East End was one thing but when you had been patting the head of a friendly, dewy-eyed creature the day before you sat down to eat well-done, severed portions of it, that was something else entirely. "I realised that I was eating something that had been running round happily the day before," he said. "It seemed immoral." That attitude didn't falter. At that young, impressionable age, Marty became a vegetarian, for good.

He was almost misty-eyed when recounting that pivotal moment for Dutch television in 1977. His vegetarian lifestyle was completely an issue of morals, not health: "It has to do with... when I was a child," he revealed. "I was brought up in the slums of London, in the city, and in the city as a child you don't see animals except cats, dogs, pigeons, horses. None of which you eat. When the war came I was evacuated into the country onto a farm and I got to play with the animals and one day George the rabbit was George, lunch."

As usual with Marty, his persona as a comedian with the laughter-inducing features meant that almost everything he uttered was greeted with a snigger. The studio audience in 1977 was no exception. He looked hurt and rather resentful but kept his focus and continued: "Really. And that was the end of it. I don't mean it to be a joke. It's a joke now. It's a bitter joke to me but it was traumatic as a kid."[12]

In fact, Marty had had his stomach turned off meat from an even earlier age, when his mother would force feed him Jewish staples of chopped liver and chicken as a child. As an adult he lived on a diet of eggs, salads, vegetables, spaghetti, bread, coffee and cigarettes. Even if the smallest bit of meat got in to his food he would turn green and throw up.[13] Barry Took maintained there was a more rudimentary reason for Marty's lifelong commitment to vegetarianism: "Later Marty was sent to a 'Dotheboys Hall' sort of boarding school, and his loathing for the food they served there was the start of a lifelong adherence to vegetarianism."[14]

However, Took did remark that he found Marty's commitment to vegetarianism later became variable to say the least. "We would go abroad on working holidays together," he said. "Marty would try bits of the local cuisine. He was a geographical vegetarian. The further away we were from London, the more meat he would eat!"

School life had made Marty's eating regime extremely difficult: "It was hard. At mealtimes, we weren't allowed to leave the table at school until our plate was clean. Meat was always served so I spent most of the time stuffing my pockets with meat in order to smuggle it out of the building. I felt like I was digging a tunnel in a prisoner-of-war camp!" It may have been one life lesson that Marty never forgot but his formal education was a mess, and not simply because of the upheaval caused by world events. After the conflict Marty had returned to the trams-and-craters life in London's East End. The family had survived the war and that post-war austerity that affected so many seemingly passed the Feldman clan by. In truth, they couldn't sink much lower than they had, but Marty's father had invested cleverly. A pushcart peddler made good, he had taken charge of a dressmaker's and was making a real success of the business. So much so that he decided to give his son the head start he hadn't had himself. As a result Marty single-handedly took on the British education system. "He put me into one school after the other," recalled Marty ruefully. "All over the country. I was thrown out of a few and left others." And it wasn't just the food that turned Marty's stomach. Whether it was Heathcote School in Danbury or an Orthodox Jewish public school, no educational establishment could keep him interested for long. "I ran away from one harsh boarding school three times. The fourth time they expelled me.

That was what I was trying to tell them in the beginning: that I didn't want to go to their school. But they kept bringing me back and beating me, bringing me back and beating me again."[15] Marty's disjointed education also kept him apart from his sibling for much of the time: "I know he was very upset to be sent away to boarding school in Brighton," says his sister Pamela Franklin. "It wasn't that long after I was born and he always thought it was because of me. It wasn't, of course. It's just what people did in those days. He was a bit angry about that. Between the time he was aged eight and eleven we didn't see much of each other at all."

An inattentive and obstinate pupil, his academic prowess ranged from ninety per cent in an English test to a big fat zero in Mathematics.[16] Despite this early aptitude for the written word, typically the British educational system still penalised the young Marty: "I used to write a lot of poetry. I was first punished for writing at the age of eleven. My school accused me of copying a poem I wrote. It wasn't very good, but it scanned and rhymed, and it might have come out of a book of children's verse or something. They said I wouldn't be punished if I admitted I copied it. I said, 'But I did write it,' and so I got punished for writing. That may have gotten me on to it. The masochist in me may have said, 'Hey! People punish you for writing – I'll be a writer!' So I started writing then." Marty's youthful imagination and delight in baiting authority led to a passion for fiction, even within his regimented homework assignments: "Writing came easy for me," he explained. "I'd be asked to write an essay on what I did on my half-day's vacation. Well, I didn't do anything interesting. So I just filled the whole exercise book with a story that I'd made up – a child's novel, set during the war, in which I parachuted into occupied France and captured a German general and brought him back. I filled the whole fucking exercise book with this. Again I was punished. They said, 'That isn't what you did.' And I said, 'No, but what I did was boring.'"[17]

Marty's features were also getting the battle scars that would make his fortune: "My face reflects the sum total of the disasters of my life," he said. "My eyes are the product of a thyroid condition caused by an accident when somebody stuck a pencil in one eye when I was a boy,"[18] and "I got hit with a cricket ball, and some bones were re-arranged."[19]

His fragmented school days also taught him a vivid life lesson: self-preservation: "When you are small and at school you have to move fast. I had to get the first punch in and then run like hell because if the guy could have caught up with me he would have killed me."[20] A quick wit also paid dividends in this: "You'll find that most comics are small and physically strange-looking," he said. "If you're small and funny-looking and you don't have great scholastic genius – which I certainly didn't have – you retreat to the position of comic. It's the only possible position you can take and survive among your peers. Unless you're great at sports. At sports I was like I am at drums – enthusiastic but not talented."[21] He did, somehow, pass his eleven plus exam in spite of rather than because of his teacher. "There were good teachers," he admitted. One in particular greatly encouraged his love of art and music. "But I know that many of the teachers that taught me were ill-equipped. Let alone to teach but to be outside of jails. They were lucky criminals who had never been caught. They were con men and bullies and all kinds of villains."

His film publicity blurb in the 1970s would reveal that Marty had become "hooked on comedy" during this time, whether through simple survival in various school playgrounds or burgeoning interest in amateur dramatics. But comedy was actually more of an escape from formal education. Marty would as often as not skip lesson after lesson in order to sneak into his local cinema to see the films of his Hollywood-based idols: the Marx Brothers, Laurel and Hardy, Red Skelton, Danny Kaye. Even the ultra-rare opportunity to see Buster Keaton in full flow.

His love of comedy took him in directions far beyond the educational system he found himself trapped in, including his first attempt at being a stand-up comedian at the age of twelve: "I'd been to see Danny Kaye at the Palladium. Having seen Danny Kaye I thought what I had to do is quite simple. I have to sit on the edge of the stage and talk to the audience with a cigarette in my hand. I stole jokes from everybody. It was an amalgam from jokes I had nicked from Max Miller, Danny Kaye, Jack Carson, Mickey Rooney; people I had seen on stage. I performed them once at a Bar Mitzvah for pocket money. I didn't see anything incongruous in a twelve year old smoking a cigarette and talking about my wife: 'Now she's a lovely woman, let me tell you about the kids...' I couldn't understand why they got annoyed with me!"

However, arguably his most prized and inspirational possession was a paperback copy of scripts from *Take It From Here*, a pioneering BBC radio comedy penned by the architects of the form, Denis Norden and Frank Muir, whom Marty would cite as influences throughout his career. Tellingly, his heroes were often writers first and foremost. He considered himself privileged to be counted within their number. Indeed, as a teenager and perhaps in petulant reaction to his school's accusation of cribbing, Marty sat himself down and scripted his own episodes of *Take It From Here*.

"When I first started writing humour, I decided I would read everything I could on it to find out what I was doing. And that will totally destroy you. You read all these different theories of humour, and they all contradict each other... It's all theory. No good. Books and theories about humour have rarely been written by people who practice it. Freud had theories of humour. Whether one questions those theories or not, I do question the standard of the jokes he quotes – they're pretty bad. Yes, they'll all work, but so will their opposites. None of them will define humour... All of the theories about humour are true to an extent, but then there's a greater truth than that, and I don't know what it is. There's a kind of Zen of humour, and if somebody is going to write it, then they'll have to write it from the Zen point of view. Except that Zen is noticeably humour-less – it really is."[22] Marty's was an obsessed and precocious talent.

A 1970 profile of Marty by John Hall noted: "As a result of this early specialisation Feldman never made the science sixth. In fact he never managed to stay in one school for very long, and notched up twelve alma maters before his fifteenth birthday. It is his proud boast that he has been kicked out of some of the worst schools in London."[23] This was no myth either. Marty's inability to follow the rules resulted in monthly upheavals to yet another leaky fountain of knowledge.

"I have been expelled a few times," he remembered, "but many times it was suggested that it would be a good idea if my parents didn't bring me back next term. I could never resist a dare. I would be ringing the bell and a teacher came in to class and said if you think that's clever go and ring it outside the headmaster's door. I knew that was exactly what I had to do. I had to pick up that big bloody bell, go and stand outside the headmaster's door and ring it as hard as I knew how. The school did come pouring out. I did get whacked. There's this kind of awful foreknowledge of what I do. It's going to work out to be a disaster and yet I kind of commit to the disaster. Actually, I think I ought to be declared a disaster area."

This lifelong feeling of alienation had stemmed from his fraught school days. "That goes back to being the only Jew in my class, being the alien," he said. "That's how I was treated. I should have been issued a green card then. When they had prayers, I was sent outside. I wasn't allowed to be there for prayers. They gave me extra maths. That's obviously how they thought of their religion – it was as complicated and as dull as maths. That's the English attitude towards Protestantism: cold showers and mathematics. It's totally sexless. Cold. The British produced a great number of mass murderers, you know? England and Germany. Passionless mass murderers. Little bank clerks. My neighbourhood doctor. They all have sort of bald, bony heads and wear pebbledash lenses and raincoats. You find out that nice little guy in fact slaughtered a hundred people and ate them or something. I think it has a lot to do with Protestant repression."

At first he was an enforced and devout follower of the Jewish faith: "I got Bar Mitzvahed, the whole thing. I was very good. I learned Hebrew. I was very attracted to Judaism, to the ritualism, the theatre of Judaism. Like Catholics. They do it even better – it's grand opera. The same country that produced Verdi produced Roman Catholicism. The costumes and the lighting are the same. I suppose some of my early feelings towards theatre were conditioned by going to synagogue and by the Hasidim who lived in the neighbourhood. They were always singing and playing the violins. They were like Sufis to me. I'm still attracted to Hasidim. I love them, although I'm no longer a Jew in any religious sense, and there is no other sense in which you can be one. It's a love of magic that Jews have. Also, a natural sense of money! Jews are storytellers, too. I can't think of White Anglo-Saxon Protestant storytellers that would go from village to village, telling the legends of the people, like the Jewish storytellers in the

shtetls."²⁴ "My parents were very religious, very orthodox," says Pamela
Franklin. "When Marty was young he too was very orthodox. He went
to the synagogue regularly with me every week on a Saturday. I vividly
remember walking with him to the temple. We also attended Hebrew
studies on Sundays. As he got older he became less and less interested. He
was obsessed about getting into show business."

In order to escape the sense of alienation of being a Jew in England
during the Second World War, Marty's parents took a drastic step,
according to Barry Took: "Around this time the family changed its name
– from what I don't remember – to Feldman, a change which upset the
sensitive Marty. It seemed to him like the loss of identity. Later came the
bourgeois family home in North Finchley, and time spent at a sedate north
London grammar school, Woodhouse, which contrived to push [him]
into the tame kind of rebellion that was commonplace among middle-
class youths in the late forties and early fifties."²⁵ As Marty testified:
"There's a lot of anarchy in my comedy."²⁶

This anarchy fully erupted during his school days. "I didn't do Bible
class because I was a Jew," he remembered. "I used to get annoyed about
this and get a Bible and put graffiti all over it. Some awful copperplate
saint; some androgynous creature with his hand out pointing the way in
an awful school Bible. I drew glasses and buckteeth and a moustache, and
they didn't like that. Again I got whacked for it."

Marty's personal rebellion would be far less pedestrian than most,
but the continual attempt on his parents' part to blur their Jewish roots
rankled. It seems to coincide with his father growing prosperous. This
attitude just made the young Marty even more cynical. "Jesus was Jewish,
I suppose," he said, "[but] he's not the kind of Jew who would be accepted
by the Hampstead Garden Suburb. He wasn't a lawyer or a doctor or the
kind of Jew my parents would have accepted. He was merely a saviour,
which wasn't a professional. You couldn't have a brass plate."

Marty's niece Suzannah Galland says, "My uncle loved his father very
much. My grandfather Myer was a very religious man and a very funny
man, so although they didn't play games Marty did grow up with humour.
My grandfather did very well in business. He had a string of beautiful

models modelling gowns for his fashion house. He would eventually become so successful that he could afford to buy himself a Bentley, but it was bang in the middle of a social change and Marty wanted to be part of the revolution."[27]

As his parents became more affluent, Marty simply became more rebellious. He was completely disinterested in money and position: "By the time I was old enough to realise, we were doing OK." It was too late for obedience. "Most comedians are either lazy or inefficient. By being the jester of the class I found I could get out of work at school. By doing that I found I didn't have to compete. You know how competitive the school thing is. I'm basically non-competitive so I just sat there and went ya-boo-sucks."[28]

Besides, Marty had long ago found his passion in life: jazz. With just two formal trumpet lessons he, once more, rejected education and taught himself: "I had a trumpet case and I had a bottle of gin. I hated gin. In fact it used to make me puke. But I used to resolutely drink it because I had read [pioneering jazz cornetist] Bix Beiderbecke used to drink gin. By some process of alcoholic osmosis, by the presence of a bottle of gin in my case, [I thought it] might turn me in to Bix Beiderbecke. I was the youngest bandleader in England. I had Marty's Gin Bottle Seven. I wanted to have a treasured destiny at the age of fourteen. By the age of fifteen I had realised I didn't have a treasured destiny, I only had a slapstick now. I've lived in that ever since."

Jazz music was hardly the image his parents wanted. Particularly not when the lifestyle invaded their peaceful home: "One night I brought a lot of people back to this house; a load of musicians. A kind of orgy took place in this suburban house and my parents came home and found it. The police were called because a bird fell out of bed onto a broken glass. There was blood everywhere. It was like cleaning up after a murder. My parents came home in the middle of all this and said: 'These are your friends? These people with beards and bare feet who play trumpets and take drugs and drink!' I said: 'Yes, they are!' They said: 'You're giving us a bad name in the neighbourhood!' So I left home. I left at my and their own volition. I had a choice [but] I knew that I could not go back to that home as long as I was with these people and I felt more at home with these people than I did with the suburban community."

As throughout his life, Marty gravitated towards Soho and the jazz clubs, cafés and pubs that bred rebellion and the community of skippers: the waifs and strays who became his closest friends. "I'd built a house from deckchairs in Green Park. We would make a house, me and the bums that were with us – me and my trumpet. We would sleep in this tent-like little house made of deckchairs. You would stack them up to make a covering. I used to get up in the morning and blow 'Reveille' in the park. It was great. Tramps learn how to sleep in a park under cover. What appeared to be an empty park at five thirty in the morning suddenly was populated. All [these] startled figures would pop up out of the bushes!"

Sleeping rough and doss houses became Marty's norm. "There were certain waiting rooms and certain stations that were fine. You could sleep in Waterloo. I don't know why [but] the police were easier there. All you had to do was to have a ticket for a train, so you had a reason to be there and you could sleep there. Waterloo was also very near to the Sally Ann." Indeed, the Salvation Army came to Marty's rescue on several occasions. Until he was barred! "You used to tie your boots to the bedpost so they couldn't get nicked," he remembered, "and you used to put your jacket and trousers under the blankets so they couldn't get nicked. So, you'll be lying in this awful bloody dormitory. One night I was lying in my shitty pit with this smell of carbolic everywhere and a guy got out of the bed next to me and pissed on the floor. [This] was fairly common. I thought: 'Well, that's OK.' I was very tired and drunk. I didn't realise he had pissed on the floor under my bed. The next morning the guy on the door said: 'You're barred!' And I said: 'Why?' 'For pissing on the floor. There's piss on the floor under your bed,' and I said: 'That wasn't me. I wouldn't piss on the floor!' He said: 'It's there. You're barred.' Barred from the Salvation Army. It's the point of no return, really!"

The solution was show business. "I answered an advertisement in *The Stage* that asked for a 'personable young man'... and to enclose a photograph. I was fifteen. I enclosed my Bar Mitzvah photograph in fact, from two years earlier. I was going to get paid thirty bob [shillings] a week. I got hired, got on a train to Exeter and was picked up by a very strange looking guy. If Orson Welles were dying of cancer and bought himself a fright wig, he would have looked like this man. He was a hypnotist and he had a strange little wife of about twenty-five – a shrewish little bird. They were playing one-night stands in village halls. On the way back to the caravan where we were going to be staying they both groped me; I had never been groped by two people, never mind one male and one female. I found out they were both bisexual and fancied me from the photo. I fought them off. I said: 'I don't want this, I want to be in show business.' They said: 'What do you do?' I said: 'I don't know. You asked for a personable young man. I'm young. I'm man, very pointedly, and probably personable. What do you want me to do?' [He said]: 'I thought you had an act.' I didn't have an act but I said: 'Oh yeah, I've got an act.' That night I walked on without any idea what I was going to do and tried to remember some jokes that I'd heard. While I was doing this, a lady in the front row started knitting and someone else had fallen asleep. I came off and cried, knowing that I had to go back to this caravan and be groped by these two strange creatures again. [For] the rest of the act I had to put on a record, 'Legend of the Glass Mountain', while this hypnotist pretended to hypnotise his wife and then pretend to hypnotise me. He couldn't hypnotise either of us. We would go to a different town or village each day. In the morning, I would have to go round with posters to the local shops to persuade them to put the poster up. I would unload the scenery, put it all up, get on, do the show. After about two weeks I had developed about ten minutes of chatter. It wasn't patter. It wasn't comedy. I didn't know what it was. It was conversation without anybody to talk to. They fed me on rough Devon cider, trying to get me pissed. If there weren't enough people in the hall, he would refuse to do a show. He would be drunk every night and when we got back to the caravan he would try and rape me again. All this for thirty bob a week! I said: 'Look, I'm going. I really can't stand it.' They paid me my thirty shillings in silver. My thirty pieces of silver. It was the night's takings, in fact, and the guy said to me: 'If you tell anybody about what we did, we'll blacken your name and you'll never work again.' That was my first experience of professional show business. I thought it was all like that, which is why I stayed in it!"

However, this was one of many final straws for Marty. "I would try and go home occasionally," he said, "but things would get in the way. I couldn't live my parents' life and they couldn't countenance my way of life because it involved all kinds of disreputable carryings on. They were right from their point of view."

At the age of fifteen and completely disillusioned with his place in life he dramatically upped sticks and tried his luck in France. Paris was the European centre of art, poetry and cool jazz. As often was the case in Marty's life his natural desire to be at the heart of creativity completely over-took him: "Needless to say, I dropped out of school early," he recalled. "You were supposed to make some half-hearted attempt at a higher education so that you would have some kind of career. Certainly that's what my parents wanted for me. [But] there were too many things I wanted to do. I wanted to write. I wanted to paint. I went to Paris to write and paint. I thought that if I went there and hung out, the ghosts of Fitzgerald and Hemingway and Henry Miller would sort of rub off on me by osmosis.[29] But it doesn't happen by osmosis; nothing happens by osmosis. I discovered that in a year or so, during which I learned to get rid of the adjectives in my writing. I realised that the verbs or the nouns were important – either the trumpet or the rhythm section."[30]

As usual every instinct and reaction to life's ups and downs was equated to jazz music. But Marty's rebellion, while dramatic, was reassuringly borne of middle-class boredom. Marty's was a very British coup.

Chapter Two

"I won the award for being the best loser."

Like most people between the cradle and the first kiss, Marty's attitude was that no one else could understand what he was trying to do. A creative mind was already hard at work and a total devotion to silly things and silly people was clouding his vision wonderfully. His mind was full of great literature and majestic pratfalls, off-colour jokes and hilarious slow burns. He had been the class clown and the class joke. He was proud of both achievements.

Indeed, comedy seemed to be his chosen profession. However, rather than the spiralling linguistic trickery of his subsequent scriptwriting, Marty chose to tread the lonely path of the long distance stand-up comedian: "I tried it once, when I was fifteen. But you know the stand-up comic is a lonely figure who is put in the position of dominating the audience. The same impulse that makes you a stand-up comic probably makes you a dictator. It's a very lonely way to make a living."

But a living had to be made. His impulsive abandoning of the educational system was reckless and fun but the harsh reality was less amusing. Away from school and away from his family, Marty was residing in a disused hut in the centre of London's Soho Square. The Artful Dodger had reared his head again and the excitement of a life living rough wasn't enough to heat his beans of an evening.

He later admitted that he was something of a middle-class teenage rebel.

His Jewish parents had worked their way up through the rag trade in the East End of London until they had owned their own shop. "I suppose I was a bit of a hippie," Marty reflected at the end of the 1960s.[1] More to the point, Marty was a romantic and an artisan to the soles of his worn-out shoes. Paris seemed the natural place to be: "I got to Paris because I thought that's where painters should go. With my trumpet under my arm wrapped in brown paper, because that's what Bix Beiderbecke did. We got to Paris and I stayed there for about a year." It was "a completely bizarre, exciting, great period in my life." Paris was the city an artist really felt he had to experience in order to call himself an artist. Suffering for your art and peace of mind in London was one thing, suffering in Paris was a statement. Marty had little education, even less money and absolutely no French but he picked up a smattering of the language from American G.I.s studying at the Sorbonne although: "They never used to study. They used to sign on the first day, get their grants and get pissed the whole of their period in Paris." One such G.I. was an American Greek sculptor by the name of "Speedy" Pappofatis. He was: "a very good sculptor – he ended up doing some work on the United Nations building – but he could never sell any of his work. I was student-looking then and used to hang around bars and accost likely looking American tourists. I would tell them I knew a very fine French sculptor and drag them back to his studio. He would put on a French accent and sell them bits of his work and I would get a commission on it. They would buy stuff from a genuine French sculptor but they wouldn't buy it from a guy called 'Speedy' Pappofatis from Illinois!"

A general tout and dogsbody, Marty would model; even make attempts to sculpt but there was always more money to be had. At fifteen, he could be "three people in one day." He was an assistant to a pavement artiste for a short time. "This guy had a perfectly viable theory that if you paint some pictures on the pavement and you are not sitting there then no one will drop money in the hat. So he used to go round about six in the morning, do about twenty different pitches and put a cap down." Utilising the indigenous students as well as Marty, "One of us would take one of the pitches and just sit there. Tourists would go by, they would see someone sitting there and they would drop a coin in the hat. We were stand-ins for a pavement artiste. We would divvy up at night."

"I worked various fringe operations – legal, semi-legal, some illegal activities," he said. "The usual street hustles, which could never quite get me hanged but could get me sent to reform school if I was caught. I was never caught." For Marty, Paris was also, naturally, a hotbed of jazz. Since he arrived in 1949, the nightclubs and bars had held a unique fascination for the teenager. He would often claim, with sincere pride, that he was "the world's worst trumpet player" but it earned him a living, of sorts.

Jazz proved his most stable source of income. He busked on the streets of Paris, played his trumpet in cosmopolitan cafés and finally ended up working at Honey Johnson's, a small jazz club in the Montparnasse. "It was an American bar and I played for beer money or wine money. All visiting American musicians would come there and I'd be terribly conscious of how bad I was." In order to mask his embarrassment, Marty concocted a lie that would see him through for several years. He developed TB. "I used to pretend that the doctor had told me that I mustn't play the trumpet so I wouldn't have to sit and play. I could lay out and say: 'I'd love to be playing with you fellows tonight!' I'd even sit up on the stand and play the odd bit I knew and say: 'You realise I can't play too much because of my chest.' Everybody would be really sympathetic. I worked there for three months!"

Still, he drifted through life. His only constant companions were his trumpet, and the bohemian jazz musicians he would hang out with: "We staggered back to my room with four musicians. One American musician had never seen a bidet before. He thought it was a place to crap. He was very pissed and had a shit in this bidet. We spent most of the night trying to poke it down with a pencil. The same night he found what he thought was the light switch but it was the bell pull. Up came the garçon, who was about eighty-five, and he saw us all in our room poking shit down a bidet with pencils. He called the concierge who came and screamed and threw us out of the hotel."

But this free-wheeling lifestyle wasn't to last. Without a regular income, Marty was arrested for vagrancy and deported, but the essence of Paris never really left him. He had been touched by the freedom of artistic expression, seen a bit of the world – albeit its rough underbelly – and fooled people into believing he was something he wasn't. Whether that had been a pavement artist or a trumpet player the result was the same. You got paid for lying. This was something worth cultivating. As was his "messy libido": Marty had had his heart stolen in Paris: "There was a bird I knew, [a] marvellous kind of *La Bohème* bit, living with a sculptor. She was every fifteen-year-old's dream; a beautiful, wild Bohemian walking around in her boyfriend's shirt. I wrote mad poems, stories about her, fantasised about her."

Once he was back in Britain, the pull of Soho was too strong and his fifteen-year-old fancy was shattered: "I was working for an advertising agency, delivering [printing] blocks, [and I] met her on a bus. I found out that she was an East End scrubber. In London she was walking around in wedge heels and a pencil skirt with her hair built up at the back, Teddy Girl style. All my fantasies have turned into that. It's always mornings after. That whole love affair that had gone on in my head was killed the day I met her on a bus." But there were other girls; plenty of them. "I've fallen in love about 500 times in my life," he said. "Sometimes 300 times in the same day. I used to write poems to a girl who worked in a tobacco kiosk outside the cinema in Charing Cross Road. I never met her, didn't know what she was like. I just used to send her poems. I was totally in love with her."

Back in the mundane and respectable Britain he had run away from, Marty's parents were still pushing him towards something, anything, that had a hint of security about it. "I did several things simultaneously," he said. These ranged from the emotionally stunting to the hilariously liberating. No sooner had he enlisted with an advertising agency than he was slung out for insubordination. "It was run by a very sorrowful Quaker," he remembered. "In fact he didn't fire me. He gave me every opportunity to let me leave. He called me in to this awful, dark-panelled, Quakery office but he couldn't fire me. In the end he had to say: 'Well, I don't think you're suited to this profession.' He was right." Drunken afternoon sessions in Soho jazz clubs were far more appealing than advertising. Certainly more appealing than the Army; another failed attempt by Marty's parents to pin him down. He failed the medical, for the Army psychiatrist believed he would be a disruptive influence. He said that: "I did not respond to totalitarian discipline. I didn't. I don't now! I need rules to break. The trouble with being an anarchist is that you have to blow up the building you are living in while you're still living in it and then run like hell."

Finally, his parents enlisted him onto an evening scholarship course at Hornsey Art College. They reasoned that if he must be an artist then at least he could be a qualified artist. A framed certificate on the wall would give them a sense that he had achieved something. "I was slung out of Hornsey before it was fashionable!" It was inevitable. The thirteenth and final seat of learning that failed to inspire him. Again, it was his anti-establishment attitude that flared and caused problems. "My teachers insisted that you had to draw perspective with rulers; rule your lines off into the distance. I said I didn't want to paint the world that way, I wanted to paint it flat. They said, 'First you must know how to paint perspective.' I said: 'But I'll never paint that,' and argued that 'Ferreo Attilio painted it flat!' 'You're not Attillo. You can't invent your own perspectives. You have to paint it our way.' I remember telling the other students that the teachers were full of shit and that all they were trying to do was brainwash them. I got expelled."

The die had been cast; Soho's tantalizing mix of drugs, jazz, women, alcohol and petty villainy had finally won. Marty was hooked. "I was hanging around a lot of fun amusement arcades in the Charing Cross Road which was the meeting place at the time. I drifted through dozens of strange, peripheral jobs. I met this great, dangerous-looking African on the Charing Cross Road. I worked for two days with him as what we called a Smudge Boy, which was a street photographer. I'd never had a camera before. People would run to the other side of the street when they saw him. He was about six-foot-five with tribal scars. I worked as a kitchen porter in a hotel until lunchtime and the dishes came. Being a vegetarian I couldn't face touching dishes with meat on. I could have cleaned up shit but I just couldn't face meat. So I walked out of there. I was a kitchen porter for three hours."

Marty still busked with his faithful trumpet and landed the ideal job, in a musical instrument shop. Well, it was ideal for his jazz musician friends: "I was fired because I gave away reeds, mouthpieces and on a couple of occasions instruments to musicians that I knew from Archer Street. They needed the reeds, mouthpieces and instruments. I could never explain this to the guy who ran the shop. That's reasonable. He was there to make a profit. I wasn't. I worked there for about a week."

Unsurprisingly, Marty was still sleeping rough. There was always just one thought in his head, depending on whether his guts were rumbling, he wanted to get completely stoned or he wanted to kip. At the time he was living in a hut above a sewer in the middle of Soho Square. "It was a little gothic hut with this great tangle of undergrowth and a hole in the railings. We used to creep in through those railings and sleep there every night." Marty's chief ally was Ray Courtney, a deserter from the Canadian Army who thought he was Jesus: "Actually, he didn't *think* he was Jesus, he was *convinced*. He probably was. Somebody had to be Jesus, why shouldn't it be Ray? I always knew Ray was there. I stayed there a lot of the time. I knew I had a bench and a sleeping bag there."

Once a new day dawned, Marty, Ray and the "bum community" would wander over to Soho and drink and talk and try and make money in the Alex or one of several cafés in the West End where all the tramps congregated. "There used to be a café called 91 in Charlotte Street," remembered Marty. "Ray was the original hippie I suppose. I was sitting with a guy called Mad Bernie Tobasis – who later killed himself, most people I knew have killed themselves. We had been brought up that Jesus was a Jew. Ray said: 'Well, I'll see you in a minute.' He went upstairs and he came down with blood all over his trousers. He had circumcised himself. Mad Bernie said, 'We ought to call the police,' but the last people you call are the police. It's a working class thing you are brought up with, they are the enemy. It's no good telling people that the copper is a friend who will help you across the street. When you grow up on the streets, the copper is your enemy, especially if you live on the wrong side of the law as I did then. So we called the ambulance. They came and Ray refused to go with them. He said, 'I am the Son of God. God will look after me.' God apparently did, because three months later he was walking around fine." [2]

As for Marty being on the wrong side of the law, it was simply a way of life. He would busk, illegally. "There was another guy called Mad Barney – everyone was mad back then. He used to pitch Bibles as pornographic literature: 'All the filth in the world, all the obscenity, all the lewdness. It's all in here!' He would sell these little wrapped packets: "'Ere you are. I'm only asking half a crown each, that's all I'm asking. They won't allow me to open these. There's all the depravity in the world here. Only half a crown each.' And everyone would buy these bloody things and find all they had got in the end was a Bible. Quite defensible because it *was* all in there!"

Other literature proved fruitful for Marty; both educationally and financially. "I stole books for a living for a while. There was a guy who dealt in stolen books. He would pay us a third of the published price if we'd steal them. So we would go and steal books from bookstores in London. And I found I was keeping a lot of them – I wanted to read them. I actually stole my education. I don't know why, but I got very high on American humorists very early: [James] Thurber, [S.J.] Perelman [both of whom contributed to one of Marty's essential journals *The New Yorker*], Ring Lardner." [3]

He cited the cynical scribblings of Robert Benchley as a favourite as well as immersing himself in the writings of Dorothy Parker, Donald Ogden Stewart and Stephen Leacock. [4] The fifteenth century Frenchman François Rabelais inspired Marty with his grotesque and bawdy writings while the sixteenth century Spaniard Miguel de Cervantes bewitched him with poetry, plays and the adventures of *Don Quixote*. There was the English strain of wit and wisdom from Patrick Campbell and Evelyn Waugh, [5] although he maintained that: "I missed the whole English mainstream. I haven't read any Thackeray. God knows what Jane Austen did, apart from writing movies for Laurence Olivier – I don't know. And yet I know all about Mark Twain, I know about Frank Sullivan, and I can tell you all about Will Guthrie." [6]

The Artful Dodger in hippie clothing was now here to stay and this literature-savvy sneak thief embraced another of his passions: writing poetry. "I was about sixteen and used to write poems on the bottom of my paintings." This was: "The only thing to come out of [Hornsey]. I had read [Dante Gabriel] Rossetti used to write poems on the bottom of his paintings. Most of the poems were verbose and imitative of [Dylan] Thomas's style. I was very hung-up on the physical sound of words at the time." His style and instincts may have changed over the years, but not that obsession with the sound of words. "It's like sculpting," he explained. "I write like a sculptor models in clay. I used to work upward, but now I work backward, chipping away the stone until I'm satisfied with what's left. A poem can start out three pages long, become four lines, then two words. I look at it and think, this isn't a poem, so I rip it up and throw it away."[7]

Producing paintings with verse written on them was a canny double indemnity against penury. It got him in with the Soho elite. He would lounge around coffee bars, jazz clubs and pubs with hip and happening friends like Bernard Kops and Frankie Norman. He met artists Stephen Spencer and John Minton and even his poet hero Dylan Thomas.[8] "Minton had talent. He had taste. He knew I was a lousy painter. I knew him around the jazz clubs but he took my painting on the bottom of which I had written a very boring Dylan Thomasish poem and showed it to Dylan Thomas in the pub – the Coach and Horses in Soho. Dylan Thomas liked my poem very much. Minton said, 'Forget the paintings, you're a fucking awful painter. But look, you can write.' I think Thomas liked my poem, not because it was a good poem but that it was an imitation of Thomas. He was flattered."

So Marty decided to concentrate on the poetry: "I even bought a cape." He was also drinking huge quantities. "I thought if I drank enough I could write poetry like Dylan Thomas. It's an adolescent mistake. The lifestyle is a manifestation of the man. I would mistake the vomiting poet that I knew for Dylan Thomas the poet and it wasn't. The man I knew was a vomiting drunk who would puke all over my blue suede shoes in various pubs around Soho. I thought in order to be a poet you had to be sick a lot and pee in the street and hit people. All Dylan Thomas talked about was how much he'd had to drink and how much he could drink."

But he got Marty published as a poet. "He bullied a publisher. There were lots of very thin poetry magazines in the fifties that folded after two or three issues. They were always called something like *Ambit* or *Miasma* or *Vacuum* or *Orgasm*. Anyway he browbeat someone into publishing some of my poems. I loved the idea of seeing my stuff in print, then I saw it there and I felt very vulnerable. This stuff was open to criticism. I wasn't ready for honesty. You need some illusion. Poetry gives you nowhere to hide. You're too exposed. It's a key to you."

Like his trumpet playing and his painting, he felt his poetry "was very bad. I didn't like being exposed and naked. They were telegrams from me to me."[9] A sense of total embarrassment took over him. He imagined people jeering at him in the street. "I wanted to hide at that time," he said. "I didn't want to publish any more poems and I haven't done since."

Still, although Marty knew his limitations as a jazz trumpeter, that was a collaborative experience. He could hide amongst musicians who could actually play. Besides, he needed the money. He also had a fine ear for talent. Legendary tenor saxophonist Tubby Hayes enjoyed his first break in Marty's line-up.[10] "We split a fiver," Marty remembered. "It was at The 52 Club. We were the relief group for Johnny Dankworth in the early days of Bebop." So, Marty Feldman and the Bebop Seven played the music the people wanted to hear. Well, at least six of them did. "They were all very good musicians except me." Marty pulled the old TB trick again. "I would sit somewhere on the stand and beam at my band. It became a joke. Marty Feldman's Remote Control Band, because I couldn't really play. Tubby Hayes has a record he made of the band and he says you can almost hear me at one point!" Poorly paid one-nighters in London jazz clubs were simply a means to an end. For Marty, it was a paid education: "When my band was performing one-night stands, there wasn't very much else to do. So books were passed around. I was a magpie with anything to read. I'd swoop down on anything that seemed to glisten, take it back to my nest, and read it. And then a book would refer to another, and I'd get that, and so on and so on. But then I realised I wanted to write fiction, not read it. It wasn't necessary to read it; I wanted to improve on that."[11]

Marty may have been giving his brain nutrition through his valued collection of books but at this same time his brain was getting a touch of neuritis as well. Again, it was Charing Cross Road that brought the detritus of Soho together. "I used to meet a guy from the Elephant and Castle who arranged fights every week. Every Saturday night he and his team would go out and fight. Like you would arrange a football match, they would arrange to fight another mob. But it wasn't a joke fight, it was a dead serious fight with broken bottles and bicycle chains. He would say to me, 'We're having a fight next Saturday night, do you want to come?' and they'd meet at 8.30 and they would fight. They would try and kill each other for an hour and a half and then all go off to the pub and get drunk. It was like a regular fixture. He could never understand it that I didn't want to go along. Once I went along to watch them fight and it was exactly like a football match. They would pick sides. This was how he got his kicks. This was the early Teddy Boy era, but I was never a Teddy Boy. I was too hung up on being a black jazz musician. I tried very hard. I hanged around with Africans in a black pub. It wasn't beautiful then, it wasn't even attractive then otherwise I probably wouldn't have tried. But I used to wear the peg-top trousers, porkpie hats. I was a Jewish vegetarian and I was wearing a porkpie hat. It should have been a smoked salmon hat! The string ties. I could swear fluently in Swahili. I became an early hipster, before Norman Mailer invented white black people. I also realised fairly early on that there was no market for white black people. White people didn't want white black people. Black people didn't want white black people and Jews didn't want either kind. I think I've consciously chosen to be a misfit all of my life because it's more interesting."

He had one impossible dream. "I wanted to be an instant Miles Davis," he said. "My fantasy was that I'd wake up one morning and be black and playing the trumpet."[12] However, there was another trumpet player that Marty could aspire to more readily. At this time "*The Goon Show* started happening"[13] and in Spike Milligan he found a trumpet-player, writer-actor lunatic whose mind exploded with anarchic comedy. He was the only hero who wouldn't let Marty down. But in the early 1950s, Marty's intake of drink and drugs only gave him the illusion of being a musician or a writer. The tangible release for his angst was street violence. Maybe not the fights his friend from the Elephant organised, but smashed out of his head punch-ups just because, like Everest, it was there. Naturally, if the violent urge within him could earn him money, then so be it. "I did box for a bit, but I was never a good boxer, although I made some good moves. I shaped up great until the fight started. That's like most things that happen to me in life," he reflected ruefully. "Some nut" had secured Marty bouts in boxing booths that turned that "little snub nose" from childhood into "this great hooter" which served him well comically. But the most influential "nut" in his life was encountered in a familiar haunt: the amusement arcades on Charing Cross Road. "I met up with an Hawaiian guy who was totally frightening. He had frizzy, black hair before it was called a natural or an Afro. He just had frizzy black hair and carried an Hawaiian knife with him everywhere." This was Joe Moe, a young, handsome drifter whose mother had been part of Felix Mendelssohn and His Hawaiian Serenaders. Marty and Joe had music in common. Then there was alcohol and dope. "This was the early days of pot when you could walk around the West End smoking joints openly," Marty remembered. "We used to do that. We used to go up to coppers and ask them for a light. They didn't know what it was then. We enjoyed defying authority in that way."

Then there were the girls. "Joe was very pretty. He was very definitely butch and he would have gone for you with this Hawaiian knife if you had suggested anything else. In fact the only way I could get Joe angry was to call him a pouf. He used to come at me with this Hawaiian knife and put it down at the last minute because he knew he could beat the hell out of me and just hit me, which is what he did."

This was the start of a beautiful friendship. What's more, Joe had a job opportunity. "He had got a job with a Red Indian act in a sideshow in Dreamland in Margate. He said would I like to come along and be in this act. We were just assistants to a Red Indian fakir called Tay Owana." A mystic, conjuror and illusionist, the biggest illusion of all was that Tay Owana was actually Jack Taylor from Peterborough.

"He was billed as Tay Owana from the Rolling Plains of North America, but it didn't really matter. They didn't know the difference in Margate! The entire company was Tay Owana, myself an East London Jew, Joe this

Hawaiian guy, another Jewish lad from the East End called Johnny Myers and his West Indian wife, Cathy. That was our company of Red Indians."

Marty's place was subservient but at least this was proper show business, of sorts. "It was a weird act. I used to fire arrows into Tay Owana's stomach as part of my duties. These were four eighteen-inch prongs on the end of this arrow and they would go in to his stomach. I would fire them from about four foot away. He would pull them out, throw them on the floor and stand there quivering. He was pitted with tiny little holes. He was mad, quite mad. He used to jump up and down on broken glass. We used to beat him with burning clubs, flay him with barbed wire and then we played bongos, God knows what that has to do with Red Indians, but we'd do all this as a sideshow at Dreamland. For the finale he used to get into a large tin box painted with dragons and while the band played 'Land of Hope and Glory' he would blow himself up! I think he must have bought a box from a bankrupt magician and 'Land of Hope and Glory' sounded impressive. God knows why he blew himself up. He was mad. We once caught him in the digs with a Red Indian headdress on looking at himself in the mirror. He began to believe he was a Red Indian in the end."

Marty's season at Dreamland also involved every other aspect of the funfair. He worked the bingo, spent time in the boxing booth and looked after the rifle stall: "Which was fixed. All the sights were bent." Still, the boxing came in handy. Fights were the norm down in Margate. "Jack and I used to fight a lot," said Marty. "We used to drink too much. That was why. I was trying to become an alcoholic. I worked very hard at it but I didn't have the dedication. If I had a hangover I would quit for the day. A real dedicated alcoholic has to start every morning whether he feels like it or not. It's like training. I was a dilettante. The people I knew who really made it as alcoholics fought through those bad times and carried on drinking. I have to admire them." Jack – in Indian headdress or not – was one to be admired.

Marty might have lacked dedication but he was invariably drunk when he performed simply to combat his fear: "I used to get so scared before I went on. I was scared that I would miss with the arrow when I fired it into his stomach. I was scared that when we lit the paraffin for the burning clubs I would burn myself and I was just scared of being in front of a lot of people."

As a result of all this alcohol intake, "Jack and I would be drunk and fight," Marty remembered. "We sprawled on the stage fighting in the middle of a performance. Joe would come out and separate us, brandishing his Hawaiian knife. He would be equally drunk or stoned and we would be totally unaware that there would be an audience out there."

Marty's libido had also arisen once more. He had fallen in love with a girl in a Western show in Margate. Even after his season at Dreamland had come to an end he was determined to see her. "I used to hitch-hike on lorries going down to Margate from Covent Garden every night! Just to see her for about two hours. A quick fuck in the back of a car and hitch-hike back to London again."

Once again, Marty's income came from a variety of sources, mostly illegal. He had stuck with Joe after Margate and was living in Brixton: "with a guy called Jarett. I lived there a lot. He would push pot or charge as we called it then. We would wrap our little half crown packets in that brown paper with tar in, very thick greaseproof paper, and we used to go round selling it. We used to hang around a pub called The Roebuck which was opposite a dance hall called The Paramount on Tottenham Court Road. There was no illegal stimulant that could not be obtained within a hundred yards of that pub. All the dealers lived around there. We used to live in there."

Petty crime was in Marty's blood. It was simply what he did. "We used to go out looking for villainy," he said. "But I was a failed criminal. I couldn't beat anybody up. I couldn't even beat anybody down. We are all villains. It seemed the only way to go. But I didn't have the bottle. You need bottle to be a top villain, like you need bottle to play the trumpet well. I was a get-away driver once but I was more worried about driving a get away car because I didn't have a licence!"

Marty would have to get drunk before he could go through with any crime. One Christmas Eve finally told him that he really wasn't cut out to be a villain. "It's like an O. Henry short story," he said. "I broke into a car. There were some parcels in the back and I stole them. We ran back home,

Jarret and Joe and I, and unwrapped them. They were fucking choirboy surplices and it was Christmas Eve. I thought maybe there is a God. If there isn't a God, I'm not cut out to be a villain. Either way, someone is telling me something. So we returned them to the church. We couldn't take it seriously so we wrote an illiterate note saying 'Dear Sir, I stole them surpluses and I seen the light. Hallelujah!'"

But show business and villainy intermingled seamlessly. Nowhere more so than Jack Spot's place, the Blue Spot club in Old Compton Street. "Some of my best friends are villains and some of my best villains are friends," said Marty and that club was full of them. "It was full of villains with shooters. When they came up to ask for requests you did them, even if you didn't know them! They would always want to sing "My Mother's Eyes" or "My Yiddish Mama"; there were a lot of Jewish gangsters around at that time. [American singer] Billy Daniels used to come down a lot. He was at the Palladium. He used to carry a shooter too and we'd have to play 'That Old Black Magic' about eight times a night for him to sing." The *People* called Spot the Al Capone of Soho. Marty called him Spotty. Disillusioned with the trumpet, Marty had had aspirations to be a drummer. He had got himself a drum kit. This had been before Paris, when his father would still guarantee him because he was under age. Almost as soon as he had picked it up jazz drummer Flash Winston had asked to borrow it. "Professor Bebop he called himself then," remembered Marty. "He had an audition for a summer season only he couldn't get into his rooms to get his drum kit because he didn't have the rent. Once he had got the audition he'd have the money, he could pay the money and collect his drum kit. I was flattered by being asked by a professional jazz musician to be allowed to lend him my drum kit, which I did. I didn't see him or my drum kit again for about two years." In the interim, Marty had got in to trouble with the hire purchase company, the police and his father.

When Marty was rehearsing a new trio act, the manager of the Blue Spot club, a friend, would let them use the club for nothing in the afternoon. "I played trumpet. One of my partners played clarinet and the third one played guitar. We'd got through our rehearsals and we were having a little bang on the drum kit and on the piano. The clarinettist was playing clarinet. We were just playing for our own benefit – very badly – but we were stoned and having a ball. The phone went and it was Jack Spot. 'Who's that playing there?' The manager said, 'That's just three friends of mine who are rehearsing down here.' 'Well, they swing. Get rid of the resident band and hire these fellows.' 'When?' said the manager. 'Now!' So we were offered a job. You didn't turn down a job anyway in those days, certainly not if it was Jack Spot offering it to you. It was regular money and you might get beaten up if you refused. So when the manager said, 'You're starting work here tonight,' it wasn't a question, it was a contract. What I didn't realise as I was banging away on this drum kit was that the drummer in the band that was fired was Flash Winston and the drums were my own drums that I'd lent him two years before! I didn't recognise them because he'd beaten the hell out of them in two years. So I got my own drum kit back and his job all in one go."

Marty would work a lot of Soho clubs at this time; grabbing a month here, three months there and usually on a different instrument every time. "I found you could fake it," he said. "I had never played bass. I can't play bass to this day. The bass player was sick and he asked me whether I would deputy for this trio. Again it was a lunatic drinking club in Soho. I said, 'But I can't play bass.' He said, 'Nobody listens as long as you go up and down on one string and keep low down they'll just be a fuzzy booming sound. As long as it's approximately in tempo nobody's going to worry about it.' So for three months I played up and down on one string. Nobody but the pianist and drummer knew I couldn't play. People used to buy me drinks. If they were drunk enough they would even compliment me on my bass playing!"

If Marty could fake it to earn a crust, then he could certainly fake it to pull the birds. The year was 1952, Marty was seventeen years old and it was hip to be an American, so, "I was an American for a long while during that period. We were known as Piccadilly Yanks. We used to hang around Piccadilly Circus tube station because that's where all the G.I.s on furlough used to hang out. If you were English the birds didn't want to know. I told them I was on furlough from Manston, that was a base I knew near Margate. So we all dressed like Americans. I had friends who were working on boats and they used to bring back ties cut square at the bottom, Prince of Wales check, argyle socks, button down shirts. We would wear our hair in crew cuts. Smoke Lucky Strikes bought illicitly on the black market from a guy called Fat Stan. We were weaned on a tradition that everything American was good. Every American you met had the cool of Humphrey Bogart or Alan Ladd."

The crew cut hair also helped make him think more like a jazz musician because now was the era of West Coast jazz and Charlie Parker. Again, as with Dylan Thomas, it was the lifestyle rather than the reality that appealed to Marty. He was so intrigued by Charlie Parker: "I thought that if I became a junkie, I would play like Charlie Parker. In the end I found out that junk destroyed some of his abilities as a musician but when you're a kid it is the lifestyle you envied rather than being able to do something." Marty's drug-taking was extensive. He lived on two kinds of speed; particularly the chemical kind. He would take Benzedrine and chew the paper in a Lyons Corner House. He would experiment with harder drugs. He even sneaked back into Paris to meet his hero. "I went in 1952 to meet Charlie Parker and all he did was talk about snooker. I was so pissed off!" Not only that, but Marty was deported again.

Joe Moe was now living in a studio in Belsize Park and Marty had a place to stay when he needed it, which was most of the time. The studio was owned by a couple of bi-sexual painters. A husband and wife, "and Joe knew they both fancied him. So Joe played them along so we would have somewhere to kip for the night. Joe knew this was his function. He was keeping them both on a hook because if either of them had fucked him, the other one would have thrown us out the next night, so Joe was prick teasing for the rent! A lot of my early life I never knew where I was living until I woke up the next day. There was a lot of living on bombsites at that time, you would just wake up and think, 'Hey, another day.' Whoever was in the room or on the bombsite with you, you would set off to face the day with and you would pool what ever money you had."

Little wonder that friend and colleague Graham Chapman looked back at Marty's early life and came to the conclusion that: "He was a B.A. (First Class Honours with Distinction) from the University of Life."[14]

Chapter Three

"I feel about Keaton the way an organist thinks of Bach."

By the time Marty turned sixteen he had experienced life as an artist. Or at least the poverty-stricken life he thought an artist should experience. He wore his successes and failures like military medals won in the battle of survival: the deportation from France, hob-nobbing with the great and good in Soho and shambolic attempts at breaking into the entertainment industry were all grist to his creative mill. Experiencing life in the gutter while gazing at the stars, gently goading authority at every turn, writing down thoughts and feelings over elongated hours and continuous cigarettes in a simple street café. That was what he was born to do.

"My generation are transition figures," he said. "We were between the old-fashioned bohemian, corduroy, bearded, sandals, bare-feet, pipe-smoking generation and the drug/pop culture of today. We were shady figures really. We don't fit in to either. In many ways we were ahead of our time. In other ways we were very much of our time and even behind it. It was the end of a period. It was the end of Soho."

He could control his nervous energy if he had something to rally against, but if there was nothing to rally against he would self-destruct and beat his head against the brick wall of suppression. That desperate drive to make sense of his inner demons had intensified. He simply had to make something of himself. As if to live his life in the clichéd way of artistic expression he had tried his luck at everything: from bouts in boxing booths that had resulted in that misshaped nose to a stint as a racecourse tipster. Eventually he would run away to join the circus, or at least the Margate Fun Fair where he had secured gainful employment as a sideshow assistant. It was as if he had picked up tips on how to break in to show business from half-remembered moments from *The Jolson Story*.[1]

Marty had worked out a music hall act with Joe Moe. Indeed, it was the rehearsals that had landed him a job at the Blue Spot club.

"Joe had been brought up knowing Hawaiian music," Marty explained. "He taught me the Hawaiian war chant and he could play ukulele as well as guitar, and twirl a war knife which seemed like a good basis to start an act off from. I could play trumpet. So when we found Mitch Revely, a red-haired midget clarinet player, we had an act. It didn't have any shape." This was the blueprint for Morris, Marty and Mitch; one of the nosiest and most disjointed acts ever to hit the circuit.

"We auditioned for lots of people and we ended up doing an eccentric dance. Eccentric was the key word. Dance was a very loose description," explained Marty. "We moved about in black tights a lot like Max Wall did. He was a corporate hero of ours. The only offer we got was from a bent agent who thought all three of us looked quite well built in tights and obviously had no intention of ever hiring us for anything else except some strange private party."

Marty and his pals made money any way they could, usually by flogging shirts and material in the local markets. They had got their first booking at the Regent Theatre in Hayes. "We didn't have any uniformity. We felt we ought to have some kind of costume for our act. We were working in a market during the day to get the props for our act that night. Except it's impossible to save. All the money coming in is in cash. You're like a sailor on shore leave. Your pockets are stuffed with cash. You're Jack the Lad every night." In the end, they could only afford a minimal uniform. "We had three matching ties which we wore with white shirts and black trousers. That was a well-dressed act!"

Putting them into a show featuring experienced pros Donald Stewart, Renée Houston and Randolph Sutton, the Regent's manager was not impressed with the act, fuming that it had insulted the intelligence of his patrons. He promptly paid them off after the Monday night performance. "We had to go back the next day and collect our props," cringed Marty. "We didn't want to do it in the evening, because we couldn't face the other actors, so we sneaked in to the dark theatre in the afternoon. We had a drum kit, a sarcophagus for some reason (it was rigged out as a telephone box inside). We had a lot of stuff we didn't need. Renée Houston heard us coming off stage and was very sympathetic about it. She gave us lots of good advice. Basically, keep well away from the theatre until you've learnt something about show business! The best advice you can give to anybody is to piss off, really!"

"We finally got an offer from an agent to go into a show called *The Saucy Girls of 1952*. They hired us because we were versatile. We would do anything in order to get on stage. We would move scenery, we would announce the nude, we would provide musical accompaniment for acts, stooge in sketches. Anything as long as they hired us. It was the first time I was offered a percentage. I thought that would mean we would get a lot of money. I found out we were getting seven quid a week between the three of us." But it was show business.

The show toured the worst theatres in Britain: "All the No. 3 and No. 4 theatres. Anywhere that would put on a cheap show." The Dean Family were the core of the production. "They really were the whole show. The father was the MD, he also did a piano act. The daughter had a dog act and did a knife-throwing act with her mother who was also the wardrobe mistress." The son, Derek Dean, later became an established comedian. He was the boy prodigy of the act. He would juggle, act in sketches, dance with his sister. When Derek was indisposed, Marty would take over: "At one point I was lead dancer," he recalled. "They really didn't need anybody else. Them and us and a load of chorus girls."

Marty was convinced that John Osborne had seen the show, because elements of *The Entertainer* were very familiar to him. Even so, he thought even that had romanticised the decline of the music hall. His experiences were much seedier. "There's very little romantic about audiences being drunker than the performers and that was saying something! Or smuggling in fish 'n' chips backstage and peeing in the sink," he said. "You can't smell dampness or taste poverty except at first hand. We were all skint. It was very seedy. The nudes used to have to stand still because an undulating tit would be calculated as a source of provocation. They would assume that if a nude moved her nipple even by a couple of inches that the whole audience would go out and rape their grandmothers. Margot used to do a series of twelve statuesque nude poses." These included Helen of Troy, the Lady of Spain combing her hair and Diana the Huntress. "Someone would bring on a stuffed greyhound and she would stand there holding this greyhound on a leash. I remember the guy who ran the show telling her to wobble her tits about. She said, 'I can't. What happens if the watch committee is in?' 'Tell them that the rostrum's rickety!' So every night she used to do a little stagger towards the end of her nude bit and just move her tits a little bit. She would end up as Britannia. All the chorus girls would come on and do a military routine around her and end up saluting. She would stand wrapped in the Union Jack with a shield, a trident and one tit hanging out!"

Marty became completely blasé to the nudity although it came as something of a shock to his father when the show arrived at Collins Music Hall. "My father had become quite well off in business at that time," remembers Marty. "He came backstage to see me and he brought his bank manager. He was sitting there talking to a nude woman and he was absolutely fascinated. He couldn't believe that I actually got paid. That this was a job. He would have hung around nude women for nothing and given up his Burtons suit." Although Collins had paid host to the biggest stars in the business, including Marie Lloyd, Fred Karno and Laurel and Hardy, "It was a really bad theatre," said Marty. "There wasn't a stage door. You used to get to the dressing rooms through some catacombs which had been there since the Plague of London. But you felt it was a showcase. That was a word agents used to use to book you somewhere where there wasn't very much money. You'll be seen. Somehow you felt maybe Cecilia Williams – who was the booker for the Moss Empire circuit – might be in. She would never be seen within a mile of Collins. The No. 4 dates that we played was a totally different world to the Moss Empires and Stoll and even the syndicate that had three or four theatres in London. They were good dates. Ours was another world entirely. It was really the dregs of show business."

To supplement their income, Marty and his two partners would hustle around the snooker halls. If the town had a market place they would work that, as often as not picking up more and more outlandish props for the act. The tour was all about survival; mainly surviving the grotty digs that they found themselves in. "We had got to Middlesbrough," Marty remembered. "We had been travelling all night from somewhere like Weston-Super-Mare. We got in at about six in the morning, very hungry, very tired, looking for digs and really feeling awful. We found some digs. We got round there at about 7 A.M. We hadn't eaten for about ten or twelve hours. We got in and sat down in this grubby little front room. The landlady brought us food and she served exactly the same food to a little fat dachshund that followed her in. We were about to eat, the dachshund wolfed his food down and keeled over on his back and died. There we were with our knives and forks poised over exactly the same food as he had eaten. We didn't eat for the rest of that day! The whole company would sit down to eat. A landlady once brought in the vegetables in a chamber pot. She said, 'You needn't worry about it, it's been carefully scrubbed out!' But there it was all the same. Another night I didn't eat. I didn't eat very often because if you were a vegetarian they didn't cater for you. They would leave out cold meat for everybody else and they'd leave out a tomato for me. It was that misconception that vegetarians don't eat at all!"

Still, the show must go on and *The Saucy Girls of 1952* was still getting regular bookings. "It used to begin with us singing: 'Saucy Girls there's something here you'll enjoy, Saucy Girls there's something here for every boy. You'll find in this sparkling revue, a smile, a song, variety too. Music and laughter we have in store and when it's all over you'll shout for more, so it's hello to you from the Saucy Girls of 1952.'"

If the tour arrived in a town it had played recently, "we changed its name," said Marty. "For several weeks it worked under the name of *Up the Girls!* It was called *Evening Nudes*. It was also called *This Is The Show*, so from a distance all you could see on the posters was 'TITS!'"

"We did it again in 1953 and we just changed the title to *The Saucy Girls of 1953* and sang: 'so it's hello you see, from the Saucy Girls of 1953.'" In the end the show ran for nearly two years: "In which time we systematically fucked every one of the chorus. Derek Dean, Joe, Mitch and myself were the only heterosexual males in the show under the age of sixty. Consequently we had the pick of all the birds in the chorus. They were coming and going at a rapid rate. On a rainy day in Bilston what do you do except pick out one of the girls from the chorus and say 'You love.' Because everyone else was either a raving queer or over sixty or very often both, they were glad to get us. So we had a randy two years.

"Joe Moe had put one in the pudding club. The whole company saved for weeks and clubbed together so she could have an abortion. It was twenty-five quid which was a lot more than anybody was making. We all saved together and sent her off to have an abortion. When they talk about show business people sticking together I often think about that. These hard-pressed pros putting their pennies down for some poor little bird to have an abortion. That's show business!" In the end, it was fun with the chorus girls that saw Marty and his act thrown off the bill. "The guy who ran the chorus refused to let any of his girls work with us anymore. He was going to take his girls out of the show. The birds were getting five quid a week out of which they had to pay for their own make-up and their digs. They had nothing. They couldn't afford to offend this guy and they could replace us easily, so that's how we got fired from that."

Marty remembered that: "We did make it on to reasonably good dates at the end," and the Saucy Girls continued without them, leaving him stranded somewhere outside Leicester. It looked like the end of the act, especially as Marty had met somebody who had joined the show during the last few weeks. "He was a hard Scot. One of those people who was as wide as he was tall. All muscle. He was a dedicated alcoholic, an ex-merchant seaman with tattoos on every inch of his skin. I imagine. He was the kind of guy who would have got his balls tattooed! His philosophy was that if you had an inch of your skin that wasn't tattooed and if you were sober after ten in the morning, you were some kind of poufter. The act had folded. Nobody else would work with this guy, so he made me rehearse a comedy act with him."

The idea was to knock some act together and play the working men's clubs in and around Leicester. "The first rehearsal was in these dirty digs in the front room. He had to be on stage and I had to come out and say, 'Guess who's in the navy?' And he'd say 'Who?' and I'd say 'Sailors!'. I balked and said, 'I can't do that,' and then he came for me. He beat me up. I said, 'No, that's shit.' Even then I knew that wasn't very funny."

With his show business cronies gone and in desperate need of money, Marty took on a job in a boot factory in Leicester. "All I did was run the sole of the boot round a machine that made a groove all the way around the sole. I would pass it on to this man on the left hand side of me having had it passed on to me by the man on the right hand side of me. I don't know what he did to the sole of this boot. I don't know what the guy on the left of me did to it after I had finished with it. But I got to care about it. I got to the stage where I wanted to make good grooves in the soles of boots. If you got the jitters or had a hangover your hands would shake and the groove would not be even. I thought: 'That's a hell of a way to spend your life. Getting up every day to put grooves in the soles of boots.' So I quit there."

It was the summer of 1953. Marty was nineteen years old and, once again, Joe Moe and Mitch Revely popped up. Having heard that American bases in France and Germany were desperate for acts they auditioned for an English agent who got them a tour.

"The Americans let you know if they didn't like you. It was very common to have bottles of Coke thrown at you on stage. They didn't want to see us. They wanted to see the girls. By then we had decided that we couldn't do anything that involved much talking because we were always very drunk. All we could do was make a lot of noise. Although we were billed as a comedy act, we did a couple of quick crossover jokes and then we went in to a drum solo. Mitch was the drummer and everybody would shut up so we joined in on a drum trio thing that went on for about twenty minutes. Which they loved. They would stomp and clap along to that. That was it!"

In order to keep working, the act needed military references from each base. "We got into a club once, on New Year's Eve. It was about five to twelve. The entertainment sergeant used to have to sign at the end of your act and put a comment. We walked in and Mitch went up to him and said, 'Would you mind signing this chit,' and the guy wrote a glowing report of our act. We haven't even been on. They didn't know. They were so drunk. We got a lot of work as a result of that! Wild days, really."

Typically, this didn't end well. "We were caught up in a race riot in France," remembered Marty. "We were doing a show near Bordeaux. I was sitting talking to a black guy afterwards; a musician in the band who had worked with Tubby Brown. This big southern sergeant said, 'Don't sit with him. There's going to be trouble if you do.' I couldn't understand what it was about. Suddenly there was this loud noise, we ran out and there was this white guy lying at the bottom of the stairs with his skull cracked open and a black guy stood at the top who had pushed him. It turned in to a riot and I was standing in the middle of it saying, 'Look fellows, you don't want to hit each other. Let's be friends!' I didn't realise what I was into. They had taken these southern whites who had never mixed with black people before and black people who had never been allowed to mix with whites before and put them on the same base! There were guns, knives, bottles, the lot. They hustled me out otherwise I was going to be killed. In fact, four people were killed that night."

The agent that had got them the booking turned out to be a shyster who was juggling payment between eight other acts. "We were left stranded in France without any money," said Marty. "This agent finally got struck off. Most people I have ever worked with have been struck off. They are the only people who would ever hire people like us." As a result, Marty got deported for the third time. "The French consul got tired of sending me home!"

Nevertheless, the act, of sorts, was still there and they kept on trying. It was a hesitant step up the ladder of comedy. It was a somewhat rickety rung, but even his ultimate slapstick hero clowns weren't finding the going all that easy at the time. Harpo Marx had toured England with Chico and found sentimentality in the Brothers' last feature film, *Love Happy*. Stan Laurel had joined Oliver Hardy for one last tour of England and dragged himself through illness to finish their last film, *Atoll K.*

Charlie Chaplin notched up feature films at the leisurely pace of one every four years and indeed his latest, *Limelight*, had seen a bone thrown to Marty's greatest inspiration. Buster Keaton was eking out a living as an often uncredited gag writer on other people's films. He was something of a broken man, between alcoholism and the ignoble fate of becoming a stooge on television's *Candid Camera*, but for Marty nobody could touch him. According to Marty's close friend, the writer David Weddle, "he would keep a portrait of Buster Keaton with him wherever he went. In his office, at home, in his dressing room, no matter where in the world he happened to be working, and... he would watch at least one Keaton film a day. He told me that this was, 'Just to remind me of my roots.' The thing that broke my heart was when he said he knew he would never be as good as Keaton. That was his dream."[2]

If the fate of the clown princes that inspired Marty told him anything at all then it was that the affection of English fans stayed loyal a lot longer than that of Hollywood producers. Still, Marty's contribution to the national sense of humour had more in tune with the gloriously groan-worthy Vaudevillian shtick of Ole Olsen and Chic Johnson.[3] Morris, Marty and Mitch had but one comedy maxim. Basically, it was, as Marty remembered: "to play a lot of instruments... badly."

Quite understandably, the bands at these various theatres were none too impressed with them. By this stage they had each rented a white tuxedo. This was their stage uniform and it simply added to the hatred they received. "We were inferior musicians," said Marty. "They would be these grizzly old miners from colliery bands in-between shifts. We would do a band call and the trombone player would be sitting there with a miner's helmet on! We were three guys in white tuxedos doing a music hall act and although they were much better musicians than us they weren't trendy or young. I don't blame them for hating our act. Compared to what they were getting paid, we were getting paid very well. We could strut about on stage in white tuxes and they had to go and work down the mines and so they took it out on us in that way. We used to do a terrible joke. We used to sing, 'Give me that old soft shoe, I mean that old soft shoe,' and the band would stand up and hurl shoes at us. We gave them a load of shoes. I knew this drummer didn't like me at all, because I couldn't play drums and I was up on stage faking it. He had the terrible needle and he picked up this hob-nailed boot and really aimed at me. He knocked me unconscious and I was off for the rest of the act. From that point on we never carried boots again, only plimsolls!"

This air of violence resonated throughout Marty's music hall days. He would find the local bar and get completely tanked up on cheap draught cider before a performance. When he was in the theatre he would drink at the bar. "Constantly I was barred from bars in theatres before the age I was legally allowed to be in them," he said. Pretty much everyone on the bills drank. In Bilston there was a tenor who: "would come after me every night with a broken bottle. We did a once nightly show there, not twice nightly, which meant there was a lot more time to get drunk. He did all his sentimental ballads about his mother but at about ten thirty at night when he'd had a few jars he wanted to kill me. We weren't friends or enemies. He just didn't like the look of me and in Bilston there's not many places to run to!"

Marty's fellow performers would be in constant flux because the act was bundled in with various touring shows. If Harry Lester's Hayseeds were top of the bill, that would be the name of the show. If it was Dorothy Squires it would be *Dorothy Squires' Road Show*. "We had stolen new things by that stage but it was still, basically, a bad musical speciality act which is what it always was."

Marty was still adamant about his lack of talent as a jazz trumpeter but, according to Barry Took, he certainly looked the part. "In those days, Marty was quite good looking – blonde and with a small goatee beard, in the hope to pass for a jazz trumpeter I suppose, as that was his ambition." Indeed, if he couldn't play the instrument well it just had to be enough to play the instrument at all. Even in the face of an audience who clearly didn't want to hear it. The result was nothing if not noisy and anarchic. It was certainly way ahead of its time, which is a polite way of saying it wasn't very good.

A quarter of a century later, Marty could look back on the early 1950s with a clear perspective of why humour was so difficult for him. Humour derives from depression. If a nation is going through a financial rut the population seeks laughter to elevate it: "I think it's unfortunate for a lot of performers and writers who were writing comedy in the fifties," he explained. "[It] was... a period when people... didn't want to laugh. Now people want to laugh. I think in the fifties we had the illusion, living in England, that we were living in an affluent society [and that] everything was fine. We felt very smug and very secure and when you're very secure the need to laugh is not as great somehow."[4]

It is debatable that even a financially struggling America of the late 1970s would have found Morris, Marty and Mitch hilarious. Still, in his most nostalgic moments Marty would liken the team to somewhere between the Ritz Brothers and Dr. Crock.[5] A music hall speciality act where, to coin the old Olsen and Johnson tagline for *Hellzapoppin'*, anything could happen and it probably will, it was unfettered insanity in the regional theatres of England. Or, as Marty reflected in a less guarded moment: "It was putrid."[6]

But it was still all about survival, whether that was getting a bed for free or merely getting out of town without your face smashed in. "Joe looked like Sabu as a young man," remembered Marty. "If the landlady looked likely, Joe would be nominated as the one who would kip with her for the week. Sometimes the three of us would get free digs, sometimes it was just Joe. At one point we were always following *Soldiers in Skirts* in, which was one of the earliest drag shows, so we always scored the week after that!"

While appearing on the bill with Harry Lester's Hayseeds in Belfast, Marty met Silver McKee, the legendary hard man who ran the city. He was very much in the mould of Jack Spot in Soho and as he knew Marty's connections he took a liking to the act. "He had a knife wound in his stomach from a time he incited and fought off a riot during the Troubles. He'd been bodyguard to Robert Cohen, who was the World Flyweight Champion at the time. He used to walk round that town, taking guns out of copper's holsters, twirling them around and putting them back and patting them on the head. He was tough. Two great paddies turned up at the theatre and said, 'Silver McKee wants you to have a drink with him tonight,' and we said 'Well, we don't feel like having a drink thank you very much.' 'No, you don't understand. Silver McKee wants you to have a drink with him tonight!' The stage manager told us if Silver McKee wants you to have a drink with him tonight, you'll have a drink with him tonight! He came round between houses, a big blond, greying, heavy but very gentle man. The old ladies used to like him in the theatre because he'd open doors for them. At the same time somebody heckled us that night and he wanted to go out and smash them in the teeth! We said, 'No, if they don't like the act, they're entitled to heckle.' Silver was all for tearing him apart and throwing him over the circle."

For Marty, the treacherous Belfast pub crawl started out badly when they visited the local Conservative Club to meet Irish Conservative politicians Silver was in with. The club itself was less happy. Only a few weeks earlier, the black singer Archie Lewis had been on the bill and when the club refused him admission Silver had wrecked the place. "They had just put it together again the night we arrived!" remembered Marty. "We walked around town from bar to bar and he'd be taking his rake off from all the street bookies. If they didn't have the money he would hit them. It was a very calm evening of business transactions for him! At one point he did not want to be observed by the police, so we knocked on somebody's front door. We walked in and there was a little old couple; the guy was reading the paper, the old lady was sitting by the fire. They said, 'Evening, Sir,' and we walked right through the house and out through the back door to lose the police!

"Silver had a passion for snooker. We got to one bar and he wanted to play and I was the only one of us three who played. By this time Silver was very drunk and obviously going to get very violent. We played [a frame until only the black ball was left] and he left the black sitting on the edge of the pocket. That's the only time in my life that I've ever taken a dive and I missed it. I thought, I've given seven away and I've saved my life."

The culmination of this evening of mayhem saw them meet Silver's grey-haired old mother. "We went to this little old house and there was this little old lady who looked like [Hollywood's favourite 'Oirishman] Barry Fitzgerald in drag. We sat down and had a cup of tea. Then Silver said, 'I'm just going to see Marty back to the digs,' and she said, 'No, you're not. It's late enough. You're going to bed!' and he said, 'All right, Mum.' This was the man who ran Belfast!"

Back on stage, the act was getting more and more bizarre. "We had always vaguely done impressions," remembered Marty, "but mostly they were impressions of people the audiences had never heard. We were pretty safe. Joe would do King Farouk [of Egypt]. Nobody knew what the hell he sounded like. He was black and once Joe wore a fez the audience would applaud and think that was very accurate. Joe also used to do an impersonation of [French painter Henri de] Toulouse-Lautrec that I took over later. Not of José Ferrer [in the film *Moulin Rouge*] but of Toulouse-Lautrec. Now, as long as you were on your knees and had a beard and you pointed out it wasn't José Ferrer's interpretation of Toulouse-Lautrec but an impersonation of Toulouse-Lautrec there was nobody in that audience who could say you were doing it badly. They had never heard or seen him. It was a terrible ragbag of bits and pieces."

The theatres they were playing weren't much better either. "We played really shitty music halls. Places like the Leeds City Varieties, where they told you to hang your clothes high up off the floor so the rats wouldn't get them. Our act was made up of run-acrosses. They didn't tell us that the front side was the only side you could get off the stage from. You'd run across to the other side and as soon as you got off stage there would be just you and blank wall. I'd be stuck on that side of the stage for ten or fifteen minutes while my partners finished the act because I couldn't get back across to change. I'd be stuck without my trousers, custard pie all over my face!"

Being paid off by various theatrical managements was an occupational hazard and one that happened to Morris, Marty and Mitch on a regular basis. But, for this particular show, the signed contract had booked twenty-two performers and there was a clause that specified that all cast members appear on stage for the finale. This was a standard clause to stop comedians doing their act and then nipping off to do another gig somewhere else. "This manager insisted on the full company," remembered Marty. "But we were paid off so we couldn't appear in the show. We just had to appear in the finale. They did a run down a wooden stairs, you would bow, the audience clapped and you would extend your hand to the staircase and someone else would run down and take their applause. Audiences for the whole week saw three strangers. They had not seen us before in the show because we hadn't been in the show up to then! I don't know who they thought we were or what they thought we were doing but they would applaud like mad. Very often we would get more applause than the acts that had been on! We would just sit in our dressing room, wait for the stage manager to say, 'Right, it's finale time,' put on our tuxedos, run down, take our call and then we would have two or three hours before we would have to take our call for the second house. We'd go to the nearest pub, get stoned out of our minds, run down and take our call again. That was a real pleasure. Later on I realised you had to do an act before taking your curtain call which was tough. I got the cream of show business at that time. Afterwards it was just the yoghurt!"

However, this spare time did enable Marty to start writing comedy material. "I had always written," he said. "We used to write our own material for the act but much like other music hall acts, you didn't actually write it, you stole it. We began to collate it, which is a writer's word for steal. Eventually I found I was writing bits, unconsciously. I was adding to what was all ready there. And I was writing comedy."

Denis King remembers that: "I was a bit of a performer in those days, touring the halls with my brothers. I don't remember actually seeing them perform but I know Mitch Revely, the Mitch of the group, was a real hustler. He would continually be trying to sell jokes to the other comedians on the bill."[7]

Marty wasn't averse to this behaviour either. "We used to line up outside the Palladium, where a comic would be playing. His manager would come to the door and a lot of us would stand there, holding out pieces of paper with jokes scrawled on them. And he paid for each one he bought. When I found that somebody would pay me to write jokes, I wrote jokes for anybody who would buy them."[8]

It was with national pride that the *Glasgow Herald* reflected on Marty's "prancing anarchic style" and remembered that: "He started off by writing radio scripts which were all rejected until [Scottish comedian] Jimmy Logan bought one for £50."[9]

"I met up with John Law who taught me a hell of a lot about writing comedy," remembered Marty. "He knew the act that I did and I became quite friendly with him while I was doing a show in Scotland. He'd seen it and we found that we had common interests, mainly in American humorists. He encouraged me to write saleable comedy. He drilled me, actually. When I got a comedy idea he would sit me alone in his flat, work out the bare bones of an idea with me and then go off. He would come back two hours later and see what I had written, then help me edit it."

Besides the extra pay packets, the music hall circuit experience gave Marty the opportunity to watch some of his homegrown comedy favourites performing live. Radio may have made stars but variety turns like Michael Bentine and Peter Sellers quickly realised that there was money to be made from resurrecting their ancient wartime material. Give Tony Hancock a pair of brothel creepers or Harry Secombe a shaving brush and they could entertain for at least twelve minutes.

Unsurprisingly, Spike Milligan was also dragging his unique brand of comedy insanity around the country: "Marty and I met in 1955 at the old Chatham Empire. He and I would talk and talk about comedy. I loved to talk to him about comedy, and he was like a scientist with the subject. He was into abstract comedy, and he told me he wanted to be like me. He loved people like W.C. Fields, the Marx Brothers and Tommy Cooper, and he absolutely worshipped Buster Keaton."[10]

A fellow lover of comedy and also of the trumpet was stand-up comedian Barry Took. However, when Barry met Marty a huge mirthquake singularly failed to shake the variety theatre to its foundations. In fact, the two didn't particularly hit it off at all. They were, after all, two playbill-filling rival comedy attractions. One may have been part of a Spike Jones-styled musical slapstick troupe[11] and the other a rather nervous Tommy Trinder-fashioned teller of jokes, but they were rivals none the less. Frankly Marty would rather chew over the comedic fat with Spike Milligan any day of the week.

"I'd met Barry when he was a solo act around the halls," said Marty. "I met him at York Empire, he was doing a stand-up act. He'd been with Carroll Levis. We were able to help each other. Again, there were very few young people on variety bills. The very fact we were under sixty gave us something in common. We found we had similar terms of reference. We'd read the same authors. We liked the same kind of music. We came from similar backgrounds. Our ambitions were similar."

Barry Took recalled that: "We chatted briefly. I watched their act. I seem to remember Marty watching my act. And that was that, or so we thought." The following week and on the same variety bill the two chatted further. "That was in Weston-Super-Mare and that time we really got to know each other. Perhaps Marty had been slightly intimidated by me. I had been a performer longer than he had, simply because I had been around a little longer. I was four or five years older than he was. In fact, I always was! It's quite a big age difference at that age. I was like the older brother he never had."

Mind you, although Marty was still only twenty years old: "He had seen so much of life already," observed Took. "He was old beyond his years really. A young man of twenty with so much experience – in everything – that there was something in those eyes. A wisdom, world-weariness, call it what you will."

Marty said that: "We became friends. Barry went his way as a performer. I went my way." As a writer Marty was still very much under the wing of John Law, as a performer it was the continued lunacy of Morris, Marty and Mitch. A few months before his twenty-first birthday Marty fulfilled at least one burning ambition; his comedy troupe made their debut on television.

Typically, any variety act worth their salt – and quite a few that weren't – invaded the little glowing box in the corner of the nation's living room. Morris, Marty and Mitch were no exception, making their first appearance on the evening of 18th April 1955. The programme, *Show Case*, was the standard variety slot under the production eye of Ernest Maxin.[12] Broadcast live from the Television Theatre, the troupe couldn't have been all that terrible for Maxin and other producers called them back for further variety appearances every few months for the next year and a half. They would conjure up their brand of musical madness on variety shows headed by the likes of Billy Cotton and Jimmy Wheeler.[13] By the end of 1956 the group were commanding fees of thirty-five guineas for each television appearance. It was the heady heights indeed. But for Marty, as was often the case upon achieving the level of success he had long craved, it simply wasn't enough.

The act had always been bad but now the strain of tatty theatres, poverty and impending violence had taken their toll. Marty's twenty-first birthday was the beginning of the end. "We were wearing our rented white tuxedos, standing outside the stage door at the Cardiff Empire and a little poisonous Scots dwarf was lurking about," said Marty. "He kept pointing at me and saying, 'It's all right for you.' I said, 'What do you mean?' 'It's all right for you in that white tuxedo.' I said, 'Look, this is my stage costume.' I tried to explain to him and as I did he hunched up more and more. I thought I was getting through to him until I realised he was hunching himself up for an assault. He finally butted me in the stomach. So I grappled with him and he hit me in the head. One of my partners came to my rescue and this dwarf butted him in the face. The third one came in. There were the three of us and this dwarf beat the hell out of us! The stage manager had called the police and this dwarf was dragged off but we had to go on stage for the finale of Harry Lester's Hayseeds. We had to promenade around, arm in arm, with the Kaye Sisters singing 'Walking My Baby Back Home'! These three blood stained characters, me clutching my groin, one trying to mop blood from his nose, the other one with blood pouring from his head, all in white tuxedos singing, 'Gee but it's great, after being out late...!' When we got off they rushed us off to hospital. That was my twenty-first birthday."

Cardiff also saw Marty's battle with the local theatre bands reach fever pitch: "The pit bands used to scrawl comments on the act all over your band parts [sheet music given by each act to the theatre's resident orchestra] in indelible ink. Because we were a bad act, week after week the band would write their comments. 'Fucking awful act!' The parts used to look like a lavatory wall. There was almost no band part left. We couldn't afford new band parts. That would cost twenty quid. So we just had to keep handing them in each Monday morning. We would toss to see who would take band call because none of us wanted to be there when the band would look at the band parts and see these comments."

The days of music hall were numbered. "It was right for us to split up," Marty said. "The act was very, very bad. Music hall was really dying before we came in to it. We were in on the last gasp and we were not the people to give it the kiss of life. We got just enough of a flavour of what it might have been like in its really good days. Just enough to work with some of the people who were really great. We did occasional bills with Sandy Powell, Max Wall, Frank Randle. I saw Max Miller playing to a near empty theatre.[14] It was the end, but I learned a lot. If I learnt anything I learnt it from the wings, never on stage."

Chapter Four

"I don't think of myself as a comedian or a clown.
I just think of myself as me."

Although Morris, Marty and Mitch had made headways into television and, as a natural by-product, seen their variety theatre bookings improve, Marty had decided what he wanted to do with the rest of his life. He wanted to write comedy; his own unique comedy. "So when the act folded it was a natural thing for me to hawk my comedy around... with no luck."[1]

"I wrote some sketches for Alfred Marks, on spec," Marty remembered. "I wrote lots of them; for Arthur Haynes or Jimmy Logan or whoever. When I got a rejection slip I'd just rub out the name and insert the next name. Rub out Arthur, put in Alfred, rub out Alfred... and send in the same script. Sometimes I didn't even know enough to do that. I sent Alfred Marks a couple of scripts when he was doing his television series. Among the rejection slips, I got a letter from Alfred saying he couldn't use the material because he didn't think it was right for him but that I obviously had merit as a writer and that I should continue. I've only met him twice since and I've never mentioned it. I don't know whether he remembers it and [to him] it's probably a small thing that he did. But it was a thing that actually kept me writing. I was just about to turn it in, not having sold anything for six months. I was thinking of going back to the markets again. I got that one letter, very elegantly written on blue note paper, just telling me to keep doing it. Not offering me any money, just encouragement. That is worth more than money. The money is gone tomorrow. The encouragement has stayed. In bad times I thought about that letter. It helped a lot. It was a generous action."

By 1956 John Law was an established writer, working with Bill Craig at ATV.[2] Naïvely, Marty thought he could just send sketches off to various television shows and be accepted. "I was twenty-two," he explained. "I didn't know that shows had writers. I tried flogging material to *The Arthur Haynes Show* which Johnny Speight was writing then."[3]

"I couldn't understand it when they said, 'No, we have a writer.'" John Law was still pushing Marty forward, however. "He drove Roger Hancock mad to make them buy something off me," said Marty. "Roger used to run *The Arthur Haynes Show* for George and Alfred Black. Roger bought a sketch from me just to get John off his back. They paid me thirty quid for it and I went off on holiday to Switzerland. From then on I was a writer. That metamorphosis happened as a result of an illicit union behind a bush between *Take It From Here* – which was the English-European verbal tradition, and the whole Rabelaisian lunacy of *The Goon Show*. *The Goon Show* is my father, *Take It From Here* is my mother. I was born on the wrong side of the blanket out of those two shows."

As Marty reflected that first sketch "was heavy on charm – which means no one laughed."[4] But it was a start.

"I was getting vaguely involved with tapes and making experimental plays with John Law," he remembered, "and the two of us would hang around with Barry Took. Barry had become a writer before we met again. It was natural that we should collaborate." Pamela Franklin remembers that: "my brother used to write with Barry Took at my parents' home in Henley. Despite the differences between them, my parents were very supportive of him. Marty and Barry would sit in the kitchen for hour after hour working on scripts. The laughter that rang from the two of them was very infectious."

"We had appeared together in Weston-super-Mare," Took recalled. "Marty said that I looked funnier in the street than I did on the stage! I used to wear a casual lounge suit and suede shoes in those days. Off duty I would sport a tweed jacket with cheesecutter cap, old school tie and an umbrella whatever the weather. He suggested I wear that gear on stage, and it worked. It gave me a comedy character. When Marty's writing seemed to be going nowhere, I was appearing in *For Amusement Only* in Shaftesbury Avenue. Almost every evening he would come round after the show and we would share a cheap bottle of wine."

It is certain that at this point in time, Marty needed Barry more than Barry needed Marty. Took's enthused attitude to the future gave Marty that sense of dependability that his insane imagination needed. "Marty was a born writer," said Took, "and I knew we could work well together because of, rather than in spite of, our many differences. Marty and I would add material to my stage act. Nothing much but the signs were there. I fell in love with his sense of the absurd and how far he would take a joke to milk every last laugh out of it. He was like a craftsman. He just seemed to know what was and what wasn't funny, instinctively."

Tellingly, Marty never gave up on this fledgling writing partnership, even when the doubts and demons invaded his thoughts.

"Marty had faith in us," said Took. But it wouldn't prove easy to sell their work. "We had these visions of sugar plums in our heads," Took continued. "We day-dreamed about series after series of television and radio comedy. We thought we were destined to become instant Frank Muir and Denis Nordens and Ray Galton and Alan Simpsons. But it was a slow start. We were the typical overnight success. It took us several years to make that major breakthrough."

Still, Marty was more a performer who wrote rather than a writer who performed. He reflected that, "There used to be an afternoon show on television which was produced by Anne [who later married runner and politician Chris Chataway] called *Fancy Free*. This was at the time I was hanging around with Barry Took and John Law. I don't know what people made of it at home. I've never met anybody who saw it, it went on every Wednesday, live. Anne would say, 'Just come down and do what ever you like on the show.' So on a Wednesday afternoon if you had nothing else to do you would stagger down to Elstree. Because we never believed anybody ever watched the show we would just lark about. There were afternoons of mayhem with Barry, myself, Lionel Blair, Amanda Barrie, lots of people. We'd sing a song or crawl about on the floor or make up a sketch. It was like a club. If you were free you'd say: 'Let's do a telly!'"

It was now that Marty started spending less time with John Law and more time with Barry Took. "We wrote an abortive crime serial for ATV which we could never sell to anybody even though we knew people there. Barry and I discovered we had a rapport. Our personalities contradicted each other enough to give us a black/white, male/female, north/south relationship which we needed to strike off each other. But we were both, at that time, with different partners. We had a literary affair."

Although Marty wasn't officially writing with John Law, "I went through a whole period of ghost writing for other people who I can't name. But I wrote for a lot of shows without any credit for them." Marty did work with Law on a new solo stage act for himself though. "What's the opposite of delusions of grandeur?" Marty pondered. "Because I suffered from them at the time. John convinced me that I could be funny on stage, so we cobbled together an act and I went and did it at the Nuffield Centre. I also had my first big part in a sketch on television the following day. I was watched by a prominent agent at the Nuffield Centre; a guy who handled most of the biggest comedians in the country. He called me up and said, 'Do you want me to be frank with you?' And I said, 'No!' He said, 'You don't have it. You're not a comic. You're a very good writer, you should stick to what you know.' He may have been right, but I so lost my bottle. There's a guy who could have destroyed whatever career I have. I asked to be let out of the television. They couldn't because it was so short notice, so I did it but I did it very badly and got no more work as an actor for a long, long while after that. I was replaced immediately. Luckily I wasn't at a very vulnerable point because I was writing, but he could have said it in a more encouraging way. He could have said work on an aspect of the act, instead of which he said, 'Forget it.'"

With his ambition as a performer crushed, Marty worked in a bookshop near his beloved Charing Cross Road. It was almost exactly like the old days because: "Again I got fired. If someone came in asking for a particular book and I knew there was a better book available on the same subject, I would recommend them to the other shop that sold that book. My boss was very reasonable. My job was to sell his books. The fact that his stock was inferior had nothing to do with me. I was more concerned with giving [the customer] the best information on the subject."

Although Barry Took was writing professionally with Eric Merriman, "We spent a lot of time together. We were friends," said Took. "Marty would go through mellow moods. He could get down in the dumps at the drop of a hat but he would always come out the other side. As often as not with a brilliant comedy notion." Comedy writing was clearly Marty's therapy. That and the firm friendship of Barry Took kept him on a fairly even keel; for the time being at least.

Some six months after Marty's ignoble Nuffield Centre performance, "John Law was still working on my career. He was convinced I could be funny and he persuaded Michael Bentine to use me in a show he had coming up on ATV. Michael had never seen me do anything, there's no reason he should. I had never done anything. Except an impression of Michael Bentine many years ago during my days in music hall. I met Michael in a coffee bar called the Act One Scene One. I used to hang out in there a lot. Michael said, 'Can you do a Scots accent?' And I said, 'Yes,' and I was hired to do three shows for ATV. The next day, [ATV impresario] Lew Grade saw me and said, 'Who's that boy? He's very good. We should do something with him.' John Law, who was waiting on hand, said, 'His name is Marty Feldman and I've written a show for him.'" John Law and Bill Craig had indeed written a series for Marty. *Three "Tough" Guys* related the hapless escapades of three bumbling criminals. "Then," bemoaned Marty, "Lew Grade wanted to use a mate of his and had forgotten who I was. So, the show that was written for me was in fact done with someone else. Long cigar, short memory.[5] So I did these three shows with Michael Bentine thinking that if I get on the box and I'm fairly good then I'll be offered work. The very first show I did with Michael was virtually a walk-on. He suddenly lit up on the idea of my face and started to invent a show around me on the spot. It was a parody of Faust. Would I like to do that? I had one line in the show we were doing. I thought, 'I'm going to be a star.' Michael forgot as well. Not by the next day, by just after lunch. I had called my agent and said, 'Don't ask for too much money.'

After lunch I said to Michael, 'This Faust idea. I've talked to my agent...' He said, 'Faust? Faust? What Faust?' He had forgotten all about Faust. He was on to something else. By then he was wondering what I would look like in drag for another sketch. So I teetered on the verge of acting. Nothing happened so I went back to writing again."

These writing sessions would occasionally involve Barry Took, but still nothing tangible came from it. "We started fairly organically, really," Took remembered. "It wasn't official. No contracts were signed or five-year plans formed. We just made each other laugh and eventually we started writing those things down. It was as simple as that. We just knew we could do something special together. We wanted to write together and we did. It was the flowering of a blissful working relationship. No, it was more than that. It was a marriage. We pretty much did everything that a married couple would do, except take our clothes off in front of each other!"

The person that Marty eventually would take his clothes off in front of on a regular basis was a young secretary by the name of Miss Lauretta Sullivan. The date was 12th April 1958 and for Marty, drunk and a writer with the sniff of success, it was lust at first sight. For Barry Took, there was something deeper about the attraction as well: "Lauretta was perfect for Marty. She was the identikit wife-in-waiting for a cool, wannabe intellectual dropout in the Britain of the 1950s." Marty and Lauretta met in a fashionable club, The Mandrake, a place that was extremely Marty-friendly.[6] "A touch of jazz clubs, a hint of drinking in sleazy West End bars and clubs." This was the very environ that Marty loved. Lauretta was "a whiff, in short, of Bohemia."[7]

Marty himself never glamourised that first meeting with "the most beautiful bird in the world." Booze, as always, was the great leveller. On that fateful night in April 1958 Marty was ten-foot-tall and bulletproof: "I met her in a club. I was very drunk, and she was embarrassed because I was very drunk. I heard her voice – Lauretta has a very husky voice – and apparently I swung right around and said: 'What an interesting voice.' She was bored by me, but we started talking, about ballet, of all things." As for the face, still without the overt popping eye, "She said she found it fascinating but she always did have strange taste."[8]

For Barry Took that instant attraction to Lauretta's voice was very telling indeed. She was "a soundalike of his mother, psychoanalysts might note, but, unlike his mother, a Catholic from Ireland via south Wales."

"Then it was supposed that the young man, having sown a wild oat or two, would go into his father's business... Marty didn't. His father, a dapper, manicured, twinkling-eyed gown manufacturer with a line of amusing, gently-dismissive patter which his son inherited, and whom I first met in the early fifties, would phone me from time to time and ask plaintively, 'Where's Marty?' I didn't know and said so."[9]

This gradual detachment from his family was nothing new, of course. First it had been the eroding of his Jewish roots through perceived betterment. Now the seeming U-turn of the fact that his steady girlfriend wasn't of the Jewish faith was causing friction within the family. Barry Took remembered that he, "as the non-Jewish best friend, helped a little to re-cement family ties but mostly it was a natural desire of a loving family to stay intact." Even though, Marty's bitter memories of feuds and name-calling would never be completely forgiven and forgotten. The fact that Lauretta was "described by the rest of the Feldman family, she told me at the time, as 'that whore,'" naturally drove the couple closer and closer together.

It must have tickled Marty that Lauretta's strict Roman Catholic father had but one complaint about the relationship. He couldn't care a jot about the fact Marty was a Jew. But he was a prosperous family butcher and took exception to Marty being a vegetarian!

Luckily while all this was going on Marty found regular work with a firm family favourite, *Educating Archie*. As Marty said, "Eventually, I got involved with writing a radio show for a ventriloquist dummy, which is a very sensible project! From that point on I was a professional writer." Peter Brough and the wooden schoolboy had been mainstays on BBC radio since June 1950. Over the course of seven series it had already given Max Bygraves his "Big 'ead" catchphrase and given Tony Hancock recurring nightmares.[10]

At the time the shows were being written by Ronald Wolfe and Ronald

Chesney, who later created situation comedy of the highest calibre but were already firmly established.[11] Indeed, Ronnie Wolfe had "already been writing for the radio series of *Educating Archie* for several years [since September 1955, in fact]. Word got round that we needed another ideas person on the writing team. One day into our office in Golden Square this very strange looking young man slouched in. He looked a bit frightening actually but he was the sweetest of people. That was Marty. He clutched a few pages of script in his hand and held them out for me to read. The moment I took them he lit up a cigarette and nervously watched as I read what he had written. It was good stuff. Very original, off the wall material. I said, 'This is excellent. It's fresh and very funny'. He stammered: 'Are you sure? You're not just saying that?' I assured him that he had a great writing talent. We shook hands and he joined us as the third writer."[12]

The recordings for the show were a riot. "Peter Brough didn't bother doing a ventriloquial bit," remembered Marty. "He just used to talk. He would open his mouth just as wide for Archie and himself. He'd bring the dummy out of the suitcase, put it on his knee and away we would go. Peter had one trick. He knew that he could spin the dummy's head and the audience in the studio would laugh. He would think, 'This joke is not going to work,' and spin the dummy's head. But there was always a time lag. You would hear the show, hear a joke die, silence, and half a second later a sudden roar of laughter. I'm sure audiences at home wondered why the hell the audience in the studio were so slow!"

Inevitably, Marty's writing partners also got caught up in his domestic situation. As did Ronnie Wolfe's wife, Rose: "We were very much a part of that aggravation with his parents. Lauretta was not the girl that his mother, in particular, wanted for her son. She wanted a good Jewish girl for Marty. All Jewish parents wanted their children to stick to their own faith and preserve the tradition, it was how things were in those days. It doesn't matter now but then it was very important. Still, no one could have split them up. They were just Marty and Lauretta: an item for life. Besides, he was just too way out for that family of his. He simply didn't belong in that household at all."

"Late one night Marty phoned me saying he had got a special marriage license," remembers Ronnie Wolfe. "It had to be secret because his family would have gone mad if they had known." But even then it had been Lauretta who had proposed to Marty, not the other way around. The date was 14th January 1959, the place Caxton Hall Registry Office: "At Marty's wedding there were only three witnesses," says Ronnie Wolfe, "me, Ronnie Chesney and Peter Brough. Archie Andrews obviously couldn't make it! Marty's parents had no idea. His mother had always said that if Marty married Lauretta they would find her in the London Clinic having a nervous breakdown! On the morning of the wedding, Marty looked green with nerves. Lauretta looked pale but beautiful. She had what Marty always called 'long, useful legs.' The ceremony was over in minutes and we were outside on a rainy pavement by ten o'clock. I asked Marty whether they were going on honeymoon and he said: 'No, we're broke,' so the three of us had a whip round and got enough money together for a room at the St. Ermins Hotel next door to Caxton Hall. Marty protested: 'But we've got a script to finish!' But Lauretta was gratefully dragging him towards the hotel entrance. I can see Marty now looking back at us and saying: 'Look fellas, if I think of any gags I'll phone them in!'"

In fact the only phone call Ronnie received was from Marty's uncle: "Members of his family were always phoning the office and almost as soon as I got back from Marty's wedding the phone rang. 'Well, did he marry that girl?' I knew exactly what it was about. 'Yes!' I said. 'Right. You can tell Marty that his mother is now in the London Clinic!' And the phone went dead."

The family problems decreased with time. They had to. There was nothing Marty's family could do to separate him from Lauretta. Marty's happiness was compounded by the regular money that *Educating Archie* gave him as well. He was making a living and this appeased his mother up to a point, as Barry Took remembered: "There were all kinds of uneasiness until Marty and Lauretta were obviously settled and Marty was prosperous." Even so, it was never fully resolved. "Lauretta became 'okay' and Marty was richer by the hour and all was well."[13]

But Marty was worried. So worried, in fact, that Spike Milligan recommended him to a psychiatrist. "If Spike recommends you to a psychiatrist you know you're in trouble!" he said. "This psychiatrist said, 'What's fucking you up, Mart?' I said, 'What's really worrying me is an insecurity about what I'm doing for a living.' I was writing a radio show for a ventriloquist dummy, well naturally you're going to feel insecure doing that. I was getting seventy quid a show. I said, 'My main worry is I'm married now and I want to look after my old lady. What's worrying me is that this is not a secure income. I'm broke now and I don't really know where next week's money is coming from.' I tell this psychiatrist I'm broke and the next day he sends me a bill!"

Marty need not have worried. His continuing commitment to *Educating Archie* was getting more and more lucrative, but still he doubted his own ability: "Marty wasn't at all confident in himself as a writer," says Ronnie Wolfe. "He was quite child-like at times. Very insecure about what he was doing. But his comedy quirks were coming out in the scripts. He was very avant-garde, even then. Way before his time. We couldn't use all the stuff he wrote because it was so outrageous but we had elements of the madness that he would later make his own."

The turning point was when Associated-Rediffusion picked up the television rights of *Educating Archie* and presented a hugely successful series. Now you really could see Peter Brough's lips move but no one seemed to mind. With Archie Andrews on television, there was obviously a lot more freedom in terms of physical comedy and slapstick and that was right up Marty's street. There was also enough money coming in to indulge himself in a used car. Ronnie Wolfe recalls "warning him about the pitfalls. I told him that I would go with him and he looked at me and said: 'Ron, I'm perfectly capable of buying a car, you know.' He had this naïve charm and I was worried about him getting taken for a ride, quite literally, so I told him to go to Henley's, a good dealer and to get a guarantee. Somehow he had got waylaid and ended up in Warren Street. At that time, every dodgy used car salesman in London traded in Warren Street. It was well known. Anyway, Marty got talked into buying this car. It was a pale mauve sports car convertible with an open roof. A real show stopper! I said: 'Did you get a guarantee?' And Marty looked at me with this sweet, innocent look on his face and said: 'No! The salesman told me that this is such a great car it didn't need a guarantee!' Soon afterwards we were going to see a show at the Oxford New Theatre and Marty excitedly offered to drive us. We all piled in to his car and Marty put it into gear with a great flourish and off we sped: 'See,' he said, 'I told you what a great car this is. Listen to that engine.' We went over a big bump and the door fell off!"

A scene worthy of Archie's televised antics, running concurrently with his radio misadventures on BBC radio. Indeed, it was just days after his television debut in September 1958 that the ninth and final series of *Educating Archie* started on the BBC. As with many of the great names of post-war British comedy, including Hattie Jacques, Bruce Forsyth, Dick Emery and Beryl Reid, Marty found his first footing in the sometimes sentimental and sometimes cynical world of the wooden puppet.

"I didn't get pissed off with Peter," said Marty. "He was a nice man. I got pissed off with this lump of wood. To be Boswell to a lump of wood is not much fun. You had to write for him as if he actually had life. You would have to go through the motions of actually thinking of him as a twelve-year-old boy. He's a lump of articulated wood!"

As John Hall later noted: "In two years on the show, Feldman learned from Ronald Wolfe all he knew about the mechanics of comedy writing. On *Archie*, he became a pragmatic humourist."[14]

But two years was more than enough for Marty. "Peter Brough was very proud that [the classic Ealing Studios film] *Dead of Night* had used his father's dummy. I've known a lot of ventriloquists who have been taken over by their dummy [as Michael Redgrave is in the film]. Peter was taken over by his dummy to a large degree. He gave me presents which were always from 'the little fellow' which used to worry me!"

In many ways, the carnivalesque scribblings for *Educating Archie* were Marty's firstborn, and if this was a substitute baby for the Feldmans it's scarcely surprising that he never wanted the real thing. "We've a Yorkshire Terrier," Marty would explain. "One does what one can."

He was very good with other people's children, though, just so long as he could give them back to their loving parents after a couple of hours. "Our daughter Kathryn adored Marty," remembers Rose Wolfe, "he would baby-sit her for us and make up these wonderful games to play with her."[15]

"Marty would often come to our house to write the scripts," recalls Ronnie Wolfe. "In fact he answered the telephone one day and was the first to hear the news from St. Mary's Hospital, Paddington that my second daughter, Debbie, had been born. He loved her too." For Rose Wolfe: "A baby simply wasn't for Marty and Lauretta. They were so involved with each other, so intertwined, that children would have been a handicap. It would have been too much responsibility and disrupted their social life. They didn't need children, they had each other." In off-guard moments he would even consider their childless life "lucky". There was simply no room for anybody else. "Not only [is Lauretta] the love of my life, but my best friend as well."[16] Marty was the eternal boy-man in any case. Call it romantic. Call it selfish. Call it practical. They were more than enough for each other. "We decided we are a family unit," Marty said. "Me and Lauretta."

One partner was enough for Marty in terms of writing scripts as well. He had grown tired of the "daisy-chain writing" that the Wolfe and Chesney team signified. A partnership with Barry Took seemed the obvious solution. As Marty explained, "When both our writing marriages irrevocably broke down it was inevitable that we should get together and write. We didn't set out to be a team." Indeed, Took was still writing with Eric Merriman at this time but, as Marty remembered, "Barry and I wrote the last series of *Take It From Here*. Frank Muir and Denis Norden left it and they asked for Barry as he had something of a reputation as a writer; having been in on the beginning of *Beyond Our Ken*. I had just become a writer and Barry asked me if I would like to write it with him." The final series of one of Marty's great influences was broadcast from the end of October 1959. "When we sat down to write *Take It From Here* we found we were very in tune with the humour and very in tune with each other," said Barry Took. "We said we'd write together and see how it goes," remembered Marty, "and you go your way and I'll go mine." In the end they went the same way for the best part of a decade.

Chapter Five

"I don't enjoy anything while I'm doing it.
I enjoy having done things, though."

Although the days of *Educating Archie* were numbered, Marty would energise the last year or so of the knowing and playful antics of Peter Brough and his incorrigible dummy. On radio, Gladys Morgan had joined the cast as the Welsh cook and the central comedy musings came from Bernard Bresslaw. Marty gave him a popular catchphrase: "'Ullo. It's me, Twinkletoes." It was simply the latest in a seemingly never-ending line of hulking idiot characters that had quickly made Bresslaw Britain's biggest comedy star.

For Bresslaw, it had all started with the ITV situation comedy *The Army Game*. The first massive comedy success for commercial television, the ramshackle boys of Hut 29 at the Surplus Ordnance Department at Nether Hopping had first fallen in and fallen over in the June of 1957. Created by Sid Colin, the premise was simple. With National Service still an on-going thing in Britain at the time, the comedy goings-on of a group of misfit squaddies struck an instant chord with the nation.[1]

By the time season four kick-started in the October of 1959, the series had notched up an incredible seventy-eight episodes. New broom producer Peter Eton took over the reins and ushered in new cast members – a standard practice, the fluid format allowing recruits to come and go – and new writers. Two such scribes were Marty Feldman and Barry Took. Still, Marty wasn't so much new to *The Army Game* as getting his just reward for the first time. *The Army Game* had been one of the many shows Marty had ghosted scripts for at £30 a go. "I found out the guy who was writing was getting three hundred quid for merely writing out my eight pages of plot and turning it in to dialogue. I thought 'that's a bit strong', but that thirty quid paid the rent." Both Marty and Barry brought something to the fledgling professional writing partnership. Barry had embraced Marty over on BBC radio and Marty had pulled Barry into Granada Television, pretty much simultaneously. Gradually "the boys" were incorporated into the established writing team, as often as not contributing additional material to scripts that Sid Colin and others had previously worked on.

Although the situation of the comedy didn't allow for great flights of fancy or surrealism, Marty and Barry were working on the nation's favourite comedy series and being paid a handsome wage. However, it is reassuring to see Marty's name come up – at the bottom of a list of five scriptwriters – on an episode based around an out-of-tune trumpet player. It could have been Marty's dream job. The trumpet player in question was "Bootsie", so called because he was "excused boots" due to his bad feet. Alfie Bass, the diminutive Jewish character actor who had been with the show since the outset, played the little tinker with charm and gusto; his soft plimsolls getting more ragged with every passing series. His chief cohorts at the time were a lanky northern bag of bones played by Ted Lune and a cockney ducker and driver played by Harry Fowler: "I came in [from series three onwards] to take over from my old mate Michael Medwin who was always playing cockneys but actually wasn't one. I was the real deal. It was bloody hard work but we had a ball on that show."[2]

Bloody hard work, indeed. Thirty-nine shows were taped for series four alone, four of which included a writing credit for Marty. The key comic conflict was still centred on the little man of Alfie Bass and his battling with military authority. The most vicious of these was in the personage of Sergeant Major Snudge. If *The Army Game* can in any way be compared to its American television counterpart, *The Phil Silvers Show*, then Snudge was the Bilko character: cunning, mean-spirited and corrupted, he would always do things by the book unless it affected him. Scottish comedian and character actor Bill Fraser played Snudge from the second series of

The Army Game and the on-screen chemistry he established with Alfie Bass elevated them both to stardom.

During the spring 1960 run of the fourth series, rumblings started about capitalising on this huge popularity. Granada Television was not foolish. If they could have one hit show syndicated on the ITV network then why not two? So it was that producer Milo Lewis, who had overseen the first three series of *The Army Game*, plucked Alfie Bass and Bill Fraser out of the show for good. The show went on for a fifth and final series. William Hartnell, the pioneering Sergeant Major Bullimore from the first couple of series, returned and a youthful Dick Emery was cast as his Bootsie-like figure of squaddie hatred.[3] Marty, already well versed with Dick Emery's characters from his *Educating Archie* days, received just one writing credit on this swan song series. Although he did bestow a lifelong catchphrase on Dick Emery; "Hello Honky Tonks!" was first spoken by Dick's khaki character Private "Chubby" Catchpole.

For Marty, it was a significant farewell to *The Army Game* because it wasn't so much "goodbye" as "let's push two of the most popular characters out of the forces and into Civvy Street. And keep this story rolling." For it was Marty Feldman and Barry Took to whom producer Milo Lewis entrusted the lion's share of the new series. Took remembered that: "Although we were fairly new recruits to *The Army Game* writing pool, everyone at Granada seemed to like what we were doing. Marty and I tended to write really well and really quickly for the characters that Alfie Bass and Bill Fraser played. We both loved that love-hate relationship they had on screen. It was almost child-like in its bickering and playfulness. Most of what we wrote that was used on *The Army Game* was for Alfie and Bill. I suppose that's why we were called in to write the spin-off series."

The new show clearly stood on the shoulders of the popularity of *The Army Game*. Indeed, the ITV schedules were almost post-modern in their cheekiness. The further misadventures of Alfie Bass and Bill Fraser first aired on Friday 23rd September 1960. In a pre-title sequence, the characters are shown being demobbed and, quite literally, leaving Nether Hopping barracks behind them. On Tuesday 27th September 1960 the reboot of *The Army Game* began, allowing viewers to alternate between their favourite demobbed army chums and the boys – including Harry Fowler and Ted Lune – they had left behind them.[4]

As for the title of the spin-off show, it would have appeared obvious but, remembered Barry Took: "The new show was called, at one time, *Alf and Bill,* then *Nice and Ugly,* but mercifully arrived on the screen as *Bootsie and Snudge.*"[5]

In modern television Marty and Barry would have got a "created by" credit throughout, as they penned the first script of the new series and eased Bootsie and Snudge out of National Service. Immediately there was a sense of quality and imagination at work in the scripts. The gang show mentality of *The Army Game* was gone and in its place the endearing play fighting of the two central characters was developed. The grudging affection and tricky wordplay, hinted at in *The Army Game,* was given full vent. We, the audience, were privy to the two protagonists' innermost thoughts. This was a trick used often through the series and it successfully broke down that fourth wall, made the characters even more endearing and showed, early on, that Marty and Barry were determined to push things forward. This was not simply an *Army Game* in Civvy Street although the first six episodes were, in fact, listed as *Bootsie and Snudge in Civvy Life* in the *TV Times.* Still, no water would be trodden with this series. At least one budding writing partnership was tuning in and taking notice: "Dick [Clement] and I were very impressed by *Bootsie and Snudge,*" says Ian La Frenais. "They had cut their teeth on *The Army Game* which was fine. That wasn't really their show and they had guidelines to follow. But *Bootsie and Snudge* was their creation. They took those two characters out of the army and created this whole new world for them to live in. It was character-based more than the broad quality of *The Army Game.*"[6]

There would be the occasional nod back to *The Army Game,* of course: witness Snudge sitting down at a piano and banging out 'Ain't She Sweet' like he used to do "in the sergeant's mess". Geoffrey Palmer, who had sporadically popped up as various military personnel in *The Army Game,* also sporadically popped up as various policemen and a fireman in *Bootsie and Snudge.* It would be reassuring to think that all these were the same man. Still, all the new show really needed was to retain the

Bootsie and Snudge dynamic. For the comedy to work, both would have to be subservient, but with Snudge slightly less subservient than Bootsie. The visual compatibility and vocal bickering of Alfie Bass and Bill Fraser simply gelled and as Bootsie muttered in one episode: "You love this cat and mouse game, don't you?" It perfectly sums up the entire series.

The decision was made to have them employed in a London Gentlemen's Club, the Imperial. Bootsie could still, happily, be called Bootsie because although he was free of army restrictions and away from the squaddies who used the nickname, he still had to clean the boots of the members. He was, however, usually referred to as Bisley throughout the series. Snudge was still in service but with rather more authority, which was perfect for continuing the browbeaten treatment of Bootsie. The real authority figure was played by Robert Dorning as the Club's Honorary Secretary, although his continual "Tut. Tut. Tut!" for quiet masked his own powerlessness against the club committee members. Rounding off the quartet of regular leads was Clive Dunn as Old Johnson, a general dogsbody and old soldier. Although Dunn was already a specialist at "old man" parts, *Bootsie and Snudge* pretty much set in stone the mannerisms of his later, most famous character, Corporal Jones in *Dad's Army*.

The stuffy club was the means to the end for the comedy and, as often as not, the two central characters would wander into more familiar places. Lengthy diatribes would take place while they lay in bed in their servants' quarters. They would chat over a sandwich and a flask of tea in the park or the graveyard. They would unsuccessfully try and pick up girls on a big night out or tackle the intricacies of a local laundrette. They would even hang out in a doctor's waiting room and earwig other people's aliments.

Once the four lead characters spent the entire episode locked in the club's washroom. In another, the still fresh novelty of television was embraced when Snudge's set attracted a group of people into his tiny accommodation. One episode had the duo debating what to do on their Sunday off, only to end up doing nothing but talking about it and not leaving their room. Another saw them plan and pack for a holiday in Bognor and never leave the club. This was the offspring of Laurel and Hardy's *Perfect Day* via *Hancock's Half Hour*.[7]

The more familiar and simple the setting and plot the better, for Marty and Barry allowed their imagination to take the characters into more fantastic places. Television conventions would be shattered with Alfie Bass looking directly into camera with disgust that his private conversation was being over-heard by the audience. A Chaplinesque sentimentality was developed with the Bootsie character as he would have full-length conversations with an ant while washing the club's front step. An ambitious re-telling of the Faust legend saw Snudge become a dashing Jack the Lad and the by-product of Old Johnson being rejuvenated: thus allowing for the historically interesting sight of Clive Dunn as he really was behind all that aged make-up.[8] Ronald Fraser took on the role of the smooth-talking Satan and was just one of many notable guest artistes who flocked to the series. Patricia Hayes and Pat Coombs were petulant gossips. Warren Mitchell added pathos as a crumbling Polish pianist and later returned twice as Reverend Dante Groper. Mollie Sugden turned on her haughty grandeur as Mrs Bonn-Bouche. Arthur Howard gave his usual touch of timidity to Vincent Lackaday-Williams. As well as displaying Marty's usual flair for eccentric names, these characters were truthful and real, adding light and shade and comic power to the scripts.

Mind you, all this inventiveness wasn't enough to crowd out more routine and obvious comedy behaviour like sloppy food preparation in the kitchen or destroyed clothing ruining Snudge's planned evening out. Just before the first series ended Bootsie and Snudge were both in drag. A sure sign that inspiration was failing the scriptwriters.

"Once I was appalled at the script and I said so," remembers Warren Mitchell. "Marty said, 'Go and write one yourself then!' And I did. He and Barry thought it was wonderful but they never did it. Marty was very encouraging."[9]

The occasional lapse into more lowbrow comedy staples was hardly surprising, however, for the workload put huge pressure on the writers. As Barry Took remembered: "In those days, ITV comedy shows ran on the American pattern – thirty-nine episodes at a time being quite common. We certainly did thirty-nine programmes in the first series of *Bootsie*, with Marty and me writing the vast majority of them."[10]

Indeed, the first eighteen scripts were all Took and Feldman collaborations and throughout the rest of the run both writers took on individual episodes as well as pitching in with additional material in other people's scripts.[11] Barry Took even appeared in one episode (transmitted on 27th January 1961) although Marty, still desperate to act, failed to step in front of the camera despite the myriad of perfectly suited tramps and vagabonds that populated the series. He said that: "I discovered that there was much more money in writing for other comics than trying to be one myself."[12]

The people who sat and watched and loved the work could never understand how a writing partnership worked. "People say, 'Do you do the plot and does he think of the funny lines?' said Marty. "Very often you don't know. If you do know there's something wrong with the relationship. It would vary from day to day. There would be days when I had a marvellous plot idea and Barry would decorate it. I would be the architect and he'd be the interior decorator. There were other days when it would work the other way around. While that existed we had a very good working relationship; probably among the best teams in the country. The total was more than the sum of the parts." Barry Took remembered "those wonderful moments when the typewriter seemed to be going faster than anyone could possibly think. Those are some of my very happiest memories. Marty would often claim that when we started writing at that sort of pace the typewriter somehow made the two of us blend in to one. He would say that a third person entered the room and did all the writing for us. A person called Barry Feldman or Marty Took. At those moments writing together felt so right. Almost easy."

Marty's solo writing credits heightened the love of the lengthy duologue between the two central characters as well as the comedy gleaned from normality and boredom. In the episode transmitted on 3rd February 1961, minutes of screen time are given over to debates about the addictiveness of smoking and the nuisance of having to pop to the shops in order to buy some cigarettes. The bickering dialogue spirals on in this fashion:

Snudge: You smoke too much y'know, Bisley. A boy of your age, it's ridiculous. I had an uncle of mine who smoked sixty a day once. Never stopped. Everywhere he went. Everywhere he went he had a cigarette in his mouth. Never stopped. Everywhere he went, he smoked.

Bootsie: What, even in the wotsit?

Snudge: Yes!

Bootsie: How do you know?

Snudge: I used to see the smoke coming out of the keyhole! Finished him, y'know. Oh yes, he went before his due time.

Bootsie: How old was he then?

Snudge: Eighty-four.

Bootsie: Eighty-four?

Snudge: I've told the story as a moral. Stop smoking, Bisley. Give it up! Tobacco is a filthy weed, which from the Devil doth proceed. It stains your fingers, marks your clothes and makes a chimney of your nose.

Bootsie: Yeah, you're right. I wouldn't like any black soot up my hooter, I wouldn't.

Typically, the episode embraced television convention and featured Bootsie bumping into Terence Brook: famous at the time as the lonely man in the series of "You're never alone with a Strand" cigarette advertisements.

The episode was something very close to Marty's heart, in more ways than one. He had always been a heavy smoker. It fitted his jazz club image perfectly. But the relentless pressure of writing *Bootsie and Snudge* had increased his intake even more. "I was writing thirty-nine TV shows a year for three years, plus two radio shows a week," he sighed. Chain-smoking and copious cups of coffee were essential for Marty's concentration. He once said: "To me it is a necessary crutch against the tensions of life." Marty's home was heavy with smoke, as Lauretta was even more of an addict, as Rose Wolfe remembers: "If Marty would smoke between courses, Lauretta would smoke between bites!" It undoubtedly contributed to the inspired hysteria within Marty's scripts. Unfortunately, it was only a matter of time before this unhealthy and mentally exhausting lifestyle took its toll.

Doctors diagnosed a severe case of Graves' disease;[13] a condition most commonly brought on by stress, over-work and cigarette smoking. The medical dictionary should have included a photograph of Marty. It was a long and painful illness but the cure was even worse. Accidentally given an overdose of the thyroid treatment, Marty's face reacted badly and that "lazy eye" that had disconcerted him for so long bulged.[14]

Lauretta was unperturbed by the change, particularly when she was advised that the operation that could, and only could, rectify the situation was potentially life threatening. "Leave it," she said, "I'll just look at the other one."

Besides, medical opinion at the time suggested that the condition wasn't permanent. "My eyes were fairly OK till I had this thyroid thing and they popped out," Marty said a decade later. "The doctor said they'd pop back. I'm still waiting..."[15]

Marty, unwittingly and unwillingly, had his comedy trademark. It was his Charlie Chaplin cane or his Harpo Marx wig but, at the end of a day's filming, he couldn't simply remove it and blend back into the background. That popped eye would be the curse and blessing of the rest of his life.

Chapter Six

"Other artists can put over my material better than I can."

For both of those people closest to Marty; his wife, Lauretta, and his writing partner, Barry Took, the appearance counted for nothing. As Barry wrote, at the height of his friend's fame in 1969, "I had never noticed the way Marty looked. We'd write sitting side by side, we'd drink leaning against the same bar, we'd eat, as often as not, at a snack bar counter."[1]

For Marty, during this time as purely a writer, he was in a safe and secure place. Looking out on the world from behind those bulging boiled egg eyes of his. His life as a writer was a cosy, isolated affair with only his family and friends around him. The press never bothered him and admirers of *Bootsie and Snudge* would never have recognised him.

Indeed, Barry Took later ruminated on "the anonymity of the scriptwriter." They had gone "back to ATV to work for a season of *[On] The Braden Beat*. We were told later that the production team had had a bet on which one of us was Took and which was Feldman."[2]

Marty's appearance might have changed but his drive hadn't. Indeed, typically one of the last episodes in the first batch of *Bootsie and Snudge* featured Bootsie in a hospital bed – plagued by unwanted visitors.

It is not too fanciful to see Bootsie as Marty's own alter ego. The little Jewish chap with a skill for playing the trumpet badly and a love of poetry: naïve, happy but with a temper on him. Snudge is Barry Took: tall, polished but a little irritable, as likely as not to cause a problem as calm the situation down. Together Marty and Barry wrote such vivid, intertwined speeches for their beloved protagonists. In October 1961, after just a four-month break, a second series of *Bootsie and Snudge* hit the screens. The show that had spawned it, *The Army Game*, had gone forever.

Happily, for Barry Took, "That second series was shorter than the first. It was only twenty-nine episodes. That was just what we were called to do, it had nothing to do with Marty's recovery. Again, the majority of the episodes were written by us."[3]

Indeed, everything was reassuringly the same. The familiar 'Pop Goes the Weasel' theme tune, Snudge's cunning, hand outstretched, tip-hungry: "I'll be leaving you now, Sir." Bootsie's resigned: "But ne'er mind, eh?" Even Clive Dunn's aged "Why heyyyy" at the sight of a pretty ankle. The characters had become almost Dickensian, such a part of the London psyche were they. Moreover, the show had been recognised by its peers, or at least Alfie Bass's performance had, when he was named the Variety Club of Great Britain's ITV Personality of 1960. Bill Fraser attended the ceremony and posed, suitably disgruntled, with his beloved co-star.

That affection and familiarity would be essential, for the second series had a sting in its tail. The shorter run may have been "a blessed relief" wrote Barry Took, "except that we had to soldier through a long Equity strike, (Equity [the Actors' Union] quite properly wanted a bigger stake in what Lord Thompson of Fleet had called a licence to print money) using only the four actors under contract – Bass, Fraser, Robert Dorning and Clive Dunn. We used every permutation of being locked in, locked out and being stranded in the middle of nowhere – soliloquies abounded and, good as the actors were, it was agony to work under such restrictions. When finally the strike was settled, Marty and I celebrated by writing a story with eighteen speaking parts, a parody of Alfred Hitchcock's *Rear Window*."[4]

It remains one of the cleverest half hours of situation comedy ever broadcast on British television. Such complex, healthily populated plots were rare in situation comedy at the time, particularly from the 'beans on toast'-geared output of ITV. Marty seized the freedom that Granada had given the writers. The budget may have been low but the scope was infinite. In one of Marty's solo credits he pitted Bootsie and Snudge against each other in a club-based recreation of a battle. For all intents and purposes the entire episode revolved around the two men at play. The limitations clearly fired the imagination and some of their finest ever scripts resulted.

"It was exactly the same with *The Goodies*," maintains Tim Brooke-Taylor, "when you are forced to write to limitations you think in a more clever way. Those episodes that Marty and Barry had to write for just the four people signed up under contract were, I think, so much better than the others. All of them were really good fun but when those restrictions were in place their verbal material was just fabulous. Tightly constructed, well thought out comedy programmes."

But for Marty, the fun of writing for the old soldiers was beginning to pale. He was still burning to act. It had been over five years since his promising jaunts on ATV but throughout those years Marty still had a carrot of fame dangled in front of him. The dangler was always Michael Bentine. "I would bump into Michael while I was writing *Bootsie and Snudge* or whatever it was," remembered Marty. He would say, 'That face. I've got to use you. Will you come and be in my next series?' And I'd rush home and tell Lauretta: 'Oh, I've got a chance. I'm going to be an actor again, Michael Bentine wants to use me.' Come the series Michael would forget. About three months later I'd bump into Michael and he'll say, 'Marty! I must use you. Come and be in the next thing that I write.' Six or seven times I believed him! I kept on going back saying I'm going to be an actor again and he'd keep forgetting."[5]

A third series of *Bootsie and Snudge*, broadcast from October 1962 through to May 1963 saw Marty's involvement decrease. He wrote less than a third of the twenty-nine episode series. Marty had simply burned himself out where *Bootsie and Snudge* was concerned. As Barry Took explained, "We wrote... at a prodigious speed... We could write twenty-four and a half minutes' comedy for commercial television in a day. There were, of course, days, weeks even, when we couldn't produce anything at all – we'd temporarily written ourselves out. There were times too when we disagreed over what to write but these occasions were rare."[6]

However you look at *Bootsie and Snudge*, and at its best it was indeed brilliant, the sheer longevity and success of the characters secures them a place in the television Hall of Fame. "There were over one hundred episodes of *Bootsie and Snudge* altogether," remembered Barry Took, "and I was associated with them all in one way or another. I can't remember what was happening in the rest of ITV during that period, and, in fact, I'd be hard put to it to remember what happened anywhere else on earth, so involved was I with the day-to-day affairs of *Bootsie and Snudge*."[7]

Barry Took had also been writing successfully for the BBC for several years. It was a natural step when, at the age of twenty-eight, Marty returned to the corporation as a contract writer. With ITV's most successful situation comedy on his CV, Marty was certainly a hot property and the BBC were keen to allow him a scattergun approach. As a result of poor management and lack of focus, his initial months led to unfulfilled commissions and creative compromises.

Bizarrely, the very first script the BBC commissioned Marty to write wasn't a comedy at all but a hard-hitting dramatised documentary on drug addiction. Having mapped out the idea in writing to Marty's agents, Fraser & Dunlop, on 14th January 1963, the as yet untitled project no. DR63/0174 promised a fee of £300. This was provided that the storyline by the author, Marty, was accepted and a sixty-minute programme was broadcast. By 1st February 1963 the BBC had commissioned Marty's idea. He threw himself into research regarding the drug problem in Britain. Tentatively entitled *Drug Addicts* the research led to nothing and the project was officially written off by the January of 1964.[8] In the interim, Marty had been commissioned for something much more up his street: an episode of *Comedy Playhouse*.

Comedy Playhouse had been an important part of the schedules since 1962 when it had been pioneered by writers Ray Galton and Alan Simpson as a platform for one-off half-hour ideas. However, since 'The Offer' had been immediately picked up for series potential – it became *Steptoe and Son* – the whole *Comedy Playhouse* strand was now seen as a place for potential pilot shows. Galton and Simpson had relinquished their hold on the show and now the BBC presented it as an active playground for scriptwriters with unique ideas to present. These were the perfect environs for Marty and he was commissioned for three scripts for the new series; two under producer Michael Mills and one for Dennis Main Wilson.

Although the script for the first of these was plain sailing, for it wallowed in the East End Jewishness that Marty knew well, the production was fraught with disaster. 'Nicked at the Bottle' concerned the exploits of a corrupt lawyer, "Mossy" Marcus and his eccentric client, Emily Trout, played by Margaretta Scott. It was packed with the seedier side of London and full of Yiddish phraseology, and the BBC immediately saw it as a series. To that end they pulled out the casting stops and approached a huge star for the role of Mossy: Terry-Thomas. Having just broken into America with the all-star comedy classic *It's A Mad, Mad, Mad, Mad World*, T-T was quickly becoming the international definition of the British silly ass. The role of Mossy was something very different and that was both the challenge and the problem.

From the first day of rehearsals, on 15th October 1963, T-T seemed uneasy with both the script and the direction. Two days later he expressed his concerns to his agent, Clive H. Nicholas, who advised him to leave the project. Nicholas himself went to the rehearsal room to drop the bombshell and, as Terry-Thomas remembered in his autobiography: "It was as simple as that. Instead of spending a few unpleasant weeks mucking about in a rotten play, I went to the South of France."[9]

An internal memo from the BBC tells a slightly different story.[10] Terry-Thomas had accepted the role on 3rd October and, already in possession of the script, had expressed how much he liked it. The star was continually trying to increase his BBC fee and it was suggested that this was the real reason why he walked off the project. On the evening of 17th October, the day Terry-Thomas had walked off the show, both Michael Mills and Dennis Main Wilson "called on Terry Thomas [sic] at his house but they were unable to gain admission. The producer thereupon contacted George Cole personally and persuaded him to take over the part."

This was extremely short notice for, as originally planned, 'Nicked at the Bottle' was recorded just days later on 21st October. The BBC were livid, however, and wisely Terry-Thomas wrote to Michael Mills on 23rd October: "I must apologise for the abrupt way in which I left you last week, but as it was impracticable for me to continue, it seemed the best way to do it. I should be the first person to agree that I could be accused of lacking in good manners, but in 'using the secateurs' a lot of discussion was avoided, which apart from being very exhausting could not possibly have altered the situation."

When the show was broadcast a few weeks later the public and critical reaction was good, but not as good as the BBC had expected. While a very fine actor, George Cole did not have the star pulling power of Terry-Thomas. Nor did Alfred Marks, Leonard Sachs or Sydney Tafler, all offered up by Terry-Thomas's agent as able and willing replacements.[11] The threatened legal action finally fizzled out by December but Terry-Thomas didn't work for the BBC until 1967. (Astonishingly enough, this was in another *Comedy Playhouse* episode, 'The Old Campaigner' written for him by Michael Pertwee. Tellingly, however, this cast him in the much more familiar role of a caddish salesman. A series followed and the BBC raised a 'we knew it!' eyebrow.)

The *Comedy Playhouse* that producer Dennis Main Wilson had commissioned Marty to write was broadcast in the January of 1964. His *Bootsie and Snudge* scripts had been liberally populated by waifs and strays and this show, 'Good Luck Sir, You've Got A Lucky Face' was very much cut from the same cloth. The central character was a roguish match-seller by the name of Gomorrah Weevil, played by *Comedy Playhouse* regular Graham Stark.[12] He fought the corner of the little man and attempted to bamboozle a scurrilous landlord, Harold Harbinger, played by Derek Francis, an actor who specialised in bluff pomposity.

Although no series resulted, Marty was commissioned by producer Sydney Lotterby to write a sketch series for Graham Stark. Having long proved himself a reliable stooge for almost every comedian on television, this was Stark's big chance to prove himself as the lead. However, in a BBC memo it was explained that: "Marty Feldman was commissioned to write the scripts for the Graham Stark series but because of some difference of opinion as to content it has been decided not to proceed with the arrangement. Copyright department have arranged a settlement under which Marty Feldman is paid a fee of £550. There is no possibility of any of the material being used."[13]

It is unlikely that Marty's scripts were too outlandish for Stark. This was, after all, a performer who would try anything for a laugh and had happily cavorted around with Peter Sellers for Richard Lester's groundbreaking *The Running, Jumping & Standing Still Film*. Whatever the problem, Marty couldn't have been that downhearted. The second of his *Comedy Playhouse* scripts, broadcast in December 1963, had proved hugely popular and the BBC wanted a series.

The episode, 'The Walrus and the Carpenter', was something more akin to the introspective duologues that had been a feature of *Bootsie and Snudge*. It was a more ambitious script than the jaded Jewishness of 'Nicked at the Bottle' as well. This would have depth of character and attempt to enrich the mild-mannered comedy with pathos. In other words it needed a bit of heart, and Marty needed Barry Took. "At that time I was still under contract at Granada," remembered Took.[14] "As a result I did work on the script with Marty but I couldn't be credited on the BBC. That was only right and proper in any case. It was Marty's idea."

Moreover, the BBC written archives reveal that Marty was originally contracted to also write the series alone. On 9th June 1964 three episodes of twenty-five minutes each were commissioned at a fee of £550 per script. The contracts were signed three days later but Barry Took's name has clearly been added and it is noted that the two writers will now share the money: "Both authors have signed a Guild Series Agreement."[15]

By 27th July 1964, Head of BBC Comedy Tom Sloan was in receipt of the first two scripts. He found them "satisfactory and would like to take up the option on a further three, making six in all." As John Law's secretary, Miss S. Bateman noted in her own hand on a memo to Heather Dean in Copyright, the series would be "five scripts in this series and one repeat of original 'Walrus and the Carpenter' from *Comedy Playhouse*."[16]

Barry Took remembered that: "Some bright spark at the BBC had wanted to call the series *You're Only Old Once* and I know Marty was very unhappy about that. Neither of us could come up with a better title than

Marty's *Comedy Playhouse* title. Thankfully, in the end, we got our own way and the whole series was called *The Walrus and the Carpenter*. It was perfect. If you know your Lewis Carroll you'll understand why."[17]

Indeed, the two central characters were as chalk and cheese: Gascoigne Quilt, a well read, gentle man whose life and career had been ruined by a sour love affair and Luther Flannery, a hard drinking womaniser who stomped through life with disregard. This was scarcely the stuff of a typical situation comedy but the writing was so finely tuned and the casting was something near perfection. Importantly, these two misfit friends were not played by comedians but by actors: Felix Aylmer as Quilt and Hugh Griffith as Flannery.

The second episode of the series, 'Return to Lumley Hoo', had, according to the script: "discovered [them] sitting in the churchyard listening to the sound of the church choir practising... this starts Quilt off reminiscing about the old days when he was a school teacher at Lumley Hoo."

The Audience Research Department report summed up that: "This was, indeed, television comedy at its best." Audience members said it was: "humour tinged with pathos but never over-sentimentalised and always delightfully human and natural. The characters of the two old men were beautifully drawn, viewers thought – Quilt, the gentle scholar and his more exuberant and down to earth friend, Luther – and their conversation just the ordinary, everyday kind of thing that such a pair would find to talk about during the long and empty days of retirement. In the words of a housewife: 'Beautifully written. This script had everything – laughter, tears, the lot!'"

Nicholas Young, cast in this episode as one of the prefects at Quilt's old school, remembers that production didn't go entirely smoothly. "The main cause for concern was its stars. Dear old Felix Aylmer (he was never young) had great difficulty with his lines and his speeches were written down everywhere for him (including his cuff). His co-star was also a problem. It would be fair to say that Hugh Griffith liked a drink. As his reputation went before him, it was decided that the best way to control his excesses was to rehearse in a club [in Putney] with a bar in situ!" Unsurprisingly, "Marty and Barry Took did appear at rehearsals to keep an eye on things (which for Marty, was difficult!)"[18]

The efforts obviously paid off for: "The majority of those reporting seemed well pleased with the overall standard of performance and were delighted with Felix Aylmer and Hugh Griffith as the two old gentlemen. Indeed, it would be difficult to fault their portrayals of these vastly differing personalities, drawn together by their mutual loneliness, viewers said, and it was to be hoped that subsequent episodes would give them ample scope to develop and deepen their happy relationship. The contrast between them enhances the liveliness of the scenes. Although Luther shows respect for Quilt's culture, one feels he is much tougher and therefore the protector of his friend. The psychology of old age is wonderfully portrayed.'"[19]

Nicholas Young recalls that: "Also in that episode was Terence Alexander. As a young actor (in name and in fact) I felt privileged indeed to work with such legends."[20]

As for the audience, "There was much praise for an unusual and entertaining style of comedy which, with its more leisurely pace and everyday dialogue, provided a refreshing change from other, more boisterous, shows."

Dick Clement remembers that *The Walrus and the Carpenter* "was the show they were really proud of. Our real heroes were Ray Galton and Alan Simpson. They were Marty and Barry's heroes as well, obviously. I recall Marty saying, years later in LA, that he thought it was the best show that he and Barry had written. He was very fond of it. They were leaning more towards that Galton and Simpson style of good, well-defined characters and believable situations."[21]

Even when Hugh Griffith's drinking got completely out of hand, Marty came up with the solution. He brought in Warren Mitchell: "Hugh was so pissed he would just mutter his line and fall asleep, so I did the lion's share of his part playing a character called Hugh Wilberforce. Hugh had this terrible tick where he kept rubbing his face. People were going round the Beeb imitating it. Felix Aylmer was marvellous. He was very old so they would do a bit of rehearsing and shooting and then rush him off to his dressing room and make him lie down. They wanted to preserve him for the rest of the series. It was a tidy show. Probably the best they ever wrote."

However, it was the show that led to the first major dispute between Marty and Barry Took: whether this was because of the pressure of the series, the fact that *The Walrus and the Carpenter* had, initially, been Marty's project, his fledgling fumbles at the BBC or, more likely, a combination of all three. "I suppose unconsciously I regarded myself as the head writer of the team – a fact that Marty came to resent," said Took. "One of our few spats arose over our credits. He'd been moody for a few days and I asked him what was bothering him. He said, 'Why does your name always come first?' I was astonished, never having really noticed, but as I was senior in age and experience, it was natural for producers to say 'Took and Feldman', rather than the other way around. I said to Marty, 'Well, if you want your name to be first that's fine by me, in fact "Feldman and Took" sounds better.' So 'Feldman and Took' it became."

The crossover between "Took and Feldman" and "Feldman and Took" saw the two scribes writing for two very different powerhouse comedy performers. "I've written for a lot of stand-up comics in the past," reflected Marty, "and they are totally self-occupied and self-centred. They rarely make good actors, because they're not used to talking to anybody else – only to an audience. They remain superior to the audience; they remove themselves from being ridiculous. A stand-up comic is not ridiculous unless he becomes his own butt, like [rotund New York comic] Buddy Hackett does. They ridicule other people."[22]

One stand-up comedian who was uniformly seen as a very bad actor was Frankie Howerd: "He was terrible," asserts regular writer Ray Galton, "but in a brilliant way. Frank couldn't act at all but he did something amazing with what you had written for him. Like a brilliant jazz musician. That's probably why Marty liked him so much."[23] Marty certainly did like him: "Writing for Frankie Howerd taught me more about timing than I would have learned in years as a performer," he said.[24]

"They got their second wind writing for craftsmen like Frankie Howerd," wrote John Hall. "[He] was out of vogue, and once paid in *Encyclopaedia Britannicas*, but delivered a line so brilliantly that he was worth the labour."[25]

Marty and Barry wrote "the BBC" side of Frankie's landmark 1963 recording *Frankie Howerd at the Establishment and at the BBC*. The Establishment material has achieved near legendary status but the BBC material is awash with the typical "Ladies and Gentle*men*" conversational monologue that Howerd had perfected. The surreal flights of fancy through his breakfast habits and foreign travel have the distinct stamp of the writers, however.

Ironically, the live Establishment club recording is notable for the haw-hawing laughter of Frankie's camp rival, Kenneth Williams, who was in the audience that evening. And it was Kenneth Williams that Marty and Barry were set to write for. At least, that was the original idea: "[The producer] Dennis Main Wilson got in touch with us and commissioned Marty and I to write a comedy spectacular for Kenneth Williams," remembered Took. In a BBC memo the producer detailed that: "The writing job will entail not only writing dialogue material but also writing any new lyrics required, and pretty well devising the format for the show, which is to star Kenneth Williams... I am sorry that this notice is rather late. Unfortunately this has been unavoidable because Marty Feldman and Barry Took did not arrive back from a continental holiday until the weekend. As time is rather short, I should be obliged if you could press on with negotiations as quickly as possible."[26]

Barry Took said that, "I suppose in light of our material for Frankie Howerd this was a reasonable side step for us and we accepted more than happily. We both admired Kenneth Williams as a performer and, frankly, after all those hundreds of situation comedy episodes, a few sketches and one-liners dripping with innuendo was a piece of cake."

In the event it wasn't as easy as that. Williams pulled out of the project before rehearsals and, without very much script tweaking at all, the show was broadcast in the December of 1964 as *Scott On...Birds*. The Scott, of course, being Terry Scott, hugely popular at the time in partnership with Hugh Lloyd in the BBC situation comedy *Hugh and I*. "Thinking about it we must have changed something!" pondered Barry Took. "I must say that a *Williams On...Birds* would have been very different to a *Scott On... Birds*. Still, it didn't seem to matter. It was a big success."[27]

So big, in fact, that two more *Scott On...* shows were commissioned on 2nd February 1965. The contract, signed three days later, was: "for the two scripts of forty-five minutes each which we wish Marty Feldman and Barry Took to write as vehicles for Terry Scott, due for production in the April to June quarter this year."[28] A joint fee of £750 per show was agreed upon, "with some misgivings," wrote agent Kenneth Ewing. "We shall definitely look forward to an increase in this fee for future programmes."[29]

As for the hope to write for Kenneth Williams, Marty and Barry certainly need not have worried. At the very time the temperamental camp comedian had pulled out of the BBC television special in the December of 1964 there was a certain BBC radio series already being discussed. It was to be the biggest ever success of the Marty Feldman and Barry Took writing team. Ooooh. What could it be?

Chapter Seven

"I am, as you may have heard, trying for the world's longest suicide attempt by stuffing live nightingales down my throat until their beaks stick out of my ankles."

A nd now the answer to last chapter's question... No. Wait for it. Wait for it!

Having turned thirty in 1964 Marty was happily entrenched at the BBC. He was deep in the writing process for *The Walrus and the Carpenter* series with Barry Took when the corporation commissioned him: "to write ten thirty-minute scripts destined for a *Comedy Playhouse* series to be written between now and the end of 1965."[1] He would be paid £600 per script. In the event, only four of these scripts would be produced and broadcast by the summer of 1966. Two of which were written with Barry Took at the usual fifty-fifty financial share.

The first of these, 'Barnaby Spoot and the Exploding Whoopee Cushion', opened the fourth series of *Comedy Playhouse* in May 1965. Undoubtedly one of the most bizarre and inventive of all the *Comedy Playhouse* episodes, it was produced by Dick Clement who, with his writing partner Ian La Frenais, was just set to unleash the second series of *The Likely Lads*. "Ian and I first bumped in to Marty back in the early 1960s," remembers Clement. "It was before we had even started writing professionally. I was on a director's course and was showing Dennis Main Wilson a little film that I had made. This would eventually turn into *The Likely Lads* but it was just a short film. I remember Marty walked in to the back of the room and watched it and said to Dennis: 'They are good writers. Put them down on the list.'"

Ian La Frenais says: "That was lovely. You see, Marty was a big name writer and we were nothing. The short film had been Dick's exam piece to get into the BBC as a director. We were young, budding writers but to have someone as established as Marty to actually praise us and acknowledge us as good writers was really something."

'Barnaby Spoot and the Exploding Whoopee Cushion' starred John Bird. "He had become a star of the satire movement with *Not So Much a Programme More A Way of Life* [broadcast from November 1964 to April 1965] but this was his first acting job," says Clement. "Actually, Marty himself should have starred in it. He hadn't started performing on television at that stage but the role would have been perfect for him. Barnaby Spoot worked in a novelty shop and he invented a walking, talking cheese! It was very madcap and off the wall. Very Marty, in fact."

As the BBC promotional blurb had it: "Have you ever gone past one of those cluttered, overflowing shops which sell practical jokes, and wondered what sort of person took the trouble to invent them? This may have been the starting point for Marty Feldman and Barry Took when they sat down to write..." The show saw Barnaby taking the rejection of his latest novelty, that "Chatty Cheddar", and plotting to eliminate the company's board of directors with the exploding whoopee cushion of the title.

"It was wonderfully mad stuff," chuckles Sheila Steafel, who was cast as the "shapeless" Miss Narcissus Font, Barnaby Spoot's love interest. "Marty was a fun and funny man. All I remember was that he had these extraordinary eyes and a very beautiful wife! He was around during rehearsals and when we recorded it and was very nice and encouraging to us actors. He seemed genuinely pleased with what we were doing with his script and it was typical Marty and Barry material. They had such wonderful imagination when it came to character names. My character was a prime example."[2]

A cross section of the audience certainly agreed, with one reviewer reflecting that: "Even Barnaby Spoot's name made me laugh, and there were plenty of other laughs to follow." Those that liked the show really liked the show, considering it: "Refreshingly unusual in both theme and setting. The characterisation was particularly good – Spoot himself, his 'lady love' and his assistant, the horror film addict who related his lurid stories with so much relish – all these were well drawn, they thought, and the dialogue was both witty and amusing, providing a really first class and enjoyable show."

However, many, many more found the comedy a little too wayward for their taste. While welcoming the reappearance of *Comedy Playhouse*: "Many of those reporting were obviously extremely disappointed in this first programme in the new series. A number dismissed it out of hand as 'puerile rubbish' – the dialogue was feeble, they said, the story 'thin' and the episode as a whole too stupid to be in any way amusing. 'I thought it was a load of tripe and nothing like the original *Comedy Playhouse* series,' wrote one Housewife."

It was seen as "slow and boring (one group finding the Vincent Price saga as unfolded by Spoot's assistant particularly tedious). Wrote an Architect: 'This was disappointing, or perhaps the splendid title encouraged one to hope for something more original. A promising theme mishandled.'"[3]

Even more bizarre was 'Memoirs of a Chaise Longue', a *Comedy Playhouse* that, as the promotional material had it: "set out to map a career of a piece of period furniture through its long and eventful life." A sort of *La Ronde* for Thomas Chippendale, the twenty-five minute script by "that versatile pair, Marty Feldman and Barry Took," squeezed in three separate vignettes related to the chaise longue in question who tells the tales from its current position; in a London junk shop.

"We were really inspired by [the current big screen hit] *The Yellow Rolls Royce*," remembered Barry Took. "That comprised three stories related to the car in question. They had two hours to play with, mind you, but I still think it was one of the very best things Marty and I ever wrote together. The limitation of the time and money was inspiring rather than depressing. Our original intention was to have the stories related by a commode but we thought better of that in the end. Perhaps we had an attack of good taste, I don't know!"

A commode would have certainly suited Marty and Barry's first choice for actor: Kenneth Williams. In the end, it was veteran writer and personality Alan Melville that played the chaise longue. Long familiar from *What's My Line* and *The A to Z...* series, Melville told the *Radio Times* that: "The BBC rang up, sounding a bit furtive, I thought. It was put to me as 'how would you like a starring role in a *Comedy Playhouse* written by Marty Feldman and Barry Took?' Of course, I liked the starring bit, and I'm a great fan of the writers, so I said fine, and asked if I may just read the script before signing a contract. It was then that the stammering started! Slowly I learned that the part was as a piece of furniture." Melville filmed one day so as his head could be superimposed on the gargoyle headpiece of the chaise longue and linked the three stories: 'Mixed Doubles', a 1890s tale of mutual infidelity between two married couples, 'Creature of Habit' which featured a 1930s widow revealing secrets to her latest conquest and 'A Warm Reception' with the children of two feuding Irish families consummating their passions.

The Audience Research Department report singled out this last instalment as: "quite the funniest part of the show." With J.G. Devlin and Shay Gorman as the couple in question it was: "typically Irish" and "a real winner." The 'Creature of Habit' segment owed: "its success... to Betty Marsden's 'excellent' portrayal of the 'much-married lady.'"[4]

Betty Marsden had, of course, already been relishing Marty Feldman and Barry Took scripts over on the Light Programme in the radio programme that finally got the writers to work with Kenneth Williams.

Barry Took remembered that: "Eric Merriman and I had written this show *Beyond Our Ken*." Kenneth Williams had been part of the frantic supporting cast of this show. The star and, indeed, the Ken of the title was the respected and respectable broadcaster Kenneth Horne. "The idea was to simply pick up from where we had left off," explained Took. The series that resulted would be the insane maiden Aunt to *Beyond Our Ken*. Took recalled that, "with wonderful originality, the BBC wanted it to be called *It's Ken Again* and in fact that was the title for quite a while. All we wanted to do was keep the fun of *Beyond Our Ken*. The title didn't really matter."

According to the diary Kenneth Williams kept in 1964, something slightly more sinister was going on. On Tuesday 29th September he wrote that his *Beyond Our Ken* co-star, Hugh Paddick "said that Merriman had incurred the wrath of the BBC, and that consequently the series was off. So that is that. That's the end of that little annual source of income, and prestige and everything." But the BBC were clearly not about to lose such a winning format or, indeed, writer Barry Took. On Monday 23rd November, Williams wrote that he had been "to the Aeolian [BBC offices] to attend this conference with Roy Rich who is now in charge of Entertainment on the Light Programme. The upshot of it all is that we're to have a new series entitled *It's Ken Again* around Mar-April of '65. They're approaching Barry Took about the actual writing."[5]

In a letter dated 26th November 1964, both Barry Took and Marty were commissioned "to write thirteen of these programmes with an option of a further six at a fee of 125 guineas per script. I shall require a pilot script during January 1965 and it is hoped that this will be acceptable as the first of the series. I understand that the broadcasts themselves will commence early in the Second Quarter 1965."[6]

But there was a problem; a problem that had the potential to become rather nasty. Although both writers had a good pedigree on radio, it was understood within the industry that Barry's radio writing partner was Eric Merriman; even when Marty wrote for *Take It From Here*. Much as Marty had hooked up with Ronnies Wolfe and Chesney. It wasn't an official situation but it was mutually understood. Until now.

Barry felt that: "Marty was key to the new series. It wasn't that Eric couldn't have written the show. Of course he could. Quite frankly, at that stage in my career, I didn't really want to write for radio anymore. Why would I? Marty and I were riding high with our television work. We were turning work down because we were so busy.[7] It was the medium we wanted to work in and it paid a hell of a lot better. But we were given the opportunity to work with the very best people from *Beyond Our Ken* and the very best radio producer in John Simmonds. I was looking forward to writing for Kenneth Horne and Kenneth Williams again, particularly with Marty at my elbow. With Marty on board the humour just had to forge ahead. It was very much in the mould of *Beyond Our Ken* just ten times more off-the-wall. Marty just put his own mark on it."

But on Friday 27th November 1964, the day after the series had been commissioned, Kenneth Williams notes his "morning began with irate & bitter telephone call from Eric Merriman saying I was disloyal to take part in a radio show which was written by other people after seven years. etc. etc. but that he should have expected it because 'I know you're only in the business for what you can get out of it...' I said that's right & eventually he rang off with the threat of court action against the new show."

Certainly the BBC were not shy in coming forward with regards the connections to *Beyond Our Ken*. On Monday 18th January 1965 Kenneth Williams told his diary that he "left Wyndham's [Theatre] at 5.45 & hurried to a meeting of the radio team at Aeolian Hall. Barry Took & Marty Feldman now writing the series. We read a sample script & I think it will provide a good sound show. I'm written in very thinly, but doubtless the weight will shift from week to week."[8]

A trial recording of *It's Ken Again* was set for 12.30-1.15pm on Thursday 18th February at the Paris in London. "This is an audience show," it was noted. "Ticket billing should read: 'Kenneth Horne in *It's Ken Again* – with Kenneth Williams, Hugh Paddick, Betty Marsden, Bill Pertwee.'" Pertwee was the only addition to the cast, in effect doubling up for *Beyond Our Ken* players Ron Moody and Stanley Unwin as a multi-purpose, dogsbody character actor. "We should like to have Douglas Smith [as Announcer], as this show is a follow-up to the *Beyond Our Ken* series," the memo unashamedly admitted. However, something historic happened before that pilot recording took place. Whether it was in light of Merriman's threatened action against the "sequel" or whether it was simply that it was considered a far, far better title – which it was – is not clear, but an internal BBC memo was issued from R.J. Marshall on 5th February 1965. "Following advice given by counsel last evening," it said, "Mr. Roy Rich [Head of Entertainment on the Light Programme] decided to adopt the name *Round the Horne* for the pilot programme which is to be performed before an invited audience at the Paris Cinema on 18th February. In making booking arrangements I shall be glad if you will now drop the former title which was to have been *It's Ken Again*."

So *Round the Horne* it was, and *Round the Horne* it was going to stay.

One of the last great bastions of BBC radio: "created at a time, 1964, when most people thought that radio was dead," wrote Barry Took. "Its abundant success however proved them wrong."[9]

Indeed, it's almost a cliché to say it, but from that very first pilot recording, *Round the Horne* hit the floor running. It, reassuringly, had one foot firmly planted in the past – the middle-of-the-road warbling of the Fraser Hayes Four could have fitted easily into a 1940s *Variety Bandbox*. But the other foot was clearly in the future – the bending of broadcasting conventions that the Monty Python generation was already developing on fellow BBC radio series *I'm Sorry I'll Read That Again*.

The show was, as John Hall noted, "the full flowering of the collaboration... a bastard descendant of The Goons and *Take It From Here*. *Round the Horne*'s cartoon characters were sufficiently close to eccentric reality to pass for a second, more swinging generation from [the earlier Kenneth Horne radio show] *Much-Binding-in-the-Marsh*. But the humour, albeit laden with triple entendres, and hung about with puns which wrung team groans from massed fans, attained to a level of surreal invention and verbal subtlety which would have died over the heads of a pre-Goon audience. It was a thing of rare beauty."[10]

The gentle mocking of authority; particularly of the BBC itself, the happy sending-up of the cast and producer, the *Take It From Here*-inspired film parodies, the galley of grotesques: everything about *Round the Horne* worked. "It was highly charged with emotion," said Barry Took. "Characters were always offering to rip the lid off, to tell all, to confess to nameless sins. The BBC censors became gripped by a revivalist fervour whilst attempting to purify the programme titles – 'We ought to do something about *Take Your Partners*. Who are they fooling, take your partners for what?'" And at its very epicentre was the man himself, Kenneth Horne.

"Kenneth Horne had a lovely, gentle sense of humour but he got all the jokes," remembered Barry Took. "He wasn't the unknowing butt of jokes. Marty and I both realised that this gallery of raving mad eccentrics wouldn't work if you had a raving mad eccentric at the centre. It all went back to the *ITMA* days when you had Tommy Handley filling the same position. All that 'Can I do you now, Sir?' and 'After you Claude', 'No, after you Cecil' stuff wouldn't have worked if you had had an equally insane central figure. Kenneth was a very straight man. He was the maypole that the eccentric characters danced around. What Marty and I tried to do and – by the grace of God – I think we succeeded, was to try and recreate that sense of a straight-laced figure of authority wonderfully hampered and hassled by these manic creations. Kenneth [Horne] had absolute solidity. The humour of Kenneth [Williams] and Hugh and Betty could dance around that. He was us. He was slightly bemused by everything that went on around him. I hope the audience identified with him but it was certainly true of Marty and I. For us, the writers, he was our representation in this crazy world we had invented."

The world and its inhabitants certainly were crazy. There was the "walking slum" J. Peasemould Gruntfuttock (played by a seedy Kenneth Williams), an unpleasant little man with delusions of grandeur who was, according to Took, "guided by voices. [He was] a sort of Rowton House version of Joan of Arc whose great aim in life was to set fire to things, not least of all himself."[11] The self-proclaimed King of Peasemoldia, he eventually married an even more undesirable creature by the name of Buttercup (Betty Marsden), the silly old cow.

There was Lady Beatrice Counterblast (Betty Marsden), the 90-year old former gaiety girl who had been married many times: "many, many times..." happy to reminisce of her exploits. Her almost as ancient family retainer Spasm (Kenneth Williams), was forever warning about impending doom. "We be doomed. We all be doomed," he would croak. The earliest days of the almost naïve, as yet unmarried Miss Bea Clissold provided Marty and Barry with the very first on-going dramatic saga of *Round the Horne*.

The regular magazine programme segment, 'Trends', was also an early hit. An excuse to send up films, television, books and other popular culture, over the years the likes of Seamus Android (Bill Pertwee) would work his cringe-worthy Irish charm on an audience, while Daphne Whitethigh (Betty Marsden) would drone on about preparing banquets, fashion shows or anything else for the self-loathing modern woman. It is hoped that both Eamonn Andrews and Fanny Craddock saw the funny side.

Chou En Ginsberg M.A., failed (Kenneth Williams) was the show's fiendish answer to Fu Manchu with plots of taking over the world as an act of vengeance over an unsuccessful audition to become a BBC announcer. He was aided and abetted in these attempts by his daughter, Lotus Blossom (played with complete lack of decorum by Hugh Paddick).

Theatrical luminaries Dame Celia Molestrangler (Betty Marsden) and Binkie Huckaback (Hugh Paddick), always cast as star-crossed lovers Fiona and Charles with too much florid dialogue were, according to Barry Took, "earthquakingly, mind-bendingly, stomach-turningly, heart-stoppingly, knee-tremblingly awful, but somehow wonderfully, terribly real and yet somehow – unreal."

The upwardly mobile, wandering folk singer Rambling Syd Rumpo (Kenneth Williams) sang of cordwanglers, pewter wogglers, throbbers and Billy-O, m'dearios. "I can remember Marty and I in a Soho sandwich bar listening to the customers heatedly discussing whether Rambling Syd Rumpo's songs were dirty or not," said Took. Of course, dirt, like beauty, is in the eye and ear of the beholder.

Those ageing chorus boys Julian and Sandy (Hugh Paddick and Kenneth Williams) knew all about the filth and depravation of the West End theatre and, having got out of it, ran the gamut of services from Bona This to Bona That. This extract from 'Bona Caterers' is relentlessly typical:

Mr Horne: What about the rest of the food?

Julian: It depends on what sort you have in mind. I mean you can have your standing up running or your sit down knife and fork.

Sandy: Your stand up fingers works out cheaper.

Mr. Horne: Yes, I think a cold buffet is best.

Sandy: Would you like us to lay on a turkey?

Mr. Horne: Well, I hadn't planned on a cabaret.

Sandy: Oh he's bold!

Julian: He goes too far. Now drinkettes. What do you plan there treash?

Sandy: Well, two dozen bottles of egg nog for a start.

Mr. Horne: But I don't know anybody that drinks egg nog.

Julian: We do, heart-face.

Sandy: He likes his egg nog, Jule does. Three egg nogs and he lets his riah right down!

"Marty and I got an awful lot of mileage from those two," said Barry Took. "We just used that familiar old camp theatre chat that the homosexual community would have recognised immediately. Don't forget that when the first series of *Round the Horne* went out [in early 1965] homosexuality was still illegal. There was no mystery to all that 'Bona' chat. It simply means 'good' but we were constantly amazed that we were getting away with some of the jokes we were getting away with. On the BBC on a Sunday lunchtime! We really did get away with murder. Here were these two delightful, fragrant old queens happily mincing about and chatting in the Polari of the gay theatrical community. All about Omipaloni [fellow homosexuals] and Lallies [legs]. I'm convinced that our scripts played a very, very minor part in demystifying the gay community in the Britain of the 1960s. When homosexuality was made legal I feel sure that Julian and Sandy helped a little. They made the nation feel safe and assured about homosexuality. There was no danger or threat from Julian and Sandy. It was something of a muted revolution."

Indeed, the show kept audiences glued to the wireless for four years: it was still an essential part of the BBC schedules when the law was passed in the House of Commons on 28th July 1967. In fact the third series had come to an end just the previous month. For Marty, *Round the Horne* gave him a major hit and helped, even more, to exorcise some old demons. "We were very successful on television and with this really exciting radio show, I think Marty just relaxed a little bit," said Barry Took. "One day he turned to me and said, 'I was a fool, wasn't I?' 'Probably,' I said. 'When exactly?' 'About all that star billing nonsense.' He admitted to me that he felt a bit foolish about it all and that, as far as he was concerned, it really didn't matter any more. I remember him agreeing with me that as long as we took half of the money each it didn't really matter which order our names were credited in. In fact, for *Round the Horne* he said: 'You know these people better than I do. You've written for them all before. I think it's only right that your name should go first.' And so it did."

The financial incentive was extremely compelling, particularly for a BBC radio series. The beloved old corporation clearly scented a hit immediately, for an opening batch of thirteen programmes was commissioned after the trial recording, with an option for a further six programmes. Although at the end of April 1965 producer John Simmonds was asked to "exercise this option on three programmes only, which means that the current series will run to sixteen,"[12] this was certainly not a lack of faith on the part of the BBC. Indeed, the same missive pointed forward. "At the same time," it continued, "I have been asked to commission Marty Feldman and Barry Took to write a second series of *Round the Horne*, consisting of thirteen programmes, which we plan to broadcast in the Light Programme early in 1966. We should like to take an option on the writers' services in up to six more programmes. We would of course be glad to continue to pay Marty Feldman and Barry Took a fee of 125 guineas per script, to cover both their interest, and a formal contract for your signature is attached."

Of course it was completely clear that the BBC knew *Round the Horne* was going to be a hit. This second series commission eight weeks into the first run was a sure sign. Marty and Barry's agent, Kenneth Ewing, was quick to pick up on it and acted accordingly. The following day, 30th April 1965, he wrote that he was: "happy to confirm that my clients will write the three additional programmes...as to the question of a future series, however, I think this will require some more thought and I would like to come back to you about this after I have been able to discuss it more fully with them. It does seem to me that a small increase in the fee would be in order, but the main question may be whether they have the time next year to write another full series. I will be back to you as soon as I can about this."

There was never any doubt in the heads of Marty Feldman and Barry Took or, indeed, Barry Took and Marty Feldman: "We would answer to both now," remembered Took, "I remember Marty saying that we had finally become that third person he always imagined entered the room and wrote the scripts for us. The order of billing didn't matter any more.

It had been a long time since that first day we had met at the York Empire but now we were almost the same person." That was the power of this wonderfully energetic, knowing, freewheeling, outrageous, affectionate and self-proclaimed "star-studded rubbish". And they were still writing at a furious pace; "a half-hour radio show took us less than two full days," remembered Took.[13] *Round the Horne* was a tonic for both audiences and writers alike: "It really was the happiest of shows," said Took. "You only have to look at the cast to realise that. Kenneth Williams would be howling with laughter with that unique braying laugh of his. Hugh Paddick would be in hysterics at what everybody was doing. Marty and I would be falling on the floor laughing and we had written the stuff! We would laugh at the material more than anybody else and it wasn't because we were being self-indulgent that we had written it. I think it was the pure joy of seeing something that we had written being performed with such care, aplomb and, yes, that old word, love. The actors were all superb."

When the contracts were signed for the second series, on 11th June 1965, the fee had been duly increased, to 140 guineas per episode. But this wasn't simply seen as a cash cow. Marty and Barry cared about *Round the Horne*. In a letter dated 3rd June, Miss D.L. Ross had also asked for an additional six programmes to be added to the schedule. Kenneth Ewing, answering the letter on 14th June, explained that: "I have to tell you that the writers are not agreeable to this at the present time. They frankly feel that the current series dropped a bit during the extra three scripts and think that thirteen is a sufficient length to maintain the standard. Possibly towards the end of the next run this matter could be raised again, but for the present we will just leave it as a contract for thirteen."

In the end, the second series remained at thirteen shows and only then at the continued expense of Marty and Barry's other writing opportunities. It certainly put the kibosh on a new radio situation comedy idea that was set to reunite them with *Bootsie and Snudge* player Clive Dunn. Over a lengthy correspondence between the BBC from the autumn of 1964 through to the start of 1966 the series was saddled with the working title of *Wilkie*. It would depend on Dunn's popular old man characterisation: an idea that had stemmed from an episode of *Comedy Parade*. Marty had written the show alone and pitted Clive Dunn against Derek Guyler as two sandwich-board men, both of whom proclaim "The End of the World is Nigh" but with conflicting opinions. One thinks fire, the other flood.

Producer John Browell wrote on 29th October 1964 to: "commission Marty Feldman and Barry Took to write six thirty minute comedy programmes in the above series for Clive Dunn. Recording dates are not yet available, but it is intended that the series should begin before week ten 1965." Both Marty and Barry dragged their feet with regards the series and Browell finally faced facts on 12th January 1965 when he wrote to Marty and Barry's agent Kenneth Ewing. "I understand... that Barry and Marty will not be able to meet the *Wilkie* commitment as we had arranged. Naturally I have had to accept this and have today written to Clive Dunn informing him of the postponement. So that we all know where we stand, I would like your assurance please that this is only a temporary postponement and that Barry and Marty will complete the scripts as soon as practicable after the Kenneth Horne assignment." Little did Browell know that the Kenneth Horne assignment would run and run and keep audiences in stitches at the Paris Cinema recordings and throughout the country until the end of the sixties.[14]

Typically, Kenneth Ewing was less keen about missing more easily fulfilled opportunities for his clients. John Browell noted that: "Kenneth... mentioned the possibility that we might like to buy the *Walrus and the Carpenter* TV scripts for adaptation to radio... and the adaptation to be done by some other writer." This was an inspired and pioneering idea. In 1966 old *Steptoe and Son* scripts were re-recorded for radio. The following year *The Likely Lads* was similarly adapted. In both cases the originals stars and original writers worked on the shows. Ewing's casting idea, somewhat desperately, was "either for Clive Dunn or the original artistes." Dunn, surely ear-marked for the aged role of Quilt, was clearly flavour of the month and, hoped Ewing, an assurance of a deal. This was not to be. John Browell dismissed it as "rather a fraught idea."

Over at BBC Television, producer Tom Sloan was much keener on *The Walrus and the Carpenter*. In a letter to Kenneth Ewing dated 31st May 1965, Sloan said that: "As I understand the position, we are entitled to a further six scripts from Marty and Barry before the end of 1965. As you know, it was my wish that these should be *The Walrus and the Carpenter* but it is now clear that the writers are unwilling to commit themselves to these…"

It was extremely surprising that Marty and Barry would actively choose not to write a second batch of their beloved series but it was born out of pig-headedness rather than disinterest. As Sloan noted, the writers would not commit to a new series: "without making it a condition that the first series should be repeated – and this I cannot agree to.[15] As far as the alternative suggestions are concerned, I think it would be best if Marty and Barry came with yourself to see Frank [Muir] and me next week when Frank has returned from Canada…"

A meeting date of 10th June 1965 was suggested and five days later Marty and Barry were contracted to write "another spectacular starring Terry Scott". This contract was also unfulfilled.[16]

A new situation comedy for BBC television did result, however. On 29th June 1965 Marty and Barry were commissioned to write six episodes for a series tentatively entitled *Home is the Sailor*. *The Walrus and the Carpenter* producer James Gilbert was at the helm and, ironically, with the Clive Dunn/*Wilkie* debacle still hanging in the air, the show was to star one of the leads from *Bootsie and Snudge*: Bill Fraser.

The first script was delivered on 7th September and the second accepted by James Gilbert on 10th November. His secretary, Sarah Bateman, also confirmed that *Home Is the Sailor* is now called *Charley Is My Darling*. However, in the very same letter Charley is hastily crossed out and amended to Barney and it was as *Barney Is My Darling* that a single series of six episodes was broadcast from the December of 1965. The premise was intriguing enough with Fraser's character, Barney Pank, returning to his wife after years away with the merchant navy. The intervening period had made them both very different and independent people and the strained relationship formed the backbone of the comedy. Irene Handl was cast as the wife, Ramona, who was in charge of a ladies hairdressers in Willesden, North London. Typically of Irene, both in performance and real-life, Ramona kept a dog: in this case a scruffy and bad-tempered mongrel whose sole aim in life was to attack Barney, a perceived interloper into its peaceful home.

Although there was no call for a pilot airing of *Barney Is My Darling*, Marty was still committed to his *Comedy Playhouse* writing contract. Heather Dean, on behalf of the BBC, had contacted Kenneth Ewing to alert him that the: "Light Entertainment Department have now decided that they wish to televise 'The Misfit', the first of the twenty-five minute scripts by Marty Feldman which we commissioned last year."[17] It was later noted that there was: "a certain amount of re-writing which it has now been decided Marty Feldman will do on the script in order to bring it up to date."[18]

The original draft was scarcely outmoded for the basic premise was an interesting and introspective one. Finally broadcast as 'Here I Come Whoever I Am' this *Comedy Playhouse* told the innermost thoughts – in voice-over – of a thirty-two-year-old loner in search of a girlfriend. Ambrose Twombly – another tongue-twisting character name from Marty's seemingly bottomless imagination – was played by *Comedy Playhouse* regular Bernard Cribbins. "That was a wonderful play to do," remembers Cribbins. "The majority of it was a monologue to myself about getting ready to go out and meet a bird. Any bird. Finally, I'm in a phone booth chatting up the bird who is in the phone booth next to me. I know this. She doesn't. Anyway she finally agrees to meet me but says: 'There's an odd looking geezer in the next booth. I'll get rid of him first!' It was very funny with a lot of heart."[19]

Bernard Cribbins would also be cast in Marty's sole entry in the 1966 run of *Comedy Playhouse*. A record five series would emerge from the run – notably *All Gas and Gaiters* and *Beggar My Neighbour* – but 'Judgement Day For Elijah Jones' was not one of them. However, it did draw a line under a couple of niggling matters. On 8th February 1966 P.D. Titheradge wrote to the ever patient Miss D.L. Ross to say: "Sorry that you don't seem ever to have been given the full *Wilkie* story... It was hoped that a series of six would develop from this and Feldman and Took were commissioned to write them. However *Round the Horne* then loomed on the horizon, and they therefore only received payment for one script written but not transmitted. It is still hoped that a *Wilkie* series might materialise in the future but this gets more and more improbable."

It was never to be, but at least Marty's 'Judgement Day For Elijah Jones' was a final practical gift to Clive Dunn. He was cast as the central figure, like Wilkie a sandwich-board man proclaiming the end of the world is nigh. So convinced was he of his own message that he planned to emulate Noah and build his own ark. Moreover he proceeded to steal a selection of animals for preservation. "We filmed it at Chessington with real animals," says Cribbins. "Clive and I were on this camel and I remember Clive dislocating his shoulder when this bloody thing turned round to bite him. Happy days!" The job did at least give Dunn two perks. Firstly his wife, Priscilla Morgan, was cast as Elijah's wife and secondly, for a refreshing change, the role called for no aged make-up.

For Marty, the show was also of crucial importance. It was the last time he would claim a solo writing credit, having finally come to the conclusion that he could only write well as long as someone else, ideally Barry Took, was sat next to him at the typewriter. Even to the extent that when Marty was commissioned to write a five-minute sketch for a *Show of the Week* starring Roy Hudd he finally did so, jointly with Barry Took.[20]

Barry remembered that: "Marty tended to become obsessed with the 'how' of writing. At one period he thought research was essential and however brief the piece we were writing he'd insist that we must visit the British Museum or Madame Tussaud's just to get the picture firmly in our minds of what hieroglyphics actually looked like or to see how Clement Attlee differed from Winston Churchill physically. The fact that you could get the information from a book close at hand wasn't enough. Strangely, this detailed research was never the slightest use for the current project but got used later on for something quite different. Another obsession he had was for quotations, and for a period our characters were forever spouting Shakespeare or Proust or the Bible." This had been particularly prevalent in *Bootsie and Snudge* but *Round the Horne* had more than its fair share of literary, classical music and historical pretensions.

Barry Took summed up the joyous mix: "Literary pastiche, name-dropping, obscure references to current show business gossip, catalogues of mythical forthcoming events: 'The washroom attendants' flannel dance and zabaglione show will be held in the coal shed at Lord's'. The splendid Over-Eighties Nudist Leapfrog Team, Rambling Syd Rumpo with his private language, Julian and Sandy with theirs."

More importantly, both Marty and Barry were determined to keep the series fresh and funny. "Marty and I never got bored with the show for the simple reason that if we did find an idea becoming tedious we'd drop it – often in mid-sentence. 'At this point we were to have heard The Three Musketeers, part III but the writers got fed up with it so instead here is a story of darkest Africa as Armpit Theatre presents Lipharvest of the River'. Another element that gave *Round the Horne* its special quality was the constant change of direction. Working on the principle that the listeners' minds would wander, we allowed our minds to wander too. Side issues would constantly crop up in the sketches – a spy story would suddenly become an out-of-touch impersonator's cabaret act. If we noticed that one of the cast hadn't spoken for a couple of pages his next speech would be a complaint that he hadn't spoken for a while and there'd be rumbles of mutiny from the cast. We noted our own shortcomings as writers. If we couldn't think of anything we'd say so and get out the best way we could."

"The scripts were full of other meanings but I don't think they were ever dirty. They were rude and often vulgar and, of course, some people objected but... it was a great lark. Because our listeners quickly got to understand that this was what the show was, they felt allowed in, able to join the conspiracy and consequently their pleasure was enhanced. It's nice to be a member of a club, even if the membership is over eight million people. Good jokes were cheered, bad jokes booed and there were plenty of both. We'd put in anything we thought was funny. We invented a character called Sir Reginald Sweet of the Football Association so that he could answer the phone by saying, 'Hello, Sweet FA'. In another script we had a headless horseman who manifested himself at midnight for a gallop over the moors. Alas his horse was headless too. They were 'just not equipped for the job.'"

What it all boiled down to was fun: pure and simple. "We never took it seriously and regarded it as an enormous romp," asserted Barry Took.

"We hurled the show at the listeners' heads to see if they'd catch it or duck. Most of them caught it."[21]

"I remember once being en route to the coast stuck in a mile long traffic jam one Sunday lunchtime. I suddenly realised that everyone in that traffic jam was listening to *Round the Horne* – everybody had their windows open, everyone was laughing – a traffic snarl up suddenly turned into a festival."[22] It wasn't just a success at home either.

Even in the very early days it was heard not just on the BBC Light Programme but on the BBC World Service as well. As a result *Round the Horne* built up a strong following across the world. "Marty and I used to have a fantasy in those days, imagining that one day David Attenborough would be in some far flung, God forsaken jungle filming an episode of *Zoo Quest* or something. He would be hacking his way through the undergrowth and come across this long forgotten tribe of South American natives who had never seen a white face in their lives before but had learned to speak English from listening to BBC Radio on the World Service. As David Attenborough broke through the foliage the Indian chief would come up to him and say: "Hello heart-face, how bona to vada your dolly old eek!"

By the summer of 1966 the show, that its star Kenneth Horne affectionately described as like "spending thirty minutes in a spin dryer" had come to the attention of the enfant terrible of satire, David Frost. *Round the Horne* was destined to go global, and that meant breaking it in America.

Chapter Eight

"Comedy, like sodomy, is an unnatural act."

At the start of 1966 Marty was on the verge of a major breakthrough. As a writer he was one of the darlings of the tongue-in-cheek and semi-avant garde set. With *Round the Horne* he was appealing to both the artistically literate and the blissfully unaware family of four.

It is the most lasting and successful achievement of the Marty Feldman and Barry Took writing partnership while Kenneth Horne, a man for whom the word avuncular could have been coined, and Kenneth Williams, chief of the manic supports, brought the words to vivid life. The characters had already become household favourites. Rambling Syd Rumpo would gleefully screeve your cordwangle as soon as look at you, and Julian and Sandy were mincing their ways into the nation's subconscious. In March 1966 they were back to have a vada at Mr. Horne's dolly old eek again. Sunday lunchtime would be a haven for innuendo once more.

Barry Took said that: "*Round the Horne* was written at a time when you've never had it so good was wearing just a little thin. 'I'm Backing Britain' didn't seem much more relevant than 'Hang the Kaiser'. The commonplace of the day were Mods and Rockers, flower power, the Beatles and Carnaby Street, the musical *Hair*, the Wolfenden Report, the abolition of stage censorship, *Till Death Us Do Part*, and *That Was the Week That Was*. There was at that time a whole loosening of public and private behaviour. By echoing what was all around us we found ourselves

absolutely in tune with our time and the show, because of this, became extraordinarily popular."

Dick Clement insists that *Round the Horne*: "fitted in to that whole range of BBC comedy. There is that thinking of the BBC bosses not understanding Spike Milligan and *The Goon Show* and that's true to an extent but the comedy heads and producers were very much on that same wavelength. People like Dennis Main Wilson understood it and embraced it. In fact it was very much the BBC house style at that time. The sixties were awash with Pete 'n' Dud and David Frost and Marty all doing surreal flights of fancy."

Now David Frost and Marty were very much swimming in the same ken. Marty's radio commitment to *Round the Horne* was being written simultaneously with a new commitment to BBC Television. On the Thursday evening before the second series of *Round the Horne* started, the satirical tsar, David Frost, had unveiled his latest offering.

Named *The Frost Report*, with all the modesty typical of the man, it was the natural step forward from the political cut and thrust that had shaped *That Was The Week That Was*.[1] Two short summers later, *The Frost Report* was all the more knowing in that its aim was to retain a slightly less firm grip on the pulse of popular public opinion and be, above all, very, very funny. In 1966 Frost knew very, very funny meant Marty Feldman.

As a catalyst writer for *The Frost Report* he would prove the only choice.

"We had all, unwittingly, been laughing at his words for years," explains Michael Palin. "Even when we were still at school. Radio and television comedy was very important to me, and Marty had been writing a lot of the best of that when I was in my teens. My formative comedy years, I suppose. Everyone listened to *Educating Archie*. Everyone watched *The Army Game*. So to be working alongside him was something of an education."

"He was always very supportive of what we were trying to do. A real champion for us and very interested in young writers. To start with Terry [Jones] and I would just send stuff in. We would get the odd line in here and there and eventually we would write little films that were included."

As far as the graduate generation of writers was concerned, Marty was the boss. Although still a relatively young man at the age of thirty-one, Marty was seen as the elder statesman to Frost's gangly collection of fresh-faced comedy scribes. He would polish, re-write and approve all the material for inclusion.

"We would have a group meeting with all the writers," recalls Barry Cryer. "Let's say the theme for that week was 'The Youth of Today'. We would have been given a brief – mainly factual – and told to go away and come up with the funnies. It was Marty who was our first port of call should we need any more information or reassurance or guidance. Marty held those scripts together and always in a very understanding way. He loved writers because he knew how hard it could be to have your material included or even read by someone in authority. He was the most relaxed and down-to-earth 'authority figure' I have ever met."[2]

At the very centre of comedy at the BBC, Marty would always enjoy the company of other writers. Ian La Frenais recalls: "He was around the bar while we were doing *The Likely Lads* and we would chat about music and comedy." Naturally, Marty relished the company *The Frost Report* offered. David Frost picked up comedy talent with the alacrity of a beachcomber picking up shells and, unsurprisingly, Marty's radio co-scribe, Barry Took, was also included in the mix, alongside fledglings like Eric Idle and Graham Chapman, and more established names like David Nobbs and Keith Waterhouse.

It was on *The Frost Report* that Marty first worked with another writer fast establishing himself, Tim Brooke-Taylor: "He was an extraordinary talent and we got on very well from the start. We always had a good giggle together. Actually we both came from such different directions, that's probably why we got on so well. I admired him greatly as a writer. That's how I first knew him, first from seeing and hearing his name on those wonderful television and radio comedies that he wrote and then from working with him on the writing team for *The Frost Report*. He was frantically prolific as a writer."

It was unsurprising then that the young Michael Palin felt rather over-awed by joining the company. "I remember the first day I met Marty," he says. "Terry [Jones] and I were contributing to *The Frost Report* in 1966 and we were going to go to a writer's meeting down in Crawford Street, a room above a Methodist church just behind Marylebone Station, where we all gathered. Generally Terry and I went together but this particular morning Terry couldn't make it so I went on my own. I think it must have been the first gathering of the writers. The whole lot. All these great names sitting there. The Dick Vosburghs. The Barry Cryers. I was twenty-two, twenty-three. Very nervous about going in to meet all these very famous writers. Anyway, I remember this vividly: only two people came over to say 'Hello'. One was Barry Cryer. The other was Marty Feldman. He just came over, shook my hand and said: 'Come on in.' He made me feel so welcome and I always remember that. A lot of writers are so concerned about doing their own thing that they forget that the young writers coming in are a little unsure of the situation. You could often ignore them but Marty made a real effort to make me feel part of the team and I really appreciated it. I was very touched by Marty's kindness and I've always tried to behave in the same way because of how grateful I was when Marty welcomed me. He was a very nice man."

Terry Jones remembers: "talking with Marty about comedy in general and the sketches Mike and I were writing in particular. He said, 'Yes, I've read your sketches and I'm sure you can make it as a writing team.'"[3]

"How wrong he was," laughs Palin, "but seriously, that was the first real encouragement we had ever had. We knew Marty as a great writer. We both loved *Round the Horne* at that time. So to get a few words of praise from someone as good as Marty was amazing."

Terry Jones reflects that: "Marty's influence was all over *The Frost Report*. We were all given a thesis written by Anthony Jay. This was a sort of themed document about the particular topic for that week's show. The way it usually worked was that the writers would go to a meeting at the start of the week and be given this thesis. About traffic or money or whatever it was and that's what everything was based on. We would write our sketches by spinning ideas off of that document. Then at the end of the week there would be another meeting when we would read out our stuff and see what was picked up. Marty was always very encouraging about our sketches and that meant a great deal to us."

Certainly not Anthony Jay, nor any of Frost's team of writers was under any disillusion. Marty was the head writer and thanks to his influence the serious political commentary bubbling under the surface of *The Frost Report* was skilfully counter-balanced with inspired bouts of out-and-out silliness. This wasn't so much satire as a variety show with a conscience.

The programme's leading lady, Sheila Steafel, remembers that: "As a performer in that group of amazing people one never really stopped to think that what you were doing was in any way ground-breaking. You just got the script and did the words. I remember the writers would gather round at the run-throughs and watch us perform their treasured pieces. [Producer] Jimmy Gilbert soon got it into his head that if we, the performers, didn't laugh at a sketch while we were performing it then it wasn't funny and out it would go. We soon learnt that if there was a sketch we really liked or, more importantly, had a good part in, we would laugh uproariously to make sure it was kept! Luckily, those wonderful writers served us so well over all of the programmes. Marty kept all the writers in order and, my God, what talent there was there."

Indeed it was Marty, along with John Law, who would write the definitive sketch for *The Frost Report*.[4] Originally included in the 'Class' edition, it featured John Cleese, Ronnie Barker and Ronnie Corbett stood in a line, expounding their position in society. Always ascetically appealing, the three represent upper class, middle class and lower class perfectly. "I look down on him because I am upper class," said Cleese. "I look up to him because he is upper class," said Barker. "But I look down to him because he is lower class." Corbett, on the end and looking sheepish, muttered: "I know my place." Even today, rarely is a newspaper article about class printed which doesn't use this image to illustrate it.

The central theme of each show, be it medicine, law or women, would always start life in the same way: David Frost's way. His linking material was structured first and foremost, purely as a hook upon which his gang of writers could hang a string of funny sketches. These links became known as Frost's "Continuous Developing Monologue" and were dubbed "CDMs" for short, although Marty and a clutch of his favourite writers would often refer to them as "Cadbury's Dairy Milk". "Mike [Palin] and

I would contribute bits and pieces to those," recalls Terry Jones. "That was the central, linking device throughout the whole show really and Frost liked to have lots of funny material in those. The whole point of those CDMs was that they were ever changing and formless. If one of the writers came up with a funny line it would go in, regardless of whether the show was just about to be recorded. Frost was clever like that. He kept his ear out for our best one-liners."

It was typical of the under-graduate, authority-baiting attitude that permeated the writing team. Frost was seen as their benefactor, certainly, but a rather self-righteous one: "We would watch the show go out," explains Terry Jones, "and at the end of each show, and before the very lengthy list of writers including me, the credit would always read 'written by David Frost'. That was a little bit naughty. 'Chosen by David Frost' would have been fairer."

Certainly the BBC's flagship radio comedy, *Round the Horne* had been chosen by David Frost as a potential hit in the United States of America. In a "strictly confidential" letter dictated by Frost on 28th June 1966 he maps out: "a general agreement between the BBC and Hartwest Productions Inc. of New York covering which we expect to exchange contracts within the next week, we propose to offer a series of thirty-nine programmes in the series *Round the Horne*, twenty-five of which have already been selected from those already produced for Light Programme."[5]

For Marty, however, there was something even more important than breaking it big in America, and that was football. And on 30th June 1966, it was not just any old football match at London's Wembley Stadium, but the World Cup Final between England and West Germany. Tim Brooke-Taylor reflects that, "I went to the World Cup Final with Marty." (Let's just pause for a moment to let the full, era-defining coolness of that statement sink in: Tim Brooke-Taylor went to the 1966 World Cup Final with Marty Feldman! Right, let's continue.) "Even more name-dropping," chuckles Tim, "I sold my standing tickets to Eric Idle! I went to all the England matches and I was standing for most of them but, somehow, Marty managed to get these seats quite close to the Queen. His father had got them from somewhere in the East End. I don't wish to suggest anything dubious was going on but these amazing tickets appeared from somewhere and there was this sense of old fashioned black market dealing going on. I didn't question it at all. It was a perfect day. There was this very funny moment when we scored the final goal and Marty and I jumped up and hugged each other like typical arty people. We pulled away from each other feeling rather embarrassed about it, looked around and saw all these city businessmen hugging each other. It was a happy moment."[6]

Marty was clearly riding on the crest of a wave but there was a feeling of unrest in the air. Perhaps in light of the impending interest from America, Marty and Barry were actively trying to re-jig the dynamic of *Round the Horne*. Head of BBC Light Entertainment Roy Rich wrote: "Whither *Round the Horne* end of term drink," which had just reunited cast, writers and production team to debrief after the second series. More over, there were active plans for the future. It was decided: "that the writers should start upon another series of thirteen, at their convenience in time, then have a considerable break, then write another thirteen – at the beginning of which second series we would start to transmit so that we should have an unbroken series of twenty-six programmes during which we can really consolidate the success of the show." The possibility of doing one special programme for Christmas Day was discussed between the key players; Marty Feldman, Barry Took, Kenneth Horne and Kenneth Williams, "all of whom were in agreement" and it was quite clearly these four men who held most clout.

As Roy Rich noted: "It became obvious that these same four gentlemen have some queries to raise before embarking on another series. I know they have in mind the dropping of the Fraser Hayes Four." Despite the musical interlude being mercilessly mocked from the very first broadcast, they were indeed becoming very twee and old-fashioned, particularly in comparison with the more hip warbling of Julie Felix that Marty was witnessing on *The Frost Report*. Even more surprising was the revelation that: "I believe they propose to raise the issue of dispensing with Betty Marsden and Bill Pertwee. I say 'I believe' because I am not sure, but I am calling a meeting in the near future to clear up these points."[7]

As it turned out the radical changes didn't happen for the next series for which, on 14th July 1966, the BBC commissioned thirteen episodes with the usual option for more. In the event, the third series of *Round the Horne* would run to twenty programmes. Marty and Barry were to net 150 guineas per show.[8]

Still, Kenneth Horne's health issues were beginning to cause concern at the BBC and by 1st November 1966 producer John Simmonds wrote to Miss D.L. Ross explaining that: "As you may have read in the press Kenneth Horne is ill at the moment and though it is anticipated that he will be able to resume work for the new series in January, we cannot be absolutely certain of this. A decision has been made, regarding the Christmas Day programme, to make it without Kenneth Horne; we shall simply 'close ranks' for this particular occasion. The writers have been informed about this and also the situation regarding the series. They have agreed to postpone and waive their four week break between the end of the thirteenth programme and the commencement of the fourteenth if this becomes necessary."

In fact Horne was suffering from pleurisy and, under doctor's orders, was to stop work for between two and three months. Marty and Barry were indeed alerted to the delay and, in a telephone conversation with John Simmonds on 11th October 1966, they were retained for a renewed starting date at the start of 1967.

Kindly, Simmonds masked Horne's illness and in a letter of 9th November 1966 explained that: "The reason for not commencing on 2nd January, which was the date that Kenneth Horne anticipated being able to start, is that the writers have accepted a film commitment to cover the period in December and early January when they had anticipated writing *Round the Horne*. This makes them unable to supply the first script of our series in time for recordings before 16th January."

In fact Marty and Barry didn't have any film commitment but there was a film under discussion from one of their champions, David Frost. He had continued to dance between the raindrops of television fame and cultivate both the established writing talents of Feldman and Took as well as the up-and-coming youngsters. He was certain of one thing: these Oxbridge chaps were the future. More importantly, having instinctively known the time for satire was long gone, he felt it was now time that the inmates should take over the asylum.

By October 1966, Frost had already moved away from the BBC to dally with Rediffusion, the London contractor for the commercial channel, ITV. More an interview and variety showcase, *The Frost Programme* was a sort of watered-down version of *The Frost Report*, complete with John Cleese and Ronnies Barker and Corbett. In tandem with his embrace of commercial television, Frost was ruefully aware of the thinly veiled contempt in which some of his writers held him. Understandably it was two of his least hostile writers, Graham Chapman and John Cleese, who were commissioned to write the script for the feature film *The Rise and Rise of Michael Rimmer*. However, the central plot – that of a media mogul who relentlessly and ruthlessly follows his path to success – was tellingly close to home. This was the comic parable of Frost's own life and his ultimate hero, Peter Cook, was cast in the leading role.

The writers took three months out in Ibiza to complete the script during which time Marty and Lauretta Feldman, Tim Brooke-Taylor and Frost himself made the trip out to pay a visit. It was a much-needed holiday for all of them but, typically, it became a working holiday almost immediately. Indeed, it was during this excursion that the idea of a new comedy revue show for ITV was discussed and developed. "David Frost came up for the day and he actually stayed over-night on the sofa," says Tim Brooke-Taylor. "I think he was just checking that John and Graham were actually writing the film they were supposed to be writing. I wasn't working on the film, I was simply there on holiday, as was Marty. We were in the same villa at the same time. That was also the time that Graham was meeting up with the love of his life. It was all very complicated but it was wonderful. Marty and I became very, very close friends during that holiday and we did talk about writing material together."

David Frost had hit upon the idea of presenting Tim Brooke-Taylor as a star comic turn in his own sketch show. "That wasn't mentioned in Ibiza," says Brooke-Taylor. "That all started to happen immediately after we got back. As far as I was concerned, David Frost asked me whether I would be interested in doing a show. Stories differ, I know, but this is the truth," he chuckles. "In actual fact, David Frost didn't want John [Cleese, as has been suggested]. Not because he wasn't brilliant but simply because John was doing *The Frost Programme*. This new show was to be my show."

The thought of holding a show together on his own was a daunting one though: "I certainly didn't want to be the leading attraction, no," confirms Brooke-Taylor. "I said to David Frost, 'Look, honestly I don't want to do it without John and Graham,' and David finally agreed. It was always in my head, ironically, that a three-man comedy team wouldn't work. I had this idea that we needed a fourth person and this was the extraordinary coincidence. I rang John and I honestly can't remember which way round it was but one of us said, 'I've got an idea for the ideal person,' and the other one of us said, 'Well, I was thinking of Marty Feldman.' We both had the exact same thought at the same time. It was one of those happy circumstances. It worked right from the word go, really, because he was so very different."

Frost however had been very reluctant to agree. Marty as a writer was one thing; a sure thing, in fact. But as a performer as well? With that lop-sided visage? "Something of a boon for a comedian I always thought," explains Tim Brooke-Taylor, "but, rather cruelly, Frost was convinced it would make people turn off their television sets. We protested that Ben Turpin [the legendary cross-eyed comedian of Hollywood's silent era] had made millions howl with laughter." Over the last year or so, Marty had still been keen to perform. "I would do anything," he explained, "even warm-ups for the shows. By the time I had reached the age of thirty-two I figured that if nobody had discovered me by that time then there was nothing to discover. It was so frustrating. I'd just given up on the idea by then. I used to go and sit in the front stalls of theatres and see the stage very near me and want to get up on there. But I had no idea what I would do if I *was* there." Unsurprisingly, Tim Brooke-Taylor remembers Marty being thrilled at the idea of performing. "I think he was amazed that anyone had thought of him, actually. It wasn't that he was self-conscious, just uncertain. He desperately wanted to do it, he was just nervous of failing. We kept telling him how funny he was. Back in *The Frost Report* days Marty would naturally act out bits and pieces of the sketches he had written and he was brilliant. And we would all just sit around chatting together as well. It was clear from these conversations that he was a very funny man indeed. I never laughed at him simply because of the way he looked."

Frost was still unconvinced – calling Marty "grotesque"[9] – but respecting the opinions of Brooke-Taylor and Cleese, he relented. Eventually. "David Frost wasn't happy about Marty for a long, long time," says Tim Brooke-Taylor. "He really didn't want him because of the eyes. I sort of knew what he meant. I think he felt people would be embarrassed by it but I knew people wouldn't be embarrassed at all because Marty would make them laugh anyway. In the end David Frost, happily, gave way." This wasn't *The Frost Report*, after all. This was to be Tim Brooke-Taylor's show and if he wanted Marty in the team then Marty was to be in the team: "That was in David Frost's head, at least," says Brooke-Taylor. "I never saw the show as my show. For me it was always going to be a happy gang show – which it was, both in terms of writing and performing. John, Graham and I all felt that Marty would be perfect in the cast. I think we had something".

However, commercial television broadcaster Rediffusion weren't all that impressed with Marty's outlandish appearance either, but, for them, this was Frost's show and, largely, Frost's money. He was the boss and if he wanted Marty to be in the team, then so be it. "We knew each other quite well before we acted together on television, of course," remembers Brooke-Taylor,[10] "and we became a very happy little team very quickly."

At Last the 1948 Show would become one of the most infectious comedy successes of the 1960s. Tim Brooke-Taylor says that: "I'm pretty sure Marty came up with that title. It was a massive dig at BBC Television Executives. We had all had experience of those at one time or another, Marty more than the rest of us. The idea was that here was this silly sketch show that had been hanging around waiting to be commissioned for nineteen years." Marty himself told the *TV Times* that: "People were confused about the title at first. People thought they were going to see a collection of post-war movies. What they didn't realise was that the title meant absolutely nothing – in fact it was a non-title."[11]

Innovative hardly covers it. *At Last the 1948 Show* positively drips with importance. In the family tree of alternative comedy it is the sturdy redwood. If *The Frost Report* was World Cup victory and the potential for change in society, then *At Last the 1948 Show* was Carnaby Street, multi-coloured kaftans and smoking pot. Its influence was pretty much immediate and continues to this day. The outrageous use of storytelling, freeze-frame photographs, captions, news links and every other trick in the book of television cliché was mocked, rearranged and generally mucked about with. A distinct left turn from the style of *The Frost Report*, this kept its comedy eye on the ball while regressing to the glorious days of music hall and variety. There was no room for topicality here; no thematic run of sketches or knowing comments on the latest headlines. Just a barrage of silliness. It was a world that suited Marty very well. Moreover, he was content to be a mere hired hand. His opinion and contribution was strongly sought in the scripting sessions but the buck certainly didn't stop with him this time around. He could relax and enjoy the work, safe in the knowledge that Brooke-Taylor and Cleese were not only the headlining comedians but also the editors for the material as well.

As a result, it was Brooke-Taylor and Cleese who were hassled, snowed-under and even humiliated during the course of the programme's production. "We wanted to have a young girl in the group," explains Brooke-Taylor. "We weren't going to have knowing monologues from David Frost. We wanted a chorus girl, like they probably would have had if we had actually been doing the show in 1948. John and I went to various nightclubs to look at their girls – for purely professional reasons – and we ended up at the Embassy. We were both rather nervous graduates at that time – I still am to an extent – and these girls were very experienced. It was all acutely embarrassing, especially when the word got out that we were looking for a girl for a new television series. The sort of girls that were offered to us were wildly inappropriate!"

In the end, Aimi MacDonald was selected. "She stood out completely from the rest. I turned to John and said, 'How can it be any other girl but her?' and he agreed." With her little girl voice, whistle-worthy figure, big eyes, blonde hair and sparkling grin, "The Lovely" Aimi MacDonald certainly stood out. As Marty said at the time: "If she didn't exist it would be necessary to invent her." She was a decorative linking device but so much more than that. Indeed, it was Marty who came up with the whole "Make Aimi MacDonald a Rich Girl" campaign. A cheeky, knowing plea for fans of the show to send in money, it added a disarming air of gold-digging cynicism to MacDonald's contribution.

Marty would himself perform a campaign on behalf of people who keep falling asleep... and would himself keep falling asleep during the appeal. Both were very much in the mode of a later variety show, *The Two Ronnies*. The seeds of Monty Python are very evident in *At Last the 1948 Show* as well. Both would resurrect particular sketches from the series. Not that *At Last the 1948 Show* was adverse to re-heating old sketches itself.

Still, amongst the re-used sketches from *I'm Sorry I'll Read That Again*, *Cambridge Circus* and other shows from the Footlights, it is Marty who stood out as the major comic discovery. It was a one-jump leap to stardom. He was adept at playing the monotonous English bore abroad – alongside his three main co-stars – in the 'Sydney Lotterby' sketches, featuring a dull irritant, named after the BBC producer and director who made his mark in the Light Entertainment department from the late 1950s. Although it was explained that John Cleese simply liked the name, Marty himself came across the real Lotterby on several occasions, including, rather tellingly, during his aborted involvement in *The Graham Stark Show*. Sydney Lotterby was the producer. Tim Brooke-Taylor would also work closely with him when Lotterby directed the show *Broaden Your Mind* in 1968. "That was a bit too close for comfort," he says. "We had been sending him up, or at the very least sending his name up, over on commercial television for months. Suddenly, there he was directing me. It's a small world!"

Marty was another mild-mannered man in a sketch all four wrote during a hilarious late-night session. Anything seemed to go and everything resulted in fits of shared hilarity. It was the secret of the show's success. If a sketch made the cast laugh it was generally accepted that it would make the audience laugh as well. John Cleese ranting on about the death cry of the ant allowed Marty to display his finest performance of beleaguered nervousness. That slightly edgy attitude and growing tension when the normal man comes face-to-face with an obvious nutter was classic, embryonic Marty.

But Marty himself seemed even happier when offered roles far removed from the meek and the downtrodden. He already looked like a victim, so he enjoyed playing the winner or, more to the point, the threatening influence. His finest appearances in *At Last the 1948 Show* are insane at best, totally barking mad at worst. The comedy of aggression appealed to him enormously. He railed against authority all his life and now, in 1967, he could attack the essence of outmoded law, questionable military action and sheer stupidity in every day life, all through the medium of a silly sketch show.

In the first batch of episodes, broadcast throughout the February and March of 1967, his comedy reached a zenith of barely contained brutality when he played a thuggish, taunting Gypsy. "Gypsy boot through your hat," he offered with menace, "nothing luckier than that. Old Gypsy saying, sir!" It is the subservient mixed with the assassin that would enrich much of his later work.

"That was Marty's great gift," says Tim Brooke-Taylor, "when you actually looked at him you thought: 'Wow! How is he going to react to this?' That was why he emerged as such an important comedy figure from *At Last the 1948 Show*. The set-up of the sketches within that show were perfect for him. We did a send-up of the popular antiques programme, *Going For A Song*. I was the host and I would pass things down, like a vase or something and you would have John talking a bit about it and then Graham would do a bit and then you would go to Marty and he would just smash it. It was one thing after another. We even had a portrait of David Frost that ended up being smashed and then we got a great big diamond and we were all thinking 'what's he going to do with this?' and he swallowed it! That was Marty's strength."

It was the essence of his comedy, as far as Marty was concerned. "Humour evolves as you evolve as a person," Marty said. "You do it for the same reason you paint a moustache on the Mona Lisa. It's a spontaneous demonstration of anarchy."

For Bill Oddie though, Marty's unpredictability "was a sign of bi-polar. Poor Tim. I think every group needed a manic depressive. First of all he had Marty. Then [in The Goodies] he had me! During a rehearsal and even sometimes during a take, Marty would put in these off-putting physical ad-libs. Instead of just throwing words in, he would throw things around. I have to confess I've been guilty of that sort of thing myself. They would groan and say: 'The puppy is out of control again!' I suppose that's why Marty and I got on so well. We were very similar. We didn't work that much together but we would have met through Tim and Christine [Brooke-Taylor]. Marty and I had a mutual love of jazz. I know Annie Ross and my first wife, Jean Hart, had connections, and I would hang out with Marty at Ronnie Scott's and various clubs and parties. I liked Marty a lot. He was good fun."[12]

A reassuring mesh of old and new material, the mentality was certainly on recycle for the musical close to the first series of *At Last the 1948 Show*; John Cleese's tone-deaf rendition of 'The Ferret Song' as lifted from radio's *I'm Sorry I Haven't A Clue*. The second series would close in similar fashion, with 'The Rhubarb Tart Song'. Both would be re-recorded in the studio and released by Pye Records. Credited to John Cleese and the 1948 Choir, Tim Brooke-Taylor ruefully remarks that: "Both Graham and I can be heard accompanying John on lead vocals. I was somewhat miffed when Marty failed to turn up for the recording sessions."

Still, by the end of March 1967, Marty was a face to be reckoned with. Not for him an uncredited appearance on a novelty recording that would barely niggle the charts. Marty did deem to join the team in the July "to take part as required and sing new recording" on *Dee Time* in Manchester. Tim Brooke-Taylor remembers that: "We were doing the Simon Dee chat show and the host was being fairly poncey. We all thought we could have a bit of fun with it. We decided that when he turned to the audience to wrap up our little bit of chat we would hide behind the sofa! He did his bit of chat to the camera, turned back to the four of us and we had all gone. Of course it was live and there was nothing he could do about it. The thought of it still makes me giggle like a schoolboy. To think of Simon Dee turning round to face his guests and find they had all vanished. When you think of it, it is quite difficult to hide John Cleese and Graham Chapman, but we did it. I thought Simon Dee was a prat anyway but he was really cross. That made us giggle even more. It was brilliant."[13]

In a few short months the unconventional face that television executives had balked at was now one of the most familiar attractions in the country. Those first batch of publicity stills for *At Last the 1948 Show* had featured Brooke-Taylor, Chapman and Cleese gathered, full-face, around Aimi MacDonald. Marty had been perched on the side in strict profile. Indeed, the most iconic publicity shot of the four principals had them all in profile. Anything, it would seem, to hide that full face of Marty's which would supposedly discourage audiences to switch on their television sets.

Still, not every fan of the series noticed that face. Marty remembered that: "I was... with John Cleese [and] a little bloke came up and asked, 'Are you the small one with the big bulging eyes?' Straight to my face. I said, 'No, I'm the tall good-looking one with the Cambridge accent.' He accepted that and went away quite happy. My view is always use what you have. Eternally pragmatic. So I've used what I've got."[14]

Tim Brooke-Taylor remembers the incident vividly: "It was John, Graham, Marty and myself and we were looking into the window of this joke shop near the British Museum. Everything in this shop window seemed so old-fashioned. There were these stink bombs and the slogan on the box was something like 'a bigger stink than Hitler!' Really ancient stuff. We were all looking at these jokes and a young lad came up and looked at us all and he turned to Marty and said: 'Are you the one with the funny eyes?' We all fell about laughing. He obviously wasn't very observant, but Marty laughed more than anybody so he had a keen sense of humour about those eyes." Those eyes were, after all, the key to his comedy fame and, at the time, at least he embraced them as a weapon of success.

Indeed, by the time the marketing machine revved up for the second batch of episodes, Marty's face was something rather iconic in itself. It had been battered and bruised during youthful days in boxing booths. During the early sixties it had been ravaged by the hyperactive thyroid. There had been a car crash, falls and punch-ups. But now, it seemed, that face had been part of his life forever. He would be the first to mock it, even when talking about experiences years before the series of events from which it had resulted.

In an interview with Marjorie Proops published in the *TV Times* at the start of November 1967, the subject was tackled full on. Indeed, the article was headed "What Did She See In Him?" Thankfully the tone is understanding and appreciative throughout, even though the journalist had been told that: "When you meet the Feldmans, you'll ask yourself why does Beauty marry the Beast?"

Proops explains in the piece that the Feldmans had been warned that this would be the subject of the interview: "Why a beautiful girl marries a highly unbeautiful man." "The strange thing was that after the first startled moment, I discovered that looking at Marty Feldman was an unqualified pleasure and I didn't really need to ask Lauretta why she'd married such a plain chap," continued Proops. "I could understand why."[15]

Marjorie Proops continued: "For a start, he told me not to be embarrassed, not to bother to be delicate about his lack of physical attributes, not to do my nut trying to be tactful. 'Speak out,' he said. 'I'm not sensitive about my face.' He may not be sensitive about his face, but he is a sensitive human being."

The article, nevertheless, did focus on his face throughout and continually explained that with Marty this is not the most important thing the visitor takes away with them. "I stopped registering his features as soon as he began to talk," wrote Proops. He was a top comedian now and one of the country's most beloved and familiar faces. "He is," wrote Proops, "like most comics, serious and thoughtful, but his solemn thoughts are punctuated with keenly sharp and witty observations." Like any bullied, abused or browbeaten youth who turns to comedy, Marty was dismissive of praise, particularly when it concerned his physical attractiveness. "Women don't want to go to bed with me," he explained, "they just want to put me on the mantelpiece." Proops herself refuted this: "I'd told him I thought he had [sex-appeal] in abundance." Unsurprisingly, Lauretta agreed and among the wistful praise for his wit and his kindness and his warmth of character, Marty's devoted wife showed genuine and understandable rage against the opinion of strangers. "I am speechless with anger when they say 'what did she see in him?' I see in him everything I want and need," she said. "I don't believe in this thing many couples crave – a total belonging to another person," said Marty. "Lauretta and I belong only to ourselves. We must be free of each other. We are each our own people, bound together by love. We both think this. If we stopped loving each other, our marriage would be over. Two people must have this sense of personal identity and freedom or love and marriage can't survive." As Proops observed, "Lauretta nodded in agreement but I sensed that she (like most women) doesn't want to feel free. She is crazy about her funny-faced husband." But both Marty and Lauretta were aware that that "funny-faced husband" had now become public property. Even then, Marty treated marriage fatalistically. "It works for me," he said, "[but] it's a man-made institution. Like others, if you need it, fine. If not, it's neither here nor there."

For Tim Brooke-Taylor: "Lauretta was a fairly essential part of Marty's life, I thought. She backed him up very strongly all the way but she was good in her own right. She was a refreshing, Bohemian figure and a very gutsy woman. I liked her enormously. She was certainly very thoughtful with my wife and I.[16] When we had our first baby she was one of the first round helping. She also had an inscrutable sense of humour. I remember we went to a football match, very early on. It was a Chelsea match and I remember Lauretta saying: 'Oh, what pretty costumes they've got on!' and I still don't know to this day whether she was sending us up or not but it certainly made us laugh."

No one outside of the business had been that impressed with Marty when *The Frost Report* compilation, 'Frost Over England', won the Golden Rose at the 1967 Montreux Festival. A thirty-five minute special culled from the best bits of the first series, this was broadcast on BBC1 just four days after the end of the first series of *At Last the 1948 Show*.

A second batch of *The Frost Report* ran from April through to June but it was the second series of *At Last the 1948 Show* that was the most crucial to Marty's standing as an ever-rising comedy star. The public didn't care who wrote which sketch; they loved the comedian who made the written word funny. Marty had the best of both worlds and was loving every minute of it.

"To have an effect on the audience, that's the most enjoyable thing," he said. "To convey a real emotion, to communicate something more than information. To be able to move an audience in some way; either to laughter or proverbially to tears. Days when you feel you've done it, when you've done a good scene, you know it."[17]

In the November of 1967, Marty knew it. The comedy was rich, surreal and joyful. "Once he got out in front of that camera there was no stopping him," says Tim Brooke-Taylor. "He seemed to swell with the excitement of it all. And he was just very, very good." Indeed, there is one sketch where he plays a burglar breaking into a shop and answering the questions of policeman Graham Chapman with matter-of-fact frankness. Yes, he's aware he is breaking the law. So what. It is a controlled, subtle and very funny piece of work and, as Brooke-Taylor had known all along, completely not reliant on those crazy eyes for the joke to work. Marty is in shadow, hidden under a cap. It is his pinpoint delivery that makes the sketch come alive.

Those in the London area, at least, were suitably enthralled by Marty firing on all cylinders. For, despite a huge audience in the capital, the fragmented nature of Independent Television dictated that some regions failed to pick up *At Last the 1948 Show* at all. Others screened the show in the wrong order. Not a problem, "when we were just a sketch show with no agenda other than to be funny," says Brooke-Taylor. It was more annoying for Aimi MacDonald who enjoyed a running joke of being joined by an additional chorus girl for every show. By the seventh episode, there were seven of them! It was Marty's idea to make the introductions more off-the-wall but, of course, because some regions were cavalierly broadcasting the shows in any order they chose, the joke didn't work. Still, the nonsensical gathering and discarding of chorus girl links throughout the run would have appealed to Marty's anarchic side.

"Marty seemed very much more relaxed about the second series," explains Tim Brooke-Taylor. "As well he might. We were a success and he loved being in a success." Brooke-Taylor had developed a close working relationship with him. Graham Chapman and John Cleese were established writing partners before *At Last the 1948 Show* so, almost by default, Marty wrote great swathes of material with Brooke-Taylor. "It was a real treat to work so closely with him. He was very intense and he was spreading himself very thinly. He would spend the mornings writing radio with Barry Took or putting our material together for *The Frost Report* and the afternoons writing the television sketches for *1948* with me. Marty was a very fast writer and a total inspiration. But even he looked up to Denis Norden. It's like that *Frost Report* sketch isn't it? I looked up to Marty and Marty looked up to Denis! All four of us respected Denis Norden and we had agreed that he should come in for the final run through of *1948*. If there were sketches we weren't quite sure about, we trusted Denis' judgement. It must have been a bit of a strain on Denis but he never showed it. He is one of the most under-rated men in comedy. A brilliant man. Because he had four egos there and we did need somebody. That was one of the good things about the Goodies. You had a majority with three but with four it could get tricky. It tended to be Marty and I writing together and Graham and John writing together but on the whole it was all four of us writing together. Of course, Marty had a staggeringly good track record."

It was in this relaxed and productive writing partnership that Marty revealed the innermost demon that drove him forward. He was a man on the run from time. "It was at that time that he said this most extraordinary thing to me," remembers Brooke-Taylor. "I think I was twenty-six and he was thirty-three and we were writing sketches together for *At Last the 1948 Show* which he loved doing and, at the same time, he was writing something else that he quite clearly felt was rubbish, and I remember saying to him: 'Well, why do you do it then?' And he said this most extraordinary thing: 'When you get to my age you'll understand.' And he was thirty-three! I honestly don't think he had a premonition of an early death, I just think he had this frantic rush in his head to get everything he could do done before it was too late and before his bubble burst. He would grab at any work offered him. He wrote fast and furious for the money and for the love, depending on the job. Sometimes it was both."

The two contributed heavily to the now legendary 'Four Yorkshiremen' sketch, which appeared in the penultimate edition of *At Last the 1948 Show* in November 1967. It is the perfect mockery of the "money won't buy you happiness" mentality, with four affluent men in white tuxedos desperately trying to out-do each other with their flamboyant tales of early poverty. "Corridor?" counters Marty. "I used to *dream* of living in a corridor. That would have been a palace to us! We used to live in a water tank on't rubbish tip! Aye, every morning we'd be woke up by having a load of rotting fish dumped on us! House? Hah!" Marty rants on about having to "work fourteen hours at t'mill, day in and day out, for sixpence a week. Aye. Then when we'd come home Dad would thrash us asleep with his belt!" Marty, with an assured Stan Laurel-like nod of the head, rests back but his companions take their experiences of poverty to even more surrealist levels. "Looxury!" says a dead-pan Graham Chapman. Marty listens to all and concludes: "You try telling that to the young people of today. Will they believe you?" It clearly pointed the way towards the relentless silliness of Monty Python. Indeed, for a long time wrongly attributed to the Python troupe and performed by them at the Hollywood Bowl, it positively pulsates with Marty's pounding beat of the absurd.

"I've said it a thousand times and I'm delighted that the penny finally seems to have dropped with people," says Brooke-Taylor. "That was our sketch. The four of us. I have clear memories of writing it, cracking up with laughter as we read it back to each other and having absolute hysterics when we recorded it. Marty would catch my eye at certain times when he knew I was at my weakest and make me giggle." The sense of danger that a moment of corpsing is just around the corner gives the programmes an air of spontaneity and sheer fun for the sake of it.

Indeed, *At Last the 1948 Show* has an endearing, student rag week feel to it. The budget was obviously limited, giving the show a ramshackle, thrown-together approach but the comic inspiration was thriving. Here are four writer-performers clearly enjoying themselves and, as a result, the audience is sucked into the fun of the situation and enjoy themselves too. "A sketch like the 'Undercover Policemen' is a really good example," says Brooke-Taylor. "I'm the police chief and John, Graham and Marty are policemen. They enter in full eveningwear drag with ridiculous wigs. I took one look at them and started to laugh. All of us break up at some point during that sketch and it's a joy for me to watch all these years later.

Now, if that had been another show a lot of that would have been cut out. But because it meant cutting the tape they couldn't do that: 'We can't cut the tape, that would cost twenty quid!' And thank God it was left in because it actually makes it. It retained the fun of us doing it and corpsing and as a result I truly love that sketch. Genuine corpsing is wonderful agony. When you genuinely can't stop yourself laughing it's like the early Pete 'n' Dud sketches. That policemen sketch preserves four friends having a jolly good time."

Marty had boundless confidence. Despite all his claims that his features were not an issue, the very nature of his success as a performer must have delighted him. Flying in the face of Frost and the executives he had made it work. Coupled with the award-winning return to *The Frost Report*, his ebullient position within the ensemble of *At Last the 1948 Show* was even stronger. Marty became more and more a mediator of quality control and advice.

Despite his verbal dexterity and skill with a dialogue-heavy sketch, *At Last the 1948 Show* also clearly displayed Marty's talent for physical comedy. There is the thief nabbed in a library by the police, dancing around the room silently as he nurses a gunshot wound. He falls elegantly on to the cushion that PC John Cleese has placed on the floor. It's a moment Buster Keaton would have been proud of. Then there's Tim Brooke-Taylor's clod-hopping guided tour through a television studio as a live drama is being broadcast. The party of Arab tourists is headed by Marty who embraces his inner Harpo Marx: grinning insanely at the young lady with devilment in his eye. That eye. That comic eye. It had finally found its focus. It is bewitched again in the Chartered Accountant sketch as Marty picks up on John Cleese's obtuseness for financial gain. By bucking the trend and claiming to be a gorilla rather than a chartered accountant, Cleese is brought into line with an increased fee. Marty, bowler-hat plonked upon his head, addresses the viewer with: "I am a chartered accountant, but I'm thinking of becoming a gorilla!"

All four principals would indulge in screaming madness within sketches. Marty would employ an otherworldly creepiness, notably in his singing Jack the Ripper: "Give me the moonlight. Give me the girl and leave the rest to me!" There was the squawking, uncontrollable craziness of Chapman and the slow build up to loony that Brooke-Taylor specialised in. Brooke-Taylor would, however, excel at the quietly spoken victim, as in a sketch with Cleese as a demonstrative psychiatrist.

"In rehearsals the scene just wasn't working," Brooke-Taylor recalls. "John was going through a phase. He was being the stage actor and deliberately underplaying the scene. He had done a bit of theatre and he was enjoying the difference of television, where every little nuance and facial reaction is spotted. That's fine if you were doing Harold Pinter. We were doing silly student comedy and I needed something to react to. I just couldn't get intimidated by this subtle performance. I needed John to really go for the sarcastic attack that was in the script. I remember going over to Marty with a feeling of frustration. I said to him, 'It's just not working, is it? I'm not frightened of him.' Marty's solution was nothing short of inspired: 'Wait until the camera has been rolling for thirty seconds and then stamp on his toe.' Marty knew that John wouldn't stop because that would ruin the take. That look of absolute fury on his face when I stamped on his toe was priceless. He just kept going but he was so angry. The dialogue had real bite and I was really frightened! I remember seeing the playback of that scene and registering that: 'That was the moment I stamped on his toe.' I always think of Marty at that moment and thank him."

Six weeks after the final *At Last the 1948 Show* was broadcast, *The Frost Report* also bowed out with a Boxing Day special, 'Frost Over Christmas'. Marty was now more than a comedy writer. He was something of a comedy "name" and the BBC had had a moment of epiphany. If commercial television could make Marty a star, it was the BBC's God-given right to headhunt him. They were very good at picking up diamonds that other people had mined.

At Last the 1948 Show was a pivotal comedy programme. Sketch shows had come and gone. Some, like Peter Cook and Dudley Moore's *Not Only... But Also*, had left an indelible mark. But *At Last the 1948 Show* really did reinvent the wheel. It had completely freed up the structure and bristled with sheer comedy fun. It allowed its stars to take it to the next, form-bending level. *Monty Python's Flying Circus* would go bonkers with the sketch show. *The Goodies* would inject the madness of the sketch into the situation comedy format. *It's Marty* or *Marty* – it will answer to both – would blend the surreal with a return to the basics of silent comedy slapstick. A sketch show, suitably, with one eye pointing to the future and one eye firmly set to Hollywood circa 1926. And Marty got there first.

The BBC had made Marty an offer he couldn't refuse and promised him enough leeway to indulge his whims totally. Marty would indulge. In twelve short months, he had gone from a nervous performer uncertain of joining a fledgling comedy team to a major comedy star obsessed with every detail of his very own show.

Chapter Nine

"I can't tell jokes. I'm the character in the joke."

While Marty's huge on-screen popularity in *At Last the 1948 Show* pointed the way forward, he was still happily entrenched in scripting *Round the Horne* for BBC radio; Marty's final series starting its broadcast run just three days before *At Last the 1948 Show* first hit the screen. His television co-star Tim Brooke-Taylor says: "I adored *Round the Horne*. I went to several recordings of those with Marty and they were as riotous as you would hope they would be."

Indeed, this twenty-episode strong series was the most constantly fantabulosa of the lot. Kenneth Williams told his diary on Monday 12th June 1967 that the recording: "went like a bomb as usual, and K.H. [Kenneth Horne] gave us all a luncheon in the loggia room at the Hyde Park Hotel. I had a conversation with John Simmonds which was v. disquieting. He said he envisaged dropping everyone from the show, except K.H. and myself, in order 'to give the writers some new impetus...' This sounds v. reckless to me."[1]

Clearly Williams had forgotten the conversation that Roy Rich had reported, in which he had agreed with Kenneth Horne, Barry Took and Marty Feldman in clearing out some of the cast. When the series returned the following year Simmonds had indeed finally given the Fraser Hayes Four and Bill Pertwee their marching orders, as well as Edwin Braden and the Hornblowers. Marty too would be absent but for a completely different reason. Still, Williams wasn't depressed for long, simply because the series was going so well.

The final recording, the following Monday, was greeted with equal enthusiasm: "It went fantastically," wrote Williams. "I have written to Marty and Barry thanking them for such a marvellous series of scripts." On the same day, 19th June 1967, Kenneth Horne put pen to paper to his "Dear Barry and Martie/Barrie and Marty" from his Knightsbridge abode[2]: "I would find it quite impossible to write entirely different 'thank you' letters to you two miracle men, so you can assume that this is 'To Took, copy to Feldman' and 'To Feldman, copy to Took'. Honestly I don't know how you've done it, but you have! And what's more every programme has been a riot. What interests me is that on the very rare occasions when we suspected that a particular show wasn't going to come over quite as well as usual, whether for scriptual, castual or audiencual reasons, the results always showed how wrong we were. It's been a smashing series – easily the best, and must have broken all records. But I doubt not that those records will be broken again when we all get together for the next group of epics. I have already turned down a suggestion that the new series should be entitled *A Song, a Smile, and Edna Purbright*, because I feel that it sounds too much like *Panorama*. May the team of Took and Feldman (copy to Feldman and Took) long flourish. What's more it's been wonderful fun to do – and if that isn't a compliment to script-writers I don't know what is. Have you ever tried working to a script in which you don't believe? Thanks again and all the best, Kenneth."

Kenneth Williams had further noted that: "The longest & warmest round of applause was for the Rambling Syd bit. It was to the tune of 'The Girl I Left Behind Me' – I broke down twice through laughing. It was a disgrace."

It was also rather opportune for exactly two weeks later, on Monday 3rd July 1967, Williams: "Went along to the Aeolian Hall to rehearse with Eddie Braden and Terry [Walsh] (guitar) for the LP of "Rambling Syd" which we are doing tonight at EMI. To EMI studios at Abbey Road at 7 o'clock. Then we did it, with about two hundred people at about 9 o'clock. It went like a bomb... At the end of the session everyone was allowed up into the control box! It was pandemonium!"[3]

One of those many thronging attendees was Tim Brooke-Taylor: "I went to the Rambling Syd Rumpo recording with Marty and it was indeed mad. The audience reaction to Kenneth Williams' – admittedly brilliant and hilarious performance – was near hysteria. The most amazing thing about that evening, however, was afterwards. Marty and I went to a club – and I don't really know much about clubs – but it was an environment Marty felt totally at ease with. Almost unbelievably, it was one of those happenings when the Stones, the Beatles and the Monkees were all in the same place, together. Even I thought: 'If only I had a camera to get a picture of this.' They were all there and getting on very well together. Marty – and all of us to a certain extent – would become part of this rock fraternity. Comedy had become a part of the in-scene and nobody took to it with more gusto than Marty."

The great success of Marty as an on-screen comedy powerhouse in *At Last the 1948 Show* had made an impact across the country and the British Broadcasting Corporation sat up and took notice. They knew Marty only as a writer, certainly over the last decade at least, but he clearly had potential as a performer. Things started to happen very quickly as soon as *At Last the 1948 Show* came to an end in November 1967.

On 28th December 1967, a letter from the contracts department read: "Would you please give me authority to issue a contract to the above artist for thirteen programmes to be originated on BBC2. The recording dates will be six programmes between April 27th and June 1st 1968 and a further seven programmes in the October/December period." It was further noted that, "Feldman has never before done any programmes of this type for us." It was as simple as that. In one fell swoop the BBC commissioned the programme that would define Marty Feldman as a comedian for all time.

On 2nd January 1968 Leslie Page agreed to the contract. That year would be a big and explosive one for Marty. Within it he would write, perform and present over six hours of his finest ever work – all but two of the shows would be broadcast before the end of the year. Crucially, while *At Last the 1948 Show* had thrived on its student styled antics and meagre budget, Marty's own starring vehicle for the BBC would be the most expensive comedy the corporation had produced to date. The show would be pure Marty, cementing him firmly as the BBC's flagship comedy turn. His contract, understandably, stipulated that: "The artist agrees that, except for the BBC, he will not, from April 1st 1968 to March 31st 1969, appear in any television programme intended expressly or primarily for transmission in the United Kingdom." If he was to be handcuffed to the BBC for the financial year then the handcuffs were particularly golden. Not only would the series make Marty even more of an instantly recognisable face on the hip London scene it would also make him a very wealthy, influential man: his BBC contract secured him £1,162 and ten shillings an episode for the performance and writing of material. What's more it was going to be in colour. Indeed, some BBC correspondence suggests that the show was to be called *Colour Me Marty* which would have been mind-blowingly apt.[4] In the event there was to be nothing as twee as *The Marty Feldman Show* hung around the star comedian's neck. In fact, this programme was to be so important it even had two titles. On occasions TV listings, BBC memos, on screen captions and Marty himself referred to it as *It's Marty*. However, in the majority of correspondence the show answered to the even more pared down title of *Marty*.

In a similar act of reassurance, Marty happily gathered around him a band of familiar, reliable and trustworthy comedy talent. Producer Dennis Main Wilson was assigned the job. Having steered Tony Hancock, the Goons, Johnny Speight and several of Marty's own *Comedy Playhouse* scripts through the muddy waters of the BBC, he was considered the safest pair of hands in Light Entertainment. The list of writers employed on *Marty* plundered the cream of the crop from the annals of *The Frost Report*, not least of which was Marty's very own rock of fourteen years standing, Barry Took.

"Marty was, obviously, too busy to keep on going with *Round the Horne*," remembered Took, "but at the same time as *Marty* was coming together I was writing the fourth series with other writers in tow, notably [*Marty* writer] Donald Webster.[5] The writing process with Marty on *Marty* was exactly the same as it had been for the years and years we had already done together. Only this time there was an added pressure on Marty himself. The work flowed well; it just wasn't as much fun as it had been."

Certainly, although Marty had been canny enough to surround himself with all the right people, he and the BBC were determined to make this his project. All his very biggest writing successes had been sequels, in a way, of other people's successes. *The Army Game* begat *Bootsie and Snudge*. *Beyond Our Ken* begat *Round the Horne*. *That Was the Week That Was* begat *The Frost Report*. Although *At Last the 1948 Show* had finally dragged Marty in to the public limelight, *Marty* wasn't going to be a sketch comedy clone. This was going to be all about Marty. Quite literally.

Indeed, the equal billing of the *At Last the 1948 Show* programmes counted for nothing with *Marty*. Tim Brooke-Taylor, who had been the intended star of *At Last the 1948 Show* and whose television fame had increased considerably by the programme's success, found that his power at the BBC was limited. "I remember when I joined Marty at the BBC my agent was trying to get me a better fee. Quite rightly, of course! He said, 'Well, he's starred in this show...' and the BBC person said, 'Well, I've never heard of him!' It's the stupidest thing to say, really, because you are immediately going to fight your corner but there was no illusion on my part. I was part of Marty's supporting team. Marty was the star." Marty was the Frank Sinatra in this particularly British Rat Pack, cleverly gathering around him the finest comedy talent in the country. Tim Brooke-Taylor and the rest could have given him a run for his money but within *Marty* the show, Marty the comedian was the unquestioned chairman of the board.

As if to emphasise the point, *At Last the 1948 Show* alumni Graham Chapman and John Cleese were also employed on *Marty*: as writers. Perhaps their funniest sketch for the show was included in the very first instalment, broadcast on Monday 29th April 1968. It cast Marty as a cockney bishop holding court on board a packed commuter train and played to his strengths as an authority-twisting performer. "Chilly?" he exclaims, "It's brass monkeys, in'it flock? I'm a Bishop, y'know! This is the proper Bishop's clobber this, all the real gear. None of yer tat!" His East End barrow-boy mentality bewilders the carriage: "Any unbelievers here?" he enquires. He is touting for trade. As well as rattling the commuters, the sketch also rattled a few cages within the viewers' committee of Middle

England which, doubtlessly, tickled Marty immensely. Despite the Audience Research Department report for this opening episode gleaning many positive comments, "Two out of every five viewers were not so struck on *Marty*, the most frequent complaint being that the Bishop sketch was in very poor taste and the bad language in it quite uncalled for ('appalled at the thought that the Bishop episode could even be written, produced and accepted by any controlling authority'; 'offensive and in bad taste'; 'the bad language was not necessary to make the point')."[6]

The bad language in question was nothing more than the odd "bloody" but in a television environ when Alf Garnett's output of "bloodies" was restricted, this was still considered a fairly fruity swear word; even more so coming from a figure of religious authority. "In fact," the report continued, "quite a number of the otherwise enthusiastic viewers also seem to have found this sketch hard to take ('let down the show because it was so tasteless', 'have mixed feelings about the bishop in the train sketch', 'I'm not a church-goer, but I don't like religion made fun of in this way')."

The report concluded that: "Though some of this section of the sample quite enjoyed the show, they said they would not go out of their way to watch it. Others, however, found nothing 'even remotely funny' ('failed to raise a titter'), and considered the show weak and stupid, with 'too many sexy interludes', unsuitable for family viewing. These were not the views of the majority of the sample, however, who, on the contrary, considered *Marty* showed great promise as a comedy show, and they were very much looking forward to the next one in the series."

The key point of appeal was, reassuringly, Marty himself. Both as performer and scriptwriter he nailed it. In fact the format is perfectly summed up in the report: "The various sketches seem to have been diverse in character, with a 'good balance between visual and aural appeal.'" That opening show included some of the best and most influential sketches Marty Feldman and Barry Took ever wrote and, indeed, they ranged from verbal to visual with consummate ease.

'At the Vet' featured Marty's little man character struggling with the roaring, squawking but unseen contents of a huge wicker basket. The oft-quoted and oft-performed routine included that most memorable of

Marty lines: "I looked him up in *The Cattle Breeders Guide*, he wasn't in there. I looked him up in *The Standard Book of British Birds*, he wasn't in there either. I finally found him in the Book of Revelation." Again the Bible was raising its head in Marty's work, alongside the ever-reliable Marty and Barry stock-in-trade of the lowly, somewhat seedy British eccentric.

As Barry Took observed, "Most of our characters had a destructive streak but, and it's a big but, they were self-destructive. Nobody was ever hurt and, looking back, I can see that we had spotted the self-destructive elements in British society at that time and invented our strange gallery of oddities to express what we felt was true of society as a whole."[7]

For Marty, writing was still the key ingredient to the programme: "I had no ambition to be a performer," he said. "I know they say all comedians are really tortured souls but I think all people are. Perhaps comedians are just more so. Work is remedial for your own personal hang-ups. You cannibalise your own experience. It can be dangerous and lead you into a very false world of narcissism. A world of images of yourself which you can get lost in. Comics are like children. They are just indulging themselves. They can play their fantasies out. I do. Perhaps it's very healthy. I'm violent. I have a lot of violence in me which I work out in the shows. If you look there is a lot of violence in my work. If it didn't go there it might come out in a much more anti-social way. The poor old bank manager has his dark suit and white collar. What can he do?"

That healthy violence was worked out of his system most strenuously in the justly celebrated elongated silent comedy interludes that hallmarked *Marty*. The opening example of this was Marty and Barry Took's 'Night Life of a Chartered Accountant' sketch which saw Marty's boring little man leaving his suburban home and frumpy wife to sample the high life via beautiful women and exotic world travel. It was, of course, a return to the pure cinema comedy of his hero, Buster Keaton. Although he would himself never be as bold to say it, Marty embraced the essence of Keaton and made it his own for a late 1960s audience. Marty was the Buster Keaton of the beautiful people generation.

That first night audience "considered it one of the best comedy shows they had seen for a long time." *Marty* was "('a real winner'; 'brilliant comedy'; 'fast moving, colourful and witty, this show is without doubt the funniest to appear on BBC for quite some time') – and viewers very much hoped the high standard would be maintained." The programme was "welcomed as 'refreshingly different', [with] this brand of 'off-beat' humour evidently appealed very much, and the show was said to have been full of original ideas and very funny. The sketch that seems to have appealed most and to have been particularly well done ('the use of slow motion and speeded-up film was very effectively employed') was the last one – 'Night Life of a Chartered Accountant'. This was said to have been hilariously funny."

It was hardly surprising then that the report noted that: "The first of these shows written by and starring Marty Feldman seems to have got off to a very good start... Marty Feldman was considered very funny and versatile, and the script well suited to him. His visual expressions were said to be a joy ('his face is his fortune'). The sample was most appreciative of the production – the fast pace, effective use of film inserts, and timing, calling for special praise, it seems."

Marty's team was also singled out for plaudits. "He seems to have been admirably supported by Tim Brooke-Taylor and John Junkin; all the artists, in fact, were thought to have been well cast, and apart from a few viewers who considered them 'not particularly good', even those who did not think much of the show seemed to feel that those taking part had done their best."

Tim Brooke-Taylor would indeed be the key supporting player in *Marty*, perhaps most notably of all as the dragged up Cynthia, wife to Marty's authority-baiting old soldier. Marty and Tim had first played the duo in *At Last the 1948 Show*, as rather timid contestants on the Nosma Claphanger Quiz Show. By the time they had been resurrected for *Marty* the ancient worms had undoubtedly turned. "I loved playing Marty's dithering old Missus in those sketches," says Brooke-Taylor. "We had such a giggle playing that couple and winding up every conceivable figure of authority, always played by John Junkin." A good example of the silliness involved comes in the second programme, with

Junkin as a frustrated travel agent:

Marty: My wife and I would like to see the Edinburgh Festival.
Tim: Edinburgh Festival…
John: How would you like to go?
Tim: Sorry, could you repeat that question?
Marty: Yes…
John: How would you like to travel?
Marty: Don't know.
Tim: Neither do I. What's the answer?
Marty: Yes.
John: I'm not asking you a riddle, madam. I am seeking information. Do you want to go by train, plane or coach?
Both: No.
John: No, what?
Both: Thank you!
John: That's better! I mean, no what?
Marty: Definitely not. We don't want to travel.
John: But you've got to travel.
Marty: Don't you order me about young man.
John: Look, you want to see the Edinburgh Festival.
Tim: Yes, we want to see the Edinburgh Festival.
Marty: Edinburgh Festival…
John: Therefore you have got to travel to Edinburgh.
Marty: Why?
Tim: Yes, answer that young man, if you're so clever!
John: Because Edinburgh is the only place that has got an Edinburgh Festival!
Marty: Isn't there one in London?

These sketches, more than any other in *Marty*, returned to the team-playing quality that had been the hallmark of *At Last the 1948 Show*. For Brooke-Taylor, it would have been better if all the show had been more like that: "Marty would steal a group sketch so there was no danger of us up-staging him. It just seemed as if he had to be in every scene, in every leading role. You need to mix it up with other people but they didn't. I hasten to add that I enjoyed doing *Marty* very much. There was just this slight feeling of unease that every sketch had to be about him. That was a shame. It certainly put more pressure on Marty."

"It wasn't that I particularly wanted more to do. John [Junkin] and I weren't exactly big stars at that time but *Marty* certainly put us in our place," says Brooke-Taylor. "I was with John after a recording of one of the early shows and someone came up to him having obviously just seen Marty. They said, 'You're the other one!' Then they saw me and said, 'You're the other other one!' which pretty much summed it up really."

It had been Frank Muir, during the days of *At Last the 1948 Show*, who had called Marty "the perfect third banana". It was exactly right. He had that ability to shine within a group effort. It's the very reason why Marty shone so brightly in that programme. It's also why Frank Muir himself had been sniffing around Marty with regards starring him in his own show.

According to a June 1968 letter from Dennis Main Wilson: "Marty Feldman offered this particular series to Frank Muir for the London Consortium [the commercial channel] originally and then double-crossed him and gave it to us [the BBC] instead. Frank Muir, therefore, has reason enough to be cross with *Marty*." That was the programme not the man but still, the Frank Muir problem had the potential to turn nasty and had blown up over one sketch. 'Opera Without Music' had been written by Frank Muir and Denis Norden and been filmed for inclusion in episode five of *Marty*. When it was broadcast in May 1968 Muir saw red. An internal BBC memo details that, indeed, it was Muir "(but not Norden) [who] is very cross that this item was not only recorded but transmitted before their permission was sought. This is, technically at any rate, an infringement. This sketch is very popular in summer shows and Muir would not in fact have granted us permission to include it in *Marty* because use on television would kill it stone dead for other purposes for a long time..." The BBC contracts department, with a typical edge of tongue-in-cheek petulance, noted that they would be "fascinated to hear why this sketch was included in the programme before the rights were cleared through us." Dennis Main Wilson was requested to answer the query.

"Further to your notes regarding 'Opera Without Music', I am not surprised that Denis Norden was quite happy with our offer of sixty guineas but that Frank Muir was 'cross.'" The producer found Muir's attitude "understandable enough" in light of the fact that the BBC had grabbed the Marty Feldman series from under his nose at London Weekend Television.

"I have spoken to Frank Muir since his return from leave and he turns out to be 'technically cross' rather than literally so," continued Dennis Main Wilson. "He made the point that the authorship of material should be ascertained before it is used. I made the point that if one is doing a weekly programme and is being let down by two major writing teams and one is under running the show by some four minutes – having made every possible enquiry as to the authorship of the piece and drawn blank everywhere – in such an emergency it is to be understood that a producer should take the bull by the horns – do the piece – and wait for the author (if author there be) to present himself. Not necessarily legal perhaps, but deadly efficient."

"I don't really believe the Frank Muir story about summer seasons – but we are obviously in no position to argue. The sketch was an enormous success and I for one will not quarrel with paying the two best sketch writers in Britain 100 guineas. (It could have cost us much more in commissioning and rejecting from lesser authors.)"

John Henderson thanked Dennis Main Wilson for the "fascinating background stuff. Clearly we have no choice but to cough up the 100 guineas that they asked. You say that in an emergency it is to be understood that a producer should take the bull by the horns, do the piece and wait for the author, if any, to bleat, which in your view is not necessarily legal but deadly efficient. It is not only illegal but usually inefficient. It is only efficient if it works. Clearly in this case no great damage has been done though it will have cost the BBC forty guineas more than it ought (and to this extent it is inefficient). In a different case where perhaps the rights in the material in question is owned not by the writer but a film company the BBC can run into big trouble and big expense. It is deadly alright but not efficient."

"So much for the legal side. There is also the matter of courtesy, and it is discourteous to use somebody else's property without their permission. If you came home after a weekend away to find me unexpectedly sitting in your armchair, looking at your television or reading one of your books, you will justifiably be stroppy, or at any rate I would be, if the positions were reversed. It would not much mollify you if I were to tell you that I had a crisis because my television set had broken down or the public library was shut until Monday. We in Copyright are here to serve you. We understand crises although of course we do not enjoy them. In future on similar occasions get somebody to ring us and we will drop everything to clear the thing for you in time."

"P.S. We have had a bleat from [agent] April Young about 'Driving Instructor' by George Evans and Derek Collyer." This sketch was featured in the sixth episode of *Marty* and appears to be a similar case of using an uncleared sketch because other material was thin on the ground."[8]

Producer Dennis Main Wilson clearly wasn't having an easy ride of it with the writing fraternity for on the very same day, 10th June 1968, he took on a query from Eric Sykes.

Sykes and Main Wilson had been close personal friends and colleagues for many years so it was a slightly hurt rather than furious man who wrote after: "Watching the Marty Feldman show last night, I was very perturbed to see a sketch in which a policeman imagined himself to be a bullfighter. I do not know whether you or the writer are aware of it, but this seemed to me to be extremely similar to a sequence in my film *The Plank*. My picture is still on release and your sketch can only be detrimental to it. Perhaps you can give me some explanation as to how it came to be used."[9]

Dennis Main Wilson replied, rather tardily: "Thank you for your note about the Marty show. Sorry to be so long in writing – I spent a week sleeping since the series finished! I'm afraid I've not yet had time to see *The Plank* so it is impossible for me to pass any judgement. I questioned Marty Feldman about it – he hasn't seen *The Plank* either – (He wrote [the sketch in question] with Barry Took and I directed the film by the way). What Marty did say, which I feel was more to the point, was that had he seen *The Plank* he most certainly would not have done his 'Bullfighting Policeman' because obviously a writer of his calibre has neither the wish nor the need to 'borrow' other people's ideas – especially the ideas of someone like yourself for whom he has such a high regard."

"I am quite confident in my own mind that this is one of those rare cases with genius thinking alike. What I will do, as soon as possible, is to see *The Plank* and then – knowing that there are repeats of Marty's programme in the offing – I will get in touch with you again." And that was that. Later Marty reflected on the sketch: "where I was bull-fighting with traffic. That was based on a real life incident, when I was drunk!" he explained.[10]

Still, having annoyed and conquered the respected old guard of British comedy writing, Marty was also courting the newish kids on the block. Even so, they had achieved enough to be dubbed "two major writing teams" by Dennis Main Wilson. Indeed, the "two major writing teams" that had proved to be the weak link in the first batch of *Marty* episodes.

Graham Chapman and John Cleese had contributed just three sketches: the controversial 'Bishop on the Train', 'Headmaster' and 'Woodworm'; a clever piece for the last episode of the series that saw pest control played out like a 1930s American gangster film, complete with Roland MacLeod channelling Pat O'Brien as the Irish Priest beetle! For John Cleese, working on *Marty*: "changed radically. Graham and I were commissioned... we sent in eight scripts; of which, to our astonishment, after initial floods of thanks, six were returned. We subsequently did five of them on *Monty Python*, so there was nothing wrong with them. It became obvious that what Marty really wanted was star vehicle sketches, whereas we were still writing sketches with three or four equal parts."[11]

At the end of May 1968 Dennis Main Wilson wrote: "With regard to writers, I feel that we have been let down by Cleese and Chapman in that they have been working on so many other television shows and film scripts that one has been unable to rely on any contribution from them at all – even though they were under contract to provide one sketch a week. When they have eventually come up with a script, it has usually been of high quality. I don't think there would be any point in relying on them for the next series."

The other "major writing" team that had been considered lacking was Terry Jones and Michael Palin. Dennis Main Wilson wrote that: "I sense that they too are doing too much and are very tired. Two or three of their ideas have been extremely good."

In the immediate wake of Chapman and Cleese forging ahead with *At Last the 1948 Show*, Terry Jones and Michael Palin had been at Rediffusion writing and performing the children's sketch show *Do Not Adjust Your Set*. It too pointed the way towards *Monty Python's Flying Circus* although Terry Jones is adamant that the writing team weren't too tired to write for *Marty*! "Not at all," he chuckles, "Mike and I were raring to go. We were busy with other shows, it's true, but not too busy. We certainly weren't holding material back from our commitment to Marty Feldman."

Michael Palin ponders: "Were we writing material especially for Marty? I think we probably were. We were thinking of him as a performer and would submit sketches we thought would be good for him. The gnome sketch is a good case in point. That would have fitted in very nicely with *Do Not Adjust Your Set*, where one of us or Eric Idle would have probably performed it but I seem to think we wrote that especially for the Marty show. It wasn't stuff for ourselves. We weren't thinking about *Python* or anything, we were just journeymen writers and writing for *Marty* at that time. It was a good source."

The gnome sketch was one of the pieces Jones and Palin wrote for the first batch of *Marty* and it remains a bone of contention for the writers to this day. The sketch stars Marty, naturally, as a green-clad gnome who happily enters the office of a mortgage advisor (played with the expected disgruntled incredulity by John Junkin).

Terry Jones explains that: "The guy behind the desk is a bit surprised but the gnome speaks very sensibly about collateral and everything else. Eventually the mortgage guy relaxes and asks: 'What's the property?' and the gnome, matter-of-factly, replies, 'It's the magic oak tree in Dingly Dell!' Mike read it out at the script meeting and everybody laughed and said 'that's great!' We were really pleased because we had got a sketch in to the *Marty* show and that was big news. However, that's the sketch that really did it for me. I started getting a bit disillusioned about writing for other people. When the show was being recorded Marty came out dressed as a gnome, which was all well and good, and he sat crossed legged on the desk of the mortgage guy. Anyway, instead of doing the first line, Marty started cracking a lot of gnome jokes. What that told me was that Marty loved to get reactions. Once they had done the sketch for a first time in front of an audience and they didn't get huge laughs, he insisted on doing it again and started putting more obvious jokes in to make the audience laugh. He just destroyed the sketch...!"

Michael Palin agrees: "I think certainly as a writer Marty was very secure. As a performer, at that time, perhaps a little less so. He had been writing for so long and suddenly he was an actor. He couldn't really act but he was a great clown. He looked fantastic. Within his certain range of stuff he was brilliant. Very much a visual performer. He always seemed a little uneasy with the dialogue-driven sketches and that was the material Terry and I were giving him. He wanted to get reactions all the time in order to make himself feel good and this sketch wasn't that sort of thing at all. It should have been done by someone like Cleese really."

Marty himself had spoken about his desire not to be too sententious about humour. "Jokes are never funny when they're done. I'm never happy with the things I've done. When you get an idea it is great. But it can never be as good as just the pure idea in your head. People let you down. I get more joy as a writer than as a performer. But a performer can make it better. I fall about at Frankie Howerd. When you do a thing yourself you know precisely what you want. The audience can say it's very good but you know it could have been better. It's a kind of cathartic thing."

For Terry Jones this was exactly how the gnome sketch affected him: "for the first time, really, I realised that I didn't want to write for other performers anymore. While we were writing for Marty – and we *were* writing for him – Mike and I really wanted to perform our own stuff."

In the end, once he had got his confidence back from the laughter of the studio audience, Marty and Dennis Main Wilson returned to the first recorded performance of the sketch and it is that version, as Terry Jones and Michael Palin wrote it, that was broadcast.

"Neither of us realised that that was what he was doing at the time," says Palin. "It was something of a relief when we saw it go out and it was pretty much as we had written it. It always makes me laugh but the studio audience certainly weren't as enthusiastic as they sound on the soundtrack. Perhaps, they used some of the laughter that Marty's gnome jokes got. Maybe that's why he had done it in the first place."

Although the first cracks had started to appear between Marty the star and his team, "We never ever fell out with Marty," insists Terry Jones. "We were both still very grateful to him for all his wonderful encouragement and support. After all the problems with the Gnome sketch, Marty invited us round to his flat [at 143 Wellesley Court] Maida Vale. It was like Hollywood in London. There was this amazing glass kitchen and a huge spiral staircase."

Michael Palin remembers that: "Marty came down this staircase in his dressing gown to greet us. It was eleven o'clock in the morning and he was still wearing his dressing gown. This is how we had always dreamed writers would live. Marty was very stylish and starry. He loved that lifestyle. He looked every inch the major comedy player that he was and for us to be asked round to his place to talk about his show was a great boost. It was a very big deal."

"I think we had picked up on a feeling of tension within the *Marty* camp. Marty was very reassuring and said nice things about what we had written. One was a sketch called 'Tabletop Battleground'," continues Palin. "It was all about these old soldiers playing out military campaigns while real-life, tin soldiers were fighting real battles with the cutlery. Marty said he had loved it and that it had been something they should have done on *Bootsie and Snudge*. I don't think he was suggesting we had pinched his idea or anything," he laughs, "but for me that was a wonderful compliment."

Marty could well afford to be relaxed and benevolent. The audience research report submitted for the *Marty* show broadcast on 3rd June 1968 was justifiably gushing in its praise. With a massive reaction index of seventy-six, "[which] would seem to reflect viewers' appreciation of the series as a whole rather than this particular edition (which a few, in fact, found rather less funny than before) it is clear that, for the great majority of those reporting, this final programme was an absolute riot from beginning to end, with a glorious 'goonlike' quality that made watching a sheer delight. The script was witty, amusing and highly original, it was said, the photography extremely clever (the woodworm sketch, for instance, and the florist-cum-jungle sequence) while the standard of performance was generally very high."

"Marty Feldman himself was a unique comedian – bizarre in both style and appearance and able, by his facial expression alone, to reduce his audience to helpless laughter, it seemed ('even before a word is spoken, one is doubled up – those eyes!') and he was very well supported by John Junkin and Tim Brooke-Taylor in what was, for many, one of the funniest shows they had seen. 'Wonderful stuff. Why hasn't he been let loose sooner?'"[12]

The report reflected that: "Comment on the series as a whole was in hardly less glowing terms. According to one group, it is true, it began well but tailed off towards the end – the invention flagged, they thought and the programmes were patchy and, at times, lacking in humour. Otherwise, however, the small sample audience appear thoroughly to have enjoyed what they saw of *Marty*. This was visual humour in the fullest sense of the word, it was said, a series which exploited the medium of television in a way rarely attempted before in the field of comedy. It was, indeed, held to be one of the most original series for a very long time, one that included a strong element of fantasy and had a zany 'way out' style of humour all its own, bringing a different approach to old and tried themes. Although all the items were not, perhaps, on the same level of inspired lunacy, the standard was generally high, it seemed – 'I remember particularly the policeman playing a car like a toreador and last night's gem of the bowler-hatted gentleman lost in the jungle behind the florists. Sheer fantasy!'"

"The whole show was of course Marty – he stamped his own unique concept of humour on to each programme, it was said, and if one was in sympathy with his view of the world (which most appeared to be) it could hardly fail. Certainly this 'new approach to laughter-making' was most welcome, viewers' only regret, in some cases, being that the series was so short; at all events, they were eagerly awaiting another in the not-too-distant future, as the following comments show: 'Just the tonic needed for a Monday evening. Marty is truly a comedian of the finest calibre. Hoping for a speedy return.' 'I think the whole series has been one of the most entertaining, amusing and original that I have ever seen. I hope we shall see more of Marty.' 'At last! A series that brings a breath of fresh air to comedy. Brings back memories of famous *Goon Shows* on radio. Let's have more of Marty.'"

It cannot be overly stressed how important all this extremely positive feedback was to the BBC's continued commitment not only to Marty Feldman as a star comedian, but also the commissioning of *Broaden Your Mind*, *Monty Python's Flying Circus* and *The Goodies*. As far as the BBC was concerned, their audience was lapping up this "unique" brand of surrealist humour, and they were going to give them a whole lot more of it.

Thus Dennis Main Wilson's outline for the next batch of *Marty*, already commissioned before a single scene of the first had been shot, of course, was for more of the same. The meeting Marty organised with Terry Jones and Michael Palin had obviously been positive. Dennis Main Wilson had, in the May of 1968, written that: "The reason for our big shortage of material was that the Cleese/Chapman, Jones/Palin writing teams did not submit scripts in the quantity and quality we required of them in their contract which left us in this rather embarrassing position." However, the following month, all four writers were being contracted for at least one sketch per show.

Importantly, it had been Marty's faithful supporting cast that had often stepped in to help plug the gaps in the first batch of programmes. As Main Wilson wrote: "I have had to get help from other writers to keep the series going. Notably John Junkin who has come up with some very good material and, latterly, Tim Brooke-Taylor and Graeme Garden who have an excellent sense of style. I recommend that they be invited to contribute to the next series, as soon as possible."

John Junkin wrote some of the best remembered *Marty* sketches, including 'Eye-o-Fry' which featured the star at his most impenetrable cockney, screaming the nonsensical word to sell his wares. Junkin teamed up with pianist and composer Denis King for several comic songs and wrote 'Pub Lunch' in tandem with Terry Nation.[13] Junkin also wrote 'The Wedding' which remains of interest to comedy historians for one reason: the amazing casting of the characters who voice objections to the ceremony taking place. At one point Marty's old *Bootsie and Snudge* star Bill Fraser appears doing an impersonation of his co-star, Alfie Bass.[14] 'The Wedding' also featured four future members of Monty Python: all of them on the writing team for *Marty*. John Cleese and Graham Chapman crop up as two back ends of a pantomime horse, Terry Jones appears as a milkman and Michael Palin is a schoolteacher correcting the grammar of the responses.

"We were just hired hands," remembers Terry Jones. "Mike and I did a few bits and pieces. There was a football match sketch, not written by us [in fact written by football fanatic Marty himself and Barry Took] but we were on the payroll and we had done a bit of acting. We had been doing *Do Not Adjust Your Set* but this was the BBC. Perhaps because we were on the payroll as writers they thought they would get their money's worth by using us as extras. We certainly didn't get any more money!"[15]

Tim Brooke-Taylor and Graeme Garden's well-received contributions included a sketch for the old couple of authority-baiters; this time at a marriage guidance counsellor. They also wrote a slapstick-heavy piece that starred Marty as a man who purposely runs down pedestrians in order to be able to visit them in hospital.

However, the majority of the material was to be kept even closer to home. On 14th June 1968 Dennis Main Wilson instructed the BBC copyright department to: "Negotiate with Feldman and Took to write twenty minutes of material per week for seven programmes. Further negotiate with Barry Took to act as editor of the scripts in collaboration with Marty Feldman and myself and to be responsible for gathering the potential material from the other authors."

"We had great respect for Barry Took," says Terry Jones. "He was something of a champion of ours. I don't remember him putting any particular pressure on us for *Marty* but if he was in charge of the scripts then Mike and I would have delivered what was required without any complaint."

Marty had become so popular with the public that Pye Records Limited approached the BBC with regards to acquiring the rights for a compilation release. In correspondence dated 15th August 1968 it was noted that Radio Enterprises were negotiating: "for the issue by Pye of a gramophone record made from the soundtrack of the Marty Feldman series broadcast earlier this year..." In the long, far off days before the BBC began releasing their own soundtracks, Pye had cornered the market in comedy releases, notably *Steptoe and Son*, *Hancock's Half Hour* and *Till Death Us Do Part*. The *Marty* release collected together original television recordings of the best of Marty's, naturally, more verbal sketches from series one under the record production eye of Monty Presky.

As a result, 'Funny He Never Married' became arguably the most familiar *Marty* sketch simply, as Tim Brooke-Taylor remembers, "because it was a single from the *Marty* album. It's a very funny bit of writing, by Marty and Barry. It's the aftermath of a funeral of a friend of these two old gentlemen, played by Marty and myself. As these two men reminiscence about their dead friend, George, it becomes clear that he was homosexual. His 'school girl complexion' and the way his 'eyes would light up' when he saw a troupe of boy scouts. It works very well on audio."[16]

The Pye record was released in the October of 1968, perfectly timed for the start of the second batch of television episodes on which Marty had been working hard in the interim. Barry Took's sleeve notes proclaimed that: "Marty's comedy is full of hidden depths. His understanding of the old and the poor and the ignorant is quite remarkable for someone who is neither old nor poor, and is far from ignorant. Time and again he returns to one theme. Whether masquerading as a working class bishop, as a father desperately trying to explain the facts of life to his thirty-year-old son, or as the cloth capped ballet dancer recently out of prison, Marty's characters epitomise 'the forlorn hope'. Endlessly justifying their actions, angry when questioned, pathetically convinced that they're right all the time, these outrageous pantaloons take us by the scruff of the neck and shake us until we begin dimly to see what a curious, sad, hilarious place the world is."

On 8th August 1968 a request came from the National Film Archive for the BBC to donate a print of a *Marty* programme. "As these programmes did not have individual titles, the Committee found it difficult to remember accurately which programme had their favourite moments... they hoped to select a programme that showed the variety of Marty Feldman's talents..." The letter, directed to Marty's producer Dennis Main Wilson, asked for his personal choice as: "The committee has recently been making sure that comedy programmes are not overlooked... they have come to appreciate the importance of preserving examples of humour of our time as well as those films of a documentary or historical nature. Very often the humour of a period of time conveys more accurately the flavour of life, say in the 1960s than the more serious documentation available."

This was a very astute stance to take and, duly on 3rd September 1968, Main Wilson wrote back to Mrs Helen K.T. Bland of the Archives: "I have had a discussion with Marty Feldman on the subject of choosing one of his programmes for you. Apart from being complimented, he reacted rather typically by saying that he wished he'd known, because he would have tried harder! (He is among the more charming and humble people one has the fortune to work with in this business.) He makes the suggestion which I promised to put forward to you that, as we are due to start a new series of seven programmes in November, would it not be a better long-term idea to defer any choice of programme until January 1969, when one will have thirteen programmes from which you can choose. His suggestion makes sense to me but, of course, I leave it to you presuming that even the National Film Archive has datelines to meet!"[17]

Broadcast from 9th December 1968, the second crop of *Marty* was of reassuringly high standard with the same mix of verbal and visual comedy material. At its peak it was being watched in fifteen million homes across the United Kingdom. Michael Palin remembers that: "Marty tended to be doing more and more of the physical comedy which he enjoyed doing. He became very Harpo Marx in those routines. There was a feeling that he didn't really like doing lines. He could do them, brilliantly. But I remember Terry and I writing more visual items for him. There was a sketch about a man who keeps on popping up in other people's holiday snaps and a thing called 'The Clothists' about a group of people who shock the nudist community by wearing clothes. Marty enjoyed all of that."

Terry Jones reflects that: "[Marty] had this great ability to put his own unique stamp on any sketch in those shows. It didn't matter if it had been written by us, or him or John and Graham or whoever. With a little tweak of the script and that look in his eye, it was immediately Marty's sketch."

The two stand-out items from series two are both elongated, silent comedy epics that have come to epitomise Marty's success at the BBC. Intricate, balletic and very, very funny, 'The Three Minute Coach Tour' employed speeded-up camera trickery, Marty's little man lost persona and the aggressiveness of John Junkin. It is a bittersweet hymn on the bland, futile and soulless British coaching holiday. The holidaymakers are crammed into a confined place with people they didn't know and forced to enjoy themselves. It is often used to capture the angst of late 60s life and there's little wonder. The extreme looks of joy and despair that cross Marty's features sum up the mood of a nation. 'The Loneliness of the Long Distant Golfer', on the other hand, is Marty's love letter to the 1920s Hollywood comedy that inspired him. Here is a man determined to beat that little white ball. Beat it scientifically rather than physically. Marty will conquer that ball, however far from the golf course it strays, through thick, thin, train journey and every other bizarre obstacle that his own imagination could conjure up. It is a relentless string of visual gags and sheer bloody-mindedness.

Denis King, composer of the silly songs in the show, was cast as Marty's dogged caddy: "We filmed it over two or three days," he remembers, "and Dennis Main Wilson drove Marty relentlessly. He drove him mad at times, but he drove Marty to do ever more intricate, dangerous stunts. Marty seemed happy. He was fearless. There was a sequence when Marty is on the top of a train [trying to play the ball from where it has landed]. I was hanging on for dear life. It was terrifying. It wasn't a flat top, it had this slightly curved top. Obviously we were tied down by invisible ropes but we did it again and again. Marty was punishing himself to get it right.

He seemed to rather like punishing himself. The train went through a tunnel and Marty emerges with a blackened face. We were walking along the track inside this tunnel and I heard this almighty bang. Marty had hit his shin and he had this great gash with blood pouring out. He just said: 'That's fine. Keep going!'"

The final fade-out as the light gets dimmer and he soldiers on missing easy putt after easy putt after easy putt into eternity is the perfect ending to a mini bear hug for the legacy of Buster Keaton. Indeed, as Marty follows the trajectory of the ball he holds up his hand to shield his eyes. It was Keaton's signature gesture. "He was determined to make it perfect," says Denis King. "Call it bravery or call it foolishness, Marty was totally focused. He hero-worshipped Buster Keaton. I think he felt he might be his reincarnation."

It is hardly surprising that it remained Marty's personal favourite of anything he had ever done. Even during his Hollywood hey-day when the film world was at his feet and he walked the thoroughfares that Keaton had himself walked, it was 'The Loneliness of the Long Distance Golfer' that he would cite. "If I'm remembered for anything," he said, "I hope it's for that."

Chapter Ten

"Once you've realised you've got the kind of face people laugh at,
rather than swoon over, you concentrate on making people laugh."

The year 1969 crystallised what the entire decade had stood for. Flower
Power had wilted, the mini – both skirt and car – ruled and the cool
people didn't have to act cool anymore. They just were. It was the year
of *Abbey Road* and *The Italian Job*.[1] Cool Britannia didn't need a snappy
brand name. England and, more to the point, London, and even more to
the point, Carnaby Street, was the centre of the known world. If it had a
comedy king then that man was Marty Feldman.

As befitting a man at the top of his profession, Marty embraced the
fame, fortune and familiarity that came as the trappings of stardom. In
the whistle-stop, rollercoaster eighteen months that had seen him emerge
blinking and feeling his way into the television limelight, he had become
an icon. A personality on the cutting edge of swinging sixties London
with his trendy Egyptian symbol of life dangling around his neck.

As the London *Evening Standard* opined: "On a bad day he can look
like the very Devil himself. But a very contemporary one. The dress is
strictly hippie. A simple tie-dyed shirt, fading denims, bare feet, a bag
hangs from his belt, the biggest I've ever seen. Into which he reaches for
his cigarette pack..."[2]

As a writer Marty kept his bare feet reassuringly on the ground. Suitably
one foot was planted firmly in the established past, the other knowingly in
the future. If comedy had a pulse, Marty's finger was pressed to it. The dim,

fading pulse of variety and sauce was embodied in the figure of Kenneth Horne. *Horne A' Plenty* had been his successful attempt at television, with the second series coming to a close on Thames Television on New Year's Day 1969. Barry Took had script-edited the programme and, for the second series, even taken over as producer. Marty contributed written material to one show. It was to be his last tangible link with Kenneth Horne, who died on Valentine's Day 1969.[3]

Although the days of these variety shows for other people were numbered, certainly as far as Marty was concerned, he and Barry Took were still furiously protective of their financial and creative hold on programmes they considered their property. One such case was the eventual resurrection of the *Scott On...* series in the autumn of 1968. Having written the first three instalments of the show, both writers felt aggrieved that the programme was back without their approval. "The result of my investigations with Bill Cotton and others is that in this case, although Barry Took and Marty Feldman provided scripts for the programmes which they wrote, they did not provide what we call a format or layout which would entitle them to control the series with regard to those scripts which they did not themselves write or which would justify a credit." Both wanted "some form of interest in the programme *Scott on Marriage*" but this was not to be and the series, with a myriad of different writers, ran with great success until 1974.[4]

The pulse of comedy was racing in other areas, however, with the BBC continuing to invest in the "unique" comedy of the surreal that Marty Feldman himself had come to personify. Marty's chief cohort, Tim Brooke-Taylor, had been given the opportunity to develop his own sketch series with *Broaden Your Mind* in which he and Graeme Garden presented "An Encyclopaedia of the Air": a convenient hook on which to hang a quick session of sketches based around a given theme. Marty was commissioned to write a thirty second quickie, with Barry Took, and that seems to be the extent of his contribution. Still, here was the guru of the movement being almost omnipresent.[5]

With Marty's fame as a performer at its zenith and with so much money having been invested in *Marty* the programme, it was little surprise when the BBC chose it as their entry for the 1969 Montreux Festival. As befitting the rules of the competition, a skilfully assembled compilation of *Marty* was broadcast on British television on 17th March 1969. Dennis Main Wilson and Marty himself were very hands-on in choosing the content and a specially filmed opening, in Montreux, was shot in the February of 1969. It was noted that: "Our expedition was most successful as regards the interior shots, but we shall have to go next week again to Montreux, to shoot the exteriors. It is quite impossible to make Montreux look as though it were in the month of May, when there is heavy snow on the ground!"[6]

Marty's new opening interlude was a clever introduction to the collection of popular sketches from *Marty*. It consisted of around ninety seconds of Marty arriving at the Festival, switching on the bank of television sets in the Jury Room and watching the jury enter to settle down to watch *Marty*.

He was treated royally by the BBC for the Montreux excursion as Bob Gilbreath, Light Entertainer Organiser for television comedy, told Marty's agent Kenneth Ewing in a letter dated 6th March 1969: "Before Marty Feldman flew to Montreux for the filming of the opening sequence of the *Marty* special we made provision for him to draw the amount of £45 in Swiss francs to cover his hotel expenses whilst in Montreux. I have since discovered that in fact Michael Mills paid all Mr Feldman's expenses, and so it was found unnecessary for Mr Feldman to draw upon his special allowance."

Still, it all seemed rather petty when concerning the star of the show. On 13th May, a further BBC memo from Michael Mills detailed that: "I should be glad if you would arrange to pay one tourist return fare London/Geneva, plus one £10-a-day allowance to Marty Feldman. This is in connection with his visit to Montreux. He himself tried to lumber us with his own fare, his wife's fare, and a bill of £52 for a 24-hour stay at the Montreux Palace Hotel. Needless to say, we would not wear this, but... we could go as far as suggested... in order to keep Mr Feldman as sweet as possible."

If the British audience was anything to go by, Marty had the Golden Rose of Montreux in the bag. The Audience Research Department report for the 'Marty in Montreux' compilation revealed that the programme was: "received with rare enthusiasm by reporting viewers, most of whom evidently regarded it as an ideal choice as the BBC's entry..."

"Marty himself was a natural clown, it was said ('something of a cross between Chaplin and Tati'). The items were well chosen and the show had pace and variety, viewers thought: this kind of humour, moreover – most of it visual – was truly international and, as such, must stand an excellent chance at Montreux 'anything that beats this MUST be good' declared one, typically."[7]

That programme was *Holiday in Switzerland*, for *Marty* was awarded the Silver Rose of Montreux. Coming second in an international television competition as fiercely fought as Montreux was no mean feat though, and Marty was delighted. Although the show had lasted just two short bursts over nine months at the tail end of the 1960s, it was pure and untreated Marty. He would never have such control again, even when directing for the cinema. The BBC may have been his bosses but they trusted him. He may have been indulging in a little diva-like behaviour but the BBC didn't really seem to mind. Besides, they wanted another series. *Marty* was being recognised. Marty Feldman himself was being recognised.

The show not only won the Writers' Guild of Great Britain Award for the Best Light Entertainment Series and a BAFTA for Best Script, but Marty was voted the Variety Club's TV Personality of the Year for 1969. As a writer and a performer he was at the top. But it was the work that mattered. Awards did little for him save give him even more clout in television production. "It's nice to know you're liked," he said, "but you can live without awards. They're only a matter of opinion, after all."[8]

A popular by-product of *Marty* was the Decca album *I Feel A Song Going Off* which boasted old friend Denis King as Musical Director: "Music had been what linked Mart and I as friends," he recalls. "Often we would journey down to Ronnie Scott's after a boozy night in Gerry's club on Shaftesbury Avenue and Mart would be there. He loved music. Both playing and listening. He would try and persuade us to play along. It was some of the happiest times. John Junkin and I had written some silly songs for Marty's television series and he said he was a big fan of them and wanted to record them for Decca Records, which delighted me.⁹ It was like old music hall songs but with a slightly hip quality to them." Indeed, there is an air of cockney knees up about 'Ilford Town Hall' performed with gusto while 'The Great Bell', probably the most melodic track on the album, wouldn't have been out of place in the Rambling Syd Rumpo songbook. Marty's little man persona is given his head on 'Cautious Love Song' and 'You Without Me', while many, like 'The Elephant Song' end on an abrupt drum sting. 'Loo' displays Marty's love of cool jazz in a number that blends Mel Tormé with George Formby. "We dug out Marty's favourites from the old ones and wrote some new ones," explains King. "I half produced the album, worked on the arrangements in the studio, played and sang backing vocals. Junkin and I were in the studio all the time and it was great fun. Zany silly stuff. We weren't expecting a great hit which was just as well because we didn't get one. I never got any money out of it! But some of the tracks got a bit of air play."

The album jam-packed twenty-four songs into its short running time with some of them, like 'Kensington High Street', lasting no more than a few seconds: "It was the law of averages," says Denis King. "If you didn't laugh at one, you would only have a short time to not laugh at another one!" In fact, *I Feel A Song Going Off* is the perfect record of that late sixties period when Marty was at his peak in Britain. "He had a great comedy brain," says Denis King. "We had a lot of fun in the studio but Mart took it seriously. We added some ad-libs and I remember Junkin and I being very proud that he was doing it."¹⁰

Interestingly, as Marty chose to immortalise some of the songs from *Marty* he was in no hurry to secure an even more lucrative deal for more *Marty* episodes on television. Instead, he turned back to a treasured writing project, *Comedy Playhouse*. Two of the scripts he had been commissioned to write in 1964 were pulled out of the BBC archives and dusted off for production in the eighth series.

'The Making of Peregrine' was heralded by the BBC publicity department as a "must for fans of the 'domestic interior' school of comedy" although the actual premise of the situation was rather more shady and down-to-earth than that. Andrew Ray played the Peregrine of the title. His father,

Stanley, played by Dick Emery, attempts to make a man of him. Taking him away from his mother's apron strings and that "domestic interior" that the BBC fanfared, the young man is shown the seedier side of life; namely the wine, women and song of a public house bar.

The other *Comedy Playhouse* for this April/May 1969 series was of even more interest. 'Tooth and Claw', like the rather ill-fated 'Nicked at the Bottle' before it, was steeped in Jewish humour and East End understanding. If it had been picked up for production in 1965 it would no doubt have starred Alfred Marks and Sydney Tafler. Now, in 1969, Marty's fame was such that his name attached to one of the roles was considered not only a good omen but also somewhat bankable. So it was that Marty himself joined Warren Mitchell as the embittered, feuding, Jewish millionaires.

Bill Harman was the assistant floor manager on the programme and remembers: "Marty and Warren corpsing throughout the recording. The script was outrageous and you could see Marty was enjoying playing the role. I must imagine it was something of a thrill to find himself mugging it up in something he had written before he himself had become a performer of note. Anyway, one scene had the two rivals both sporting a bandaged nose. The entire story was simply one of one-upmanship. Each time Marty said a line Warren would collapse into laughter and every time Warren started to laugh Marty would join him. This scene took what seemed like hours to record. Finally, after take six or seven, [director] Roger Race stormed down from the control room shaking his fist in fury and bellowing: 'If you two bastards don't behave, I'll make sure you are wearing real bandages in a minute!' Marty and Warren behaved after that!"

Indeed, a note from Roger Race to Marty clearly hinted at the exasperation of the director: "Just a brief note of my thanks to you for taking part and greatly contributing to the success of the *Comedy Playhouse* Tooth and Claw production. I felt it went very well indeed and after all the editing that we have obviously had to do on it, I think we have a very fine programme."[11]

Bill Harman recalls that Marty was a relaxed and informed

conversationalist but relished the opportunity to shock: "It's the only other thing I can remember about Marty (apart from that face which, once seen, could never be forgotten). There was a conversation we had with Warren Mitchell about Jewish idiosyncrasies. Marty claimed that no matter how much you might hate and despise someone, once they die, as a Jew, you would never say a bad word about that person. As an example he said, 'If someone told a Jew that Adolf Hitler had died, they would say, 'Oh no, and such a young man.' Warren Mitchell couldn't believe he was hearing this from Marty."[12]

While the cross-section of the viewing public had been so confident in Marty's Montreux effort, they were less impressed with 'Tooth and Claw'. As the Audience Research Report read: "Perhaps viewers had expected too much from this story of two Jewish millionaires (played by Warren Mitchell and Marty Feldman) whose only zest left in life was to outdo each other: at all events, the programme evidently came as a sad disappointment to the sample at large, who found it, at best, only mildly amusing and, in a number of cases, slow, tedious and repetitive. In fact, only just over a quarter of the sample can be said really to have enjoyed this edition of *Comedy Playhouse*. For them, it was all great fun – not 'belly laugh' material perhaps, but amusing in a gentle, more subtle way: these were two excellent characters, just as determined to get the better of each other now as in their poverty-stricken youth, and their rivalry, their attempts at one-upmanship and their 'love-hate' relationship provided an original basis for comedy. 'Entertaining and full of home truths. However much you have, you must still achieve and win over someone'; 'Let's have a series. The scriptwriters are clearly masters of their art.'"

Warren Mitchell agrees that: "It had the potential to become a series but Marty was busy and I was busy. The script was perfect. Marty very rarely lost it [corpsed]. If he did it was for a real purpose and he got what he wanted in the end. He liked to get it right and he would fight for his corner."

The Audience Research Report continued, "An equal number, however, reacted in a distinctly unfavourable manner and the rest evidently considered it no more than a very 'average' show – not poor, exactly, but certainly hardly up to the standard they had come to expect from these two artistes. The basic idea had promise, and there were the odd flashes of humour, it was said, but there was too much talk and too little action (the scene in the restaurant, for instance, seeming endless) and the show was repetitive and predictable."

For Warren Mitchell, that scene was at the heart of the show: "We played them as about sixty years old and they met every week and they would argue over the menu in this posh Park Lane Hotel restaurant. I'd say, 'I'll have six oysters'. 'I'll have seven,' said Marty. 'What sort of a number is seven? I'll have eight!' It was so childish and very funny as a result. Of course oysters are a forbidden food for Jews. That was a joke not many picked up on. In the end we had pease pudding and faggots like we always did!"

But some viewers simply found: "little amusement to be had from watching grown men behaving like children, and their bickering and squabbling grew decidedly wearisome. Indeed, had it not been for the fact that these were two artistes who 'couldn't give a bad performance if they tried', viewers said, this would have been really dire (some, in fact, having no hesitation in describing it as 'absolutely rubbish')"[13]

The *Daily Express* reviewer opined that: "Two of TV's most successful funny men, Marty Feldman and Warren Mitchell teamed up last night on BBC1's *Comedy Playhouse*. Potentially they should have forged one of the strongest links of talent since *Steptoe and Son*. But somehow it did not quite come off. Feldman… is essentially a better clown than an actor. *Comedy Playhouse* has sparked off many a good series. I doubt if this one-shot play will turn into another – it would be too hard to sustain such a series of repetitive ideas even with such stars in hand."[14]

"In a few opinions however brilliant they were individually, Warren Mitchell and Marty Feldman did not make a good comedy team, at least on this showing," continued the Audience Research Report. "Their respective styles were cramped and neither appeared at his best – 'possibly' as one suggested 'because thirty minutes was not long enough for them both to do full justice to their great talents.' It is clear, however, that the programme's lack of success was due to the script rather than the performance and, as has been said, in lesser hands, the show might have been even more of a 'flop'. Those who enjoyed 'Tooth and Claw' attributed much of their pleasure to the performance of these two very accomplished artists ('well, what can one say about Marty and Alf. They were both splendid')." It is interesting to see that even at this early stage with three series of *Till Death Us Do Part* under his belt, Warren Mitchell was already completely cemented in the public eye as the ranting Tory bigot Alf Garnett.[15]

Johnny Speight, the creator of *Till Death Us Do Part* and a regular companion of Marty's, was instrumental in a more serious venture into acting, however. Both Speight and Marty, it was remarked, were: "from working-class backgrounds, were professional jazz musicians, are mad about football, and became top comedy script writers functioning at their best in the unlikely setting of the BBC."[16] Shortly after the recording of 'Tooth and Claw', Johnny Speight and the BBC had approached Marty about revisiting two television plays that had previously starred an on-the-cusp of stardom Michael Caine. 'The Compartment' and 'Playmates' cast Marty as Bill, a downtrodden, rather irritating man seemingly with a grudge against the rest of humanity. The double header, cleverly presented as 'Double Bill' under *The Wednesday Play* umbrella in the November of 1969 saw Marty playing it straight for the first time. (Alas, it is now missing from the archives.)

"One usually dreads meeting English comedians," wrote *The Observer*, "they're always such miseries... [Marty] described himself as a manic-depressive. But the words seemed to roll too easily off his tongue, and we couldn't resist saying that it's a rather fashionable thing to be nowadays: 'It may be fashionable but I was there first. Why didn't you believe me? I was telling the truth. I was being honest'. He's a gentle man and, one suspects, an open book: 'Why else be a comic? It's a self-defence mechanism. Find me a perfectly-formed comic from a secure background.'"

With the BBC and Marty still talking about the possibility of more *Marty*, in some form or other, and his acting career pointing towards more substantial material it seemed the only natural move was into cinema.

It was John Antrobus, another of the writer fraternity long associated with Marty, that adapted the play *The Bed Sitting Room* for a feature film. Antrobus had written the play with Spike Milligan and its rather cheerful, satirical examination of a post-nuclear war Britain had struck a chord with late sixties audiences. United Artists, who had already capitalised on swinging Britain with the two Beatles films, invested in the project and with predictable haste signed up the Beatles' director Richard Lester to make it. Lester had, more crucially, helmed the Goonish short subject, *The Running, Jumping & Standing Still Film*. *The Bed Sitting Room* celebrated the British eccentrics and their dogged attempts to carry on as normal: Spike Milligan wanders through the rubble as the last deliveryman. Harry Secombe babbles away as a very Welsh representative of regional government. Frank Thornton personifies the BBC, still delivering the news – in person and in a tattered dinner jacket – from within the shell of a television set. Peter Cook and Dudley Moore are the demonic remnants of the police force. Jimmy Edwards is a piece of left luggage. Little wonder *Variety* praised: "A carefully-chosen roster of British character thesps who contribute stellar bits in almost impossibly difficult roles."

The fact that Marty was included in the sparkling cast at all is testament to his respected standing within the with-it comedy scene. Moreover, making his feature film debut, he is given a special "introducing Marty Feldman" billing. His performance as the remnants of the National Health Service relies heavily on his little man persona; fussing and fawning in his nurse's uniform. Richard Lester, seizing on that face, introduces him with a musical sting and a directionally opposing pair of binoculars before giving Marty his first big screen close-up. Subsequently, he shares a scene with the seasoned old pro, Sir Ralph Richardson. That's what you call starting at the top. Marty later issues a death certificate for the still living Mona Washbourne and is in hot pursuit to collect. There is a streak of softly spoken violence throughout his performance. It was the perfect, surrealist introductory vehicle for Marty and although it proved a box office disappointment it remains a silly, affectionate, occasionally moving and always very British reaction to the nuclear winter as told by the great and good of comedy.

Although they had discussed it on several occasions, Marty had yet to actually write a feature film. With Barry Took, naturally, in tow and with Denis Norden in the writing mix as well, British Lion took on a satirical look at the advertising industry. Ned Sherrin was to be the producer and would find himself in that role for several big-screen comedies over the next few years.[17]

According to Marty, the film wasn't originally intended as his starring vehicle: "It wasn't my idea, honestly," he said on the Shepperton set in November 1969. "When I started work on it with Barry and Denis I was just a scriptwriter, not an actor at all. But by the time we finished it I was, of some sort. And I suppose there wasn't anybody else around nutty enough to do it."[18]

The premise was indeed nutty: a comedy about a wacky advertising man whose challenge is to come up with a sexy campaign for frozen porridge. His marriage is rocky, his twelve-year-old son collects knickers in a stamp album and the man himself lives life through a fantasy of commercial breaks. If one word could sum up the experience of sitting through the film, that one word would be surreal. In a good way.

On set, visiting journalist William Hall reported that: "[Marty] had spent the morning sitting on a plastic dragon belching flames and smoke... all over Dinsdale Landen, playing the unfortunate vicar... Mr Feldman reached the end of the line before losing his balance, hanging like a huge spider from the invisible wire round his waist. 'Not bad,' said the producer... 'I think it'll work,' said the cameraman, rather more cautiously. 'The last frame might be a bit off.'

"Enormous eyes like poached eggs floating sunny-side-up in a minestrone of facial expressions. Hair wandering off in all directions. A voice that makes itself heard in firecracker bursts: 'Hey! Was that okay? Did you get it? Hey, someone! Hey! Absurd, isn't it? Here am I, a grown man, sitting on a dragon while someone pushes lighted fireworks up its nostrils and 60 highly skilled men stand around watching us!'"[19]

Although a domestic comedy focused on Marty's failing marriage, the "sex-sells" advertising fantasies throughout embrace vivid daydreams and a string of costume changes; Marty is indulged as everything from Count Dracula to the hero of a silent melodrama. Indeed with its hair-brained slapstick and quick-fire sense of the absurd, *Every Home Should Have One* – the title referred to au pair girls much more than it did to bathrooms

– was for all intents and purposes the big screen spin-off for *Marty* the series. There's even a tail-end cameo from Marty's coarse archbishop. (In full regalia, complete with crozier, Marty encounters a television studio security guard: "'Ere, you a Bishop?" "Well, who do you think I am with this then, bloody Bo Peep? Course I'm a Bishop you twit!")

Modestly Marty claimed that producer Ned Sherrin had gone through a lengthy list of other potential stars. He had peered round at Marty sat behind his trusty typewriter and sighed: "It looks as though you'll have to do it." Still, in the dying days of 1969, there was nobody else in the industry who could or should have done it. The darling of television comedy and an award-winning performer and writer, Marty was ideally situated to make his major break into feature films.

The *Photoplay* reporter visiting the set was: "convinced that *Every Home Should Have One* is going to be the funniest comedian's film for many years. It's also going to mark the arrival in the cinema of a zany genius who could grow to the stature of a Buster Keaton or a Jacques Tati. 'I'm learning,' said Marty, when we lunched together at Shepperton. He came late to the restaurant (he won't miss the day's 'rushes') and cheerfully attacked his vegetarian's green salad."[20]

Marty's lunch during the shoot would always be a frugal one; typically one cheese sandwich and a glass of water. "I'm a vegetarian and I'm not hungry anyway," he would explain. "Not, after [the dragon incident] I went through back there." It was more than physical discomfort though. He was nervous. "I've put three inches on my waistline in the last ten weeks. People eat more when they're insecure, did you know? Success goes to my stomach, I reckon."[21] But this was after seeing the rushes of the morning's filming. If he wasn't relaxed then, he was clearly worried about what he saw.

"I know a lot of actors are put off by seeing themselves in rushes," he admitted, "but I go as much as a writer as an actor. They have taught me a lot about how much or how little you need to push a point home. If your face is twenty-feet-high, one word will do the trick. But if you think you've got an idea over from one half of the screen while some bird's taking off her clothes on the other half, you're wrong."

Having left the safe confines of his own BBC show, Marty was certainly in no hurry to direct a film himself, although the possibility was already in his head at this stage.

"You pretty soon learn how small you are. In television, it's easy to feel a big shot. It's your programme, the camera's on you and there probably aren't many other people around. But a film belongs to the director. He controls those dozens of blokes all round you and you depend on every one of them. And when it comes to the finished film, it's not what you do that makes it good, it's the way they stick the bits together."

The man that had landed the job of filming everything and sticking the bits together was, suitably, Jim Clark, an experienced editor on such controversial and cascading sixties classics as *Charade*, *Darling* and *The Pumpkin Eaters*. This was his first film as a director and Marty's small screen acting technique learnt from both *Marty* and, perhaps, most importantly *The Wednesday Play*: 'Double Bill', paid off.

"There are two things that have really surprised me," Clark said. "I wasn't sure that it would be possible to think of [Marty] as the husband in the straight scenes he plays with Judy [Cornwell] – Britain's Shirley MacLaine. But he handles them beautifully. And having the scriptwriter as the star has brought no problems at all. He never objects if I cut a line, and it's very handy to have him around to come up with a new idea when something doesn't quite work."[22]

Marty's performance is something of a revelation. He had proved himself as a good sketch comedy performer week in and week out on television, but to sustain that energy and interest over a feature's length took much more. Certainly it is a given that he excels in the Walter Mitty-like vignettes but only because we, the audience, have warmed to the complex man behind the day-dreaming. Thus, we believe his marriage is threatened because of his apathy. The domestic scenes have an under-current of kitchen sink despair that Marty laudably refuses to send up for a quick laugh. We sympathise with him when his obsession with work makes him fail to pick up on the initial advances of another man towards his wife. We certainly believe his sexual attraction to Julie Ege. The Norwegian actress and model was, arguably, the most decorative of decoration utilised in British comedy and horror of the period. Producer Ned Sherrin used her several times, notably in the film version of *Up Pompeii*, and recalled Marty didn't have to act very much while he was around her. During the shooting of the Ingmar Bergman-inspired fantasy of Swedish sex both Marty and Julie Ege were completely naked. Although the camera angles were skilfully designed to protect the audience from seeing Marty's manhood, Marty himself had little control over it. Who would? As the two naked lovers ran through the fields Marty got erect. So excited was he at the sight of Julie Ege in the buff that the scene had to go for a second take. Marty's penis had kept poking up into shot![23]

Even at the end of 1969 there was talk of Hollywood stardom but Marty was happy to bide his time. He had plenty of clout on *Every Home Should Have One* but he was relaxed under the control of Jim Clark, who he dubbed as: "marvellous. I'm sure he's going to be one of the greats."[24]

The *Monthly Film Bulletin* reviewer was rather less impressed, writing that: "This feature debut by Jim Clark (formerly editor for [Jack] Clayton and [Stanley] Donen, and director of several TV documentaries and theatrical shorts) is a strictly hit-and-miss affair which reveals, once again, the dangers of trying to be fashionably contemporary and satirical at the same time. The targets are familiar enough (bizarre advertising campaigns, clean-up TV propagandists, au pair girls with funny accents and plunging necklines), and they are parodied in a manner somewhat akin to the *Carry On* tradition – except that the verbal jokes are even bluer and, occasionally, offensively dirty in their obsession with phallic symbols. In an attempt to keep the whole thing lively and effervescent (bright decors, heady colours, animated inserts, and so on), writers and director have gone for a spanking tempo in which one noisy gag is quickly superseded by another on the basis that if you don't like one, you may love the next. Unfortunately this method is no guarantee of genuine wit, and it is surprising that such a film buff as Clark should make so little of his fantasy parodies of horror films, Swedish nude love scenes and silent melodramas. He fares much better with the decor and props, though, like the little van in the shape of a toothpaste tube which capers all over London.

"In some respects, of course, the whole thing is a gigantic in-joke: most of the creative talent involved know the television world from practical experience and proceed, gleefully, to blow it up – almost literally – at the end. The sight of the disintegrating studio prompts the TV producer calmly to remark, 'This has the makings of real television material'; and the film's better moments contain nice little throwaway lines like this. Most of the cast, however, are encouraged to punch away at everything in sight, which results in a good deal of unfunny mugging. Marty Feldman himself is probably an acquired taste; in close-up, his facial expressions and googly eyes make Jerry Lewis' gyrations seem quite sober, and his film technique is as yet too limited to take the weight of a whole feature. If he could be calmed down a bit and encouraged to develop his sly, mean look, he might have the makings of a genuine grotesque, but the film's particular brand of slapstick offers him little opportunity."[25]

Marty himself was confident the film would be reasonably successful: "I have high hopes for it," he said. "With any luck it'll turn out better than good, even if it's less than fantastic." That modest, understated and certainly achievable level certainly was achieved. It is his only British-based starring vehicle and one that, on its very rare television screenings, reminds a jaded nation of just what Marty was doing during his super stardom of the late 1960s.

It also consolidated his rock 'n' roll lifestyle. Marty still might have felt a little uneasy about being a cultural icon at the age of thirty-five but if he had to be one he was certainly going to enjoy it. Throughout *Every Home Should Have One* Marty donned flamboyant clothes designed by Mr. Fish of Piccadilly. The style perfectly suited Marty's swinging sixties clout.[26] "His first starring film role was very important in terms of this embracing of the sixties," remembers Ian La Frenais. "Being a star on television was one thing, but being a star in your own film was something much more again. I remember seeing him entering a very trendy club with a very attractive woman on his arm – an attractive woman who wasn't his wife. It was Julie Ege and she was in the film with him. I stopped him to say 'hello' and this woman on his arm was *really* stunning. We chatted about it a little later and he gave me that off-kilter smile and said: 'Success has gone to my crotch!' That was the first time I had ever heard that. That was a very Marty line."

One can almost hear him thinking to himself as he chatted to William Hall over lunch in Shepperton that, no, it wasn't his appetite for food that had increased because of his new fame but his appetite for sex. "But he really was a fifties man," says La Frenais. "Very much of radio comedy, jazz cigarettes and that bohemian lifestyle. Suddenly he was a sixties man with floral jackets and revolutionary ideals. You see, he was older than all those other sixties people. Even though it was only by a few years, Marty was very conscious of it. Everyone famous was twenty-four at that time. Marty wasn't."

Dick Clement agrees that: "In a way, to use Marty's own musical allegory, it was the difference between Elvis Presley and John Lennon. It may have only been a matter of five years but that was a huge chasm in the sixties. Marty probably felt like a fraud or a fool but he went along with it because it suited his career. He was a comic icon of the late sixties with the brain of a mid-1950s writer."

Marty also quite clearly enjoyed it and one can scarcely blame him when his showbiz lifestyle culminated in hotel bedroom romps with Julie Ege. For Tim Brooke-Taylor, his unfaithfulness was an isolated incident: "There was a time when Marty suddenly flipped. He went off with a lady and did drugs and drank too much. He did everything wrong... for about a week, and then he went back to Lauretta. He got through it! I remember saying, 'Well that was probably a good thing that you did that.' He tried it all out, got it out of his system and went back to his wife."

However Bill Oddie remembers several such instances. "Lauretta was long-suffering beyond belief. People would say: 'She's really putting up with that?' Marty was back and forth from America. All these different girls would be around. I don't even think it was the power of stardom. It was an era of Beauty and the Beast anyway, I promise you. It occasionally benefited me. There was a syndrome of glamorous models going out with wizened photographers. They all had these incredibly glamorous models as girlfriends. You felt like it was almost a fashion accessory for the girl."

Warren Mitchell recalls that: "Marty's close friends had a joke that his eyes went like that because he once found himself in bed with two lesbians! He was very attractive to women and he was happy to oblige."

"Mart was such a lovely man that you could almost forgive him anything," says Denis King. "I didn't see that dark side of him but you would hear stories of his moods. We were very good friends. Marty, Lauretta, Anne and Ted Levy. In fact, Lauretta was a bridesmaid to my first wife. We would spend a lot of time together. Mart was taking a bit of dope. Well, a lot of dope really. He would go off on a bender; simply disappear and then reappear a few days later. No-one knew where he had gone."

According to Marty, the rot had set in quite early. Back when he was just finding his feet on *At Last the 1948 Show*, the seven-year itch kicked in. "Suddenly I was going through my adolescence at thirty-two instead of fifteen," he said. "Marriage isn't easy. In fact it's bloody difficult. All intense friendships are difficult." He remembered that he and Lauretta separated for only a few months but that she was patient and forgiving. "She did the only thing a friend can do when there is trouble... be there," he said. "She was. When I phoned her up and said, 'Can I come home?' She said, 'Yes'. Otherwise I might not have survived or I'd have gone under through alcohol as so many of my friends did."[27]

But Marty would return again and again to the heady cocktail of sex, drugs and booze, particularly at times of stress and depression. It would block out the pressure of work and dull the pain of critical failure. Lauretta would always stand by him. Whether the period of separation would be a week or a few months, she would always take him back and always nurse him through his insecurities. However, Marty's other marriage couldn't withstand the fame and frailties that plagued him. Barry Took filed for a "divorce".

Chapter Eleven

"One of the nicest things about success is that I've been able to get tickets very easily to see Chelsea play."

The writing partnership that Barry Took had long likened to a marriage had finally gone sour during the summer of 1969. Nothing can put a friendship at risk more than the ultra-success of one of the friends. For two men who had been equals for so long – ever since bumping into one another on the same variety bill at the York Empire – the sudden escalation of Marty as Britain's favourite and most influential funny man must have rankled. "After the initial anger had worn off," wrote Barry Took, "a friendship developed that has lasted, with a break of an hour or so here and there, ever since."[1]

However, Barry Took remained adamant to the end that it had been: "a delightful time. But all lovely things must come to an end. You realise that. We used to write very fast and we wrote literally hundreds of scripts together. Films, television, radio, everything and then one day we both looked at each other and said: 'We've done it all!' and we really had done it all. But we were never happier than when we were writing together."[2]

Although the friendship had been an occasionally rocky one it is impossible to deny that the writing partnership was every bit as prolific and successful as Took would claim: "We worked together for ten years and we finished every day screaming with hysterical laughter. Marty would sit at a table cracking gags we couldn't possibly use and I would be flat on the floor laughing."

Sheila Steafel maintains that: "I don't think Barry was particularly jealous of Marty's success. No more than anyone is jealous of anyone else in this business. I've got a very lengthy list of people I hate! But Barry was doing his own thing and stayed friends with Marty. I'm sure it smarted to some extent because they had such a long partnership. Suddenly, or so it seemed, Marty was this huge international comedy figure and Barry was hosting *Points of View*."[3]

Moreover, Barry Took was still a major player within BBC comedy. "Barry was someone we all respected hugely," says Michael Palin. "He was the respectable man in the suit at the BBC but he had also worked the variety circuit and written all this wonderful comedy. He was someone we felt very privileged to have in our corner."

Terry Jones concurs that: "Barry was always very encouraging. He was instrumental in getting Python going. I suspect if it hadn't been for him Python might never have happened." *Monty Python's Flying Circus* debuted in October 1969.

The final straw for Barry Took must have been *Marty*. Although Barry was heavily involved in most of the scripting, this was seen as Marty's personal triumph. *Round the Horne*, by the very virtue of their non-involvement in the performance, had always been a joint success story. On *Marty* no one gave a second thought for Marty's co-writer when Marty's comedy stamp was so firmly on the entire product. Took was picking up a respectable £350 per episode for his written contribution but, perhaps, the most galling thing of all was that he was also performing the warm-up routine before the studio audience: "For this work we [the BBC] offer you a fee of fifteen guineas for each programme."[4] There was an embarrassed sense of tossing an extra coin in a beggar's tin cup.

Marty had already initiated writing with old friends like John Law and new, like Tim Brooke-Taylor, in a series of trial separations from Barry Took. "We would come back together refreshed," Marty said. "It worked for a long while until, over a long period of time, I became an actor and Barry's acting ceased and he became totally a writer. We no longer shared the same terms of reference and our writing relationship drifted apart. I used to spend eight or nine hours a day with Barry, five days a week, and when you write with someone, you know them mentally naked. You know their hang-ups, they know yours. You tend to get to know your writing partner probably better than you know your wife. You certainly spend more time with them. You know each other very, very well. And it's difficult having known each other very, very well to be social friends again. You know each other too well. Once it became predictable, once the surprise went out of it, we had nothing more to learn from each other. We had no more reason to go on."

This feeling of losing control and position while Marty flew ever higher was undoubtedly intensified during the spring of 1969. A BBC documentary crew was following Marty's every move for a programme eventually screened as *One Pair of Eyes*. Barry Took's gritted teeth admiration was palpably clear in the piece the *Radio Times* commissioned him to write in promotion of the programme: "In the past year more newspaper space has been devoted to Marty than to QE2 and Concorde combined, and I've no intention of adding to the work of the press cutting agencies more than I have to, but Marty's curious temperament is worth considering for a moment. He's a man of great contrasts and great contradictions. Belligerent but a pacifist, an extremely shrewd business man but indifferent to money, fond of children but so far without any of his own, a vegetarian but a lover of bullfighting. He has a bubbling, frivolous sense of humour but is subject to moods of great depression – a poet, a footballer, an intellectual who lives, it seems, entirely on his emotions. As the song says, 'A Strange Harmony of Contrasts.'"

They are the words of a bickering spouse who, in the dying days of a marriage, rather enjoys point scoring against the person they have shared a huge slice of their life with. It was a very public bit of bitching.

"Television has married its latest star at the Chapel of Our Lady of the Sorrows, Wood Lane (better known to some, perhaps, as BBC's Television Centre)," continued Took. "The carousel is spinning, the organ is playing 'Here we are again, happy as can be, all good pals and jolly good company,' and Marty has his pick of the horses.

"In *One Pair of Eyes* (Marty's comment on the aptness or otherwise of the title is stated in the programme) you can explore with him his feelings and attitudes and meet his heroes, colleagues and friends. It should be a fascinating programme. With Marty in it, it's certainly not going to be dull."[5]

The last major collaboration came with Marty's BBC special for the Easter of 1970. The corporation had waited patiently for over a year while Marty moved away from the sketch show format that had made his name. With a ratings-winning repeat season of *Marty Revisited* throughout February the BBC happily offered him a £750 contract for a one-off *Marty* programme.

The contract that Marty signed on 10th February 1970 was under the agreement: "Should a series of programmes starring Marty Feldman be mutually agreed (30' duration) to be performed on dates within one year of the above recording date [23rd March 1970], our engagement fee will be £1,750 (covering the right to one repeat) and the copyright fee can remain unchanged... unless the series becomes the subject of a co-production involving Marty Feldman as a producer. In that case the terms will be subject to re-negotiation."[6]

The forty-five-minute special, subsequently broadcast as *Marty Amok* on 30th March 1970, was in effect the very last edition of *Marty*. His usual supporting cast was in place: Tim Brooke-Taylor, John Junkin, Mary Miller. The scripting team included Terry Jones, Michael Palin and *Round the Horne* salvagers Johnnie Mortimer and Brian Cooke. The director was *Marty* and *Comedy Playhouse*: 'Tooth and Claw' war-horse Roger Race.

It was the last time that Marty and Barry would write together. "When a writing partnership breaks up people treat it like a marriage," Marty said. "They say, 'Oh, I can't invite Barry Took because Marty's coming,' and they talk in hushed tones about it. They don't understand that a marriage can break up but people can still be friends. But I have custody of the scripts. He visits them weekends!" Lauretta would later recall the gales of laughter that she would hear coming from the room where they were working. She thought that Marty's ideas and imagination ran riot without Barry being there to rein him in. "I appreciated her saying that," Took commented.

Now the mooring rope had gone and the complete lunacy was free. The opening gamut of *Marty Amok* was typically wild as waiter Marty welcomed a couple to a restaurant, offered them the octopus within the fish tank, dived in fully clothed and yelled: "Would you like it off the bone, Sir?"

It was clear during filming that Marty was back in his element. "Watching them shoot this part," wrote Rose Marie Wiltman in *The Sun* on the 21st March 1970, "is like watching early movies being made. There is the same speed – they rarely shoot a scene more than twice, and the same rapid improvisation, by Marty and everyone else in the cast. Ideas come up at the rate of two a minute." The reviews were universally favourable. "There is a mixture of crafty innocence and know-all devilment that tears you two ways," thought the *Daily Mirror*. "Laugh? Or run for the hills? It's a toss-up. I mean. Would you like to be trapped in a lift with Marty at his manic best? Would you even like to serve him in a bookshop? It is the uncanny side of Marty that can give you nightmares while you are laughing at the picture jokes. And it is the nightmarish ability to transgress normality that he exploits best. Take his last sketch last night. Little man in a bowler at a Western, peacefully smoking a pipe, when Red Indians return the cavalry's fire – but from behind him in the circle. They ride through the audience and drive him into the screen, and the film. He is chased into the bar of a Wild West town where it turns out he is the villain all the characters have been expecting. Which is the sort of thing that happens to me in bad dreams when I haven't got the option of heading for the end of the film and making a quick exit, as Marty did. It is Funny Ha-Ha and it is Funny Peculiar. He's looking at you from the inside of his head. Palming off his uncomfy moments... [in those] ten sketches in forty-five minutes, each with its alien edge to give it his signature."[7]

However, despite the continued high quality of his output, the BBC was fast losing their grip on Marty. Moreover, they wouldn't tolerate the odd special every so often. Marty couldn't drag his feet over the signing up for a proper series for much longer. But he was determined to bide his time for one simple reason. America had sat up and taken notice.

It was all with the blessing of the BBC at first. As early as May 1969, the BBC Managing Director Paul Fox was in discussion with Ed Saxe, the President of CBS International, with regards to sharing Marty's BBC programmes with the American network. Saxe had asked for 525 line video tapes of the two best *Marty* programmes and, as Paul Fox wrote:

"CBS are anxious to get involved in this series in some way or another."[8]

It was naturally agreed that the Silver Rose of Montreux-winning compilation would be one of these shows. It included the very best of Marty's work and, as Dennis Main Wilson wrote to Michael Mills on 9th May 1969: "I suggest that the second one should include those items which just missed the Montreux show. Please consult with Marty about the items to be included, and please stress to him that this is not a sale, nor an offer for a sale, but an opportunity for CBS to assess Marty's suitability for their programmes with a view to a co-production deal." The second compilation included 'The Flying Rabbi', 'Table Top Battle' and the 'Elephant Song' so that, as Dennis Main Wilson noted: "CBS will have a complete, overall appreciation of Marty's talents."[9]

As it turned out there was no new series of *Marty* for CBS to co-produce but, as Barry Took wrote: "This recent TV series is being shown all over the world. Offers flow in from every quarter. Sheldon Leonard (executive producer of *The Dick Van Dyke Show*) is convinced that Marty is the best thing he's seen in years. George Schlatter (the man who created *Rowan and Martin's Laugh-In*) calls himself Marty's number one American fan. The words 'brilliant', 'genius', [and] 'unique' fall like confetti."[10]

On 30th May 1970, just two months after *Marty Amok* was broadcast, *The Sun* newspaper was reporting that Marty was "starting work on a new series for American television... [with] one interesting co-star... Julian Chagrin." This show was to be a landmark in Marty's career: *The Golddiggers in London*. As another *Sun* headline screamed on 25th July 1970: "Our Marty slays 'em in the States: Marty Feldman, the comedy scriptwriter who turned performer only three years ago, is making a smash hit on American television. The series *Golddiggers*, which was made in Britain for NBC, and has been shown in place of *The Dean Martin Show*, is gaining him as much praise from a rather startled American press as his performances did here. *The Dean Martin Show* has been one of the top American shows for some time now, and there was some doubt about how well Marty's sense of humour would show up. But it seems nobody need have worried. [Jack Pitman, of the] *Daily Variety*, the show business magazine, tips him as possibly 'the first British comedian to make it on

American video since Bob Hope.' It says that 'no show ever moved faster.'"

In a landmark August 1970 article, 'American Dreams', John Hall lavished praise on "US TV's latest find". Hall noted that the explosion of interest in Marty was on: "the occasion of his present airing to the press [and] his ecstatic discovery, suddenly this summer, by the usually taciturn and knife-cruel television writers of the United States."

It had been the *Los Angeles Times* that had described Marty as "the find of the year", while *Variety* called him a "wacky gas".

"Apparently," continued Hall, "the villains are throwing their hats in the air over Marty's guest appearances in a show called *The Golddiggers*, which is the summer replacement for the regular Dean Martin programme. Anything which replaces *The Dean Martin Show* merits tumultuous applause in my book, and our American cousins are celebrating their release from the syrup opera by heaping upon Marty comparisons with Danny Kaye, Buster Keaton, Chaplin, Cantinflas, Fernandel, and Mutt and Jeff, to begin with."

Dean Martin need not have been concerned with Marty's immense popularity. The Italian crooner hadn't been usurped by the *Golddiggers* show. In fact, he was "presenting" it in a break from his usual mix of song, comedy and dancing girls. Jack Hill could reveal, however, "more specially, Feldman is booked to appear on the actual Dean Martin groan-in later this year." These appearances allowed Marty to dust off some old routines and, delightfully and incongruously, have Dean Martin appear as his grinning, self-mocking second banana.

"I remember Marty telling me about his experiences with Dean Martin," says Tim Brooke-Taylor. "It was obviously an amazing opportunity for him but Marty was a wreck afterwards. Dean Martin simply refused to rehearse. He would prefer to spend all his time playing golf. Now, I can understand that but not when you have a show to do. Marty wouldn't have even met Dean Martin by the time the show was being recorded. Marty would have to pop his head round the curtain after Dean Martin had finished a song and go straight in to a sketch without rehearsal. Marty would know his lines, of course, but Dean Martin would be reading his off idiot boards. It was insane."[11]

The news of his instant fame in America meant little for Marty. When it broke he was holidaying in Elba and, upon returning home to England, commented: "I've no strong feelings about what is happening in the States. It's all over there and I'm over here. It's like nothing to do with me."[12]

Marty soon found a taste for the Hollywood lifestyle though. He had started going over for work assignments and at one point he was an uncredited script doctor on Mike Sarne and David Giler's film *Myra Breckinridge*. Vera Day remembers that: "My husband, Terry O'Neill, was out there photographing [the film's stars] Mae West and Raquel Welsh and we spent quite a lot of time with Marty and Lauretta. We were sitting round the swimming pool and Lauretta and Marty were sunbathing. My first husband, Arthur [Mason], had been an East End boy and I could relate to Marty. I said something like: 'All these East End boys love the sunshine, don't they?' and she snapped: 'Marty actually came from Hampstead!' Now I knew he came from a working class Jewish background but she was having none of it. Marty was very quiet and didn't correct her. I found Lauretta rather snobbish. She would find the latest sensation and go completely overboard with them. I remember she had taken this young pianist under her wing and we were dragged along to some nightclub to hear him play. She just turned her back on him during the performance, smoked her cigarette and behaved as though she was his agent. It was very strange. Marty always looked a little embarrassed about it and although he wasn't exactly under her thumb he was always very softly spoken and careful what he said when she was there. He was a lovely, softly spoken man anyway but he certainly seemed more relaxed when she wasn't around. He was marvellous with our daughter, Sarah. The place he was renting had a swimming pool and he taught her to dive. He was lovely with Sarah. She was a lovely little girl. Very well behaved. Marty would say she was nothing like the typical showbiz kid he would meet in America. He didn't like pretentious people."[13]

The American success did open further doors for Marty, however. Producer Larry Gelbart started talks with him about a second starring vehicle for the cinema. The tentative title was *Nobody Loves an Honest Cop, or The Other Kind Either* but this comic romp through the streets of the New York Police Department was typically gearing Marty's humour towards the blunt end of the American market and, thankfully perhaps, came to nought. A third film project, this time for television, was more intriguing. Marty hoped to achieve the almost impossible and film one of his favourite books, *Don Quixote*. He would be in support as Sancho Panza, with either Anthony Quinn or Peter Sellers as Quixote. Moreover, there was talk of an American television series that would capitalise on his success with Dean Martin and force him further into the international limelight.

Reassuringly, Marty had his feet firmly on the ground regarding all these aborted projects, particularly where the move into American television and its questionable output was concerned: "Well, when the first prize is a bag of shit..." he pondered.[14] He felt that British television would give him the opportunity to make the sort of programmes he wanted to make: "I want to get back to the fundamentals of comedy without the clutter of storylines," he said. "No talkie-talkie bits. Get back to where it all began." His plan was to produce, star and direct in a series of self-contained thirty-minute silent films for television. The BBC was the perfect home for them.[15]

Thus, Marty certainly had no qualms about signing up for yet another special for BBC television, although his involvement in the actual writing of the programme wasn't as much as usual. Indeed, when the idea was first mooted on 15th July 1970, producer Michael Mills instructed Jack Beale in the copyright department to: "negotiate a fee for Marty Feldman with his agent, Kenneth Ewing of Fraser & Dunlop Ltd., for a half hour all-filmed script to be written by Marty Feldman and to star himself. It is proposed that the filming should start in the last week of September, and one would like to have a fairly definite script by the end of August. I am not commissioning Marty Feldman's performance until I have received the script, so in this case his script fee will be separate from his performance fee."

On 12th August 1970 it was noted that Marty wanted the scripts to be written with or by other writers and was arranging to meet with Michael Mills the following day. The final outcome of this meeting was detailed on 20th August 1970, the day after John Hall's 'American Dreams' piece had been published.

The project, now discussed as the *Marty Feldman Special Film Programme*, was to be written by Johnnie Mortimer and Brian Cooke [also of Fraser & Dunlop]. "We are aiming to film this in England and in Spain in October. Marty Feldman is himself making some contribution to the show, but as [agent] Kenneth Ewing represents both parties it seems to me that it would be best to negotiate a complete fee and let Ewing tell us what proportion is to be applied to whom."[16]

After the usual debate over fees, Marty finally signed the contract on 28th September 1970.[17]

It was agreed that Cooke and Mortimer would receive the major writing credit: "with Marty's name coming separately at a position to be agreed with the director."[18] Finally, on 6th October 1970, the programme was unveiled as *Marty Abroad*. It was filmed on location in Spain and in Britain from 19th October 1970.

As well as the cutting back of the writing team, Marty's supporting players were curtailed as well with only John Junkin joining him for the programme. Tim Brooke-Taylor was busy filming the first series of *The Goodies* but re-teamed with Marty for the most prestigious night in the variety calendar, The Royal Variety Show. "Funnily enough that was the night after the first transmission of *The Goodies*," says Brooke-Taylor. "I remember Roland MacLeod[19] and I watched it go out in the dressing room because we were at the London Palladium rehearsing for the Command Performance. Marty didn't watch it with us and I felt slightly disappointed. I remember wondering why not, mind you he was probably mixing with the biggest showbiz people at the time."

As for the actual Royal Variety Performance on 9th November 1970: "That was the biggest disaster ever," chuckles Brooke-Taylor. "I think we must be the only people to finish our act and not quite be able to make it round the corner to take our bow before the applause stopped. It was so little. When they put it out on television [BBC1, 15th November 1970] they had obviously put on a little extra applause to save our embarrassment. The sketch died the most almighty death on the night.

Marty a few short years after his
"Gothic Shirley Temple" phase
(above left). He looks unhappy
about being on camera, unlike
his proud mother.

A rare shot of Marty looking
cheerful in school uniform (above),
here away from war-torn London
with his sister, Pamela.

Every inch the smart young son
of a Jewish immigrant family.
A Little Lord Fauntleroy of the
East End.

The relaxed variety turn, complete with poised cigarette, and his dressed-to-the-nines parents Cissy and Mossy, and sister Pamela.

In the early 1950s Marty embraced the new wave of jazz culture. Here he sports the hip goatee. Pamela makes for a stunning companion.

The famous Marty eyes haven't quite developed but already he is promoting a shadowy, man of mystery image.

Two comic minds as one. The writing partnership with Barry Took would last over a decade and produce successful film, television and radio. It was Marty's second 'marriage'.

Four comedy legends in profile: John Cleese, Marty, Graham Chapman and Tim Brooke-Taylor. The celebrated *At Last the 1948 Show* team.

The black humour of death would be a recurring theme in Marty's work. Here he dons the undertaker's garb for his BBC series *Marty Back Together Again*.

In 1969 Marty took on more serious work as the disconcerting Bill in Johnny Speight's 'Double Bill', part of *The Wednesday Play* strand.

The 'lovely' Aimi MacDonald joins the *At Last the 1948 Show* publicity session. Marty is still just concealing his idiosyncratic features.

A publicity portrait as Teddy Brown in his first starring film vehicle, *Every Home Should Have One*. The cool fashions mirrored Marty's own taste.

Marty took on American television guest spots in such fare as *The Sandy Duncan Show*, *Hollywood Squares* and *Flip*. His smiles usually masked his disinterest in the work.

Marty always seemed non-plussed about the big hand American audiences gave him. A memorable scene from the TV special *Lights, Camera, Monty!*

Marty gets playful with Julie Ege – cinema's definitive Swedish au pair girl – in *Every Home Should Have One*…

… and dances the night away in a blur of late-sixties psychedelia. The partying would go on well after the cameras stopped rolling at Shepperton Studios.

"I ain't got no body!" Marty's most potent and lasting legacy is as Igor – that's Egor! – from Mel Brooks' *Young Frankenstein.*

Marty puts on the Ritz to join Peter Boyle as the monster and Gene Wilder as Frederick in the musical interlude. Marty's contribution was heavily edited.

Director and co-writer Mel Brooks joins the chaps and Teri Garr on the Fox Studios sound stage.

Marty returned to England to co-star in Gene Wilder's *The Adventure of Sherlock Holmes' Smarter Brother*. The good guys are at the mercy of Leo McKern's Moriarty and Dom DeLuise as Gambetti.

Marty was wrapped up in film all his life. He gave his most personal Hollywood salute to his slapstick heroes as Marty Eggs in Mel Brooks' *Silent Movie*.

Crime does not pay as Marty's dogged Scotland Yard Sergeant gets his man (Roy Kinnear) in *The Adventure of Sherlock Holmes' Smarter Brother.*

Making his cinematic directorial debut, Marty cast Hollywood royalty Ann-Margret as his mother. Well, he was the writer as well!

Monty Hall's TV special *Lights, Camera, Monty!* utilised much of Universal's contracted talent including Marty, here getting a taste of things to come…

…in his first Hollywood film as star, director and writer, *The Last Remake of Beau Geste.* He did his own stunts to re-capture the silent era magic of Harold Lloyd's thrill comedies.

Marty searched far and wide to find a young man who looked like what he *should* have looked like as a young man! With Michael McConkey on location for *The Last Remake of Beau Geste.*

The last laugh. Marty enjoying himself on location for his final film, *Yellowbeard.* Its posthumous release would be dedicated to him.

Cigarette nervously in hand and in full monk costume, Marty directs a scene from his second production, *In God We Tru$t*. It was universally and unfairly panned.

Fifteen years since teaming up for *At Last the 1948 Show*, Marty and John Cleese joined forces once again for *Yellowbeard*. Comedy heavyweights all at sea.

Marty was with his "bird", wife Lauretta, for half of his life. She was his rock, soul mate, best friend and sharpest critic.

Good friend and fledgling writer Alan Spencer joins Marty in his beloved dune buggy on the back-lot during the making of *Silent Movie*.

Never at ease with the glamour of show business, Marty accompanies his mother to a glitzy affair.

The embodiment of the freedom of artistic expression that the 1960s cracked open, Lauretta and Marty were certainly among the beautiful people…

…but into the 1970s Marty was still happy to clown and send up his supposed clout in Hollywood.

A relaxed and healthy-looking Marty shortly before his death. His thoughts were on a return to the world of British TV he knew and loved.

I was a city businessman and Marty came in and said, 'Give me some money or I'll take my clothes off'. Then Roland MacLeod came on and arrested him."

Marty remembered doing: "A sketch at the Royal Variety Show for Mum. Liz [The Queen Mother]. And she was very offended because during the sketch I had occasion to divest myself of my trousers, which upset Mum and family and Phil the Greek [Prince Philip]. They got very upset. They said you shouldn't take your trousers off in front of [royalty] and I thought, 'Well, Philip must have done or where did Anne and Charles come from!' The Queen's seen a man without his trousers before. She must have done, I hope, otherwise there's another Immaculate Conception that I didn't know about."[20]

For Tim Brooke-Taylor: "It was one of those times when as I was standing there and the curtain went up I was thinking, 'I'll know when Marty has come on because the applause will start.' Anyway, the applause didn't start and he was stood next to me so I thought, 'Oh God, we're not in good nick here already.' It was one of those embarrassing silences – a virtual silence – all the way through the sketch and we had to hurry off, round the curtain, bow to the Royal Box and then get off. It was a disastrous occasion. Funnily enough it was the Royal Command on which Freddie Starr was the hit of the show. He was very shy and obviously on his own and Marty and I adopted him. It's just ironic because we died the death and he tore the place apart."[21]

Marty was well aware that he had poked fun at the Royal Family and he was rather proud of that: the public reaction was always very good. "The reaction with regards the thing I did about the Queen [in *Marty*] she never actually admitted she'd seen it. 'We hadn't seen this!' sort of reactions. The Palace did not admit it but I found out afterward that she had. I've often thought the British national creature should not be the bulldog, you know, it should be the ostrich. You stick your head in the sand and pretend it hasn't happened."

This wasn't a case of Marty bristling with confidence years after the event. He had a sense of bravura at the time. Tim Brooke-Taylor remembers: "Marty wasn't nervous on that occasion. Not as nervous as me! Because he had this history of performing in music hall and variety, he knew where he was on a stage. You never quite knew with the group thing how it was going to work on stage and I suppose our style of comedy was out of its comfort zone. Maybe we were just terrible. I don't know. But Marty took it all in his trouserless stride. The line up after the performance wasn't very major for me because I wasn't even in it. Just the leading lights were presented to the royalty present. I just hung around backstage and quietly slunk off when it was all over."

Marty was certainly confident enough on stage to be having ongoing conversations with Spike Milligan about staging *Waiting For Godot* at the Roundhouse in London. Indeed, over the course of several years, talk would invariably turn to presenting this most eagerly anticipated production of Samuel Beckett's masterpiece but, with Marty's typical sense of comedy, the only trouble was that whenever they met they couldn't decide who was going to be Estragon, and who Vladimir.

Although this tantalising project never came about, Spike seemed to be a near constant talisman for Marty. Indeed, it was almost as if *Every Home Should Have One* hadn't been made when Marty bowled up to Pinewood Studios for a cough and a spit of a role in *The Magnificent Seven Deadly Sins*. The film was directed by Graham Stark for Tigon Pictures Limited. "The governor was Tony Tenser," says Stark, "and we didn't see eye to eye on anything. My initial hope had been to have the film's stories flow into each other in a similar way to that wonderful French picture, *La Ronde*. I was going to link all the stories. It wasn't supposed to be a film of seven sketches but that's what it became because of Tenser. He said: 'I've been to see the cartoonist!' And I said: 'What?' 'Oh yes, I've signed up Bob Godfrey to do the cartoons to link it.' I said: 'You do realise that you have absolutely cobbled it now. The film will stop. It will stop six times before the final end!' It became sketches instead of one complete film. But it was a joy. I have never enjoyed myself as much. The absolute power of being a director. Suddenly everyone is your best friend and everything is down to you. I had a marvellous time, particularly doing the 'Sloth' sequence with Spike Milligan. It was very funny. I simply popped down to the dining room at lunchtime and saw a lot of actors: "Ere mate. What are you doing tomorrow?' You see Spike was the sprat to catch the mackerel. Once they knew Spike was the star of this segment everyone said 'yes'. They all loved him. Marty Feldman. Ronnie Barker. Peter Butterworth. You know. All these great comedians."²² A homage to the silent cinema, the segment was shot in sepia and told in a series of very brief vignettes, each moment illustrating an extreme example of sloth. Marty, sporting the bowler hat and scarf of his familiar irritating little man from television, prefers to wait for a tree to fall down rather than walk around it. His patience wears thin and he tries to chop it down without much luck. And that's it. He also gave Stark an old story outline to script for the 'Lust' segment. A free adaptation of Marty's *Comedy Playhouse* script 'Here I Come Whoever I Am', this time Harry H. Corbett played the forlorn would-be lover, Ambrose.²³

On television too, Marty was embracing his inner Goon and hanging out extensively with Milligan. However, *The Marty Feldman Comedy Machine* would not be a BBC series. Importantly, this would be a best of both worlds situation for Marty who, while reluctant to throw himself completely into American television, was well aware that success there would be very lucrative indeed. Marty's love of Britain and familiarity was catered for. Spike Milligan would be a regular member of Marty's supporting team on screen. Indeed the two were practically a double act in several sketches; a silent partnership, you might say, notably in 'The Undertakers' when each tries to out do the other by burying the opposition. The 'make love not war' country yokel bomb disposal team also showcased the Marty and Spike partnership. "Whatever a genius is I believe Spike Milligan to be one," said Marty. "But you can not predict what genius will do. The media – plural of medium meaning somewhere between excellent and lousy – doesn't understand him." Spike also contributed greatly to the scripts: notably various vintage nonsense poems recited over interpretative dance by the Irving Davies Dancers. *Round the Horne* mince machine Hugh Paddick also supported Marty on screen, as did Benny Hill's regular rotund stooge Bob Todd. Monty Python animator Terry Gilliam – an American in London already more English than a wet Bank Holiday – contributed the breathtaking credit sequence. A conveyor belt of manufactured men is churned out until the never-ending stream of identical heads is interrupted by a Marty Feldman head. The product causes the machinery to overheat and Marty is rejected. It was a typical work of Gilliam genius.

The demand for this new series was clear: thanks to the success of *The Golddiggers in London*, Marty had quite literally become an overnight sensation in America. One newspaper reviewer went so far as to observe that: "The reaction of American audiences to Feldman has been so good, even those who say they never watch TV have heard of him." Such was the interest that American television executive Larry Gelbart floated the idea of a Marty series especially designed for the American market. Gelbart was based in England at the time and had watched the *Marty* shows with great interest. With a keen eye for the American exploitation of Marty, Gelbart approached the most sensible choice for such a venture: Sir Lew Grade at ATV.

With firmly established in-roads into American television and a seemingly limitless budget, Sir Lew tempted Marty back to the other side. "Marty was obviously highly susceptible to being made a star," says Bill Oddie. "I think he would have rather liked all that. He was perfectly happy to go off to ATV and do his own series. I can hear Lew Grade saying: 'Take the money, Marty my boy!' and he did." Indeed, although Marty was still wary of Grade after the *Three "Tough" Guys* debacle in 1957, he did want the potential international fame that the series promised. The television mogul had long been making this kind of colourful, comedy variety show in Britain for consumption in America, and with that in mind the programmes would be stuffed to the gills with American talent. International singers like Thelma Houston and Randy Newman would contribute. Familiar faces from American situation comedies would guest star: Art Carney from *The Honeymooners* for example, and Barbara Feldon from *Get Smart*. Moreover, Hollywood legends of the calibre of Orson Welles and Groucho Marx were imported. Marty must have been in pig heaven. In terms of working with such heroes, at least.[24]

Often brilliant, often terrible, *The Marty Feldman Comedy Machine* secured a late night slot on British television. At its very best it displays flashes of imagination and the epic near-silent comedy that had marked out Marty's BBC work. 'The Fly', for example, had Marty as a manic cymbal player chasing a persistent fly through a full-on orchestral recital. The presence of John Junkin as the disgruntled conductor added familiarity and reassurance. 'The Wheel' clad Marty in a Buster Keaton porkpie hat and saw him engage in a battle of wits with a spare tyre. In both, there is a touching sentimentality towards the object of Marty's frustration, but although displaying his brilliance as a clown the location filming seems cheap and uninspired compared to his greatest work of the late sixties.

Tim Brooke-Taylor was aware of a fundamental problem with the series: "When Marty went to ATV there was a definite shift in the material. It was playing more towards an American audience. A whole lot of different writers were brought in from different places."[25]

"Marty approached a lot of us to work on that show," remembers Michael Palin. "Perhaps he felt he was running out of ideas or he wanted some familiar people around him. He was losing that quality of English eccentricity. I know he asked a lot of us. Terry and I. John [Cleese] and Graham [Chapman]. Bill Oddie and Graeme Garden. Tim Brooke-Taylor. Barry Cryer. The idea was to get all the writers he knew to go down to Elstree Studios and sit in a big room and work there. They were going to practically lock us in! This was quite against everything comedy writers did. It was a cottage industry. You worked from home, from your attic. You didn't go out and work in a factory production line. That was very much a Hollywood thing that Marty obviously was warming to. I got the feeling that the American audience wanted something high energy and whatever they had seen in Marty in his British television successes they wanted that times ten. We were asked and we were very reluctant. I don't think Barry Took actively advised us against it but he was certainly more interested in us doing our own thing on television. As were we. Frankly, we didn't have the time or the desire to write for Marty at that point."

Of all of Marty's old cohorts, only Tim Brooke-Taylor took up the challenge. "I wasn't in those shows," he explains, "but simply being a very small cog in the writing team was enormous pressure. Far more than we had had on *Marty*. I think it was too much material [fourteen hour-long programmes in a single series] and the pressure on him must have been impossible. I felt Marty lost his unique comedy identity in that series and that, coupled with the pressure of delivering the goods must have been a big strain. I found the pressure on me was pretty hard to bear, even for an external writer. It was always a case of: 'Why haven't you written more?' They worked us very hard."

Still, Marty had picked up a useful trick when the pressure of work was getting too much. He hurt himself.

Chapter Twelve

"I let my energy express itself in physical terms that
often leads to broken bones and injuries."

The art of physical comedy is a very dangerous thing. One must only look at the track record of Marty's hero, Buster Keaton. Tim Brooke-Taylor says that: "There were moments on *Marty* where I hurt myself. Marty, John and I did a sketch about the Bavarian wine-treading dance which involved us stepping in and out of wine barrels. My shins were black and blue afterwards. Comedy can be very painful."

It is quite natural to come across a BBC Accident Report concerning an incident on the set of *Marty*. One is dated Saturday 11th January 1969 and reports on an accident from Television Centre, Studio Six. Marty, importantly, was the cause not the effect. "The accident occurred shortly after a scene which involved thirty-one extras some with galvanised buckets and ladders. The artistes were kneeling at the time and we had just gone into the Closing Titles when Marty Feldman started to clown around and pushed the end persons in two of the lines of artistes. This caused a ripple effect along the line of artistes – knocking all the artistes over. One of the extras a Mrs Mary Denton fell badly against one of the buckets. This caused a swelling on the upper part of her right arm. The floor assistant – Christopher Fox – took Mary Denton to Sister but, unfortunately, it was her early night off so the Senior Fireman was called. He inspected the arm and recommended that she should have it x-rayed. Christopher Fox accompanied Mary Denton in a taxi to Hammersmith

Hospital [casualty department] where her arm was ex-rayed [sic]. The results... proved to be negative." Mrs Denton was taken back to her home and probably dined out on the story for several months. But for Marty perhaps a seed had been planted. If this woman could be fussed over by the television company and, most appealing of all, get a few hours away from the studio, then why not him?

The second accident report that quarter directly affected Marty. This was issued on 30th April 1969 during work on *The Wednesday Play*; a fresh and challenging project. Producer Graeme McDonald verified that: "During the performance [at Television Centre, Wood Lane] the artist was required to knock loudly on the door of set. Whilst doing this Mr. Feldman, using an unnecessary amount of force, grazed his hand." Graham Benson was cited as the witness for the BBC records and Marty got a few moments away from the studio pressure.

By the summer of 1970 seemingly every interview with Marty starts with his explaining about some broken limb or other. On one occasion it was a broken wrist: "My wrist? Yeah, I broke it. I fell off a wrestler. It could have happened to anybody. I was standing on a wrestler and fell off. That's all."[1]

Under the rather apt but haunting headline: 'Your Laughs are Killing Me', the *People* reported that Marty had started *The Marty Feldman Comedy Machine* with a broken wrist in plaster, suffering from a couple of concussions and two torn ligaments. Marty, it was said, thought of himself as a fatalist but, providing he doesn't kill himself, he plans on being around for a long time to come.

Tim Brooke-Taylor is clear that: "Marty knew what he was doing. You can't be a student of Buster Keaton for all those years without knowing what damage certain stunts will do to your body. Marty could fall in such a way to make it look good – by which I mean dangerous – and claim major injuries. I'm not saying that all his accidents were deliberate by any means but there were certainly stories during the making of his ATV series. There was such great pressure on him during that time that there was a story of him deliberately injuring himself by falling off something on set."

The stunt called for Marty to cling to a rising curtain and when the mechanism went wrong he fell twenty-feet to the ground and broke his arm. "I wasn't there for that," says Brooke-Taylor, "but that certainly did ring true. I knew him for a long, long time and I understood what he was going through on that show. He just had to have some time off. Some time to get his head together. It certainly wasn't anything against the production and he was certainly no wuss was Marty. I know he got back to the set to finish the sketch but that brief respite from the pressure of it all, it must have been heaven for him."

Indeed, Marty was no wuss. After treatment, he went back into studio to film the rest of the segment with his arm in plaster. "Don't you think it looks like a swan's neck grown from the shoulder?" he told the *People*. But "that most visual of TV entertainers" would not give up the business for anything. "Mr Feldman may think he's killing himself for your laughter. But he'd hate it if you stopped laughing."[2]

Unfortunately, one person who had stopped laughing was Marty's producer, Larry Gelbart. He had got increasingly annoyed with his star's behaviour. Spike Milligan, never the most diplomatic of men, tried to mediate between star and producer but, as Spike's erstwhile manager Norma Farnes notes in *Spike – An Intimate Memoir* a chance meeting with Larry Gelbart and his wife Pat in a restaurant started and ended with the exchange: "How's Marty?" "Marty who?" The tension was not only as a result of the hushed rumours that he was causing himself injury on purpose and thus, in the eyes of Gelbart, holding up production, but also through his erratic behaviour away from the set. Marty's drinking, drug-taking and partying habits were at their height in the early 1970s. He was a personality who courted attention. He was working which kept the majority of his insecure demons away and he was seemingly master of his own destiny, but he enjoyed the celebrity lifestyle. If he wanted to take a break from filming, he would. If he wanted to go out and get wrecked into the wee small hours, he could. The show was *The Marty Feldman Comedy Machine* after all. He called the shots.

Larry Gelbart thought otherwise and, despite the show being his brainchild, told Sir Lew Grade that he was abandoning the project in the middle of the run. Finally, after much persuasion, Gelbart stayed on until the fourteenth episode was ready for broadcast in January 1972. He then returned to America to adapt the film *M.A.S.H.* for television. Gelbart had initial hopes for a second series with Marty but his disillusionment notwithstanding, these plans were abandoned by ATV simply because *The Marty Feldman Comedy Machine* had failed to live up to expectations in terms of ratings. With a scheduling slot running to half past eleven at night, this was scarcely surprising. The late night slot allowed Marty certain freedom in terms of content, but with great swathes of his audience either in bed or down the pub, the ratings were certainly affected. Typically, murmurs of his decline were already in the air. The British love to see a success story on the verge of tumbling and Marty's case was no exception. Once you are down, the people start kicking.

The British establishment was certainly up in arms over *Oz* magazine, which had been charged under the Obscene Publications Act and accused of trying to corrupt public morals. The editor, Richard Neville, and his assistant editors Jim Anderson and Felix Dennis had opened the editorship out to secondary school children. The resulting *Schoolkid Oz* was the cause of the case, as many had mistaken it for a publication for children. John Mortimer QC in defence said that the case: "stands at the crossroads of our liberty, at the boundaries of our freedom to think and draw and write what we please." As a result John Lennon and Yoko Ono joined the protest and Marty was amongst the show business witnesses for the defence during the Old Bailey trial in June 1971. Marty was typically irreverent throughout his time in the dock, asking Justice Argyle: "Am I speaking loud enough for you, or did I wake you up?" As Marty left the witness box he called the presiding judge "a boring old fart."[3]

This was a little bit of rebellion away from the television studios. In its own way it released some tension but in the end, as he had done as a teenager, when things got too much for Marty he simply ran away from home. This time, however, he ended up in Australia and he was a visiting star.

His stage cabaret act *Marty Amok* picked up on the title of his BBC special from two years earlier and had its world premiere in Australia.

The reason for this was many-fold. British comedy had long been popular down under and during the 1970s the likes of Sid James, Dick Emery and the Two Ronnies would be treated like the Second Coming when they made the trip. Marty, again, was something of a trailblazer but the reasons were purely self-centred. It would have needed one almighty accident to bury himself away from the comparative failure of *The Marty Feldman Comedy Machine*. In Australia he was assured adoration and a lot of money. Frankly, the cabaret performances were an easy and lucrative escape route. He would be paid to perform a collection of old material. Indeed, he told one Australian journal that he saw himself as a re-actor rather than an actor: "I don't have any visions of standing alone on a stage," he said, "I just want to be better than me."

As journalist Diane Blackwell observed: "any similarity between the shy, contemplative man with a soft cockney accent and passion for poetry and Berlioz and the wild-eyed, tangle-haired lunatic before the cameras is strictly physical."

"I don't really even know what my achievements are supposed to be," pondered Marty, honestly. "They are not clear cut. I can see several goals to aim for – each performance is in its way a separate goal – but there are no high spots, just higher and lower spots."[4]

Marty would liken himself to a court jester performing for his king: his television audience. Immediately that was an Australian television audience for whom he starred in the one-one special *The Marty Feldman Show*: again to become a common practice for visiting British comedians.

The British-born director of the show, Brian Trenchard-Smith, remembers: "I had admired Marty for years. *Round the Horne* had been a Sunday lunch ritual with my family. We would listen and guffaw at that and then my father and I would go over to Aldershot to see the latest film that I wanted to see. I was a self-taught filmmaker and left England in 1966 because I just couldn't get established in the British film industry. Within three weeks of being in Australia I was editing television – mainly news. I had forged references and I was being paid sub-union rates but these TV promos were good enough for me to be stolen away by the 9 Network.

"I would be loaned out to British companies, like Hammer Films, to work on trailers. I had made the trailer for *Every Home Should Have One*, so I had watched him back and forth culling the best bits of Marty from that film.

"I became a roving creative person and eventually the 9 Network asked me to direct. This had been my cunning plan all along. I directed a few programmes including a film about Australians who had won the Victoria Cross, and then the Network told me that Marty was coming over to make a half-hour TV special. It was the first time I directed an actor in a proper show. It was certainly my first attempt at comedy."

Originally the Network had assigned Bill Hughes to direct. He was busy directing the successful situation comedy *The Godfathers* but would produce the Marty show. The directorial reins were handed to Trenchard-Smith: "Marty had a clear idea of what he wanted, he did allow me the freedom to get on with it. We got on fine. I never saw him get drunk or take drugs. There were no problems or concerns. He was never critical of anything I did and he was always on the ball for the show. I am a happy-go-lucky director. Part father confessor, part court jester. I like to have a happy atmosphere and that show was very happy."

The concept for the show was Marty and the animals. To that end, the unit filmed for three days at the Taronga Park Zoo in Sydney. "It overlooked the harbour," recalls Trenchard-Smith, "and as zoos go it was quite a lovely place. Marty did make the comment that if we were like the lions and stuck in a cage it wouldn't be so nice though!

"That was the whole point of the show. It allowed Marty to rant on about cruelty to animals and his own vegetarianism. It treated everything one puts in one's mouth for food as subjective. There was one scene in a restaurant where Marty harassed a man eating a juicy steak. I hasten to add that this was all very funny as well as political. 'Have you ever heard the death rattle of a celery?' Marty yelled. 'Listen to those screams as carrots are pulled up by their roots!'

"The sketches were linked by Marty singing 'If We Could Talk to the Animals' from *Doctor Doolittle*. I took great delight in breaking that song up and filming Marty alongside as many animals as we could get: giraffes, lions, rhinos…

"This rhino was in his enclosure but we tempted him with food to go as close to Marty as we could. Throughout the linking song Marty was wearing a cloth cap. It was continuity. During the rhino scene he took the cap off, dangled his arm over the fence and hung it on the rhino's horn. Because we had stopped bribing the rhino with food it started to move away and Marty's immediate response was to climb over the fence to get his cap back! We had to physically restrain him. Eventually the zookeeper we had on hand did get the cap back and we could finish the filming.

"The deal was that the show could only be shown in Australia and I have never seen it since, but we got some very good reviews. It was fairly unique to have a big British comedian tour and film in Australia at that time."[5]

Though the Australian show was a success, Marty was still wounded by the perceived failure of *The Marty Feldman Comedy Machine*. He retained enough standing in Britain however for Sir Lew Grade to consider him for the Montreux Festival.[6]

A half-hour compilation edition of *The Marty Feldman Comedy Machine* was prepared and, as this was intended for the international market, the emphasis was on physical comedy. The musical interludes were gone and the only guest star to make the cut was the imposing, impressive – in many ways – figure of Orson Welles, who boomed the narration for the appeal on behalf of the British Aristocrat. It cast Marty as the aged Lord Plumdick: "Often I'm compared to birds, and this is strange because I recognise in myself a bird-like way of moving." Indeed, Marty plays the Lord like a rare breed throughout, brooding, bobbing and preening himself. "Actually, I have a phobia about birds," he said. "I'm terrified of them. If a bird was let loose in here I'd go crazy."[7]

The film was a wicked send-up of those travelogues that had long been the stock in trade of Orson Welles. Although he would gravitate to any job that provided him money for his own filmmaking – advertising everything from wine to the latest Hammer *Dracula* film – Welles still had that indefinable something. He was a giant of Broadway and Hollywood wrapped up in a corporate emblem and if *The Marty Feldman Comedy Machine* needed an edge in Montreux, Welles' presence certainly provided one.

When the winner was announced in May 1972, *The Marty Feldman Comedy Machine* was awarded the Golden Rose. The Silver Rose went to *The Goodies* episode 'Kitten Kong'. Unsurprisingly, with tongue planted ever so slightly in cheek, Bill Oddie remains furious: "Basically Marty Feldman cheated!" he chuckles. "Well, Lew Grade at least. He took fourteen hour-long programmes and cut them down to the very best twenty-three minutes. Even then it wasn't that funny. That actually annoyed me and Graeme and split Tim right down the middle. I'm not really blaming Marty but the rules clearly stated the programme had to have gone out as a proper show. I was somewhat resentful. Our show was pretty much how it had first been broadcast, with a couple of extra visual things added to impress the judges. But with Marty's show the gloves were off. Everyone started writing things for Montreux tailor-made for foreigners with no sense of humour after that!"

Marty may have had a Golden Rose of Montreux in his grip in the summer of 1972 but he didn't have a renewed contract with ATV. Unsurprisingly, he used his free hand to pick up his cap and toddle back to the BBC. Having basked in the dimmed light of Spike Milligan, to a certain extent, Marty hooked up with an equally renegade heavyweight comedy hitter in the shape of Peter Cook. Producer Duncan Wood noted that: "Marty Feldman and Peter Cook came in to see me recently accompanied by Pat Freeman who, I understand, will represent both of them in negotiations apropos the following proposition. They are offering us a Feldman/Cook forty-five minute special written by and starring the two of them. BBC2 is very interested in the proposition but, of course, is equally interested in the cost of it."

Requesting a "total performance and copyright fees involved for Messrs. Feldman and Cook", Wood warned that: "There is likely to be quite extensive filming for such a special programme, and I would therefore suggest we give them an all in fee in this respect."[8]

Marty's reputation for expensive programmes was well known, of course, and although this interesting collaboration with Peter Cook failed to materialise he was still etching out plans for a series of comedy shorts for television based on the quality and filming techniques of the greats of the silent screen. To this end Marty had set the wheels in motion to form his own production company and develop films starring himself which would mix and match the very best of Buster Keaton and Jacques Tati. "There will be sound but not particularly the spoken word," he explained. "The dialogue won't be important. Of course, they'll be in colour and there will only be one reel [as opposed to the silent 'two-reelers']. The idea is to make short films for use anywhere in the cinema or on television."[9]

This project, with its canny eye on the overseas market, using the international comic language of mime and slapstick, was ultimately put on the back burner. Sir Lew Grade's winning compilation of *The Marty Feldman Comedy Machine* had been only the start of his full exploitation of the series. The intended market for the programme had always been America and the ABC Network had started a lengthy run of the show from the April of 1972. Rather frustratingly, ABC edited down the fourteen hour-long programmes to fit fourteen half-hour slots; thus a forty-eight minute running time was pared down to just under twenty-four minutes (minus the commercials). One wonders why Sir Lew didn't initiate this for British television. Of course, in terms of commercialism, the hour running time would have netted him more money and that's exactly why he did it. Marty was fully aware of this: "The media is dishonest," he said. "It operates on the profit basis. Produce the most for the least and get the biggest return. If the product is too good it will detract from the commercial and the commercial is the reason you are there. We're there to sell baked beans, love. We're not there to do good shows!" But when the American television company it was chiefly aimed at only required a half-hour programme and the pressure on Marty himself would have been greatly lifted with a fifty percent cut in his workload, the success story and continuation of *The Marty Feldman Comedy Machine* could have been very different. ATV could have nurtured an on-going relationship with Marty rather than burning him out for the immediate big pay packet.

However, when the series came to the end of its US transmissions in August, Marty's star was on the ascent again. The series hadn't done that well in the States and certainly hadn't caused such a sensation as his earlier work with Dean Martin, but even a mild hit was a crucial hit in America.

Marty spent the rest of the year cropping up in guest spots and panel games: *The Johnny Carson Show, Hollywood Squares, The Sandy Duncan Show*, pretty much anything that was offered to him, in fact, and why not? The main objective was maximum exposure and, besides, amongst all this smiling the right smile on chat show settees, the odd gem of an assignment would emerge, such as the *Hallmark Hall of Fame* production of 'The Man Who Came to Dinner', broadcast at the end of November 1972.

Marty's heavyweight film pal, Orson Welles, took on the role of pompous and acid-tongued playwright Sheridan Whiteside played on Broadway and in the original 1942 film production by Monty Woolley. Welles had been approached for both previously. The all-star cast gave a nod to the past with Mary Wickes reprising her original film role of Nurse Preen while Marty eagerly grabbed the opportunity to play the wild, girl-chasing comedian Banjo. Jimmy Durante had etched the role in the film. Harpo Marx was quite clearly the seed of inspiration for the character. This was manna from heaven for Marty, and an opportunity to inject all the manic, wacky and knowing humour at his limitless disposal.

Instead of fully consolidating his American exposure, Marty chose to grab international work offers and concentrate on breaking back into the BBC. These even included attempts to place weary old sketches – as often as not co-written with Barry Took – for the likes of Frankie Howerd and the Two Ronnies.[10]

Marty's on-screen British television work at this point was restricted to guest appearances. He cropped up in the BBC variety show *It's Lulu* for example. A sense of declining power must have swept over him when he stopped and realised that this was *It's Lulu* and not *It's Marty*, particularly when his contract was for both performance and scripting the item. Once again, he fell back on an old routine: the 'Ballet' sketch that he had written with Barry Took, as his contract noted, "for an original Marty series, and which we will be using with Marty on a guest spot."[11]

Ironically, Marty had been invited to write, choreograph and even dance in a ballet for the Hamburg Opera House. He admitted that his experience was "none. I've never written a ballet and never danced. But

I want to do it. Hopefully this will not be a formal ballet but dance based on free movement. I'd like to go back to the source of movement and learn how to do it." It was yet another intriguing project that failed to materialise.

He did manage to fulfil slightly less taxing assignments, such as being the guest celebrity on an edition of *What's My Line?*, the chief joy of which was the presence of Kenneth Williams on the panel. However, it didn't exactly set the world alight as Williams recorded in his diary entry of Wednesday 19th December 1973: "Arrived at Manchester. First show was restrained and dull. Marty Feldman was the guest celebrity. In the second show, it was the wonderful Mike Yarwood. He was splendid." The following day Williams noted that: "Marty gave me a lift home and said, 'You have become much more relaxed over the years... quite different from the old days...'" Marty himself was still living life to the full, and in Manchester in 1973 that meant partying with footballer George Best. Marty kept up with the notorious drinker throughout the evening. As Williams himself later recalled: "Marty Feldman was coping with George Best's drinking bouts in Manchester!"[12]

This excessive lifestyle was doing Marty no good at all and, at times, it threatened his new project for BBC television. As with the aborted programme with Peter Cook, this would try and team Marty with another established comedy personality. This time it was the writer, Johnny Speight, who had long collaborated with him. But more and more press speculation surrounded Marty's health. Concerns were raised about his hectic social life and relentless working schedule. There were even suggestions that he had already suffered a heart attack. Derek Griffiths, who gave his considerable musical and comedic talents to the Johnny Speight enterprise, remembers that the final title of the show was very apt indeed: "*Marty Back Together Again* was exactly what Marty was trying to do. He was trying to put his career back together again, as well as his reputation. The title of the show was certainly reflective of a national concern for Marty's health. I mean, he was all right but there certainly was a heart scare during the making of the show. I remember vividly Marty trying to dodge the press in order to avoid talking about it. He didn't want any health scares getting out, hence why the show poked fun at the whole scare."[13]

Originally entitled *A Speight of Feldman*, the BBC had started production in the summer of 1973 but, almost immediately, Marty was injuring himself. Correspondence from BBC contracts noted that the star had: "sustained slight injuries to the palm of your left hand whilst rehearsing..."[14]

The incident had occurred on 11th July when two skin cuts appeared on the palm of his left hand. Antiseptic and dressing was applied to the injury by a fireman on set and Marty was taken to the King Edward VII's Hospital for an anti-tetanus injection in the Casualty Department. Filming was taking place in the water tank on Stage 3B at Ealing Studios and, as the accident report recorded, "During shooting Mr. Feldman was swimming in the tank (splashing and leaping about) as directed. When shot ended he emerged from tank and noticed the cuts. It was assumed that these had been caused either by 1) Length of fish line used to position some furniture floating near Mr. Feldman in the tank, or 2) Nails which may have come loose from a piece of scenery in the tank."

The BBC Television Film Studios at Ealing were clearly a dangerous place for Marty. Earlier, on 2nd July, the first day's work on the show, he had been filming on Stage 2 when he received a small cut on his left shin. Antiseptic and Elastoplast had been applied. Typically, Marty's injury had an air of surrealism about it: "Mr. Feldman," it was reported, "was removing a violin bow, which he had previously secreted up his trouser leg. As he extracted it, the tip appeared to graze his shin causing a small cut." David Perrottet was the witness to both accidents. All filming for the series was completed in two blocks during the summer of 1973, from 2nd to 22nd July and from 6th to 12th August.

Derek Griffiths doesn't feel that Marty was under an undue amount of pressure and thus this was not a return to his ATV trick of deliberately disrupting the shoot. "These were accidents, pure and simple," Griffiths says, "he was always doing something extremely harebrained in the name of comedy. I suppose it was an occupational hazard. Mind you, he wasn't doing his body any favours. He was a hell of a drinker. I was the one they called boring in that company. Everybody drank."

For Marty still subscribed to the lifestyle rather than the reality. "When I became a comic," he explained, "I knew that drinking before a show would slow my reflexes down. But I knew the myth of Buster Keaton the alcoholic, Tony Hancock the alcoholic, Sid Field the alcoholic. The comics that I admired were alcoholics and I thought that if I drank enough maybe I would be funny too. I don't think I've really learnt."

"In fact, the drinking became a problem," says Derek Griffiths. "I used to try and get Marty not to drink at lunchtime because it obviously wasn't doing him much good. He was a very addictive personality: alcohol, cigarettes, coffee, once he was hooked he was well and truly hooked. Most days we would finish rehearsing at one o'clock for lunch and Marty would usually slope off for a liquid lunch with Jimmy Villiers. Now Villiers was one of the most terrible boozers in the business, by which I mean he was very good at it! The gang was completed by wee George Claydon; now dwarf actors are notorious. I've directed them in pantomime and they are all dreadful for the sauce. Still, Villiers was by far the worst. He would have a little flask on set to keep him going during the morning and after Claydon had taken two sips out of that he was out for the count. Claydon's toleration made him good for up until 11am. The rest were out by 1pm!

"Unfortunately our director, Dennis Main Wilson, would be no help. He would join them in various pubs along the Kensington High Street. The lunch was always a liquid one. We were supposed to be back for two o'clock but they would never be back until 3.30pm. Absolutely plastered. They were no good to anyone. Eventually, I realised it was pointless sticking around so I decided to take a lovely half day and go home at 1pm. The following day, Marty said: 'Here, where did you vanish off to yesterday afternoon?' I said: 'Oh, you remember, you said we had finished at lunchtime and we could go if we wanted.' 'I did?' he said, 'Oh yes, that's right. I did.' He was so pissed he couldn't remember what he had said.

"I remember one time we were filming a car sequence involving a load of pallbearers and, sure enough, Dennis Main Wilson, said: 'Lunch!' and I grabbed Marty. Usually, they would all slope off to the pub and we would get nothing done in the afternoon. This time I said: 'Look, there's a fantastic fish 'n' chip shop near here.' So I tore off with Marty and purposely steered him away from the drinkers. Marty and I were getting our fish 'n' chips when suddenly I spotted Jimmy Villiers walking up the road towards us. He was wearing a five hundred quid Duggie Harwood suit and looking for us! I said to the man behind the counter: 'Look, we are filming for the BBC and that bloke outside in the flash suit, he's from the Inland Revenue. He's already cornered us this morning. Don't let him in!' Marty and I always had a lot of fun sending up Jimmy. Anyway, I didn't believe for a second that this fish 'n' chip shop man would go along with it but, sure enough, Jimmy got to the door, flung it open and bellowed: 'There you are chaps. I've been trying to find you...' Where upon the fish 'n' chip owner said: 'Oi! Get the fuck out. You are not coming in to my establishment. I don't owe you bastards a penny!' Jimmy was so shocked he just looked at us and walked away... to the nearest pub, no doubt!"

Regardless of Marty's reliance on alcohol during the making of the series, Derek Griffiths is adamant that: "Marty was an absolute joy to work with. There was never any problem when we were filming it and he had this charm about him. Even if he was slurring slightly in the afternoon, one forgave him. I've worked with so many other comedians over the years and a lot of them are very nervous about where the laughs are. No names, no pack drill but other comedians would frown down on you if you got a laugh. Marty never did that. He saw the show as a whole and we were part of his team. A laugh for the show – regardless of whoever got it – was a good thing."

For Marty it was something of a relief. Being back at the BBC with good people around him released the pressure. "Because of the way things have happened I have become a star," he said. "Star is to do with the money you get and to do with the box office. It's nothing to do with your value as an actor. I don't want to be a star per se. I want to be a part of making something which is good. Just part of the team."

The closeness of the *Marty Back Together Again* team was further illustrated in another joint sending up of James Villiers. "We were rehearsing in the Beavers Hotel on Kensington Church Street," remembers Derek Griffiths. "Jimmy looked at Marty and I one day and said: 'Do you know, chaps, I have never worn jeans!' We couldn't believe this. It was what we wore all the time but Jimmy was always immaculate in a tailor-made suit. Anyway, we took him down to a stylish boutique and equipped him with a few pairs. After a few moments there was this terrible puffing and wheezing and groaning coming from the changing room. We said: 'Are you all right, Jimmy?' There was this strained reply, 'Yes... Well, actually, no. Not really. No. Where the *hell* do you put your do-dah?' Marty and I were in chronic fits of laughter."

"Marty was a very stylish man. I remember Marty and I visited BIBA when it first opened, which was in the old Derry and Toms department store. We waited by the ornate lift gates, when the gates suddenly opened, and it was packed, and nobody was getting out. The porter driving the lift stared at Marty as if he was a lunatic. Marty smiled at him and said in a loud silly voice, 'Child molesting department?' The doors closed abruptly. It was a joyous time."

Dennis Main Wilson was well respected in the industry and, remembers Derek Griffiths, "The joy of him was that he was the best talent scout in the business. He had this natural gift for finding the right writers and the right performers." Indeed, amongst his credits were *The Goon Show* and *Hancock's Half Hour*. He discovered the comic talents of Kenneth Williams, John Sullivan and Johnny Speight. "He was the guv'nor at the BBC," asserts Derek Griffths, "he just gathered together all the right talent, wound them up and let them go. He wouldn't really do anything else. He just knew we could do it. He would say: 'Right, make me laugh,' and, thankfully, we did." Still, as Warren Mitchell, the man who brought Johnny Speight's Alf Garnett to life for Dennis Main Wilson and took on his fair share of Marty Feldman scripts says: "Dennis was that very rare creature. A real amateur. That is not a pejorative term. It means a lover of and that's what Dennis was. He was the original amateur. He loved what he did and he would go to any lengths to do it."

He certainly kept an eye on the writer credits for the show. Johnny Speight was the leading light and was a talent Derek Griffiths admired greatly: "To talk to him you wouldn't think all these great scripts would be inside that little frame but his mind was so sharp. He personified that old

phrase: 'don't judge a book by its cover'. He was a peerless scriptwriter."
Marty agreed, often talking of Speight in the same vein as Charles
Dickens. "With Johnny's series it's collaboration. It's perfect. When I do
a series with Johnny I collaborate with Johnny. Not as a writer. I perform
Johnny's material as an actor would perform a playwright's material but
collaboration is the only way to go."

The series utilised other material as well, as a letter from Dennis Main
Wilson indicates, Marty was happily plundering material from *The
Marty Feldman Comedy Machine* archive. But gone were the days when
sketches could be handed round shows like confetti. This was material
from American writers and was causing concern. Steve Kennis of the
William Morris office was roped in to try and: "check actual authorship
with Marty tomorrow. My secretary will then ring Copyright and give
them the facts about 'Beach – Test Match' and 'The Undertaker'."

Barry Took, it seemed, had been attempting to get back into Marty's
world by resurrecting even older material: "With regards to the material
that Barry Took supplied from *Round the Horne* I confirm that this was
not used. Of the two sketches written by Graham Chapman and Barry
Cryer – 'Mel Garfin' was used, 'Indian Restaurant' was recorded but will
not be broadcast. I have, in fact, passed this sketch on to Terry Hughes
for possible use in *The Two Ronnies*." This common practice of passing
sketches around the various sketch shows at the BBC was accepted by
most, although it could lead to disputes as witness the earlier complaint
from Frank Muir and suspicion of Eric Sykes.

Perhaps the most inspired and certainly most satisfying use of vintage
material was in the songbook of Tom Lehrer. Although it was new to
Derek Griffiths: "that connection with Lehrer was amazing, in retrospect,"
he says, "but frankly at the time I had never heard of him. But he had
written these wonderfully satirical songs back in the 1960s and Marty
was a huge fan of his." Indeed, Marty had first heard them during the
days of *That Was the Week That Was* and *The Frost Report* and jumped at
the opportunity to work with Lehrer. Marty's own show gave these classic
compositions a contemporary 1970s edge and the hilarious renditions
of songs such as 'The Varsity Rag' and 'National Brotherhood Week'

are the most relaxed and effective moments of the series. "Marty was a writer, first and foremost, of course," says Griffiths. "He had been at the cutting edge of British satire. Lehrer's lyrics were perfect for him. I would accompany him on the banjo or guitar or whatever it was."

Even so, despite Griffiths' acknowledged musical talents, the re-working was left entirely to Marty. "We didn't move that far away from the original and, obviously, Lehrer himself was consulted, but the new lyrics I would leave to Marty. It was his show. As often as not he would update the lyrics or add his own line here and there during rehearsals and we would pass the changes to the Musical Director. It was a very quick and easy working relationship when we did the songs."

The joy of making *Marty Back Together Again* masked a severe worry for the star, however. His BBC contract earned him £1250 per programme, in a deal that covered both his performance and contribution to the scripts. Dennis Main Wilson was somewhat aggrieved to be left in charge of the editing of the series because, "Unfortunately Marty shot off on tour and at the moment of writing is still in Germany. I believe he is due back tonight. At the same time I am, myself, going on holiday tonight."[15]

The European touring production of *Marty Amok* also picked up several film and television contacts. As with the Australian premiere of the live cabaret act, Marty's incentive was purely financial. Indeed, according to Derek Griffiths, Marty was severely in need of money. "We were filming some inserts in and around Ealing and Marty had this old blue Rolls Royce. He came up to me and said, 'Look, I've got a bit of a problem, do you want to buy it?' I said, 'I'm sorry. What?' 'The Roller. I'm selling the Roller. It's yours for two or three grand?' 'No, Marty I really don't want a Rolls Royce.' That was not my sort of thing at all. 'Why are you selling it?' I asked. He said, 'I need the money, quickly.' He had loads of debts. He owed money to everybody. The question of Marty's move to Hollywood was never really discussed, although I got the sense he was running away from Britain."

In their obituary for Marty, the *New York Times* reported that, "A BBC tribute... yesterday recalled that when he left Britain in 1974... [he] owed

$118,000 in taxes but was convinced that he would repay his debt and become a financial success in Hollywood. The BBC went on to report that Mr. Feldman had succeeded."[16]

But it certainly wasn't easy. His beloved home in Hampstead was put on the market and plans were set in motion for Marty and Lauretta to permanently up sticks and grab any opportunity that America may offer. Hampstead had been perfect for Marty; as near to a village life as is possible in London, while the house was a Gothic, church-like structure: "built by a lunatic Victorian industrialist".[17]

The Hampstead mansion was kissed farewell in style, however, as Michael Palin remembers: "We all went to his house up in Hampstead. It was a big house and there was a surprise party for him. It felt like it should have been for his sixtieth but it must have been for his fortieth, just before he went off to Hollywood. Anne Levy organised it. She was Peter Sellers' first wife which was pretty apt with hindsight. There hadn't been a major Hollywood success for a British comedian since Peter Sellers had made it. It felt like a good omen for Marty and we all hoped he would find success and happiness in America. I think he found one of those things, for a short time at least. I remember we all got together and had to hide behind furniture and curtains. The lights were turned off and a little later Marty arrived and was ushered in through the door and Anne was saying: 'Come in, you're early...' at which point the lights were turned on and we all jumped out screaming and shouting. It was a fun way to say goodbye and good luck."

Derek Griffiths reflects that: "I never saw him again. He went to America and that was that."

Chapter Thirteen

"If it's overnight success it's been a very long night."

"Perhaps it's with hindsight," muses Bill Oddie, "but it came as no surprise to any of us that Marty went to Hollywood. He had done the ATV series so we all knew he was being floated in those American waters, being lauded beyond these shores and beyond logic, frankly. He had done this bloody long series, cheated his way to a Golden Rose of Montreux and so it was only a matter of time until he was thrown to Hollywood. That was the next step. Take him over there and make him a star. They had done it with Peter Sellers and they would do it with Dudley Moore. It never ends well for our blokes over there."

The Marty Feldman Comedy Machine had indeed struck a chord with a huge number of Americans. His pursuit of work there was inevitable: "A mountaineer wouldn't hang about in Wales," he said. "He'd go to the Himalayas." Although it hadn't been the massive commercial success that ABC had hoped for, it did consolidate Marty's cult status amongst students and the self-proclaimed intellectuals. It was certainly enough for a tempting five-year television contract to be put on the table. However, despite the promise that the series would make Marty a millionaire, he turned down this much needed financial boost in favour of a film to be shot in black and white over at the 20th Century Fox studios. For one of the great and good of American film comedy, who had been bewitched by *The Marty Feldman Comedy Machine*, was Gene Wilder: "I picked up my pad and pen and wrote the title *Young Frankenstein*. I had been a lover of movies ever since I was a child and I think the name *Young Frankenstein* came from the film *Young Edison* which I had loved as a kid. I just thought what sort of things would have happened to the great grandson of the original Frankenstein. I loved the original *Frankenstein* films. My script was particularly inspired by the 1931 original and *The Bride of Frankenstein*. In fact, originally, my Frankenstein was going to end up over the precipice and the monster was going to hook up with the fiancée."[1]

The concept also called for a comic grotesque to play the hunchback. A sort of cross between the hunch-backed assistant played by Dwight Frye and the broken-necked assistant played by Bela Lugosi in the Universal series. Marty Feldman was a gift from God. Indeed, having been inspired by the *Comedy Machine*, Gene Wilder wrote the part especially for Marty. It was he who gave Marty his big break in Hollywood. He practically told him to pack his bags and go West, young man.

"I play the part of Igor [pronounced Eye-Gor for affectation] the assistant to Frankenstein," Marty told a visiting Mexican television reporter on the set. "He's actually a hunchback. I don't have the hump with me at the moment. It's optional. You only wear it in the evenings, you know."

"I am the only guy ever to appear in a horror film without make-up," he quipped again making the first joke about his appearance before anybody else could. "Not even size six eyeballs."[2]

Fortuitously, Marty was being represented by Wilder's agent, Michael Medavoy. Delighted when Medavoy suggested doing a film with both Marty Feldman and Peter Boyle in the cast, Wilder was struck by the thought and asked, "How did you ever come up with that team?" He replied that: 'I have all of you on my books!'" As Wilder solemnly mused: "Well, with a wonderful artistic basis like that, it can't go wrong!"[3]

Marty remembered the moment when the film collaboration was hatched: "Peter Boyle and I were in this agent's office and the agent suggested that we should do a film together. He said he knew just the guy for us to work with and he got Gene Wilder on the phone. 'Hello,' I said, 'I'm Marty Feldman.' Then we talked about ideas and Gene said he would send one in the post. One paragraph arrived the next day and within twenty-four hours they had a producer and director and a million dollar film had been set up."

The paragraph that had hooked Marty and everybody else was the train station meeting between Frankenstein and the hunchback. It was written exactly as it appears in the finished film and became something of a lucky mascot throughout the production, post-production and distribution of *Young Frankenstein*. It certainly appealed to director Mel Brooks. Gene Wilder remembers that Brooks was: "Mike Medavoy's suggestion. He had read the script, loved it and said: 'I think we can get Mel Brooks to direct this.' I said: 'I don't think Mel would want to direct anything he hasn't conceived himself, but if you can get him he'll be wonderful.' The very next day Mel called me and said: 'What have you got me in to? And I said: 'Nothing that you don't want to get in to.'"

Wilder had just wrapped on Mel Brooks' cowboy film pastiche, *Blazing Saddles* which, after critical successes with *The Producers* and *The Twelve Chairs* would put Brooks firmly at the top of the list of American film comedy directors. Brooks was still uncertain about lending his name and talents to a project that wasn't entirely his but he had a solution. He would contribute to Gene Wilder's completed script and claim a co-writing credit. His name attached to the project also helped get the budget upped from 1.7 million dollars to 2.3 million dollars. Producer Michael Gruskoff secured the support of Alan Ladd Jnr over at 20th Century Fox when Columbia Pictures pulled out.

Mel Brooks, choosing not to appear in the film, gathered together his familiar repertory company of stars; Madeline Kahn as Frankenstein's snobbish fiancée and Kenneth Mars as the often impenetrable Germanic police officer.[4] The distinguished Cloris Leachman had recently won an Academy Award for Best Supporting Actress in *The Last Picture Show*, while Teri Garr was a film novice who had caught the eye of Brooks through her television success on *The Sonny and Cher Comedy Hour*. All of them were brilliant. All of them were over-shadowed by Marty. "For me he is probably the heart and soul of the film," says producer Michael Gruskoff. "The bizarre world that we all entered into when we walked onto that set was epitomised by Marty."[5]

Mel Brooks agreed, explaining that, "When you're a comedy writer you pray for Marty Feldman because what you pray for is that they'll meet the material. They'll do what you wrote. Marty Feldman not only met your material, he lifted it. He gave it that extra magic. That magic touch."[6]

It is clear that Marty's performance served as a pick-me-up and an inspiration to the American cast and crew. His Igor would be, at turns, sensitive and mischievous. Genuinely frightening at times, "Marty was," according to Mel Brooks, "the hunchback assistant as played by a music hall comedian. Or vaudeville if you were American. That's why we put in all that Yiddish shtick. He throws in lines straight out of the pages of *Variety* at certain points. The whole thing is dripping with Jewish humour, of course, and the scene that I consider closes the second act is when the monster breaks out of the castle and goes off on his own. Gene shouts out the line: 'What have I done!' Which is the line that would close every second act in every Jewish play in New York. Marty and Teri reacted beautifully to it by copying [Wilder's] hand to mouth gesture. Lovely. There were bits of the [Catskill] mountain[s] comic in there. When Gene goes in to face the monster and Marty throws away the line: 'Nice working with you.' That was what every mountain comedian would say when he sensed impending danger. Everything was thrown into the mix."

Everything is right. Marty would lapse into song within a scene: the slow pan across the "three years dead", "two years dead", "six months dead", "freshly dead" heads is one of the film's stand out moments. For the "freshly dead" head is a very much alive but perfectly still Marty, who suddenly bursts into both life and song with a rendition of 'I Ain't Got No Body'. The first two skulls were the genuine article as borrowed from a local laboratory, the third was constructed within the Fox Art Department and the fourth – Marty – was "one only God could make" as Mel Brooks remembers. The scene was one of many where Marty would add something extra to the script. "He loved the drums. He was learning or about to start learning. I know he loved music and he knew that I played the drums a little. There are drum passages called rim-shots. [After the song] Marty did them for me. To make me smile. It worked. I loved his reading of that scene."

Marty, like a kid in a Hollywood candy store, would also include elements of his comedy heroes that had now become friends and colleagues. Groucho Marx proved extremely useful in a particularly difficult scene. It's what Gene Wilder calls: "Mel's most brilliant day on set. Madeline [Kahn] arrives as my fiancée and Mel had us improvise this on the spot. Marty says, 'OK, you take the blonde, I'll take the one in the turban.' He was doing Groucho Marx, basically, but Mel wanted more than that. He told Marty to bite the head off the fox fur that [Madeline] was wearing. I would say, conservatively, that it took eight or nine takes because every time he bit that fox fur there was always fur left in his mouth and we couldn't not laugh. We tried. We just couldn't help it. We finally got to the eighth or ninth take. I held in the laughter. It took great moral strength but I held on. It might look like I'm trying to hold back some kind of anger toward him but I was really holding back the quivering mouth of not wanting to laugh. We laughed all the time. Marty was just so funny doing all his bits of business."

Mel Brooks remembers that scene as: "Just impossible to get. It was pure gold, of course, but every line got a laugh. On the set while we were filming none of the actors could keep it together. It took me about twenty takes and hours and hours of cutting and cutaways from one to the other to cobble together that scene and make it look like the actors played it with a straight face. It was outrageous. Quite certainly the best and the worst day of my life!"

Marty's performance is also awash with those beloved elements from his silent slapstick heroes. The scene where Frankenstein is attacked by the monster and desperately mimes out a message is a case in point. Mel Brooks remembers that, "Marty lights a cigarette – something he was very capable of doing – and he throws the match up in the air with overplayed energy. It's a marvellous moment of visual comedy worthy of a Keaton or a Harold Lloyd. We did sixteen or so takes on this. I think we finally went for take nine but Marty's performance didn't lose any of its power and fun and energy. Children love this. He remains a hero to kids simply because of that two minutes or so of film."

Marty's contribution to his character was constantly inventive. The "werewolf" banter with Frankenstein en route to the castle was worked out between himself and Gene Wilder on set. The revelation that the mere mention of the name "Brocker" (as played by the frosty-faced Cloris Leachman) would get a terrified whinny from the horses was seized upon by Marty. During the largely improvised arrival of Madeline Kahn it was his idea to re-emerge from the castle entrance and shout "Brocker" one last time to close the scene on a laugh. It was Marty's idea too, to add "not the third switch" and a bit of music hall business when lightning is beginning to pump life into Frankenstein's creation.

The silent comedy creep through a darkened laboratory also gave Marty's imagination flight. Ruining the normal brain – as Dwight Frye had done in the original – Marty is forced to unwittingly pick up the abnormal brain: his later reflection that the brain belonged to "Abby Someone" is one of the laugh-out-loud moments of the film. During the scene, Marty added the exaggerated point to the glass-cased brain and a knowing glance into camera. Marty gave several of these throughout the film, with the blessing of Mel Brooks, and it effortlessly underlined the power of the joke and added an endearing quality to the performance. In many ways, he is our amazed representative within this insane "world of gods and monsters".

"His comedic mind was extraordinary," testifies Mel Brooks. A blessing to the comic energy of the film, the subdued chat in the laboratory when Frankenstein finally realises that Igor has provided an abnormal brain for the monster made several seemingly unrequired cutaways to Inga (as played by Teri Garr) necessary "not only because she looks gorgeous and brought such sweet naïvety to the film but because Gene was continually breaking up with what Marty was doing. I had to have some straight footage to fall back on and break up scenes that were originally intended as continuous pieces. That was the genius of Marty. His comic mind was so fertile."

So much so that he contributed greatly to the very look of Igor. Elements were, of course, taken from the various assistants Frankenstein had had in the original films and the black, hooded attire was very much reminiscent of Vincent Price's appearance in *The Tower of London* (1962). A horror film fan's nightmare vision of Richard III, if you will. "I could probably walk down the King's Road on a Saturday wearing this lot without anybody noticing," he said. "I might even pull a bird!" But Marty added a playful, potentially destructive edge of comedy to the image. Over the first few days of filming he would systematically shift the hump on his back from one side to the other. In the script, the character of Igor was already oblivious to his physical defect. The "What hump?" line being one of the most oft-quoted of all Marty moments. As soon as Marty's moveable hump trick was spotted in the rushes, Gene Wilder scripted a surprised: "Didn't you used to have that on the other side?" It was that kind of film. Luckily. Marty's little bit of merriment could have caused all sorts of continuity problems and re-shoots.

The hump itself was, in fact, as Marty said: "What they call a pregnant pad which means it was used in films for showing ladies when they are pregnant. A hunch front rather than a hunch back." His contract included an addition clause that he could keep the hump after the filming was completed.

Liz Beesley, who was cast as the Little Girl in the film, remembered: "Marty was the first person that greeted me at the door... and he was in costume! So we opened this big stage door and there's Marty opening the door for us. He came up to me and said, 'Hey little girl, you wanna play with my hump?'"[7]

Marty was obviously happy. The glitter of Hollywood was still twinkling and he gushed: "I like making movies." On the set of his first Hollywood film and some five years since his last decent sized film role (in *Every Home Should Have One*, belatedly released in America in 1978 as *Think Dirty*) he said: "What I do is make films. Make comedy and I suppose I don't care where I am. One studio is much like another. I love studios. I'm at home when I walk in and see the lights and the cameras. When I get the chance to do the thing that I do, which is to try and be funny, I don't mind where I go. If you're a miner and they close the mines down you either change your job or you go and look for new mines."[8]

Marty's bright and fresh passion for Hollywood, coupled with his boyish love of movie history may have given the film its heart and soul, but the element that made it a masterpiece was simple: the sheer, undiluted affection for the vintage horror film.

Amazingly, the original plan was to have made the film in colour. No big studios were investing in black and white films in 1974. Both Gene Wilder and Mel Brooks were adamant that it needed to be in black and white: "Because," as Wilder said, "I want the film to be the way the old films used to be in 1932 not 1960, 1970 but the way they used to be with Boris Karloff and Bela Lugosi."[9]

Mel Brooks took influence from "Fritz Lang, Murnau, James Whale obviously. Whale made the *Frankenstein* films in Hollywood, of course, but they were full of British actors. That's partly why I wanted Marty in the film. I wanted an essence of English eccentricity within the main cast which Marty brought to it in spades. I always wanted as many of the small part villagers to have a cod English accent. You watch those old Universal *Frankenstein* films, the entire village sound cockney!"[10]

This homage to the vintage films that had inspired *Young Frankenstein* was made all the more tangible when the MGM backlot was used for both the European village scenes and the graveyard sequence. The original 1930s Universal *Frankenstein* lab sets designed by Kenneth Strickfaden were located; still in full working order. Designer Dale Hennessy worked his magic and fitted the rest of the sets to match. Even the directorial techniques themselves were cleverly ignorant of modern filmmaking: "I asked Marty to hold the picture up and hold it in place as I moved the camera slowly in," remembered Mel Brooks. "Then he just let it go when I told him to and it swung. I could then cut to the dead body swinging in the rain. It was old-fashioned movie making but it worked."

But only in black and white. Cinematographer Gerald Hirschfeld came up with a compromise: "My thought was that it should begin in black and white to replicate the original *Frankenstein* but that we could segue into colour when it became the modern day with young Frankenstein."[11] Brooks stuck to his guns, however, and threatened to withdraw from the film if it wasn't shot entirely in black and white. 20th Century Fox backed down, despite the fact that cinemas in Europe were simply not booking black and white films anymore. *Young Frankenstein* would change all that.

It is this tangible affection for old time Hollywood that makes *Young Frankenstein* such a lasting treasure. For Mel Brooks, "That classic theme of an innocent trapped in a disfigured body is still there. Even though we were doing a ridiculous comedy we stayed true to that basic idea of Mary Shelley's *Frankenstein*. I think that's why it still lives." It was "not how can we make this fun, but how can we make it real which will be more fun," Gene Wilder explained. "It was made with love for the whole gamut of horror movies of the thirties," said Marty. "It isn't burlesque. We felt that if the frightening bits weren't frightening, then the funny bits would not be funny."[12]

Marty's performance embodied that. He was "half sinister, half jester" and, according to producer Michael Gruskoff: "Just the sweetest man. He was a lovely, co-operative, funny, talented comedy genius. What he brought was his own interpretation of those old *Frankenstein* and *Dracula* monster movies."

It wasn't all sweetness and light as far as Mel Brooks was concerned, however. In Marty Feldman, Gene Wilder had found an ally. Undoubtedly, as a writer to the very core of his being, Marty accepted that this was Gene Wilder's vision. For once Mel Brooks had been a hired director. Brooks certainly put his stamp on the material but there was a sense that, despite what the poster may scream, this wasn't just 'A Mel Brooks Film'. Indeed, the character of Delbrook was so named: "to sound a little like Mel Brooks just so I could remind myself that I was part of all this fun."

The scene that completely split the opinion of Brooks on one side and the Gene Wilder/Marty alliance on the other remains the defining moment of the film for many: "The famous scene of Gene dancing with the monster I didn't want to do, originally," says Brooks. "I thought it took the joke too far. But Gene loved it and Marty loved it. You have to look very closely to spot Marty's involvement in the scene. He's the pianist during the performance of 'Putting On the Ritz'. I did shoot a couple of close-up cutaways but never used them for some reason. But he's there if you look. That scene was perfect. Science meets entertainment. And that was the feel of the entire film, really."[13]

Both Mel Brooks and Gene Wilder were having such fun on *Young*

Frankenstein that neither really wanted to wrap. Brooks kept on filming extra scenes which were tacked on to the film and clearly had become so convinced by the musical interlude that he decided to end the film with a 1930s Busby Berkely style curtain call for the leading cast members. Alas this final flourish was removed from the final cut.[14]

Gene Wilder remembers that Mel Brooks could be a strict director when he wanted to be: "If I or Madeline [Kahn] or Cloris [Leachman] were not doing what Mel wanted he would pull on the reins and if he wanted more he would start tugging. Marty didn't respond well to the tugging. I'm not saying there was anger but as soon as the reins were loosened Marty would respond like anyone with freedom. That means that maybe he would go off half-cocked in the wrong direction but the next take he'd go off full-cocked in the right direction!"[15]

But on his very first day of filming, Marty was reining himself in. He was fully aware that this was a Hollywood film and he wasn't the star of the show. That opinion quickly evaporated as more and more of the cast and crew fell under his charm, but that first scene was a nerve-racking experience for Marty. Ironically, it was the very scene that Gene Wilder had sent over to tempt him to take on the role: the scene in which Igor is introduced on the platform of the Transylvanian Station. "That was the first movie I did in Hollywood and the scene was actually my first night's filming on a Hollywood movie and I was scared bleepless!" he said. "Gene's lovely. His timing in that is like Oliver Hardy. It forced me to be Stan Laurel because his timing was so like Oliver Hardy… it was a night shoot, very cold, and I was freezing and very scared. [On the 'walk this way' line] he pauses… and I sort of adlibbed ['this way' and handed him the stick to come down the stairs like the hunchback] – it's a terribly old music hall joke. I did that to make the crew laugh and Mel Brooks said, 'Let's shoot it'. I said, 'Mel you can't, it's an old joke!' and Mel said, 'I want to shoot it!' So we did it and we did it the other way without that joke and afterwards Gene said to me, 'Are you going to tell Mel to take that joke out? It's terrible.' And I said, 'Well, I don't want it in. You tell him. You wrote the script.' We both said, 'Mel, please take that out,' and he left it in. He said, 'I think it's funny.' Audiences laugh at it. Gene and I were both wrong. Mel was right."[16]

The scene was lovingly constructed almost solely to introduce Marty's character in a startling manner. The platform set of over thirty feet and the train, permanently fixed on the MGM backlot, were beautifully lit by Gerald Hirschfeld. As Frankenstein is left on the platform and the laugh that the "Pardon me boy, is this the Transylvanian Station?" line gets dies down, the tension is built up with sound effects and a shuffling from off-camera. As Mel Brooks says of that moment: "Anybody who knows anything about movies will remember and cherish the laughter that Marty Feldman has given to the world." But that terrible old joke that rounded the scene off was one that Marty probably would have winced at even during his variety days with Morris, Marty and Mitch.

Still, Mel Brooks seemed determined to keep it in; until the final cut. Assistant editor Bill Gordean says that: "After several preview screenings with employees in the studio the panic set in about whether the film was getting bogged down and too slow. Mel was starting to take out some gags. He said: 'We're going to take out the gag at the railroad station at Transylvania when Marty says to Gene: 'Walk this way,' and Stan [assistant editor Stanford C. Allen] said: 'No! Please don't do that,' and Mel said: 'No, it's coming out. It's a cheap joke.' Stan said: 'Yeah, it's a cheap joke but it's funny. Please don't take it out!' So finally Mel relented and said: 'OK it can stay for the preview but it's coming out Saturday.' That scene came on, the audience howled and we came up to Mel afterwards on the sidewalk and said: 'OK, well, do we take it out tomorrow?' And he said: 'Get outta of here!' And I give Stan the credit for that because Mel may well have taken it out of the movie and you would never have seen it."[17]

Mel Brooks has subsequently admitted that: "I like cheap jokes. If they made me laugh then I would keep them in. For me there is never really an audience. I don't know what will make them laugh. I have an audi-I. That's just me, folks. If I laugh I hope other people will too." The "walk this way" line certainly made them laugh. Brooks tries to include it in: "every movie I make since, certainly *To Be or Not To Be*."[18] The line had such a cultural impact that Aerosmith recorded 'Walk This Way' after attending a late night screening of *Young Frankenstein*, and included it as a tribute on their album *Toys in the Attic*. It became arguably their best-known song: all thanks to a silly ad-lib from a very nervous Marty Feldman.

Marty may have been nervous but he wasn't too preoccupied to ignore the interest of a young fan. "I was fourteen years old and snuck on to the studio lot when Mel Brooks was making *Young Frankenstein*," recalls Alan Spencer. "You could do that kind of thing back then. The first time I did it the guard on the gate didn't ask me anything. The second time he did stop me and I told him I was Mel Brooks' son. He said he could see the resemblance! Then I saw the man I really wanted to meet. That was Marty, in full Igor garb. He saw me and said in this sing-song voice: 'You're not supposed to be here, are you?' I admitted that I wasn't and Marty said that I would be his guest for the day. He reported back to Lauretta that night saying that he had met the only person in Hollywood who truly knew his work... and he was a kid!

"It was true. I had already started writing jokes for some local radio comedy shows and I think Marty saw something of himself in me. He would give me specific advice about writing for certain comedians. He had also started writing early and snuck in to meet his heroes. And his middle name was 'Alan'! We had a lot of connections. I admired him so much. He was the only person who could literally make me convulse into hysterics. I told him that he had the power to kill me if he wanted and he said, 'I promise never to use it!' I had seen him with Dean Martin in *The Golddiggers* and had decided to research his work. I had gone to the library and looked up stuff about his British films like *Every Home Should Have One* and got hold of the records of *Round the Horne* and his BBC shows. I found out about everything he had done. Marty's eyes opened even wider than usual when he heard that. No one knew his early work, particularly not his work as a writer."[19]

Still, Marty's immediate future in Hollywood was as an actor, specifically an actor in the hands of Mel Brooks. Amazingly, there was one sure-fire line that didn't get a reaction. When Frankenstein bellows at Igor: "Damn your eyes!" and Marty points at his misaligned opticals and answers triumphantly, "Too late!" As Mel Brooks remembers: "No one got it during the preview screening or press releases. It was a bit of Victoriana from England and the cliché wasn't known [in America]. I loved it and I trust the English audiences got it." Indeed, it became a signature line for not only Marty's career but his subsequent legacy. No other actor could have made that line of dialogue work so well.

Having given Marty's character the full build up it was also important for the director to see the character end the film well: "The four principals had paired off into wedded bliss at the end of the movie so I had to give Marty a nice farewell," said Brooks. "In fact, he's the very last person you see in the picture. Playing that French horn from the earlier scene. Happy. Sat up in the battlements like a friendly gargoyle, next to a real gargoyle, like Charles Laughton in *The Hunchback of Notre Dame*. It was a beautiful performance and, for me, remains the heart of the comedy."[20]

When *Young Frankenstein* opened in America at Christmas time in 1974 it was an instant hit and although he failed to get the expected Oscar nomination,[21] Marty did pick up the inaugural Best Supporting Actor Golden Scroll at the Saturn Awards, devised by Dr. Donald A. Reed to honour the neglected genre of science fiction and fantasy. By the time the film arrived in England at the start of June 1975, Marty was a film star to be reckoned with. While, with the double barrelled success of *Blazing Saddles* and *Young Frankenstein*, not only was Mel Brooks firmly established as one of Hollywood's top directors but the spoof movie was seen as a commercial guarantee.[22] In 1975 Mel Brooks could have sold anything: even a silent movie to 20th Century Fox. These were Marty's perfect Hollywood environs: "I've always had a love-hate battle with words. I suppose I'm a bit schizoid about it. Part of me says I don't like words. You can't trust words. They can mean different things. Anyway my pronunciation isn't so hot. I can't say them too well. I'm better equipped to do the physical thing. You've just got to look at me."[23]

The premise of *Silent Movie* is simplicity itself. Mel Brooks cast himself as washed-up film director Mel Funn. His attempt to sell the idea of a silent movie as his comeback project meets with disbelief from the studio head (played by Brooks' old television boss, Sid Caesar). Recklessly promising to include all the biggest stars in Hollywood in the film, the director goes off to persuade the likes of Burt Reynolds, Anne Bancroft and Liza Minnelli. "Lots of stars did guest shots in it," said Marty. "Even Paul

Newman. There's one scene with him where we have a chase in motorised invalid wheelchairs. It's wild. He liked the chair so much he took it home with him. Doesn't sound much, maybe, but each chair cost £20,000."[24] The most delightful star cameo of all comes from French mime artiste Marcel Marceau. Having made a career out of never speaking, he utters the only dialogue heard throughout the film. When Brooks telephones him to enquire whether he wants to appear in a silent movie he simply says: "Non!" As *Variety* reported: "The slender plot... is basically a hook for slapstick antics, some feeble and some very fine..."

Alan Spencer remembers that "Marty loved the company of other comedians. He would learn from them. I was on the set of *Silent Movie* a lot and he and Marcel Marceau really hit it off. They would be in the corner exchanging routines. They spoke the same language. The language of physical comedy. I remember Marty watching Sid Caesar work and in-between takes he would give Sid a few comedy ideas to work into his routines. They were all part of the same club. Marty was amazed to be working with some of the old school comedians. Fritz Feld was playing the Maître d'. He always seemed to be playing the Maître d'. But he had been working in Hollywood since the 1920s. He came over to Marty to introduce himself and say what a big fan he was. Marty couldn't believe it. He was so flattered. 'You're a fan of mine? I'm a fan of yours!' Marty would always do that. He would instantly deflect the conversation towards you. My friends at school would never believe that I knew Marty, and he would invite them to the set and be lovely with them. Even when friends of mine might meet him independently, they would say that they were friends of mine and Marty would say, 'Then you have very good taste!' Often when I was with him talking about writing comedy I would say, 'I can't believe I'm actually here talking with Marty Feldman.' He would look at me and smile and say, 'Stop it, love!' He wasn't threatened by anybody. He was just so encouraging."[25]

A silent comedy made in the Hollywood of 1975 was about as perfect a project for Marty as could ever be conceived and, indeed, he mugs, gesticulates, grimaces and body pops throughout every sight gag in the book. His curly locks are almost continually dampened down under an old style flying helmet, his ever mobile body clad in a tight fitting tracksuit, his mobile eyes forever searching out the next attractive female. This is Marty channelling Buster Keaton and Harpo Marx as never before, and relentlessly for nearly ninety minutes. "I know how Buster Keaton fell on his arse. In the same way I do. We both fall on our respective arses because we thought it would be funny at that time. We didn't write a thesis on it before we fell and say to the director, 'Hang on, I can't do a pratfall yet. I have to work out the motivations for my pratfall. The theory behind my pratfall. The art of my pratfall.' You say, 'There's a mark on the floor, I'll hit that mark when I fall.' Bang. There you go. Anything you do is intuitive." There is something very satisfying in seeing him clown on the Hollywood thoroughfares once occupied by his screen heroes.

But he was still modest about his place in the pantheon of great clowns: "I can't get rid of the umbilical cord I have to Europe or to the European tradition that came to me via the silent movies – Keaton and Langdon and Laurel and Hardy," he said. "I've had to accept the fact that I will never be as good as those people have been. That's the hardest pill to swallow – that I'll never be in the same league as those I admire." Yet there was a stronger emotion about his favourite clowns. Certainly stronger than simple admiration: "I admire Chaplin," he said, "but I never loved Chaplin. I loved Laurel and Hardy. If I could have chosen a couple of uncles, I would have liked Laurel and Hardy. If I could have willed genius, I would have been Keaton. But you can't. And you can't aspire to be that any more than the average organist can aspire to be Bach. They are so pure and so much above anything you understand. You can't aspire to it. That's the hardest thing to swallow. You say, 'Well, all I have is me, and I have to do the best I can with that.'"[26]

Marty is knocked to the ground, double flips and is catapulted onto a crowded dance floor and at every turn it really is him doing those things, just like his slapstick heroes in the Hollywood of the 1920s: "I think if you can do a thing yourself you ought to. I think you cheat the audience otherwise," he said. "It's part of your responsibility. It's what you're paid for. I like to do my own stunts when I can but I couldn't do anything very specialised. If I had a tightrope walking sequence I'm not a tightrope walker and I couldn't learn in time to do the movie but if it's a matter of falls and jumps and leaps and crashing through things then, yeah, I'll do that myself."

"I had arguments with Mel about letting me do my own stunts. A stuntman can do them better than me. He can do a marvellous graceful fall but he can't do it funny. It's not his job to be funny... I have funny feet. I have funny legs. Jacques Tati said: 'Comedy is mainly a matter of legs.' I think he's right. If you're a clown you use every part of your body. If the director chooses to use a close up of me... I'm still using the rest of it. Like a piano has eighty-eight keys, I'm using all of the keys. The director chooses which part he wants to photograph but I use every part – that's my instrument."[27]

Although again he was not featured on the list of scriptwriters, Marty's influence is all over *Silent Movie* and, tellingly, *The Marty Feldman Comedy Machine* writers Rudy de Luca and Barry Levinson joined Mel Brooks and Ron Clark on the script. *The Monthly Film Bulletin* was left rather unimpressed by it all. "Brooks' grotesquely lunatic style of comedy has little real connection with the silent clowns his film supposedly celebrates: one would search long and hard through the works of Chaplin or Keaton to find a frog leaping from a breast supposedly throbbing with romantic passion or an outsize fly winging its way from the top of an Acme Pest Control van to a restaurant customer's soup... The film is further harmed by having a triumvirate cutting the capers rather than Brooks alone: all the nearest jokes are centred round Brooks himself... or appear as throwaway details... while Marty Feldman and Dom DeLuise only provide unfunny mugging. Despite the large number of agreeable gags, it's hard to join in the closing festivals... the comedy seems too ingratiating, the clowns too self-satisfied."[28]

This completely misses the point. *Silent Movie* was a film about the extreme audacity of Mel Brooks actually making a silent movie in the Hollywood of the mid 1970s. It was one long joke, both in terms of a skilful re-imagining of the slapstick traditions of the past as well as at the expense of the studio boss at 20th Century Fox. The very idea of anyone making a million dollar, colour silent movie in "this day and age" is ridiculous. The fact that Brooks and his little knockabout gang made it work both artistically and commercially is nothing short of a miracle. No wonder Marty once dubbed Brooks "an incredibly intelligent pixie."[29] Marty's deadpan salute to his comedy roots is at the very heart of the film. He effortlessly holds his own alongside veteran masters of the art like Harry Ritz of the Ritz Brothers and Fritz Feld of the legendary "pop!" In that beat-up old car careering around the Hollywood hills, the stars embrace the legacy of the Ritzes and the Marxes and the Stooges. There is even a dash of Morris, Marty and Mitch about them. And as the director, Brooks takes full advantage of Marty's unique, mobile, funny face: "The only way you could hide from Marty was by standing right in front of him," he said. "He was the very opposite of cross-eyed. He just couldn't see you if you were stood right in front of him!"[30]

There were times when hiding from Marty was Brooks' only respite. Tempers had flared up during the making of *Silent Movie* and at one point Brooks, who was often given to phrases in the extreme, muttered: "Marty was heaven and hell to work with. He is probably the most complicated human I've ever met. [He] has peripheral vision in his soul." Alan Spencer believes that: "Mel Brooks was a good person for Marty. They were opposites but both had great creative integrity. Mel knew how hard Hollywood was for Marty."

The love-hate relationship between Marty and Mel Brooks may have gone deeper than just artistic differences, however. There was something Freudian about their relationship: "I'm... drawn towards Mel Brooks," Marty admitted. "With all the things that are wrong with Mel, he has such an energy. He's volatile. There's no container big or strong enough to put his energy in. We're totally opposite. I'm the introvert; he's the extrovert. That's my father's generation. That's the generation that came out without any education, that hustled and pushed and said, 'I want to get to the top of the line' – and got to the top of the line and pushed their way beyond it. I recognise so much of my father in him."[31]

A year after *Silent Movie* was released Marty explained that: "I've worked with Mel Brooks twice. I've done two movies with him... Mel has a great instinct for comedy. There's a Yiddish word 'tummler'. There's no translation into English... Mel talks comedy. He can demonstrate it more than he writes it and his instincts are usually right. You can't explain why but you can't explain comedy. You talk about a sense of humour so therefore it can't be defined and all I know is when Mel says: 'Let's do it,' chances are he's right, even if you don't know why. He knows something. Possibly he has his finger up the pulse of the American public! You can take a pulse anally as well... his humour is a little broad but he knows what people will laugh at. There's some kind of instinct which is nothing to do with talent, it's something separate. Clowns sometimes have that, like musicians have a sense of what swings. You know the old story about Duke Ellington when a woman said to him, 'What is jazz?' He said... 'If you have to ask, you'll never know.' Well, it's that. It swings or it doesn't. If your foot taps it swings and if you laugh it's funny. Mel has that. What ever it is he's got a lot of it."[32]

Marty would never again star in a Mel Brooks film. *Young Frankenstein* had become such a hit at the box office that studios were falling over themselves to make parody films with the recognised Mel Brooks repertory company. By 1976 the inmates had well and truly taken over the asylum.

Chapter Fourteen

"I don't want to be a director, I want to direct. There's a difference.
I'm not interested in the lifestyle."

With *Young Frankenstein* about to become the hit of the British box office in the summer of 1975, Marty had been back in his home country to support Gene Wilder in his directorial debut *The Adventure of Sherlock Holmes' Smarter Brother*. Filmed at Shepperton Studios from the April, the presence of the stars of *Young Frankenstein* just ahead of its British release was perfectly timed. Indeed, this wasn't by chance. The Holmes film was 20th Century Fox's own follow-up to their monster success from Mel Brooks. This time Wilder would single-handedly claim the writing credit and star as Sigerson Holmes; the supposedly smarter brother of the title. Madeline Kahn was cast as a kind of parallel universe Irene Adler to complete Fox's *Young Frankenstein* star line-up.

Marty had formed a strong friendship and on-screen chemistry with Gene Wilder during the making of *Young Frankenstein*. "We were very close. Gene loves to play tennis which he plays about as well as I play drums," he said. "We go off and do whatever it is we enjoy doing."[1] As a result Marty gladly accepted the role of Orville Stanley Sacker: a compound of a Doctor Watson and an Inspector Lestrade for Wilder's Sigerson to interact with.[2] As with Brooks before him, Wilder the director delighted in building up Marty's first appearance. Giving a fine piece of back of the head acting, he flexes his ears (he has photographic hearing) and jiggles the hat on his head à la Charlie Chaplin. This trick is repeated as he awaits an answer to his knock upon Holmes' door and the sudden close-up of Marty's blank expression is as effective as the first appearance of Igor. The photographic hearing also allows Marty to indulge in physical abuse (he whacks his head to kick-start the process) and mimicry (he recreates bursts of conversation in character). Still, this is more than yet another addition to Marty's gallery of Victorian freaks. Alongside the dressing-up and mucking about, there are moments of tender reassurance for Madeline Kahn's lady in distress and a real sense of companionship with Gene Wilder's manic detective. Certainly *The Adventure of Sherlock Holmes' Smarter Brother* is a charming period piece with snatches of faux music hall songs – Marty joining in with 'The Kangeroo Hop' is arguably the film's most delightfully surreal moment – but it lacks the sharp focus that Mel Brooks brought to *Young Frankenstein*. As the *Monthly Film Bulletin* noted: "This Sherlock Holmes has little to do with the original: the period sets are unnecessarily cluttered... [although] the climactic opera farce [has] the players weave all the plot threads together with a fast and effective display of old tricks: mistaken identity, pratfalls, visual gags and nonsensical patter. For all its shaky construction, and uncertain inventory of styles... [it] is a promising movie; better in its parts than as a whole, and essentially a showcase for the individual performances of Wilder himself, Marty Feldman, Madeline Kahn and, particularly, the perpetually energised, rubber-faced Dom DeLuise."[3] (If anything, the love of music hall and opera is given too much emphasis; at one point in the theatre, an uncredited Albert Finney turns to the audience and mutters, "Is this rotten or is it all terribly brave?")

Perhaps all it was lacking was black and white photography: an easy trick to fall back on the *Young Frankenstein* style but one which would have linked it with the 1930s world of Basil Rathbone. As a parody of the more contemporary Sherlock Holmes adaptations, Gene Wilder could not compete with Billy Wilder's *The Private Life of Sherlock Holmes*. Still, the fruity British cast of superior character actors includes Roy Kinnear and John Le Mesurier, while the chief delight for Holmes scholars is the presence of Douglas Wilmer and Thorley Walters as the real Holmes and Watson.[4]

Although the return to Britain for the Sherlock Holmes film was something of a personal delight for Marty, his life was becoming a three-ring circus of international assignments. As often as not Hollywood was also forcing him to eat his words: "I enjoy making people laugh," he had said. "That's why I do it. It isn't just for the money. I was getting well paid before I stepped out from behind a script. I laugh at a lot of things, usually when cause and effect don't work out. Without a laugh at the end, the circus isn't complete."[5] Although he was still getting enjoyment out of some of his work, Marty was forced more and more to take the money and run. "I went through a bad time in Britain before I left," he admitted in May 1976. "No work. Nothing. Then *Young Frankenstein* came along, and I flew out here to make it. But before it came out things were difficult. Most of the money I made from the film went to pay British taxes. I had to live very carefully here. I did some TV commercials – one for cat food; another for a bug-killing spray [d-Con bug killer] and some TV game shows. When anyone asked I'd admit I was out of work. Then friends told me to keep quiet. 'Over here' they treat failure like a contagious disease, they think they might catch it if they hang around you. Then *Young Frankenstein* came out and suddenly I was in demand. I did *The Adventure of Sherlock Holmes' Smarter Brother* and now Mel Brooks' new film *Silent Movie*."[6]

Marty had been such in demand in Hollywood that he had had to reluctantly turn down Ken Russell's offer of a supporting role in his film of the Who's *Tommy*. Cast as the sadistic Cousin Kevin, the schedule clashed with another commitment and the role subsequently went to Paul Nicholas. Marty had longed to do it, if only to return home. The English filming dates for the Sherlock Holmes film had been a very attractive prospect.

Although financially secure again, he often lamented his lack of roots. He had nowhere he could really call home. He had once said that: "There is danger of just jetting about from city to city. Like Charlie Chaplin. It's a pity he went to live in Switzerland, living with millionaires. No ordinary people are millionaires. You lose touch with life and people."[7] But, this was exactly what had happened to him by 1976. Los Angeles was his base and he was back there to film *Silent Movie* after the Holmes film had wrapped. Still, work took him all over the country and all over the world. One month it was the film in England, the next it could be a film in Italy. He had become the one thing he had always dreaded he would become: a transatlantic celebrity.[8]

Always highly suspicious of the American way of life, Marty had also become bored with the stardom and the money. Once he had become entrenched in America, the disillusionment wasn't far behind. Even before filming *Young Frankenstein* and still hopelessly in debt, he had taken his cabaret act to Las Vegas. But he would rather talk about the English football results than discuss the contents of the show. Lauretta would sigh and lament that any normal human being would be thrilled by the prospect of a show in Las Vegas but, she would say, "You're not a normal human being, Mart!" The fact that even his wife had been bitten by the insanely competitive world of American show business and self-promotion had been the hardest thing to bear. It simply all boiled down to the fact that he was homesick. He would often write to old friends in England. Spike Milligan would be in receipt of several letters over the years. One, while Marty was residing at the Chateau Marmont Hotel, read: "If you don't write, I will. If you don't answer my letter, fuck you. I won't bother to write in the first place." The back of the envelope included an additional comment: "From a man posing as superjew Feldman, last seen sitting by a pool in a flash hotel getting angry about being rich." Milligan's reply read simply: "OK. Love Spike. P.S. Don't say I haven't written to you."[9]

Still, Marty and Spike were cut from the same cloth and enjoyed each other's company enormously. So much so that Marty persuaded Spike to make the dreaded journey to America to join him in a television commercial for the orange drink Solo. It was shot in October 1975 at the Key West Studios, home of the Tom Mix westerns. Spike was in love with the old Hollywood but not enough to take on regular work in America. Perhaps he sensed the danger of luxury. In that respect he was certainly more canny than Marty.

Even closer friends had already seen the cracks beginning to appear in Marty's life. "In no time at all he had become a star," wrote Barry Took.

"He developed what he described to me years later as 'the mania'. A belief that he was not just good, but somehow blessed by the Almighty (a common disease among comedy performers)."[10] Indeed, although he always tried to retain his modesty in interviews, in private Marty was becoming overwhelmed by the sheer pressure of being Marty Feldman.

Bill Oddie asserts that "once somebody is beginning to believe his own legend – a legend that has been forced upon him by American critics and American universities that read the art of Marty Feldman – that's when I thought to myself, 'Uh-oh, Marty's in trouble now.' I can hear them now linking him in with the tradition of the Commedia dell'arte: 'He is what we used to call a grotesque.' I can hear them now." Indeed, the University of California had held a seminar on his work shortly before he had even shot *Young Frankenstein*. "Marty started to believe all this rubbish," says Bill Oddie. "He was having lectures about him and before you know where you are he's beginning to lose the sense of being a person. It's international. I know he was very big in France. That makes perfect sense to me. A country where people like Fernandel and these ugly buggers became big comedy stars. These physically slightly weird looking people, the French love that."

"Everybody is trying to convince me that I'm a genius," Marty lamented, "but it's a word that's thrown about loosely in this town. I suppose I am a sort of cult figure, though." He was also aware that the intelligentsia adored him. He would describe himself as "Dada on legs".

It was a mixture of concern and envy from the clutch of writers and performers that Marty had left behind in England. As Michael Palin says: "He had a great writing career. He had carved himself a very good performing career in England. Maybe that dream of Hollywood success wasn't all it was cracked up to be. I always think he would have been happier if he had just gone over to Hollywood, done his brilliant turn in *Young Frankenstein* and come straight back home again, his star in this country even higher than it had been before. Who knows? But Gene Wilder and Mel Brooks loved his work and were encouraging to him. He must have been flattered to get that kind of international recognition. We were stuck in England doing Python! The last TV episodes and the *Holy*

Grail and that sort of thing which we, admittedly, had more control over, but Marty had leapt over all of us."

Although Marty had left television far behind him (he once said, "Television was a nice place to visit but I wouldn't want to live there again, you never get a chance to get it right; usually you settle for third best, second best would be terrific"), he was still an English writer at heart. He loved being in the company of other English writers, particularly old chums like Ronald Wolfe and Ronald Chesney, from the *Educating Archie* days. "We went to the States two or three times and Marty was very good to us," remembers Ronnie Wolfe. "We were doing *Lotsa Luck*, the American version of [hit British TV sitcom] *On the Buses*, and Marty showed us the Hollywood ropes and looked after us. It was delightful to see my junior writing partner as this big Hollywood star and he seemed to enjoy sending his American neighbours up. He would tell them the most outrageous things with a straight face and they would believe him rather than admit to not knowing what he was talking about.

"He didn't like the flashiness of Hollywood at all," Wolfe continues. "He said: 'When you hire a car here don't try and compete with the Americans. You'll never do it. Go to Hertz and hire the smallest car you can find; a little Japanese number.' I did just that. Marty said: 'I've told everybody that you are a very wealthy writer from England and that you're an eccentric millionaire in your baby car.'[11]

"He would say: 'Look at my friend Ron. He doesn't need a big car. Just a little run-around. He's a millionaire, you know!' It was Marty the film star with his eccentric British friend. Marty soon realised that you couldn't beat the system, you had to attack it subtly. Even when he traded on his stardom he did it in a devious way. He would book up in a restaurant, ring the maître d' and reserve a table saying: 'I don't want a table where anyone can see me because people are always coming up to me. Find me a little table at the back so I can have my back to the door and I can eat in peace.' Marty knew this would titillate them and when we got there we had the best table in the house!"

"It was lovely to have someone like Marty around," remembers Dick Clement. "He was so welcoming. He certainly took Ian and myself under his wing when we arrived in America in around 1976. He loved to surround himself with writers."

Ian La Frenais says: "We were spending lots of time with him. The legendary parties at Marty and Lauretta's house were epic. It's that old cliché about the sixties but it's true about Marty's parties. If you can remember them then you probably weren't really there!"

"I was there and I do have vague memories of them!" says Dick Clement. "It was a big, jolly mix of actors, funny people, writers and musicians. [The likes of Georgia Brown, Van Dyke Parks, Brenda Vaccaro and Harry Nilsson were often amongst the guests.] Lauretta would serve the drinks from their speakeasy bar. Marty's drums would be up and he would jam with anyone else who could play an instrument. Actually, I remember having a lengthy conversation with him about his theory between music and comedy. He thought the timing of a joke was exactly the same as a timing of a musical note and he cited lots of comedy writers that could also play. Woody Allen was one. Spike Milligan another."[12]

"A sense of humour is like a sense of rhythm," he said. "It all comes back to music. That's my prime source of information. Rhythm is the prime source of everything – the sound of my heart beating, a pulse, the drum. Originally somebody thumped away on some hard surface before they ever blew through anything or pulled on a string. It's the most accessible thing to do. Primitive societies – that's the kind of society I want to live in."[13]

Marty had kicked a football around with the kids on Hampstead Heath, now once a week he kicked a soccer ball around with Italian waiters, high school teachers and his manager.[14] It kept his feet on the ground: "I don't do anything consciously to keep in touch. I play soccer so I meet other people I play soccer with [these included rock star and football fanatic Rod Stewart] and I've now got to like baseball quite a lot so I go to baseball games. The only way I can relax is by using up all my energy." He would take two dips a day in his swimming pool. "I swim my anger out," he said, "it's cheaper than an analyst. I'm strong but extremely unhealthy."[15]

Marty's health wasn't improved by his drink and drug habit, and life with Lauretta was contributing to his downfall. "We would go to parties at Marty's home and sit around drinking for hours before they would even appear," remembers Ronnie Wolfe. "When they did finally join us they had obviously been taking something. They started behaving very oddly.

"Lauretta was very ambitious for him to be known for doing everything," he continues. "Every British writer wanted to make it big in America, of course, but it was the best of times and the worst of times. The American scene is very, very different. You really have to be tops all the time and eventually it just got a bit too much for Marty. He was never really tough enough for Hollywood."

Marty would play the American fame game with gritted teeth. Sometimes this would work in his favour: he made a big impression at a UNICEF concert in January 1975 alongside Danny Kaye and Marcel Marceau. Other times it would be a public relations disaster: he gleefully smashed an Academy Award at the 1976 Oscars ceremony as an act of vengeance for being overlooked the previous year. It was also a two-finger salute of joy. The popularity of parody films meant that both Marty's American champions, Gene Wilder and Mel Brooks, had spoof projects they were writing, directing, producing and starring in: Wilder was taking on Rudolph Valentino with *The World's Greatest Lover* while Brooks was tackling Alfred Hitchcock in *High Anxiety*. Marty could have easily fitted into both films, but he was far too busy. Hollywood had given Marty what thirty-five years earlier Orson Welles had described as "the biggest electric train set any boy ever had." Marty had landed a contract to direct.[16] It would be 'A Marty Feldman Film' in every way but alas, he should have had a long chat with Orson Welles. Just as it had been with Welles back in the 1940s, Hollywood's gift of filmmaking would only be a temporary one, and Marty's "toy" would be snatched away just as the "boy" was beginning to enjoy himself.

Still, for a few months at least, Hollywood had redeemed itself and Marty was genuinely looking forward to the process. It had been a long haul to get to this position of power in the American film industry. Immediately after *Young Frankenstein* had made him a bankable star in cinema, Marty's agent and manager Michael Medavoy had starting pitching him as what they called in tinsel town a "triple threat": a star actor, a writer and a director. Medavoy had attracted a trio of producers to a Marty project: it was these three, William S. Gilmore, Howard West and George Shapiro who had first approached the Walt Disney Organisation and got nowhere. Driving away from a disheartening meeting at the Disney Studios the three producers started talking about the trend for spoof remakes of classic Hollywood films. This was hardly a revelation. Since *Blazing Saddles* and *Young Frankenstein* every producer was talking about spoof remakes. Discussing possible subjects with Marty, the producers finally decided on *Beau Geste* and approached Universal Pictures with the epic to end all epics: *The Last Remake of Beau Geste*.

There was something very right about Universal, the home of the original *Frankenstein* films that Marty's breakthrough Hollywood role had been inspired by. Marty's bubble of delight was squashed a little however: "Because I made a mistake," he groaned. "I was hustling for a job – and suggested [*Beau Geste*] to Universal, who own the rights. When they ran the old Gary Cooper version for me I realised the film I'd actually wanted to remake was *The Four Feathers* [the 1939 classic from British-based producer Alexandra Korda]." But by that time the deal was signed. But what a deal it was.

Talking from "his house high above the canyons" and "curling up on the settee in a blue caftan", Marty revealed that Universal had just handed him five million dollars to direct and star in the film: "I'm bloody excited about it," he said. "It's hard to believe they're giving me all this money. I mean; I have no credentials as a director at all. And you know what? I've got Cary Grant's old bungalow office at Universal. That knocked me out. Cary Grant's bungalow!"[17] Universal was sensing money. No doubt a scene not unlike Sid Caesar's cash register eye-roll in *Silent Movie* was going on at the studios as a vision of Marty's major future in film was mapped out. While making Gene Wilder's *Sherlock Holmes* film in England, Marty had started storyboarding a project which would tempt Universal to exercise its options. In between takes as Scotland Yard's finest, Marty was sketching *Beau Geste* joke ideas onto cards and sticking them up on his dressing room wall: "When I'm finished with this picture I'll have covered all the walls," Marty joked.[18]

Marty had hooked up with Chris Allen, who had been one of the leading writers on *The Marty Feldman Comedy Machine*, and took less than a month to whip up a *Beau Geste* script. "It's not really about Beau Geste," he explained. "We used that as a point of departure. It's about all Foreign Legion stories really. The whole Foreign Legion genre, which includes pictures like *The Four Feathers*, all the adventure pictures which took as a premise that the greatest thing a man can achieve is to die nobly in a battle, which I think the English probably still believe. And that whole ethic is one of the things we are parodying. It's a parody of adventure pictures of the kind I used to see as a kid. I wanted to make the sort of picture which is an affectionate parody of the kind of movies I used to enjoy."[19]

Delighted with what they saw, Universal immediately started signing cheques. As the producer William S. Gilmore explained: "Marty is like a throw-back to the old silent comics who could do it all. It doesn't matter that he's British [Charlie Chaplin and Stan Laurel obviously slipping his mind], because physical gags travel. That's why he has a major future ahead of him, and that's why we've made a major, major investment in Marty at Universal."

It was also destined to be a long-term commitment. Universal had an option on a five-picture contract with Marty, "meaning that he can keep on writing and directing films, but only as long as Universal thinks they'll make money."[20]

They were calling Marty "a future renaissance man" and it was hoped he would be Universal's big comedy box office winner, in answer to Mel Brooks over at Fox and Woody Allen at United Artists. If Brooks represented his father in Hollywood, then Allen was the brother Marty never had. "I feel very close in some ways to what Woody is doing in his pictures," Marty said, "although it's not like anything I could ever do. I think his frame of reference is the same as mine. We're both Jews, about the same age, self-educated, wanted to be stand-up comics, wanted to be comics, became writers. So I feel drawn towards Woody, although I hardly know him. And I think if I had a brother, he might have been like Woody. So I feel caught between those two cultures. Woody Allen is not a stand-up comic; he's a lie-down-on-the-couch comic. His stand-up act becomes an extension, I suppose, of what he tells his analyst. But again, he's dominating the audience when he stands up there. I don't want to dominate; I prefer collaboration. You're together with the rest of your group, and you all take your clothes off and stand naked with the lights on. Show all the warts and everything. The gut. Varicose veins. You have to show all that to each other before you can really work together. You say, 'Look, these are all the bad things, the bad ideas. Maybe you can improve on them. Here are my failings. I'm not afraid to show them to you.' Writers and actors both have to be able to do that. I must say Americans find it easier than the English do, because the English process is very much a matter of acting at arm's length. They don't touch. American actors touch. I have to touch people to know that they're there, I think."[21]

The crucial difference between his film vision and Woody Allen's however was in the way Marty saw himself as a screen persona: "My heroic instincts don't rise," he said. "They really don't. I don't think I have any. Woody Allen made a picture called *Play it Again, Sam* – a lovely picture. Now his hero was obviously Humphrey Bogart. As a kid when I had fantasies and when I dreamed I was never the lead. I never had the leading part in my dreams. I was always the supporting part. Therefore my fantasy was always to be Peter Lorre... I never thought of myself playing leads, I suppose. I like playing either the hero's best friend or the villain's best friend. The supporting part in my own picture."[22]

Indeed, in Marty's directorial debut he cast himself as the hero's best friend or more precisely: "I play Beau Geste's identical twin. So to make it funny Beau has to be the handsomest man in the world. We're looking for him now. I'd like Robert Redford. But, listen, he'd cost more than the whole film put together..."[23] Marty became increasingly obsessed with Robert Redford's matinée idol good looks. He saw him as the ultimate Hollywood star and himself at the opposite extreme. The clown character actor. Even when he thought audiences had learnt to look beyond his googly eyes he was convinced many considered him inferior: "I'm sure Robert Redford would for instance. He is so perfectly made."[24] In the end, "the handsomest man in the world" turned out to be the dashing and much more reasonably priced Michael York. "Beau Geste in the original picture was played by Ronald Colman and later on by Gary Cooper," said

Marty. "In my version of the picture they are identical twins. Michael York plays my identical twin, naturally. I had a lot of trouble finding someone as handsome as myself. Michael plays my identical twin and I play his identical twin. Well it seems only fair. Ann-Margret plays our mother, so it's typical Hollywood type-casting as you can imagine."[25]

Michael York was immediately bewitched by Marty's humour: "I got this note from Marty which I have kept," he remembered. "He said: 'Delighted we are going to be together again, at last for the first time as never before. Hope you don't mind having your nose and eyes fixed! Ever thine, your identical twin. P.S. I know you don't drive so empty bottle of champagne is following."[26] (Later, Marty's directorial eye would even make Michael York's teeth sparkle like stars every time he smiled. His crestfallen narration put the relationship in perspective: "Beau couldn't help being a hero. Nature cast him for the part. Physically he was perfect. As his identical twin I must have been perfect too, only it didn't show so much on me.")

All was ready, but if Marty had been nervous when he first stepped onto the set of *Young Frankenstein*, the morning of 10th August 1976 must have been real pressure. That first day as a proper film director saw him thrown in at the deep end, but for producer George West, Marty's presence on set was nothing short of a revelation. As a director he appeared to be a habitual promise-keeper. He listened to advice. He remembered people's names without being overly familiar. As a performer he was always ready to switch on the comedy while keeping a lid on his manic behaviour. As West put it: "Marty is a very human being," something of a rarity in Hollywood. "If a new director completes his first day on schedule, it's an accident," said West. "If he does it the second day, it's a coincidence. The third day it's a pattern and the fourth day it's a habit."[27]

As far as Marty was concerned, he was finding his feet throughout the shoot. It was direction as work experience or, as he put it himself, "A case of self-defence. As a writer, you want to protect what you have written." Importantly, despite being his fourth film for a major Hollywood studio, this was the first to give him a writing credit. "I'm still a writer. I want a trade to fall back on when my looks go! I think that's important. No, once you're a writer you're always a writer whatever else you do. I've stepped from writing to directing. Whether you do it well or not is a judgement that audiences will make. People will either go and see it or they won't and critics will make judgements, but every writer is a director... in the making. If you write, then as soon as you've written anything, you know what you want to see. Even if you're on holiday and you write a postcard home. If you describe what the weather is like, what the beach looks like. Do we see the whole beach? Do we just see you on the beach? Do we see your head? Do we see your whole body? You'll know because you wrote the postcard. From that point on, really you're a director. [It's] technique, which I'm learning. I've done one picture as a director. I have the title director. To earn it it's going to take me quite a while. You don't become a director with one picture. I think I'm quite good for a first time but in about five years' time I think I might be very good. I think it's a natural thing that all writers want to direct and all writers should certainly have a great say in how a thing is directed."

As with any actor who was directing himself in a film, Marty fell back on the invention of a fellow comedy filmmaker, Jerry Lewis: "I use a video tape playback. Jerry Lewis used it first about fifteen years ago. Mel Brooks uses it. Gene Wilder uses it. I think Woody Allen uses it. I know Laurence Olivier used it. It seems the only way you can work, if you're this side of the camera and that side of the camera. You don't really know what you're doing so I have a link video playback which photographs through the lens of that camera and plays it back on a television monitor. Instant replay. I can see what I'm doing and what I should be doing and I put myself into the scene and tell myself what to do. As an actor I get on very well with me as a director because I slept with me to get the job! Frequently. And the writer. The three of us in one bed."

Marty also had a secret weapon in the same bed. It was called a wife. Lauretta would stand behind the camera for every shot Marty directed. As soon as he shouted "cut" to the crew he would look immediately to her to see whether she thought it was a good take or not. As far as Marty was concerned, Lauretta was the only person on set whose opinion he trusted implicitly. He would often refer to Lauretta as both his worst enemy and his best friend and that was no joke, but he did trust her sense of humour: "She's a marvellous critic. I rely a lot on her. She laughs a lot but she doesn't laugh indiscriminately. I think if she doesn't laugh, she has a reason for not laughing."[28]

Lauretta's presence must have been crucial in all sorts of ways. Not least of which was keeping Marty focused on getting the job in hand done on schedule. There was no way out of this assignment. If he hurt himself on set and delayed production, then his Universal bosses would not be happy. The threat of injury was very real, of course, for *The Last Remake of Beau Geste* indulged Marty in his usual blend of verbal nonsense and slapstick routines: "My job is not to get injured," he told *The Guardian* during filming. "I got a massage last night and she said, 'That isn't a body, it's a minefield.' Actually they're just small bruises. Small bruises for big laughs."

Unsurprisingly, Marty made the connection between what he was doing and what his heroes of the Hollywood of the 1920s had done. For much of the slapstick in his film was in tribute to the thrill comedies of Harold Lloyd and, as with *Silent Movie*, Marty was determined to do the stunts himself: "I'm shooting danger for danger," he explained. "I'm following the Harold Lloyd principle, which is to make the audience feel the risk. They won't feel any risk if there isn't any risk."

Following location filming in Spain, Marty's unit had moved on to Ireland in September 1976.[29] They had erected scaffolding within the old Kilmainham Jail in Dublin. This imposing edifice with its cobblestone courtyard was not dubbed the "Bastille of Ireland" for nothing. Marty saw it as the perfect backdrop for the most dangerous stunt in the film: walking across a plank thirty feet up in the air. Moreover he performed the stunt twice; once with his right hand attached to a safety wire and once with his left hand attached. Swift cutting between each take: "will convince most viewers that Feldman the director really is pushing Feldman the actor to the brink of death... Excuse me, I've got to go hang from a ladder."

He certainly wasn't intending to hog the camera just because it was "A Marty Feldman Film". "I like long shots," he said. "Doing a close-up would have been ego. I'd just as soon act with my back. Some pitmen in an orchestra wear tuxedo tops and jeans. They're only concerned with what people can see. Even if it's a shot of my little finger, I act head to toe."

He was also conscious of not over-using the unique face and googly-eyes that Mel Brooks had embraced so effectively. Marty was keen to show his film audience that he wasn't just a grotesque sideshow. In long shot he could prove his ability as a physical clown without relying completely on those eyes to get the laughs. If that told the media that he had his ego under control as well, then all to the good: "That's a question you'd better ask someone who does have a huge ego. I would say I have a healthy ego."[30]

It was an opinion that a disgruntled Terry-Thomas, cast as the withered old prison guv'nor, would not have subscribed to. It had been over a decade since T-T had almost spoken Marty's dialogue during that *Comedy Playhouse* debacle. In 1976 the gap-toothed comedian couldn't be so fussy and accepted a role that amounted to nothing more than a cameo. His script suggestions were certainly not welcome. "It was a joke I wrote for the bedroom scene between Ann-Margret and me," he later recalled. "We were in bed together. I wanted Ann-Margret to ask me, 'Why are you wearing that overcoat?' And I would have replied, 'A man in my position can't be too careful.' But Marty Feldman, who was enjoying himself hugely both directing and playing a big part, decided not to use it. I don't know why, it wasn't blue. Yet he allowed the line where, as Ann-Margret's exhausted victim, I told her, 'You have made a happy man very old.' That didn't make much sense either."[31]

More to the fact, it was probably complete preoccupation with his "triple threat" responsibilities on the film that forced Marty's blinkered attitude. His camera angles certainly did Terry-Thomas no favours as they clearly captured the shaking hand that pointed towards the debilitating Parkinson's disease that would halt his career. The fact that he was in the cast at all does highlight Marty's delight in the English school of comedy, though, and it was an element that both Mel Brooks and Gene Wilder had embraced in their films. Marty's cast was awash with familiar faces from home: old pal and inspiration, Spike Milligan, bowled up for a cough and a spit as a decrepit butler. *Marty* stalwart Roland MacLeod featured as Doctor Crippen. There was Irene Handl and Burt Kwouk, the imposing presence of Trevor Howard as the personification of the English upper crust, a one-legged, bear-hugging Peter Ustinov, and, most enjoyably of all, *The Walrus and the Carpenter* star Hugh Griffith, now completely pickled in alcohol as the Judge.

"I wanted to make a picture that is purely entertainment," Marty explained. "It has nothing very deep to say except: 'Laugh'. I wanted to make an audience laugh so I put as much comedy into it as I possibly could. It really has nothing else to say. It's an entertainment."[32]

Perhaps that was the problem. Too much inventiveness, too much panic, too much slapstick, too much slapdash, just too much of everything. There was certainly something very unfunny happening after the film had wrapped. Marty had wisely embraced the perfect talent to see the rushes through to the final cut. John Morris, who had worked on all three of Marty's Hollywood films, was commissioned to write the musical score, while Jim Clark signed up as the editor. Not only had Clark just cut *The Adventure of Sherlock Holmes' Smarter Brother*, but he had also been the bright young thing of a director who had helmed *Every Home Should Have One*, Marty's first and only film starring vehicle in Britain.

The Last Remake of Beau Geste was one of Universal's big blockbuster releases for the summer, but the film that emerged on 15th July 1977 was something of a mess. In truth, the mess wasn't completely of Marty's doing. As with his weary film pal Orson Welles' *The Magnificent Ambersons*, studio bosses had got cold feet and waded in. Marty himself had suddenly realised the full magnitude of what he was doing and relied more and more on the advice of Jim Clark.

Marty later reflected that: "My first job directing a film," had been a failure. "I just hated the film. It wasn't my project. It was offered to me. I wrote it [so] I can't not take responsibility for it. I take responsibility for it. I take responsibility but not the blame. There's a difference between the two that has to do with loyalty and culpability and guilt. I may be guilty, but I'm not culpable. Maybe I was insane or acting under stress, or I did it at the point of a rolled-up chequebook... I was raped. But I knew what I was doing at the scene of the crime."[33]

The original screenplay had certainly changed since Marty's co-star, Michael York, had first been handed it. "[My wife] Pat and I had been in a horrible car accident in Italy and were recuperating in hospital when I got Marty's script. And Pat read it, and laughed so hard, all her stitches came undone! It was such a brilliantly funny screenplay. Unfortunately, the studio cut the guts out of the final film. Although there were some very funny moments. There's a great movie out there somewhere, and it's one of those films that I hope someone will restore one day, to the specifications that Marty had wanted. Hopefully the excised footage still exists."[34]

Marty was irked by the press relentlessly linking him to Mel Brooks. *People Weekly* was no exception: "Of late, of course, his now forty-three-year-old looks have served him handsomely. In the three years since he landed from Britain to become, in effect, the third Brooks brother (Mel's Brooklyn-Hollywood branch also includes Gene Wilder), Feldman has been the loveable hunchbacked Igor in *Young Frankenstein*, the Stan Laurel-like sidekick in *Silent Movie* and the nutball detective sergeant in Wilder's *The Adventure of Sherlock Holmes' Smarter Brother*." But the very association that had got him the directing job in the first place had, according to Marty, dictated how he had handled it. "I did it because it was offered to me and I wanted to make a movie," he later admitted to *Penthouse*. "I wanted to direct. I was out of work. They wanted a Mel Brooks kind of spoof, and I wrote it to order. And I wasn't very comfortable doing that."

But the Mel Brooks juggernaut just kept on going through 1977. Ironically, despite his misgivings about *The Last Remake of Beau Geste* it proved to be critically and commercially successful, in America at least. It might not have been the huge, all-out smash that Universal had hoped for but, as *People Weekly* had it: "This turns out to be perhaps the best summer in Hollywood history to release a movie – just as long as it's *Star Wars*. Inevitably, for a lot of other pictures the year's been a bitch. Smarting most of all, presumably, would be the studio behind *Jaws*, whose all-time record may now be in jeopardy, but Universal has come up with a unique counter-weapon to *Star Wars*. It's not exactly a Droid of its own, but as close as is humanly possible. It's Marty Feldman of *The Last Remake of Beau Geste*. Beyond the creative powers of special effects, Feldman is a wonder of wisdom and wit of the highest Force."[35]

Variety considered: "Marty Feldman's directorial debut... as an often hilarious, if uneven, spoof of Foreign Legion adventure films. An excellent cast, top to bottom, gets the most out of the stronger scenes, and carries the weaker ones..."

When the film opened in England in November, the British press would be less kind. The *Monthly Film Bulletin* opined that it: "opens with stylish promise as the camera pulls back to reveal that the familiar old Universal trade-mark is in fact being projected on a screen in a vast, empty hall; a door opens in the darkness, a mysterious figure appears with a lantern (Marty Feldman, of course) and pops up above the screen to bring the spinning globe to a halt and brush away the glittering Universal lettering with an irreverent hand. That, unfortunately, is the last moment of either style or promise." The gleeful disregard for Hollywood was enforced when, as the *Monthly Film Bulletin* bemoaned, "Even poor Gary Cooper (there ought to be a law against such humiliations) is subjected to the indignity of being press-ganged as an involuntary participant in this fatuous farce, with his magnificent Beau Geste cut into a scene with Marty Feldman's pitiful Digby."[36]

This skilful mirage sequence is actually done with great affection and Marty spoke of "the late, great Gary Cooper" as one of his favourite co-stars, albeit with his tongue neatly stuck in his cheek. "I play a scene in the picture with Gary Cooper – through the magic of movies. He's been dead for a number of years [since 1961, in fact] and therefore it's easier to work with a dead actor because he's always there on time, he knows his lines. Done by trick photography. It was done as an afterthought after we had finished the movie."[37] (Marty's trick with vintage Hollywood stars was of course later extended into an entire film by his good friend Carl Reiner, when he cast Steve Martin opposite the likes of Humphrey Bogart, Cary Grant and Lana Turner in *Dead Men Don't Wear Plaid*.)

The Monthly Film Bulletin continued: "Anything goes here in the desperate quest for laughs, and although the storyline sets out as a broad parody of the romantic jingoism of Wren's original, most of the gags are so irrelevant to any sort of parodic context that they simply aren't funny: the courtroom run as an auction house, for instance, with Digby's sentence being bid up to 956 years by an excited spectator, or the hideously inept pastiche of a silent two-reeler for Digby's escape from jail. Buried amid the frenzied mugging by actors and director alike (significantly enough, by playing straight, Michael York and Ann-Margret provide more amusement than all the rest of the cast put together), there are one or two nice throwaway ideas like the blind legionary tacking his Braille pin-up above his bunk, or Sir Hector's wild cry of 'Out of my way, Dr. Crippen!' as the doctor emerges from the maternity room with the sad news that his son is a daughter. For the most part, though, ideas are either done to death (the interminable business with Markov's wooden leg) or so juvenile as hardly to bear mention. Beau's 'Viking funeral', for instance, is translated into a shot of Digby flushing his brother's supposed ashes down the toilet."[38]

The Last Remake of Beau Geste is undeniably terrible in places but there did seem an air of Marty-baiting within the British media. Certainly within the BBC. Throughout the seventies and beyond, extracts from his biggest successes of the sixties, *The Frost Report* and *Round the Horne*, were included in everything from *Open House* to *Christmas Morning with David Jacobs*. In the June of 1976 the BBC were putting together a special 40th anniversary festival of television and wanted to include a clip from *The Frost Report*. Throughout his days in America, the BBC were continually trying to locate him to sign release forms for vintage material. A cheque for £3 would be considered a pressing matter. £140 was offered for this particular programme and, as the BBC said, the programme: "requires a large amount of advance planning, and I would be grateful if you would ask the American agent to expedite the contract. If it is necessary to edit Mr. Feldman's contribution out of the programme it will be essential to know as early as possible."[39] There is a note explaining that: "Jane Annakin phoned to say that the contract for Marty Feldman's contract to *Frost Over England* should be coming back from USA within the next week – apparently Marty is producing, directing and starring in his own film in America and they can't pin him down to sign the contract!" There is a sense of a disgruntled 'how dare this Marty Feldman keep us, the BBC, waiting while he larks about with these Hollywood Johnnies.'[40]

The lingering fragrance of *Round the Horne* was rather strong for

Marty, for the writer had begged Barry Took to join him in Hollywood and help with the *Beau Geste* script: "[He] finally negotiated a... deal with Universal where he wrote, directed and starred in his own films," wrote Barry. "He asked me to join him in this venture but I declined. I had too many obligations of my own to fulfil in Great Britain. His first picture, *The Last Remake of Beau Geste*, was pretty grim."[41]

As far as Universal was concerned though, Marty's first venture as a movie auteur had been profitable. As *People Weekly* revealed in the August of 1977, "Universal, happily surprised by the success of *Geste*, has renewed Feldman's option for the second of a promised five films. 'I have a five-picture deal,' he cracks, 'until the first picture bombs.' He's still insecure enough to lose his lunch at a screening of his own work."

Marty's painful insecurity and self-doubt was never going to be quelled simply by happiness and reassurance from Universal. He was all too familiar with the disrespect that MGM had steeped upon Buster Keaton. As far as Marty was concerned, Universal didn't understand him or his comedy. "We who work in the medium – for us it's a medium for the people who run it it's an industry – what they want is not flashes of brilliance, they want the predictable average. They used words about us; product, property, commodity. None of these words allows for the existence of a human being. There's a new phrase now, actors are bankable or they're not. Nothing to do with talent. It means a product you can raise money on. You can't computerise comedy. It's a personal thing." In his view, this first attempt at directing a film had been turned into something impersonal. Marty had wanted the opportunity so badly he had accepted the compromise: "I was so keen to direct that first time that I'd have made *Oedipus Under Water*, if they'd asked me."[42] Following the release of *The Last Remake of Beau Geste* Marty would put himself through a lengthy period of soul-searching, re-evaluation and unpleasant questioning of his own talent. Added to that, a certain comedy troupe from England was making unexpected waves in his new backyard.

Chapter Fifteen

"I won't eat anything that has intelligent life,
but I'd gladly eat a network executive or a politician."

The lengthy shadow of Mel Brooks may have been a slight irritation but it was one Marty had to live with. Even when Marty was forging his own directing career, every interviewer seemed to ask him about the films he had made with Brooks and Gene Wilder. The ones where he had been very successful and very popular. Publicly, at least, Marty would take it with good grace, explaining that a reunion was: "not likely in the immediate future. I'm now writing the next picture I shall direct. My contract calls for me to write and direct so if I was to do a comedy I'd probably do the one that I write. If Mel wanted to do *Oedipus Rex* I think he could probably make a marvellous comedy out of it. I'd like to play the shepherd. It's a marvellous part!"[1]

More hurtful was when the *Monthly Film Bulletin* dismissed *The Last Remake of Beau Geste* as: "A ragbag of a film which looks like nothing so much as a Monty Python extravaganza in which inspiration has run dry and the comic timing gone sadly awry." By 1977 the Pythons had successfully launched themselves upon the world stage, following a loyal five-year apprenticeship at the BBC and a British-based film success in *Monty Python and the Holy Grail*. The film had opened the floodgates into America and now Californian journalists were revering Marty as: "Not just a creature of Mel Brooks movies but a one-man Monty Python on his own."[2] Marty's early connection with the Monty Python team was also picked up upon and he was continually forced to look back to the past rather than solidify plans for the future: "By the age of about twenty-one, I'd become a successful writer of television situation comedies. Again, without realizing what I was doing. It was just fun to do. And one thing led to another. I wrote for David Frost's show and worked with John Cleese and Graham Chapman, the future Monty Python people. I didn't have a sense of it as a movement or anything. I'm always on the fringes of movements; I never see them. I think I'm always looking the wrong way. There's a photo of the assassination of the Archduke of Serbia, which started the First World War. Everybody in the photo is looking towards the murder except this one guy in the corner of the picture, who's looking somewhere else. That's me. There's always somebody looking the other way. While they were crucifying Christ, there was a guy walking down the street, stoned, on his way somewhere, who looked up the hill and saw them banging away, hitting some nails into a guy's hands. He just looked away. He didn't know he was witnessing history. That would have been me, always looking the other way."[3]

When he had first taken on Hollywood, Marty would no doubt have sent himself up, pointed at his eyes and smirked: 'I can look at something and look the other way at the same time, of course!' But no longer. The curse of the crazy eyes had worn extremely thin. "Comedy is what I do, not what I am," he said. "First I'm a human being, a man. If I stopped voicing my feelings to conform to the image of a performing clown, I would be a complete fake."

He had always been an intellectual with opinions on most subjects, of course, but as Tim Brooke-Taylor recalls: "He had a slight chip on his shoulder about not being taken seriously. He was a comedian with these mad eyes and I felt he was often more intellectual than he needed to be. That's not a bad thing but you did feel he was trying to prove something to people. He felt they thought he was lacking, I suppose. He wasn't. He was a very bright man and he didn't need to do that but he would make a serious point and people would laugh. I remember saying to him once: 'You don't have to be serious all the time, Marty. When you're serious it's actually more funny than when you are being funny.' I presume that if you were Marty you would forget you looked the way you looked and be rather hurt when a serious point you were making was laughed at. Not out of malice. Simply, because people were used to laughing at him and they laughed at everything he said."

Indeed, Marty said: "After a while all those jokes about the way I looked became boring. I wasn't really aware of my appearance anyway. If you live inside Big Ben you don't know what time it is. So I lived inside myself without looking to see what I look like."[4]

Bill Oddie believes that: "Marty was very comfortable with being a successful writer. It's not how you look, it's how you think and how you write. As a performer he was obviously not unaware that if you said: 'Do you know Marty Feldman?' Everybody would say: 'Oh the bloke with the big eyes!' It was overwhelming. I can imagine that Marty often thought to himself: 'Am I funny? Or am I only known because I look like this?'"

"I got to feel about my eyes the way Dolly Parton does about her boobs," Marty said. "She has to say, 'But look – I can also sing.' I had to show that I was an actor and not just a pair of pretty blue eyes."[5]

"Marty Feldman's melancholy, I could only think, must have derived in considerable part from a worry that nobody could at first glance see the sensitive, intelligent, and charming writer lurking behind the frizzy hair, the battle-scarred nose, and the distended eyes," wrote Charles Champlin in the *LA Times*, "but part of the sadness you feel about that sweet-sad face is that, like astonishing beauty in either a man or a woman, it became a kind of entrapment, closing off, or at least making harder to achieve, whatever it is that goes beyond appearance."[6]

"There's a tragic person inside all people," Marty said. "Comedy heightens your self-awareness and causes you to go out and parade your neuroses... I have this feeling that the human condition is not a particularly jocular condition. But I don't think it's a great tragedy, either. I find it rather amusing. Absurd."

"God re-made me," Marty said. "I used to look like Robert Redford until I grew into this Gothic mask." It is a very telling phrase that; the Gothic mask sums up his eternal dilemma. The Gothic mask that always hid the profound man behind the funny image. "But," he reasoned, "if I didn't look like this, I wouldn't have become a comic."[7]

In a nutshell, Marty was a serious man trapped in a clown's body. He saw himself as a man first and foremost. He was a comedian because that was his living. The rest of the world just saw the comedian. When Marty started questioning his ability as a comedian it was the fateful point of no return. He was now programmed for a destructive descent into self-pity and deep insecurity.

Articles about him that started: "A lot of people don't find Marty Feldman at all funny," couldn't have helped very much. "They avoid his films, and television shows and refuse to read about him," continued the piece that revealed Marty was determined to re-learn the clowning skills that were his stock in trade. This "self-confessed physical aberration" simply didn't think he was good enough and with self-doubt came a keen desire to prove his dessenters wrong. "The reason is that the driving hunger behind those lunatic features is for a place among the great clowns of cinema history." Back in Britain to promote *The Last Remake of Beau Geste* during Christmas 1977 he was ensconced in the lavish finery of the Dorchester Hotel. As often as not, journalists would listen to his thoughtful pontificating and snigger as they printed them, and Marty's enthused attendance of the Circus World Championships in London was no exception. "Cross-legged... below a gold and black striped cap a size too big for him," Marty vowed that a great proportion of 1978 would see him studying at a circus school in either Europe or America: "I want to learn all the techniques of a clown, and to do that I'm prepared to join a circus school, spend a season with them, and be taught by a really good clown. I think that would help me to develop an identifiable comic character, just as Jacques Tati did with Monsieur Hulot."[8]

At the time, of course, Marty was still publicly proud of *The Last Remake of Beau Geste* and eagerly promoting it as "the act of idiosyncratic comedy" and "a romantic slapstick melodrama." Hollywood had grown to trust their own judgement in Marty but Marty was seriously distrusting himself. It was a lethal cocktail. Suddenly he realised that Hollywood was in the palm of his hand. Even though he considered what he was doing as sub-standard, everyone was hailing him as a comic genius. "He became so international that he really didn't have to do much, any more," says Bill Oddie. "I think he got very lazy. We got this picture of him being completely feted as 'the great Marty Feldman' and he was smothered by a world where if you were susceptive to drink and drugs then you were going to get it. He was and he did. It was a hyperactive, truncated life. The whole thing was speeded-up."

"I must have a Niagara of adrenaline," Marty said. "I've got to keep at it."[9] "In this little Volkswagen of a body there is a Ferrari engine," he said. "I've only one speed: full out. So if I looked back I'd crash. Maybe once I have arrived – wherever it is I'm going – I'll slow down. But not yet."[10]

The problem was he was using the wrong kind of petrol. Ian La Frenais confirms that: "Marty was drinking an awful lot of alcohol at that time. He smoked weed as well, but that was all right. He smoked pretty much anything! The parties got wilder and wilder as well. The drugs he was taking got harder and harder. Marty and Lauretta were fighting more and more. They had always fought but now it seemed like a full blown war had been declared."

"We argue," Marty admitted. "We shout and scream at each other – a lot. We're both very difficult to live with, but we can't conceive of living without each other." Marty had anger management issues too. That was why work was so important to him. "Most things I do are cathartic," he admitted. "There's a lot of energy in me. A lot of violence. If I didn't work it off I'd probably hit people, which is not a good idea, because I'm smaller than most." Lauretta was always furiously competitive and ambitious on his behalf and was getting increasingly frustrated with his refusal to behave like a Hollywood star. "When you're rich you do the same things you did when you were poor only more of it," he said. "I used to drink brown ale out of a bottle. Now that I'm rich I drink champagne. But I drink it out of a bottle. Lauretta gets very pissed off with me because I lack style. If I wear a smoking jacket – I wore one because she got me one – I walked about without my trousers on, unshaven. I just don't have the flair to be rich. I was cut out to be poor however rich I am." There was one thing that Lauretta couldn't tolerate. That was Marty's ever-increasing criticism of America in press interviews. The funny looking British clown with a passion for baseball and "a thirst for Wild Turkey bourbon" was perfect. He would use American icons as his impossible ideals: wishing to be "either first baseman Steve Garvey or jazz trumpeter Miles Davis."[11] While all the time retaining that quirky English eccentricity that was charming America.[12]

Marty never had any illusions about what his job was. He was not a politician. He was a comedy filmmaker. But that didn't prevent him from having opinions about what was going on in the world. He was cautious at first. His comic digs at America were sugar-coated. "I feel it would be presumptuous for me to make any statements about American politics because I'm a guest here." And so saying he would take a deep breath, smile that winning, crooked smile of his and twist the knife ever so politely: "I do wish that more straights would come out against [anti-gay rights campaigner] Anita Bryant. If gays do it, it doesn't mean anything. I mean people like John Wayne..."[13] Thoughtful of going too far, Marty would always end a political diatribe on a joke: "I would have no objection to running for President," he said.

He was proud of his humble roots: "I'm strictly working class, then and now," he said. "The difference is that then I got on a bus, went to my job in a factory and returned at night to my tenement. Now I have a bigger house, and I ride to work in a Rolls. But I'm still working in a factory, only now it's called Universal."[14]

Now, almost completely fuelled by drink, drugs and megalomania, Marty would speak his mind in print and in broadcasts: more often and more cynically.

Hollywood film executives were fair game. "I think they treat most comics as clowns rather than as writers-producers-moviemakers," he said. "They treat us rather like autistic children. They know there's nothing actually wrong with us and that autistic children may make them a lot of money. They know we can be a highly profitable commodity. So, they leave us alone, mostly, but they don't understand the process of making people laugh."[15] But discussing and dismissing the Hollywood hierarchy was one thing. Expressing opinions on America's position in world politics was quite another. The powder keg situation in Jerusalem was something he felt strongly about. "I'm not anti-Arab. I'm not anti-

Israeli either. I really feel rather strongly about the Palestinian refugees. Sorry to get serious and political but there's an old American saying: 'You can't make an omelette without breaking eggs.' Why is it always other people's eggs they have to break? The Palestine refugees: it's their eggs. So my stand on the Middle East situation is very ambivalent, I'm afraid. I feel more for the people whose eggs are being broken."

If he could question the political scene and find the humour at its centre then that is what he would do: "This is a truism but at any time of economic depression, whenever the world is going through a pretty rough period, there seems to be a great need for comedy. People want to escape, understandably, which is fortunate for me because I came along at the right time. If they want to escape, here I am folks. Things are pretty rough all round now and we need to laugh. I came along at a useful time... for my bank balance and my career."[16]

The Hollywood dream he was living tended to appal him though: "I live in Beverly Hills," he moaned. "You see the rich scrambling for rich people's toys. Around Christmas it's obscene. People scrambling past each other to spend thousands of dollars and throwing charity balls for cripples. I would like to take someone with muscular dystrophy along to a charity ball for muscular dystrophy and say: 'Look, he doesn't want your money. He just wants to come in and dance, okay? He's wearing a tuxedo. Let him in.' Everybody would sit and feel so fucking uncomfortable. They'll raise a thousand dollars – that's easy. But they don't want to see the reality. 'Don't show me a leper,' they say. 'I'll send him money. Don't show me a starving child. Yeah, I'll do telethons. I'll do anything just don't show me the child.' That's Beverly Hills."[17]

"If there was one thing my uncle hated more than anything it was hypocrisy," says Suzannah Galland. "He liked England a lot. If you were anti something there, you were anti it. In Los Angeles he would see all these people going against their personal beliefs simply to support a cause that might help their careers. He couldn't stomach any of that. He was a big influence during my teens. My uncle was my hero. He had a passion for life and truth. He taught me to be loyal to your craft. He trained me to do that throughout my life. He certainly never liked the showbiz razzamatazz. I remember Aunt Lauretta telling me once of a trip they made to Las Vegas. My aunt would cringe at the memory of it. They were sitting watching Frank Sinatra in concert. Everyone loved Marty. From performers to Presidents. Sinatra was singing and bang in the middle of his performance he stopped and announced that one of his favourite people was in the audience. That was Marty. Sinatra was very complimentary. After the show he sent two of his security men over to invite Marty and Lauretta backstage. Marty just got up and walked out of the theatre. Lauretta was saying: 'What are you doing, Mart? It's Frank Sinatra!' He just said: 'I don't like his politics!' That was Marty."

It was this trend of biting the hand that fed him that Lauretta desperately tried to calm. But Marty was adamant. He saw in America a corrupt society that he was all too ready to expose. As Marty's self-righteous arrogance wickedly bubbled to the surface, he was confident that Universal Pictures would be grateful for his ethical stance against the tarnishing of the American way of life. In the America of the late 1970s nothing was as touchy than a satirical questioning of organised religion, so that was going to be the very next topic Marty's comedy would attack.

In fact, as Marty revealed at the end of 1977, "I've got two projects in mind. One would be called *Marty Feldman's First Second Movie*, and the other would be about commercialised religion. I'd like to call it *In God We Trust... Up to A Point*." It was always conceived that the "S" in "Trust" would be written as a dollar sign. "There will always be people and institutions I will want to offend," he said. "I'll always offend the establishment, for example. In the same way, there will always be people who will loathe me. I'm idiosyncratically made, both mentally and physically – it shows, doesn't it? I know that some people react strongly against me. But some prefer processed cheese, and I think of myself as a chunk of Roquefort."[18]

Alas, the problem with Roquefort is that after a while it begins to stink. And the writing of *In God We Tru$t* was a very long and painful process. He still loved Americana, of course. It was just America that he was uncertain about. Or at least its politics. The American people still loved him.

Denis King remembers that: "I last saw Mart in the late seventies. I was out there doing some work and we would go for lunch and visit jazz clubs down in the [San Fernando] valley. Real legends were playing every day. He seemed very fit and happy in those days. In fact I met my new wife in America in 1980. She knew Marty through his films, of course, but was fascinated by my earlier connection with him. I said: 'He's often back in England. We'll meet up with him'. Sadly we never did."

Away from jazz, "His other passion was baseball," says Dick Clement. "Both Ian [La Frenais] and I were baseball fans as well and we would go to matches together. Marty was an established Hollywood star and so he got a lot of recognition. He wasn't difficult to spot, of course, but he was a very big star and there was real love from the people who greeted him. He was a star who made them laugh. The audience love you for that."

Ian La Frenais agrees "that people were very nice to him. Overly nice, I suppose. It used to annoy him a little. He could never escape the attention. I think that's why he took so many drugs and drank so much. It was an escape from a reality he wasn't really enjoying. He used to say that baseball was like cricket on speed. Marty was like a comedian on speed."[19]

"If you are known for comedy most people approach you smiling," Marty said. "No one is looking to hurt you. If you're Charles Bronson someone may want to take you out in a bar because you look tough and you play tough parts but I'm a comedian... most people feel that I'm some sort of pet. I could bite but not severely."[20]

"Writing was the one thing he truly loved to do," continues La Frenais, "but he was so pumped full of stuff at times he couldn't even do that." He loved the company of writers though. Dick Clement says that: "Marty was a catalyst for writers. Just as he had been all those years before at the BBC, that was his great strength. He brought a comfortable feeling of home to Los Angeles. We were writing the film version of *Porridge* at that time as well as developing *Auf Wiedersehen, Pet*, so we were deeply rooted in Britain. We might as well have been in Soho, apart from the fact it wasn't raining!"

"Those days are amongst my happiest memories of Marty," confirms La Frenais. "Marty could talk for hours and hours about scripts and comedy. He was a great encouragement to young writers."

One such writer was David Weddle, who was as obsessed with the silent era as Marty was himself: "I began reading movie books in my early teens," Weddle remembers. "I didn't really see eye to eye with my father. He was a gruff man who had been a Marine fighting some of the most savage battles of the South Pacific during World War II. His temper was volcanic but we had a love of slapstick comedy. We only really connected when we sat and watched television together: Jerry Lewis, Dick Van Dyke, Red Skelton. He brought back these wonderful books. *Classics of the Silent Screen* by Joe Franklin, and Kevin Brownlow's *The Parade's Gone By*. I devoured these books, poring over them for hours. The chapters that I pored over most of all were those dedicated to the great silent comedians: Laurel and Hardy, Charlie Chaplin, Harold Lloyd and, in particular, Buster Keaton. I got a paper round, and as soon as I had my own money I began collecting silent films and buying my own books. *Mr. Laurel and Mr. Hardy* by John McCabe was my favourite, until I read *Keaton* by Rudi Blesh. For a decade after reading that book, my life's passion was Buster Keaton. I became obsessed with Keaton's head gag man, Clyde Bruckman.[21] I began to fantasise of myself as Bruckman: pulling up to the Keaton studio in my Pierce Arrow roadster; sitting around the gag room with Joe Mitchell, Jean Havez and Buster himself, cooking up elaborate sight gags based around deserted ocean liners, runaway locomotives and daydreaming projectionists."

Then the young Weddle saw *The Marty Feldman Comedy Machine*: "It was a summer replacement for *The Dean Martin Show*. My father's laugh was as uproarious as his temper. Big and overpowering, it came out of his thrown-back head like a wind. One night I heard this roaring laughter coming from the living room. 'David!' he bellowed, 'get in here, quick, you've got to see this guy!' I came in to see Marty. It was the sketch about walking on the grass. Then there was the statue routine, putting the cat out and, best of all, 'The Loneliness of the Long Distant Golfer'. As soon as Marty put his hand up to shield his eyes I knew I had found a new hero. That was Buster Keaton's signature gesture. This comedian from England understood Buster completely. My mind went spinning off into the realms of Walter Mitty fantasies. I dreamed of Marty Feldman coming to Hollywood to make feature films. I could then go to work for him and become his gag man. It would be Marty and me, sitting around the gag room, knocking out harebrained comedy ideas. I would be the Clyde Bruckman to his Buster Keaton. The fantasies became so palpable I began to believe they were almost pre-ordained."

Then Marty *did* come to Hollywood, on what Weddle describes as "a fantastic opportunity for him. This was his ticket to the big time and my opportunity to get to meet him and, hopefully, work for him. The wheelchair sequence in *Silent Movie* was shot just near to where I lived. I was so mad at myself for not getting to the location and trying to meet him. However, a year or so later, I did manage to sneak onto the Universal lot to meet Marty. That was in the summer of 1978. I was a recent graduate of USC film school and had actually been shown a rough-cut of *The Last Remake of Beau Geste* there. For the whole of my last year I had been writing a screenplay about the life of Buster Keaton. My script included lots of elaborate silent movie sequences, of course, but it was essentially a drama. Like Blesh's biography it explored the connections between Buster's art and his private life as both began to disintegrate.

"It was really easy to get onto the Universal lot. I had a friend who was a delivery guy who told me that you can get on to any lot in Hollywood just by telling the guard at the gate that you have a package for someone. They would never check. Sure enough, all I did was pull up to the gate and tell the guard, 'I have a delivery for Marty Feldman.' 'What company are you with?' he asked me. 'Dino De Laurentiis,' I said. That bit was true. I had recently got myself a job in the mailroom there, and was squeezing this stop at Universal in among my many other drops to various studios around town. The guard directed me to Marty's bungalow and I drove over there. As I walked up to his door I had the script for my Buster Keaton film gripped in my sweaty hand. I saw a small polished brass nameplate attached to the front door. It simply said: 'Marty Feldman'. I am still a nervous person. Back then I was trembling. My pulse was hammering as I pulled the latch down and entered. A middle-aged blonde secretary [Pegi A. Brotman] looked up from her desk. I stammered: 'Umm, is Mr. Feldman in?' This lovely blonde secretary didn't shout at me but instead smiled a warm, welcoming smile and told me that Mr. Feldman was out at present. Everything is a bit of a blur for me after that.

"I spewed on about the screenplay I had written and that I was hoping Mr. Feldman could read it. The secretary was still smiling, thankfully, and she said, 'Well, Mr. Feldman won't be in at all today, I'm afraid, but I'll be sure to tell him that you stopped by when he comes in tomorrow.' She explained that she was only a temporary secretary, assigned to him just a few days ago, and that she had no idea if he would be willing to read an unsolicited screenplay or, indeed, whether he would have time. Unbeknown to me he was already working on the screenplay for *In God We Tru$t* at the time. She said that she would be happy to ask him for me and see what he said. I was babbling on about how much of a fan of his I was and then she paused and said, 'Would you like to see his office?' That was an amazing experience. The first thing you saw as you entered was a life-sized mannequin of Marty staring right at you. It was sitting on a couch, flipping you off! There was the bulldog on wheels which Trevor Howard had had in *The Last Remake of Beau Geste*, a little portable Remington typewriter – almost comically small and almost an antique even then – which Marty wrote his scripts on, a mobile of various photographs from his favourite Laurel & Hardy films and, yes, a huge portrait of Buster Keaton. It was Marty's perfect working environment. To me it was like being delivered to the Promised Land.

"The secretary took down my name and asked me to telephone the office the following day. This I did and the same secretary said, 'Oh yes, I told Mr Feldman all about you. He said he doesn't have time to read any scripts right now, but that he'd be glad to talk to you if you called back when he was in.' I stammered, 'OK, that would be great, thank you.' The secretary then said, 'Actually, he's in right now. Shall I put him on?' My pulse starting hammering again. 'Umm, sure!' I heard myself say. I felt like someone was smashing my head in with a hammer. My mind started racing. Is he really just about to come on the phone and talk to me? What do I say? Just then the line clicked, 'Hello,' purred this soft English voice. 'Umm, hello,' I blurted, 'Mr. Feldman?' 'Call me Marty,' he said. 'My name is David Weddle,' I stammered. 'I'm a huge fan of your work…' I went on and on, explaining how I had first seen him on television and really admired him. I told him that I was a graduate of USC film school and that I had written a script about Buster Keaton that I would love for him to read. 'Well, I'm getting ready to shoot my next film.' he explained. 'I don't really have time to read anything right now.' Then he started dropping in test questions. 'You know, they already made a film about Buster Keaton which starred Donald O'Connor. Have you seen that?' I recognised it as a probe immediately. I knew the movie: 'Yes, *The Buster Keaton Story*, but that's a complete whitewash. It was terrible! It had almost nothing to do with Buster Keaton's real life', I said.

"Marty continued: 'There was another film that Carl Reiner made.' It was another probe. 'Did you see that one? It was called *The Comic* and starred Dick Van Dyke. It was a fictionalisation of Keaton's life.' I began to warm to my theme. 'Yes,' I said, 'the last half an hour or so when he is an old man making television commercials is really good, but I think the first two thirds are pretty weak.' I then decided to push for my screenplay. 'My script focuses on Keaton's years at MGM, when his life and career all started to fall apart,' I explained. 'That's an interesting angle,' said Marty. He sounded genuinely intrigued now. I gushed on about the plot in an enthused and breathless rush. Marty interrupted me here and there with pointed questions. 'Is there a 'Fatty' Arbuckle character? Do you deal with his relationship with his wife?' We chatted on for over thirty minutes and finally Marty said, 'Right. Well, why don't you send me a copy and I'll read it!'

"About a week later I was in my miserable, threadbare apartment doing chin-ups. My phone rang and it was Marty: 'I've read the screenplay and it's brilliant!' he said. Now, I didn't know then that the English use brilliant merely to mean 'Good' but I didn't care. Marty Feldman liked my script! He said, 'I've always wanted to make a movie about a silent comedian and now you've gone and done it.' He laughed. He wasn't annoyed but full of admiration. He was the first person in this business to ever give me any encouragement at all. He said that he felt the script had a few rough passages that needed to be worked on. 'I wonder if you might want to stop by the office sometime this week to talk about them,' he said. I almost dropped the phone. 'Umm, sure! You bet!' I stammered. That was how it all began."[22]

It was the start of a beautiful friendship. There was immediately talk of collaboration on a shooting script and Marty would advise Weddle over several re-writing sessions. Marty also had an idea of making a family comedy alongside Michael McConkey (Young Digby from *The Last Remake of Beau Geste*). "He's never really acted before," Marty said. "I think he's a very good actor. It depends whether he wants to or not. I asked if he wanted to act and he answered very seriously. He said, 'If I'm any good.' [He's a] very sensible child, unlike me when I was eleven. If he wants to be an actor he'll be a very good actor I think. But I like his approach to it. I'd love to make a picture where he plays my son, in fact."[23]

But first Marty was preparing to play a child-like innocent himself: "I don't think of myself as an innocent, but rather as a four-and-a-half year-old child," he said. "I try to hang on to what I remember of the child in me and put some of that on the screen – and when it works there is a whoop of recognition in the audience when people recognise themselves as they were."[24] The character was the bewitched, bothered and bewildered monk, Brother Ambrose in his long awaited "difficult second album", *In God We Tru$t*. The script saw Marty collaborate with Chris Allen once again, but unlike *The Last Remake of Beau Geste* the writing didn't come easily. Marty was anxious about failure and indulging in recreational substances that were weakening his comic powers. "I've wanted to experience things through my body, through me," he explained. "If assimilated, every experience, including putting needles into every part of my body, taking every kind of stimulant drug, exposing myself to all kinds of experience, then I would regurgitate it in the form of art."

Universal Pictures were getting increasingly disorientated as well, mainly through waiting for Marty to deliver a final draft of the script. The title page of the screenplay read 'Immaculately conceived and wrought by Marty Feldman and Chris Allen'. David Weddle had read the first draft, "and it was marvellous. It was full of these wonderful silent movie sequences. In the finished film most of these were jettisoned in favour of a pretty heavy plot. The silent movie sequences are still the scenes that stand up best, but in the first draft there was much more time spent at the monastery. There was a delightful scene when Marty attached a paintbrush to each foot and shimmered up to the roof. He then did a little dance to music with these brushes on his feet. It would have been wonderful. The final script lost a lot of that magic. Marty didn't want to sell out. He didn't want the big money. All he passionately wanted to do was make a series of great feature films. To follow in the footsteps of Keaton and leave his indelible stamp and his own point of view on his films." By the end of 1979, a shooting script was ready. It was the sixth draft and had taken the best part of eighteen months to perfect.

Purely by coincidence, two films were to be released at the end of 1979 that boosted Universal's confidence in Marty's latest offering. Peter Sellers was being hotly tipped for an Academy Award for his performance as Chance the gardener in *Being There*. Having spent his entire career displaying his chameleon-like acting ability, Sellers presented a portrait of a nobody.[25] Marty's vision of his Brother Ambrose was very similar. In *God We Tru$t* had sprung from the basic one-line premise of an innocent man opening up a door to the outside world for the first time. He is a middle-aged man but has absolutely no grasp on modern society. Marty, again starring in his own film, was naturally intending to play this innocent from the outset and, thus, "Since the character was my age he had to have led an institutionalised life and that was how I arrived at the idea of his being a monk."[26]

The idea of a religious satire had raised eyebrows at Universal but they still trusted Marty's judgement and, more crucially, his box office bankability. *Monty Python's Life of Brian*, which caused controversy, but also cash registers to ring must have bolstered Universal's confidence. A big studio could face upsetting the Bible Belt so long as the controversy made them money. The Pythons were bruised but wealthy after *Life of Brian* was released. Marty's film seemed extremely well timed.

Again, his religious satire had been bubbling along for nearly two years and rather than setting his film in Biblical times, Marty's attack was a finger pointing at contemporary American evangelism: "I had my main character – Brother Ambrose – and then needed a dragon for him to slay. That became the commercialization of Christianity and the fringe religions which have become big business," he explained. "I've had a flirtation with Christianity that's been going on most of my adult life, and the subject of religion has always fascinated me. But my story deals only with its commercialization and the kind of people who treat it like show business."

Indeed, for the first time in Marty's Hollywood career he completely moved away from his comfort zone of Englishness. His parodies had folded the corners of literary greatness from Mary Shelley, Sir Arthur Conan Doyle and P.C. Wren. Even his embrace of Hollywood values stretched no further than the 1920s tradition of slapstick, more steeped in European pantomime than the American dream. The influence of his own, beloved "religious" icons were less devoutly praised throughout *In God We Tru$t*. "I have a holy trinity, which is Buster Keaton the father, Stan Laurel the son and Harpo Marx the Holy Ghost," he said, and that was as good as a summary of Marty's comedy universe as you could get.[27] This was no idle soundbite. Marty genuinely believed in this trinity of comedy deities. He would concede that Buster Keaton and himself: "have the same methods. [But] he had genius and I merely have talent. That's the difference. I'm not being stupidly modest, but to compare myself to Keaton is almost an act of blasphemy."[28] It was certainly not more of an act of blasphemy than exposing the money-grabbing cancer within the bowels of American organised religion.

The comedy is not from the Mel Brooks school of parody that Marty had become associated with. It is a return to the silent slapstick tradition he loved. Much of the film is in long shot. The internationally famous Marty face is used, but used sparingly. Mostly, the comedy is physical. Marty is a human puppet. He tumbles over people, strolls through impressive outdoor locations and clings on to a moving vehicle as if the spirits of Buster Keaton and Harold Lloyd were possessing him.

He had to admit that he didn't understand what made something funny: "But you can't say that to someone who is going to hire you to make a comedy. You have to say, 'Of course, I know why people laugh!' You have to say that to your audience, too. You can't admit insecurity about what you think is funny. You can't offer a tentative joke or routine. You have to believe you're funny. Humour is all a cumulative thing."[29]

It is a more mature film than *The Last Remake of Beau Geste*. Marty's direction is assured and fluid, while his characterisation is a believable one. The innocent figure coming to terms with the Los Angeles population of hookers, faggots and junkies is a likeable one, played with a deadpan delivery and devout belief. The domestic scenes of romance and broken friendship are not played for comedy. For Marty, the comedy was in the situation and the reaction of his character to the corrupted world he finds himself in. The only intentional humour was in the slapstick. Marty was a pawn in an insane world.

In one scene, Marty's prostitute acquaintance, tellingly named Mary and played by Louise Lasser, tries to explain the basics of mortal sin:

Mary: You really are an innocent, aren't you?

Ambrose: I suppose so.

Mary: It's touching. It really is, it's touching. In a disgusting kind of way.

Ambrose: You see, I know a lot about the theories of sin but I don't know anything about the practice. I mean, for instance, fornication.

Mary: What?

Ambrose: The Bible's full of it. You mustn't do it. It's sinful. You'll go to Hell. But it doesn't tell you *how* to do it, so how do you know you're not? I mean, for all I know I might be sitting here right now fornicating.

Mary: No, you're not. If you were, I'd tell you.

Ambrose: Thanks. That couple over there sucking each other's mouths…

Mary: Will you keep it down a little bit?

Ambrose: I'm sorry. Are they fornicating?

Mary: They're kissing. They're just kissing.

Ambrose: Kissing?

Mary: That's phase one. You see now when they get home they'll probably move into phase two.

Ambrose: Oh, you fornicate in phases?

Mary: Oh yeah. That is if you're not pressed for time.

Perhaps the fatal flaw within Marty's screenplay was that, however hard he tried, he just couldn't out-satire the madness that was the reality of America in 1980. Within a year of the film's release, President Ronald Reagan would be shot and John Lennon, someone culturally bigger than Jesus, would be shot dead. In the five years between first conceiving *In God We Tru$t* and finally releasing the film, many of the satirical elements Marty had come up with had actually come to pass. The script included a drive-in church; months after writing the sequence, Marty discovered that several were under construction. He was particularly tickled by his concept of a "broadcasting religious network". By 1980, the Trinity Broadcasting Network actually existed. The end of the film set up the possibility of merging the three main religious conglomerates in an attempt to combat war and violence in the name of a chosen God. As the film was being shot, there were advanced talks about a knowing "media-punch" of various evangelists settling their religious differences and forming a coalition.

Marty, who professed himself to be a "Marxist-Christian", saw the humour in the situation and, perhaps, an even more timely poke at America. "God has used all kinds of men throughout history, why not me?" he pondered. "It makes sense. I have access to the media. Joan of Arc had access to the King. I am also familiar with the Bible. It's a good piece of work and, like all good writing, you don't question if it's fact or fiction. Still, I am moved by the power of my own prophesies."[30]

While baiting the media – one of his favourite occupations – Marty did seem to take on the role of God's comic messenger with unreserved relish. His film, designed to protect the good name of religion by highlighting the outrageousness of the modern packaging that surrounded it, made him some sort of insane, divine weapon. God was, for all intents and purposes, using him to attack the charlatans who were corrupting His message. The central theme of the film was: "that Christ could no longer drive the moneylenders out of the temple, because now they own it, and he'd have to pay to get in... So it's about the loss of innocence, the idea that one may have to be a little corrupt in order to survive. There's a great line in it: 'The meek will inherit the earth, but not until the strong are finished with it, by which time it won't be worth having.' That represents my own belief."[31]

This wasn't a satire any more. It was a documentary.

Terry Jones, who had directed *Monty Python's Life of Brian*, sympathises: "Marty felt things so strongly. It's a bit like me, really. He felt things so strongly that he couldn't be funny about them. His attack on the American church isn't funny. It's a serious attack on the commercialism of religion. So, if he was given his head and left to his own devices he couldn't be funny about something he passionately believed in. If I hadn't have been part of Python, who knows how my film on religion would have turned out."

And Universal Pictures certainly did leave Marty to his own devices: "I'm the guy with the whistle," he said. "Anybody can make suggestions, and I'm glad they do. Some of the best things in my latest picture were suggested by the prop master. I think the thing a director can do is create an atmosphere in which creativity is encouraged. Just because a guy is key grip doesn't mean he won't have a very good idea for a line, or a guy who is lighting a scene. Everybody makes suggestions. Then the director makes the final decisions as to which way to go. He carries the whole picture in his head, or should be able to."

Marty still juggled with the Jekyll and Hyde life of being both writer and actor: "Dr. Jekyll writes, and Mr. Hyde acts and has all the fun. Writing is a continuing process that gets interrupted by acting. Writing and directing at the same time is easier – the two are inter-related. But it gets very complicated. I can be in the middle of a scene with Louise Lasser, for example, I'm acting opposite her. But then I'm suddenly aware that I'm directing her. I want to make a change in the scene but don't want to stop her, because she's going well. And I can't do anything, because the camera is on me as well. That's pretty schizophrenic." Even so, directing a feature film had lost some of its mystique the second time around: "I've learned that it isn't as difficult as I thought it would be," he said. "Most directors, like most writers, like most actors, like most plumbers, are competent at their jobs, but they're not geniuses. There are very few really great directors. Most of them create a mystique around themselves, like doctors do. It isn't that difficult to do that. If you're like [Luis] Buñuel, you don't choose to be a genius – you are one. You can't work at being a genius. You've got it or you haven't. I've learned to have the confidence in placing the camera, and I know what lens to put on. I've realised that there is no great art or secret to that. There isn't any secret in directing a film for me. There is for Robert Altman, but I suspect the secret is just that you and I can't do it and he can.[32] Directing a movie is like directing traffic. You're surrounded by experts. What director knows as much about the camera as the cameraman? Directors are mostly ex-writers or ex-producers, or they've been first assistants. They have a general knowledge of it all. But they don't have specific technical knowledge of any one department. Maybe writers are the best people to become directors. Or maybe actors – they're probably the best."

His surrounding experts were largely unchanged from *The Last Remake of Beau Geste*. Lauretta was now officially involved, claiming an Associate Producer credit alongside George Shapiro and Howard West. The heavenly music was composed by John Morris while, tellingly, the film was edited by David Blewitt and not Jim Clark.[33] But in a way, the film was edited by the people. The preview audiences who saw the film took on great importance for Marty: "I get more control," he said. "I have the cutting rights to *In God We Tru$t*. Actually, it's the audience that does the final cut in comedies. You show it to a few audiences, and if none of them laugh at a part and you don't cut it out, you're a bloody fool, you know? The cliché that the audience is a failure but the show a success does not apply in comedy. If I make you laugh, it's comedy. If you don't laugh, I've failed. Smiles don't count – you can't hear them."[34]

Of the supporting cast, only Peter Boyle joined Marty from his Mel Brooks hey-day. Indeed, Madeline Kahn and Dom DeLuise had been mugging it up opposite the latest English comedian in town, Dudley Moore, for his low-rent *Life of Brian* cash-in *Wholly Moses!*, which was released in June 1980 to a thundering silence.

Richard Pryor, fresh from Dud's dud, popped up as an energetic God in Marty's film. Although this was a computer-generated God, under the control of a silver-haired evangelist, played by another big-name comedy star, Andy Kaufman.[35] It was just one of the elements that set the pulses of the God-fearing American population racing. A black Father. A monk falling in love with a prostitute. Religious leaders seen as nothing more than Las Vegas hustlers.

For Suzannah Galland the film proves her uncle as: "a truly intelligent, creative visionary. Hollywood didn't want that. They just wanted silly comedy films. But here was Marty, a Jew, playing a monk. He had Andy Kaufman voicing the political innuendos that the script was littered with and he cast Richard Pryor, a black comedian, as God. Marty was asked about that a lot at the time. 'How could you cast a black man as God?' Marty was non-plussed. 'He was very apt, I thought,' he would say. And of course he was! He didn't care if he upset people."

Universal were ready to take the risk of upsetting people too, and opened *In God We Tru$t* on over 600 screens across America in August 1980. It was the most complete professional disaster of Marty's career. *Variety* cited it as: "A rare achievement – a comedy with no laughs." It was one of the kindest critiques.

"When reviews are shown to me – and people generally only show you the bad ones – I'm devastated. Always. Totally devastated by anybody who thinks I've done anything badly," Marty told *Penthouse*'s Richard Kleiner, in a major interview conducted while the film was in production, but not published until after its release (and, ironically, after the appearance of plenty of devastating reviews). "It's a sort of public insult or humiliation to which you can't reply," he continued. "When you see yourself lambasted across the pages of a large newspaper as a fool, as an incompetent, or just as unfunny, you're humiliated, because you know thousands of others have read that and are saying, as you walk by: 'There he is, inept and unfunny.'"

In the wake of the film's dreadful first week at the American box office, Universal Pictures pulled it from the majority of screens. With that, they informed Marty that his contract would not be renewed. His services as a film director would no longer be required.

"Marty was always a realist," maintains Alan Spencer. "He told me that he had a five-picture deal. 'If the first one doesn't succeed, I'll have a no-picture deal!' he said. He bit the hand that fed him. He mocked the studio and embraced the irreverence that his home audiences in the United

Kingdom would have loved. It didn't go down well in America. Not with the flesh peddlers that ran the studios, at least. Universal actively rooted against Marty and the film. Preview audiences liked the film but the studio didn't support it. They didn't know him as a satirist and they didn't want him as a satirist. He had a raging intellect and he had very serious things to say about the corporations. Universal wanted their clown to be loveable and look silly. The tragedy was that he wasn't allowed to develop as a filmmaker. When he was cleared out of the bungalow he seemed to be less approachable than before. Lauretta would answer the phone on his behalf. Marty hadn't grasped studio politics. Marty was very sensitive and he had values. He was loyal, non-competitive and supportive of others. These were not the values that prevailed in Hollywood. It must have hurt him when he wasn't shown loyalty and support by Hollywood. I was too young to talk to him about it. He was very protective of what emotions he showed me. I do know that a party was organised in his honour and no one came because he was considered a failure."

"When the film bombed and Universal turned away from him, he took it very seriously and probably a little too personally," says Ian La Frenais. "It was a very heavy weight to carry, having starred in it and written it and directed it. There was no one else to blame save himself."

As Marty's character, Brother Ambrose, said in the film: "Doubts are about the only certainties I have right now."

In November 1980 it was reported that Marty narrowly escaped death following an overdose of sleeping pills. It was confirmed that the comedy filmmaker had been depressed following the critical slamming of his latest film, *In God We Tru$t*. Talking a few months later Marty said, "I know there have been rumours I tried to commit suicide. But it's not true. Anybody who knows me knows the one thing I don't want is to die yet because I have got so much to do. I am a manic depressive, but I really love life."[36]

For Marty's old friend, Barry Took, his failure in Hollywood was the final, inevitable blow to a lifestyle he had never really liked anyway: "Marty had a craving for stardom which, when it came didn't satisfy him, and when it left him, destroyed him."[37] While for Bill Oddie the fact that

Marty apparently attempted suicide: "doesn't surprise me at all. Talk about the classic figure of the person suddenly finding fame beyond anything that was intended or, in some respects, wanted. As he saw everything he had in Hollywood crumbling away around him he must have thought: 'What the fuck do you do to get back?' What could he do? This bug-eyed, curly haired clown. He wasn't going to be able to carve out a career as a romantic lead."

All Marty could do was swallow his pride and play the fame game. He was still a personality. "If I aspired to be Robert Redford, I'd have my eyes straightened and my nose fixed and end up like every other lousy actor, with two lines on *Kojak*," he explained. "But this way I'm a novelty."[38] He went back to what he was used to. The only thing he could do to make money quickly. Looking funny in front of a camera. But, now, depressingly, he wasn't also behind the camera calling the shots.

Chapter Sixteen

"I'm too old to die young, too old to grow up."

It was the cruellest possible fate for Marty when Hollywood disowned him," says Dick Clement. "He was always conscious that one or two flops would damage him but after *In God We Tru$t* no one in Hollywood wanted to know him. They had given him the opportunity to write and direct and star and he had let them down. In their eyes. Marty had blown it by making them a film that didn't make money. Hollywood is the most fickle place in the world and no one wants to associate themselves with yesterday's man. It gave Marty's confidence a mighty blow." Ian La Frenais recalls: "That was the time we started to see Marty pretty much every day. Once Universal booted him out of his bungalow he rented an office in the building we worked from, just off Hollywood Boulevard. Because of all the shit he had got over at Universal, he found [our production offices] WitzEnd something of a haven. We worked like British writers – obviously. But he was drinking a lot of alcohol. I actually remember admiring him for being so frank about it. Marty would turn up at the office in the morning and join us for a coffee. He would matter-of-factly say, 'I'm an alcoholic!' I would say, 'No you're not!' 'Ah,' he would say, 'but I've had a bottle of vodka already this morning!' That *is* an alcoholic."

He seriously thought about moving to New York but, at the start of the eighties, with little opportunity of work there and far too many ready temptations, that could have been disastrous. Marty's reputation as a director was well and truly shot and as an actor, in the eyes of other producers, he was comically typecast. Even his stock in trade as a writer was a challenge: "I haven't had an idea for a movie in months," he admitted to Richard Kleiner. "Yesterday I suddenly had a clutch of ideas that all came to me from different directions, three of which I like very much. They started to nag at me. And the one that nags, 'Write me! Write me!' the loudest and the longest is the one that gets itself written. I know that there are thousands, millions, an indefinite number of possibilities. And they just sort of arrive. I suppose it's the same if you're a photographer with a trained eye. A photographer does not consciously go around framing compositions. But he has a trained eye for a good shot without even knowing it. [Photo journalist] Cartier-Bresson will just pick up his camera and snap, whereas I would spend hours with the viewfinder. He has a trained eye. And I suppose, in a similar way, I have a trained sense of what will work in the written form."[1]

David Weddle was still in constant touch with Marty, discussing the Buster Keaton biopic: "Marty liked my script but there was always room for improvement," remembers Weddle. "In all, Marty helped me through five drafts. I would go and see Marty on the lot all the time. I would tell work that I had errands to run and be yelled at when I returned two hours later! I didn't care. The job meant nothing to me. The script and Marty was all I was interested in. By the time I had a finished screenplay, there was hardly one scene left from my original version. Marty gently pushed me. He was my mentor. Time after time he would suggest I dig deeper into the psychology of Keaton. Marty told me to be more daring with the structure of the script. He did this without ever once sapping my enthusiasm for the project.

"He never tried to be funny. He wasn't 'on' all the time like some comedians. He had a dry wit, like an English professor. He didn't have much of a formal education but he was extremely well read. I went through some rough times and worked through every shit job you can imagine. I was not managing to sell anything that I wrote, but the main reason I kept going was because Marty had seen something in me. I looked forward to those writing sessions with him. They were full of laughter and we would bristle with ideas bounced off of one another. Marty taught me not to dread the re-writing process. He taught me to be excited about it. With every re-write you would be improving the screenplay and, besides, he would say that you can always go back to what you had before if you want. As good as those early scenes were they could always be made better. It was never tedious with Marty around. It was always thrilling. After each session he would say: 'Well, David, I hope I haven't dulled your pencil.' He never did, he always sharpened it.

"He tried to secure financing for our script, *The Final Chase*, but found no takers. Although he had got a line producer to budget the film, most producers at that time thought of him as a Mel Brooks comedian. They wanted him to be a Mel Brooks kind of director, and he really wasn't that kind of filmmaker. *In God We Tru$t* pointed him in a different direction. A direction that really suited him. Hollywood producers were certainly not about to give Marty several million dollars to make a tragic drama about a silent movie star. 'You know, David,' Marty said sadly one day, 'if I was Dustin Hoffman, I could get this movie made tomorrow.' I knew he had to be disappointed with the turn his career had taken, but we never spoke about it; I didn't know how to broach such a painful subject. I couldn't bring myself to ask him about it. I did see him about six months after *In God We Tru$t* had opened and he had gained a lot of weight and grown a beard. He had always been very fit prior to that and I took this as a sign of his depression. I spoke to Lauretta about it years afterwards and she said that Marty had been crushed by the failure of the film. The constraints of Hollywood had taken his vitality away. He was a weakened man in comparison with the joy of his work for the BBC."

Marty was still enthused about the future for his friend Alan Spencer as well. "He was convinced that I could make it as a writer," remembers Spencer. "Marty was remarkably patient with me but would say that he could tell I had what it takes simply by talking with me. He was thrilled when I got my first few bits and pieces on television. He was a bohemian. For him it was the writers versus the system."[2]

Harshly critical of his own writing ability, Marty lacked the focused drive that he seemed so readily to encourage in others: "When an idea occurs to me, I jot it down – on a napkin in a bar or on the back of a menu," he explained. "When I worked at home, I would give these napkins and things to my secretary, who would type them out and file them for me. But I'm terribly disorganised. My mind is like an attic full of junk. When I'm writing, I rumble around through my head to see what's up there and I don't know where anything is. I'll stumble across something, and I'll think, 'Oh, that might be interesting,' and take it down into the daylight and polish it up and look at it and get some of the slop and mildew off it and say, 'Oh, that's quite a good idea.' Other things I'll leave up there – they're best left in the dark, you know? That's exactly what it's like when I write. It's a sort of stumbling around in the dark, in the attic of my head, knowing that the stuff is up there because everything I've seen and done and have been told about and have experienced has been assimilated. It's there somewhere, so I just wander around. It's very aimless and rather dangerous. You can bruise your shins and get some very bad ideas. I fear [that my ideas will dry up] so often that I've gotten used to it. It's like living in the slide area in California. People who live there don't worry about it. They know it's dangerous and that their house may not be there tomorrow. It's like the house in Chaplin's *Gold Rush* – the one that's tipping backwards and forwards. I feel like I live in that house. Eventually I hope to get out, before the house goes over the cliff. But really I'm used to panicking early to avoid the rush."[3]

The only thing Marty could do to make money and make it easily was perform. "That was all that was left to him really," remembers Dick Clement. "We would talk about it and he wasn't happy about it but he needed to work. He needed the money. He hated doing that whole celebrity turn thing, appearing on *Hollywood Squares* or some such rubbish but we couldn't blame him. I would have taken the money to record a week's worth of programmes in an afternoon for the sort of money he would pick up. But happy? I don't think so. It was something to do and something to keep him in the public eye. He wanted to be liked and America was quickly falling out of love with him. The huge disaster and commercial failure of *In God We Tru$t* still loomed large."

So much so, that Marty accepted a bizarre role in the religious drama series *Insight*. A sort of *Twilight Zone* for Jesus freaks, the series had been running since the 1960s. 'The Sixth Day' would be the 230th episode of a run of 265. Marty was saddled with a white Harpo Marx wig, a minute pair of wings and a huge carrot to play an Angel opposite Keenan Wynn as God. Although written in modern speech by Lan O'Kun and steeped with comic asides, this was an earnest, right-on take on the Bible and the Day of Creation. Keenan Wynn looked the part of God. He had a white beard and everything. He certainly wasn't Richard Pryor, in any case.

Suzannah Galland explains that: "[Marty] loved his craft. He was an old-fashioned writer but he wasn't allowed freedom to write in Hollywood. No one in that town saw Marty as a writer. He was simply a silly clown. A personality. In fact, he couldn't get back home to England quick enough. He knew he would be free to write in England but he had projects he was committed to. Hollywood kept on thwarting him. He longed for the freedom to write but once you take that away from the sensitive creator, you clip their wings. Hollywood may as well have put him in shackles. He became more and more depressed, and little wonder. I know for a fact that going home was in the back of his mind for several years. Today, of course, he could write, produce, direct and star in films in both England and America, communicate and commute between the two countries with ease. He didn't have that luxury. The US was where his career was.

"I often would talk about this with my Aunt Lauretta and wonder how he would cope with the Hollywood of today. She always said that he wouldn't. If anything, it had got worse. The creative talent has less and less power against the corporate heads. She would say that Marty would have gone home to England in a heartbeat. But he knew what he had to do. He had to fit in and conform in Hollywood. When you did that, they went and changed the rules. They would beat you down to a pulp. They did beat Marty down, but he had been stuck in a contractual agreement and he still had to promote *In God We Tru\$t*. He would never walk away from responsibility. Time and time again in America he was simply misunderstood. He would do all those game shows and chat shows simply to promote the latest film. He would play the game, but a piece of him would die after every one of them."

Marty's sister Pamela agrees: "He wasn't a happy bunny at all. As soon as his career in America had started to unravel he desperately wanted to come back home to England. The last time I saw him was in his beloved Hampstead. We enjoyed a wonderful six hours talking together. He didn't like the Hollywood parties. It wasn't that he was anti-social. He just didn't suffer fools gladly and hated the falseness of Hollywood. Lauretta loved Hollywood. Marty had loved living in Hampstead. He loved walking. He loved drinking in the little pubs there. He loved the simple life. He was a lovely soul."

Undoubtedly the happiest of Marty's 'looking funny in front of a camera' gigs was *The Muppet Show*. He fitted into Jim Henson's affectionate resurrection of burlesque with ease and importantly the show came at the end of his happiest period. Marty would probably never be as happy again. He recorded *The Muppet Show* in the July of 1980, not long after *In God We Tru$t* had wrapped. By the time the show was broadcast at the end of the year, Marty's film had come and gone.

There is certainly something bittersweet about the show now. Marty is described as "the master of nuttiness" by Kermit and wallows in his very Britishness. He makes his entrance bellowing: "The British are coming! The British are coming!" Before muttering, "I'm British and I'm coming!" Sam the Eagle's snobbishness is fired up at the thought of having a distinguished artiste from the old country, but his pride turns to disgust as he is introduced to Marty dressed in full drag, complete with Bette Midler wig.

The theme is the 'Arabian Nights' but the heart is pure vaudeville. Marty involves himself heavily in the lowbrow antics. He enjoys a cockney knees-up and sing-song on 'The Laughing Policeman'. There's even a Marty-a-like Muppet who is cast as Ali Baba. Perhaps the most touching moment is during the final curtain call when Marty plonks his baseball cap on the head of his Muppet doppelgänger.[4]

Marty also jumped on the comedy alien bandwagon, along with Jerry Lewis and Madeline Kahn, in *Slapstick of Another Kind*. Marty played a grey-haired, bespectacled dial-a-Peter Lorre butler whose sinister streak is gradually eroded away to reveal a sentimental compassion. Although

– as the title suggests – he spends much time with food smeared over his face, Marty displayed a subtle quality that gave dignity and a touch of class to the insane script. It had been done before and it would be done again, many times: visitors from Outer Space wind up on Earth and desperately try and cope with the strange ways of human beings. But Marty's performance had a sedate charm and relaxed quality that was rarely seen in his previous film performances. Indeed, his introspective champagne-fuelled chat with Ben Frank is perhaps his most truthful film moment.[5]

The television sketch show had got a punch in the face with the arrival of *Fridays* on ABC. Created by Bill Lee, it gathered together a clutch of comedians including Jack Burns, Mark Blankfield and Brandis Kemp and let them loose on the morals of American society. Marty's guest appearance in the autumn of 1981 was high profile certainly, but it also painfully highlighted the extreme change in his physical appearance. His lengthy abuse of drugs and alcohol had taken their toll and although he tried to keep fit through working out, swimming and playing football, his weight loss was profound. At his best in a parody of Paddy Chayefsky's *Marty*; the gag commentary team judge his spoof of Ernest Brognine's Oscar-winning performance as if it were a baseball game, discussing: "The humourist juxtaposition of casting British comedian Marty Feldman..." His lean look lent itself to the seedy New York butcher in this black and white snippet. But in full colour – during his final resurrection of his late sixties 'At the Vet' sketch – he looks fraught rather than fit.[6]

"Marty told me that his attitude was that of the jazz musician," explains Alan Spencer. "He would go along with whatever came his way. He was very philosophical about it. There was talk of him having another shot at directing a film for Polygram but that never happened. Then he wanted to write novels. He was also telling me that he would bounce back. I asked him about his career trajectory and he told me he had nothing planned. He viewed himself as a cartoon character. If he walked off a cliff he would just stay there in mid-air... as long as he didn't look down! He didn't need movies to perform. I once asked him what he would do if he suddenly couldn't do movies. He didn't hesitate. He said: 'I'd perform on the street.

I love performing." As a writer he was nothing more than 'an aging whore'. His attitude was very down-to-earth."

"I've never thought beyond the present," Marty told Richard Kleiner. "I've never thought in terms of either routes or destinations. The only time you concern yourself with a destination is when you have arrived, retired, and stopped doing things. Then you say, 'Where I am was my destination,' and you look back and say, 'That was an interesting route I came by.' Thinking about destinations gets in the way. I may come to a fork in the road, and if I'm worried about destinations, I may miss that pretty road down there because I'm on the freeway. But I pretty much enjoy doing what I'm compelled to do by whatever inner demons I have. I present it to an audience in the hope that they will like it, too. That's all I can do. As long as they like it, I'm in business. If they don't, then I have to get out of it and do something else for a living."

The road back to Hollywood had been completely blocked off for Marty. He would get frustrated that studio bosses wouldn't give him the opportunity to direct another film. His days as a filmmaker seemed an awful long time ago: "I half liked the first but in the second I tried to make something important and that is always a mistake," he said.[7] He later admitted that: "Secretly I always wanted to be famous," and when that fame began to dwindle he became reflective. "I lost my values in America. I got caught up in the comet of success. I was spending too much time in Hollywood."[8]

Marty was still pushing ahead with more projects for David Weddle, however. Although the Buster Keaton film seemed to be dead in the water, the great comedian was still an inspiration. "I was writing a play about Buster's time as a gag man at MGM when he was reduced to writing jokes for Red Skelton films," says Weddle. "I would often have lunch with Marty at Musso and Frank's on Hollywood Boulevard, or at his new little office at WitzEnd Productions on Highland Avenue. Marvellous brainstorming sessions. He was still very encouraging to me. He would tell me about F. Scott Fitzgerald and the Pat Hobby stories. In my play Buster shared an office with Fitzgerald and I included a Pat Hobby-like hack scriptwriter. A character that Fitzgerald himself had feared he was becoming while working in Hollywood. That was all down to Marty.

"This was during the writers' strike of 1980/1981 and Marty asked me to write a treatment for a World War One fighter pilot story. He said that he didn't have time to write it, but thought that somebody should. 'That person might be you,' he said. I worked on the characters and the scene breakdown and ended up with a twenty-seven page treatment. Marty couldn't get the film made but I do remember turning in a draft of the treatment. I spoke with him a few days afterwards on the telephone and Marty said, 'I was so high after our meeting the other day, I sat down and wrote several pages. But then I saw yours, and they were so much better, I threw mine away.' I don't know of any other star in Hollywood who would have said that. He wasn't being nice or humble. He was being sincere.

"I was very young and we didn't have that kind of relationship where he would open up and talk to me about his troubles. He would hint at it indirectly, in respect of the building of the sympathy of my character. Mainly in relation to Buster Keaton. He would say, 'People say to me, you are driving a Bentley, you are getting laid regularly, you have no financial worries, you are not concerned about where your next meal is coming from... Things aren't that bad!' He was resilient. He was still a star. He was certainly not a broken man but he was nursing great disappointment. I remember I was on the phone with Marty and he sounded quite down. I wanted to let him know how talented I thought he was and what a great comedian he was and how much he meant to me, personally, and how grateful I was to him. Just as I was about to take a big breath and launch into this long speech his secretary interrupted him. When he came back on the line he said, 'You were saying...' and I didn't continue. The moment had gone and I didn't want to sound like an ass-kisser. I hesitated and he said, 'Well, anyway, I'll talk to you soon...' I think he could have used hearing me say that but I didn't. I regretted it. I felt I let him down.

"Still, the very last time I talked with him was after he had made *Slapstick*. We spoke of Jerry Lewis. He was still keen on talking about comedians. He told me that he was thinking of doing a supporting role in a film in Yugoslavia. He was moving forward and picking himself up.

There is no dishonesty in stumbling in Hollywood. He had planned big without knowing what that town was like and what the industry was like. He had wanted to beat the Hollywood system but he couldn't."[9]

While Marty was trying to move on to a new chapter in his career, the insecurity would simply not go away. As a teenager he lacked the determination to become an alcoholic. No longer: "I didn't have enough grounding," he said. "It's a thing that comes later in life, like being a monk. It's a vocation."

Bill Oddie remembers that: "We would all get little snatches of news from friends in America saying that Marty wasn't in great shape." Spike Milligan: "wrote to Marty a number of times [at this time], giving him my support. I knew he was in need of friendship, and I was offering mine. I had heard he was very depressed and into drugs. I knew he felt permanently repressed and that he had enormous talent which was screaming to get out. I said how silly it was to get into the drug scene, that it was only harming him. I invited him to come and stay with me. I told him he had talent, an enormous amount, but things out there were tough. I was trying to give him a lot of love, trying to keep him going. But he never answered the letter. I guess that was [in February 1982]."[10]

"It was around that time that Marty started seriously talking about going back to England," remembers Ian La Frenais. "There really was nothing left for him in Los Angeles. He would be a little drunk and wish he could move to New York but he was well aware that there would be nothing there for him either. Nothing that would do him any good, at any rate. He had always been a little part of England in LA. Now he wanted to go home. I remember him saying: 'I would love to go back to England.' America was killing him. Or he was slowly killing himself."

"Peter Tinniswood had written a series of *Mog* books which we felt would make a perfect show for Marty," says Dick Clement. Mog was a burglar by trade who resided in a mental hospital and avoided capture by the police by returning to his room after each job. It would mark a return to Marty's little man character fighting against authority. Although he found the idea of being: "A comic, to be a clown, to invite an audience to ridicule you... a rather strange thing for an adult to do. I'm not really an adult, of course; otherwise we wouldn't be talking this way. When I grow up, I shall stop being a comic and start doing something responsible."[11] But to be an actor was seen as something slightly more mature. The character of Mog perfectly suited Marty's desire for honesty, both as a man and as a performer. His characters had always been generally losers who win: "I know it's true that I play characters who are vulnerable," he said. "I'm attracted to vulnerability in people generally. I don't see vulnerability as a flaw. I see it as a manifestation of humanity." Marty saw himself as a comedian who was never sure where the next laugh was coming from. Mog would be very much like him. "I'm very far from being calm," he said. "I'm contented."

Marty had long nursed a regret that no offers from British television had come his way: "They thought I was a movie star who wouldn't be interested," he lamented. "That was wrong. I sometimes regret ever leaving Britain, but I had to come out here to earn some real money because I owed the British taxman £60,000. I've paid all that off now from my movie earnings. Money has never really concerned me. If I have it, I spend it. If I don't have it, I steal it. I will always get by – I am a survivor."[12]

"We were due to go to England to do re-writes on the James Bond film *Never Say Never Again* and told Marty that we would make the approach to the television companies," remembers Dick Clement. "It all looked very promising."[13]

"I am going back to England to work in TV," Marty proudly told the press in 1982. "I went to America because that's where movies were being made. But I temporarily lost the values that had made me become a writer in the first place."[14] Marty had always considered American television bland and unchallenging. So much so that he had fallen out of love with television completely. Now he had fallen out of love with film. "I love working in television," he said. "In films you lose contact with people, you're tied to the script. Improvisation is more me. I'm very intuitive. When it feels right it usually looks right." At least as long as it was television in England and the brand of off-the-wall comedy he loved. The promise of *Mog* gave Marty a new lease of life. So much so that Spike Milligan saw a complete change in him: "It was in mid-October [1982], he phoned me, and we talked a long time. He seemed to have won the battle he was fighting. He was in a fantastic mood, so relaxed, and excited about the future again. It was like the Marty Feldman of old, and I was happy for him again. His enthusiasm for comedy had returned."[15]

However, before he was set to return home Marty had to do a film. It wasn't the best script he had ever been sent but he was as loyal to old friends as they were to him. Off the successful back of the Monty Python films, Graham Chapman had landed a contract to write and star in a project of long standing: a pirate romp called *Yellowbeard*. The cast was a wonderful mishmash of familiar comedy groups. There was the Mel Brooks fraternity: Madeline Kahn, Kenneth Mars, Peter Boyle.[16] Cheech and Chong brought their own unique drug-addled style to the fun, while the British end was kept up by a roster of Marty's pals from the old days. Spike Milligan had contributed a cameo back in Britain but the likes of Peter Cook, Eric Idle and John Cleese would be fooling around on location in the sun.[17]

Again Marty was the catalyst that linked the different comedy factions together and he seemed to enjoy the mix. His sole ambition was to give the best possible performance he could give. He never complained about the tight shooting schedule or the filming conditions. He charmed crew, cast and locals alike; Gillian Eaton playing the dockside whore in the film, said that Marty: "[is] probably the nicest man I've met in a long time. He really is. He has an ability to become one of the natives wherever he goes; people flock to him, he magnetizes people."[18] He didn't even complain about the script which, "he had obviously read!" groans Michael Palin as he shoots his eyes skyward. "Sorry Graham! I think that as soon as Marty had read the script he would have realised it wouldn't work!"

"Marty remained upbeat and positive about it," says Alan Spencer. "He did not like the script but he liked the fact there was no pressure on him and he liked the people he was working with. He made new friends. He became very close to Cheech Marin, and of course there were lots of old friends around."

Graham Chapman was simply: "very pleased when [Marty] agreed to appear in it. I'd known Marty for years. He started off in television in a little show called *At Last the 1948 Show* with John Cleese and myself many years ago. Actually, jokingly at the beginning of filming, [Marty] said that John and myself started his career, it looked as though we might finish it..."[19] Joking apart, the premonition of an early death had always been in his mind. In 1977 he claimed in a rather jovial manner that: "I'm more than middle-aged... If I'm forty-three and I was middle-aged then I would expect to be eighty-six. I don't expect to be eighty-six. I think I was middle-aged when I was twenty-five. I don't think I'll pass fifty!"[20] Shortly before filming began on *Yellowbeard* he was even more candid: "I don't expect to live to be old enough to retire. I am going to kill myself from the pace I am keeping. I am sure I will burn myself out... [That] probably accounts for this urgency I have. A need to do everything and do it fast. Perhaps that is not so bad. I have no desire to be a grand old man..."[21]

Lauretta had visited the location at the end of November. While sitting in the shade of a palm tree in Ixtapa, a bay on the coast of Mexico, Marty discussed his own death with a journalist: "I don't think there's a death wish among actors," he said, "just a desire to experience everything. Even death... I must go on running all my life. Comics are acutely aware of the fears of disability and death. Those are our demons, and I'm trying to exorcise them from me. I don't think people who make others laugh are necessarily miserable men. Melancholic possibly, because they are more aware of their melancholia than others. We are indulged and we are children and we want to hang on to the childishness within us. Which means that we are vulnerable, and just as kids do, we go from tears to laughter very quickly."[22]

The circumstances surrounding Marty's death have been garlanded with mystery over the years and it's true that several bizarre events occurred during his last few days. However, it can also boil down simply to the economics of filmmaking. In order to lower the budget on *Yellowbeard* an English galleon was constructed in the bay at Ixtapa, and then the unit moved to Mexico City's Churubusco Studios to complete the film; a much cheaper option than using facilities in Hollywood or the UK.

Despite the location being way above sea level and the air thick with pollution, Marty embraced his ultra-unhealthy regime. Nervous as ever while working, he would continue to smoke over eighty cigarettes a day with his lighter permanently worn around his neck like a good luck charm. He also drank copious cups of black coffee. His heart scares had increased over the years of drug and alcohol abuse; with his strict vegetarian diet doing little to alleviate it. He would consume eggs by the basket-load. Drenched in cholesterol these would further block his arteries making it difficult for oxygen to get to the heart. Mexico City was one of the worst places he could possibly be. As Mel Brooks reflected: "That place was not good for his health."[23]

Still, the only medical complaint Marty suffered during the filming was constipation. It became the big joke on set. But even with his wife and friends around him he still wasn't a happy man: "Why should we expect to be?" he reflected. "We are told we should be happy, but no one tells us how. George Orwell said that all lives, when viewed from within, are a series of failures and I agree. I'm somewhere in the middle and I have occasional excursions into happiness, and other periods of total misery. But most of the time I am neither. I just survive."[24]

His heart had, apparently, been weakened by a shock caused by the legendary *Mad* cartoonist Sergio Aragones. In Mexico City filming a different project, Aragones claims to have put on a military policeman's uniform and visited the set of *Yellowbeard*. Aragones approached Marty with stern authority and violently accosted him. Allegedly, Marty was so shocked and frightened by the encounter that he staggered away clutching his heart. Aragones would dine out on the "I killed Marty Feldman" story for several years.[25]

Filmmaker Michael Mileham, shooting the behind the scenes documentary *Group Madness*, maintains that it was food poisoning that caused, or at least contributed to Marty's death: "We both jumped off the [ship] one day and swam to a little island where there was a fellow selling lobster and coconut. I had the lobster. Marty had the coconut. There was just this one guy on a tiny little island and the next day I got sick with shellfish poisoning. Shellfish poisoning can sometimes take days to affect the body and we figured that the same knife was used to cut his coconut. That could be one reason why he was sick. He was also weak for other reasons."[26]

Still adamant that his brand of comedy only worked if he himself did the stunts, Marty had been doing a scene aboard the mock galleon when he had fallen from the rigging. He did himself no serious damage but breathless and shocked, he had given his heart a thump that he could have well done without.

The film's director, Mel Damski, remembered that: "We had about ninety-five percent of Marty's scenes in the can at that time. We just had no more time or money to finish everything in the script. But we had enough for the film to work." Typically, Marty refused to go home immediately after he was released from the film. Worried that the director didn't have all he needed, he had waited until the very last day of filming... just in case.

Michael Palin confirms that: "Graham told me Marty was there until the very last day of filming. He had done a scene that morning, apparently, and seemed fine. He was looking forward to going home to his wife. He had been counting down the nights until the end of the filming schedule. But Marty wanted to be there until that last day."

Having completed his work on that morning of Thursday 2nd December, Marty had gone tourist shopping in Mexico City. The film's associate producer and Graham Chapman's adopted son and business manager, John Tomiczek, said: "[Marty] was totally devoted to his wife. When I saw him in the street he was looking for things to buy for her."[27]

Late that evening, Marty was alone in his room at the plush Galeria Plaza hotel and telephoned Tomiczek complaining of feeling very ill and having severe chest pains: "[He] called my room in the hotel and asked me to come to him. He was gasping for breath. I went to his room but Marty didn't even have the strength to come to the door. I had to get a key. Marty was lying in the room dying. I cried as I held him. I gave him oxygen and tried my best to save him from dying. I did my best to help him but in the end it was too late. I am shattered that I couldn't save him."[28]

"I found Marty in great pain and began giving him mouth-to-mouth resuscitation. All at once Marty began to talk. He wanted me to say certain things to those close to him. They were personal messages and I can't repeat them because they were private from a dying man."[29] Marty's agent confirmed that: "[Marty] knew he was dying and wanted his wife to know that he loved her dearly. They were a wonderful couple. Lauretta was like his minder. She looked after him when times were bad."

But it was the *News of the World* that screamed the headline: "Blunder killed Marty". It reported that Marty lay dying for one and a half hours before the doctor and ambulance successfully battled through the heavy traffic in the roads surrounding the Mexico City hotel. John Tomiczek was quoted as saying that: "They told me they had got stuck in traffic and couldn't get there any faster. When they finally did arrive, Marty was too far gone even to move. God knows what might have happened if they had managed to get him to a hospital. They did what they could in the room and I just sat there crying and watching the heart monitor machine. Then came that awful moment when it just stopped bleeping." He had given Marty oxygen but it had not helped. "I could see him just sinking before my eyes," he said. It was Tomiczek who rang Lauretta in Los Angeles to relate the last, tender message to her: "They were personal messages between a man and his wife and, when I told her what he had said, she just broke down and wept. It was a heartbreaking thing to have to do."[30]

Some of Marty's friends have privately suggested that his final thoughts were actually of his work rather than his wife. He felt he was letting the film down. Just as on his wedding day, the joke was of paramount importance. Whether Marty's thoughts were with his wife or his work (no doubt it was both), Tomiczek concluded that *Yellowbeard* was a return to form for the comedian: "[It] is pure Marty Feldman at his best," he said. "He is absolutely marvellous in it. It will be a fine tribute to a great man who will be sorely missed."

It was Mr William Whitton, the British Embassy Consular Official in Mexico City, who made the official announcement that Marty had died of "a massive heart attack" at the age of forty-eight.

Marty's co-star, Kenneth Mars remembered: "Somebody said to me, 'Marty's gone.' I said, 'Oh, that's great. They finally let him go home...' And he said, 'No! I mean Marty's *gone*'... We all went out to have dinner afterwards to toast Marty."[31]

Marty's body had been taken from the Galeria Plaza to a local medical centre where Doctor Gabriel Rodriguez-Weaver performed the autopsy. Several friends had said that Marty had been taking drugs as painkillers for a back injury and wondered whether these had contributed to his death. These same friends described Marty as: "Often a sad and sensitive person."[32] But the doctor immediately dismissed rumours that Marty had died of a drugs overdose.[33]

Bill Oddie remains sceptical: "It honestly wasn't surprising that Marty died. Whatever it was. Suicide? Who knows? It's called a heart attack. Amongst the showbiz deaths of recent times of people I've known there have been three I'm not entirely certain about. And all of them were in that bloody film! Marty's one, Graham Chapman is one and Peter Cook is the other. Marty had a history of heart problems but the cause of the attack was cumulative. It was the state he had got himself in. The indulgence of drugs and drinks and the insecurity. All of that."

John Tomiczek said: "I don't know what brought [the heart attack] on. It was natural causes. It would be sad and distressing if people are thinking otherwise."

Tim Brooke-Taylor believes that: "Marty was obviously an ill man. I certainly didn't think he would die at such a young age even though he always said he would. But he had this thyroid problem and you felt that he possibly knew he was more ill than he would let on."

The *Yellowbeard* production office had suppressed the news of Marty's death for eighteen hours but subsequently informed the press that he had finished work on the film just hours before his death: "He had finished his part and... arrangements were being made to ship his body to Los Angeles."[34]

Barry Took was devastated at the news of Marty's death and remembered "a loveable and sensitive man. We were good friends for twenty-five years – ten of them spent writing together."[35] Took told reporters that Marty was even funnier in private than he had been before an audience: "He was a very giving man and would give help to anyone who needed it. I saw him as someone who wanted to do it all – write, perform, direct, produce. He never accepted that no one really can do it all."[36]

Took likened Marty to Tony Hancock in that respect: "He wanted to do everything himself and that is why he went to Hollywood. Marty was one of those men whose career was up and down – he had successes followed by failures, followed by successes, followed by other failures. But people liked him and he was a brilliant comedian."[37]

Benny Hill said: "Marty was brilliant. He was always just that bit ahead of his time."[38]

Eric Idle accompanied the body on the flight back to America while on the evening of 4th December London Weekend Television screened *The Last Remake of Beau Geste* in tribute as a replacement to the scheduled late-night movie.

Alan Spencer remembers: "Marty just went away and never came back. I was determined to attend the funeral. I had never been to a funeral that wasn't for a family member before. I was old enough to drive but still living at my parents. The traffic was dreadful. It was bumper to bumper. I was so worried that I was going to be late that I got into a car pool lane. I was pulled over by a black officer on a motorcycle. He could see I was upset and I asked him if he could quickly write my ticket because I was late for a funeral. He said: 'Are you telling me the truth?' I said: 'Well, look at what I am wearing.' I was in a dark suit and tie. 'You could be a lawyer,' said the cop. 'Whose funeral are you going to?' I told him it was Marty Feldman. 'Are you telling me the truth?' he repeated. 'Yes, really. He was a friend of mine.' This cop said: 'He was a good and funny man. I'll give you an escort.' And sure enough, this police motorcycle escorted me all the way to the cemetery. Lauretta told me that Marty would have loved that."

Marty's erstwhile colleague Henry Polic II[39] cracked jokes and shared anecdotes with the 100 or so mourners who gathered in Forest Lawn in Hollywood Hills Cemetery in the Garden of Heritage in Los Angeles: "Marty never liked funerals," he said, "so I guess he is especially upset at having to come to this one." A five-piece Dixieland jazz band played a selection of his favourite songs including 'I Can't Give You Anything But Love, Baby' while the thirteen-minute service reflected on the laughter that he had provided. "The world will seem sombre without him," said Polic. Rabbi Scott Sperling spoke a few words in Hebrew. Dom DeLuise and Mel Brooks represented his Hollywood film career. "The service was very nice," said Brooks. "Marty was a great fan of comedy and jazz and this helped ease the pain a little. He will be very sadly missed."

Graham Chapman reflected that: "It was just the way Marty wanted it. His close friends decided it was the best kind of memory for his widow. It was a sad day but Marty didn't believe in sadness and he would have loved to have been here to see this."

Fellow expat Brit Ian McShane was also in the congregation as Henry Gibson explained that: "[Marty] died having the last laugh – he is going to end up buried here overlooking Universal Studios."[40] The burial immediately followed the service and was attended by Lauretta alone. Marty's gravestone reads: "He made us laugh. He took my pain away. I love you. Lauretta." He is buried on that Hollywood hillside, just yards away from his lifelong hero and inspiration, Buster Keaton. Stan Laurel is buried a short walk away. Marionettes of men, forever willing to put themselves through physical and mental torture in the name of comedy, together in a foreign field a part of which will forever be England. It was the greatest accolade Marty could have wished for.

Epilogue

"I do not disbelieve in anything. I start from the premise that everything is true until proved false. Everything is possible."

M arty may never have quite come to terms with why he was funny. He just was. The only reaction he could judge by was: "because I can hear people laughing. I can't tell you why they laugh. I can tell you the devices I use. Anybody can develop devices, but that's not being comic. I won't take bets I can make you laugh. I never know if I can do it again. If a joke falls flat, it's no good saying it was a lovely joke. If there isn't a laugh, you have no cop-out. If they don't laugh, it wasn't funny. You said you'd make them laugh, and they didn't. In fact, I'm always amazed when anybody laughs. I'm not as good as I want to be. I'm always aware of what I'm striving for, though the audience marks me on their own yardstick. They may give me eight out of ten, and I'll say I was only worth four."[1]

When *Yellowbeard* finally emerged in September 1983 it was a gift: "For Marty". The press release said that the role of Gilbert was: "destined to be this great actor-comedian's final portrayal... It is fitting that the beloved Feldman's final role should also be one of his finest. He slides in and out of seven different characterizations, ranging from a waterfront hag to a Lionel Barrymore look-alike..." As an epitaph, *Yellowbeard* is certainly a flawed one but as a jamboree of past-their-sell-by-date comedians gathered together for one last over-the-top jape it is hard to beat. In the end, Marty died in harness, at the centre of some of comedy's finest talent. Many friends cited his performance as his very finest film work, although it was certainly not going to trouble the good folk at the Academy. For David Weddle it was "like watching Buster Keaton stuck in one of those dreadful 'Beach Party' movies. You waited for the flashes of brilliance. However bad the film was, Marty could never be anything but brilliant. Even at the end there was no sign of his joy in physical comedy failing him. He was still a creative person, expressing himself through slapstick comedy. Marty was still trying to fight the good fight."

"He was on very good form, I'm glad to say," said Graham Chapman. "He'd had a couple of sad years before that which is why I was very keen for him to be in it. Suddenly everything looked great for him again and then that happened."[2] As Marty explained: "I better laugh because if I don't laugh I'll go mad." Graham Chapman had given him something to laugh about again.

"My own theory is that if Marty had lived he would have been in great demand," says Alan Spencer. "There were distinct signs of a renaissance for him. He was a wonderful actor. I can see him being cast in Shakespeare. I can see Peter Jackson casting him as Gollum in *Lord of the Rings* and I can certainly see Tim Burton using him all the time."

As the *Daily Express* noted at the time, Hollywood may have chewed him up and spat him out, "[giving] him his posthumous Oscar by burying him next to his hero, Buster Keaton, [but] Hollywood society will find its dollar-digging grief shallow. It'll be jumping out of it this morning, and running along the road towards the next sunrise of a British comedian who can add gold to its glitter." But Britain had tended to forget Marty as well. Despite the press noting in December 1982 that: "It's the little people who first spotted him on the little British box who'll miss the frog-eyed Cockney who looked like a cross between a chameleon and two poached eggs in a very non-stick pan," the passing years have left his legacy largely uncelebrated.[3]

A footnote to the achievements of the Oxbridge generation, Marty's work for British television has enjoyed just a handful of repeats since his death.[4]

As an actor, *Young Frankenstein* remains Marty's most potent and familiar contribution to popular culture. It ranked at number thirteen on the American Film Institute list of the 100 Funniest American Movies, while in 2003 it was considered sufficiently "culturally, historically or aesthetically significant" by the United States National Film Preservation Board to warrant a copy being preserved in the Library of Congress National Film Registry. But this is largely seen as a nod to Mel Brooks. Indeed, in 2007, Brooks staged *Young Frankenstein* as a Broadway musical. Susan Stroman directed the show and, suitably, Christopher Fitzgerald emulated Marty and stole all the plaudits as Igor.

As a writer, *Round the Horne* remains Marty's most lasting legacy. The BBC have endlessly repeated and repackaged the entire run of programmes until the shrill jabbering of Julian and Sandy, Ramblin' Syd Rumpo and Chou en Ginsberg have become shorthand for everything that is gay – in every sense of the word – about Britain. But again, this accolade is largely hung round the camp, limp wrist of Kenneth Williams. A successful London stage play, *Round the Horne... Revisited* recreated a typical recording session.

No, it was largely just two British citizens who protected, cherished and celebrated Marty Feldman. His two partners in life: Lauretta Feldman and Barry Took. One – Lauretta – did it quietly and privately. She gave only a handful of interviews about her life with Marty. Her memories were so many and too precious.[5] "I'll never get over it," she said. "It was twenty-five years of my life. I still haven't let go, and that's my problem... Marty's still in Mexico as far as I'm concerned – and he's coming home."[6] For decades after Marty's death, she kept the home in Hollywood's Laurel Canyon exactly the same. Just in case.

But when it came to protecting the Marty brand and his huge back catalogue, Lauretta could be ruthless. She would often visit the Venue Theatre, Leicester Square where *Round the Horne... Revisited* was being performed and count up the number of Marty lines that were being used.[7]

"Marty was a very generous, creative man," explains Suzannah Galland. "He wasn't possessive about his work. His great traits were that he was loyal and that he had great honour. He didn't care if someone else used what he had written and took the credit. Lauretta however would hit the roof!"

Tim Brooke-Taylor was grateful for such perspicacity: "I spoke to Lauretta not that long ago because we were having problems with the *At Last the 1948 Show* rights. We were making sure that Paradine or whoever bought it up were not going to get everything. She was very good at that behind closed doors, legal rankling."

Lauretta had continued to smoke, drink, enjoy jazz and visit nightclubs with her inner circle of friends. She died, aged seventy-four, on 12th March 2010, a few days after being diagnosed with a brain tumour. Both Alan Spencer and David Weddle had kept in touch with her over the years. "About six months before she died we took her out for dinner," remembers Weddle. "It wasn't a boastful thing but we had both done well and we wanted Lauretta to know that Marty had obviously seen something in us that had eventually come out. She was delighted to know that he had passed on the flame to Alan and I."

Barry Took was the public side of Marty's lasting legacy. A regular television and radio broadcaster, he would often discuss his comedy career and always cite Marty's contribution to *Bootsie and Snudge* and *Round the Horne*. Through documentaries, retrospectives and chat show reminiscences, Barry would haul out the familiar stories, laugh along at radio snippets and celebrate the Golden Age of Comedy that he and Marty had contributed so greatly to. In 1993 London's National Film Theatre included Marty in its "Funny Men" season. Barry Took attended without fuss and happily chatted about his old colleague in the bar after the screening. Barry was a peerless comedy pundit up until his death on 31st March 2002 at the age of seventy-three. John Cleese spoke at his memorial service, putting forward Barry and Marty's *The Walrus and the Carpenter* as an example of the perfect television situation comedy. Coming from the co-writer of *Fawlty Towers*, that's high praise indeed.

Now that both his closest champions have gone, it falls to those admirers who still smile when they see Marty Feldman in action. His legacy is a long and hilarious one; a precious body of work of truly inspired lunacy that leapt from deep behind those outrageously diverse eyes of his. "I could have them fixed," he once said, "but what the hell? This face is a map of what I am, where I've been and what I've done in the past. The tragic turns to slapstick in my hands. I can only see the absurdity."

"I hope there is a heaven," reflected Barry Took in 1983.[8] "When I get there Marty will greet me and say, 'Hey, love, terrific. Now – er... I've got this six-picture deal with St. Peter... why don't we... put it together – like we did when we were alive."

Marty's Credits

"The pen is mightier than the sword, and considerably easier to write with."

Show Case BBC Television: 18th April 1955, 7.45-8.30pm. Producer Ernest Maxin.

Variety Parade BBC Television: 23rd July 1955, 9.45-10.45pm. Producer Ernest Maxin.

Comedy Item BBC Television: 12th September 1955, 5.10-5.20pm. Producer P. Newington.

The Billy Cotton Band Show BBC Television: 29th March 1956, 8.30-9.15pm. Producer Brian Tesler.

The Jimmy Wheeler Show BBC Television: 9th June 1956, 8-9pm. Producer Harry Carlisle.

August Bank Holiday BBC Television: 6th August 1956, 8-9pm. Producer Ernest Maxin.

Fancy Free: ATV. Wrote and performed.

Educating Archie BBC Radio series 8: From 25th September 1957.

Educating Archie: Associated-Rediffusion. Series 1. 13 episodes. 26th September 1958 – 20th February 1959. Fortnightly, Friday 6.10-6.40pm. Episode 1: Written by Ronald Chesney & Marty: 26th September 1958. Episode 2: Written by Marty & Barry Pevan: 10th October 1958. Episode 3: Written by Ronald Chesney & Marty: 24th October

1958. Episode 4: Written by Marty & Barry Pevan: 7th November 1958. Episode 5: Written by Ronald Chesney & Marty: 21st November 1958. Episode 6: Written by Marty & Barry Pevan: 5th December 1958. Episode 7: Written by Ronald Chesney & Marty: 19th December 1958. Episode 8: Written by Ronald Chesney & Marty: 2nd January 1959. Episode 9: Written by Marty & Barry Pevan: 16th January 1959. Episode 10: Written by Marty & Barry Pevan: 30th January 1959. Episode 11: Written by Ronald Chesney & Marty: 13th February 1959. Episode 12: Written by Marty & Barry Pevan: 27th February 1959. Episode 13: Written by Ronald Chesney & Marty: 20th March 1959. Directed by Christopher Hodson. Series 2. 14 episodes. 18th September – 25th December 1959. Weekly, Friday 6.30-7pm. Episode 1: 'The Man Who Couldn't Grow Up' written by Marty & Ronald Wolfe. Director Christopher Hodson: 18th September 1959. Episode 2: 'The Prune Mutiny' written by Marty & Ronald Wolfe. Director Christopher Hodson: 25th September 1959. Episode 3: 'The Day the Bongolis Left' written by Marty & Ronald Wolfe. Director Christopher Hodson: 2nd October 1959. Episode 4: 'The Man Who Lost His Pants at Monte Carlo' written by Marty & Ronald Wolfe. Director Christopher Hodson: 9th October 1959. Episode 6: Written by Marty & Ronald Wolfe. Director Christopher Hodson: 23rd October 1959. Episode 7: 'Don't Put Your Nephew on the Stage' written by Ronald Chesney, Marty & Ronald Wolfe. Director Christopher Hodson: 30th October 1959. Episode 8: 'The Case of the Missing Aunt' written by Ronald Chesney, Marty & Ronald Wolfe. Director Christopher Hodson: 6th November 1959. Episode 9: 'The Day We Fooled the Fuhrer' written by Ronald Chesney, Marty & Ronald Wolfe. Director Pat Baker: 13th November 1959. Episode 10: 'Brough and the Bald-Headed Bandit' written by Ronald Chesney, Marty & Ronald Wolfe. Director Bill Turner: 20th November 1959. Episode 11: 'The Man with the Golden Feet' written by Ronald Chesney, Marty & Ronald Wolfe. Director Bill Turner: 27th November 1959. Episode 12: Written by Ronald Chesney, Marty & Ronald Wolfe. Director Bill Turner: 4th December 1959. Episode 13: Written by Ronald Chesney, Marty & Ronald Wolfe. Director Bill Turner: 11th December 1959.

Educating Archie BBC Radio series 9: From 28th September 1958.

Take It From Here BBC Radio series 13: From 22nd October 1959.

The Army Game Granada Television: Series 4. 4 episodes: 20th May 1960: settings by Stanley Mills, written by Sid Colin, Lewis Schwarz, Maurice Wiltshire, Barry Took & Marty. Director Gordon Flemyng. Producer: Peter Eton. 3rd June 1960. 17th June 1960. 1 unidentified. Regular cast: Private Montague 'Excused Boots' Bisley: Alfie Bass. Sergeant Major Claude Snudge: Bill Fraser. Private Leonard Bone: Ted Lune. Corporal 'Flogger' Hoskins: Harry Fowler. Captain T. R. Pocket: Frank Williams. Private Bill Baker: Robert Desmond (not in 2nd, 3rd). L/Cpl Ernest 'Moosh' Merryweather: Mario Fabrizi (not in 1st). Series 5. 1 episode. Tuesday 4th October

1960: Designer Stanley Mills. Written by Barry Took & Marty. Director Max Morgan-Witts. Producer Peter Eton. Regular cast: Sergeant Major Percy Bullimore: William Hartnell. Major Upshot-Bagley: Geoffrey Sumner. Private 'Chubby' Catchpole: Dick Emery. Private Leonard Bone: Ted Lune. Corporal 'Flogger' Hoskins: Harry Fowler. Captain T. R. Pocket: Frank Williams. L/Cpl Ernest 'Moosh' Merryweather: Mario Fabrizi.

Bootsie and Snudge Granada Television: Series 1. Broadcast Friday 23rd September 1960 – 16th June 1961, 8.55pm-9.25pm. Episodes 1-18 written by Barry Took and Marty. (Note: Episode 5 includes an on-screen title: 'A Day Off'.) Episodes 20-22 and 24 written by Marty. Episodes 27-29 written by Barry Took and Marty. Episode 33 written by Barry Took and Marty. Episode 35 written by Barry Took and Marty. Episode 38 written by Ray Rigby, Barry Took and Marty. Episode 39 written by Barry Took and Marty. Designed by Stanley Mills [except episodes 4-6, designed by Bernard Carey]. Directed by Milo Lewis. Produced by Peter Eton [except episode 33, produced by Eric Fawcett]. Regular cast: Montague 'Bootsie' Bisley: Alfie Bass. Claude Snudge: Bill Fraser. Henry Beerbohm Johnson: Clive Dunn. Rt Hon Sec Hesketh Pendleton: Robert Dorning.

Bootsie and Snudge Granada Television: Series 2. Friday 27th October – 29th December 1961, 8.55pm-9.25pm. Then, from episode 11, Thursday 4th January – 10th May 1962, 8.30-9pm (except episode 24, 7.30-8pm). Episode 1 by Barry Took & Marty. Episode 7: 'Higher Purpose' by Marty, David Cumming & Derek Collyer. Episode 8: 'The Second Second World War' by Marty. Episode 9: 'End of the World' by Marty. Episode 10: by Marty. Episode 13: by Marty. Episode 14: by Marty. Episode 16: by Marty. Episode 17: by Marty. Episodes 18-20: by Barry Took & Marty. Episode 21: by Marty. Episodes 23-24: by Marty. Episodes 26-29: by Marty. Designer: Stanley Mills. Director: Milo Lewis. Producer: Peter Eton. Series edited by Barry Took & Marty.

Bootsie and Snudge Granada Television: Series 3: 39 episodes, Thursdays 8th November 1962 – 30th May 1963, 7.30-8pm. Episode 1: 'Come in Eskimo Nell' by Barry Took & Marty. Episode 4: 'The Importance of Being Jumbo' by Barry Took & Marty. Episode 6: 'The Toerag' by Barry Took & Marty. Episode 9 by Barry Took & Marty. Episode 10: 'The Man with the Golden Guts' by Barry Took & Marty. Episode 11: 'The Incredible Tattooed Bisley' by Barry Took & Marty. Episode 12 by Barry Took & Marty. Episode 14: 'Cupid in Paddington' by Barry Took & Marty. Designer Stanley Mills, Directors Eric Fawcett, Derek Bennett (episode 4 & 11) Producers Peter Eton (1-15) & Milo Lewis (16-29).

On the Braden Beat ATV. Written material by Barry Took and Marty.

The Dick Emery Show BBC Television: additional material for first series in 1963.

Frankie Howerd At The Establishment And At The BBC The Decca Record Company, 1963. Side two material by Barry Took and Marty; by courtesy of the BBC

Comedy Playhouse: 'Nicked at the Bottle' BBC Television 16th November 1963. 9.25-9.55pm. Written by Marty. Producer Michael Mills. Mossy: George Cole. Mrs Emily Trout: Margaretta Scott. Mrs Martin: Doris Hare. Jeremy Trout: James Villiers. Mr McMurtrie: Charles Heslop. Samantha Trout: Gabriella Licudi.

Comedy Playhouse: 'The Walrus and the Carpenter'. BBC Television. 14th December 1963. 9.35-10.10pm. Written by Marty and Barry Took (uncredited). Producer Michael Mills. Gascoigne Quilt: Felix Aylmer. Luther Flannery: Hugh Griffith.

Dee Time: 1964. Marty as guest.

Comedy Playhouse: 'Good Luck Sir, You've Got A Lucky Face'. BBC Television. 31st January 1964. 7.35-8pm. Written by Marty. Producer Dennis Main Wilson. Gomorrah Weevil: Graham Stark. Harold Harbinger: Derek Francis. Jessop: Frank Thornton. Mrs Harbinger: Thelma Ruby. Lord Fenwick: Geoffrey Dunn.

Comedy Parade: 'Wilkie'. BBC Radio, the Light Programme. 24th September 1964, 8-8.30pm. Written by Marty. Starred Clive Dunn with Derek Guyler, Doris Hare and Keith Smith. Music by Alf Edwards. Producer John Browell.

Scott On...Birds BBC2. Saturday 19th December 1964. 9.25-10.10pm. Written by Marty & Barry Took. Producer Dennis Main Wilson. Starring Terry Scott and Rita Webb.

The Walrus and the Carpenter. BBC1. Written by Marty and Barry Took. Producer James Gilbert. Episode 1: 'Return to Lumley Hoo', 2nd March 1965. Episode 2: 'The Coffin They Carry You Off In', 9th March 1965. Episode 3: 'Luther Flannery Revisited', 16th March 1965. Episode 4: 'Luther and the Golden Fleece', 23rd March 1965. Episode 5: 'The Quarrel', 30th March 1965. Episode 6: 'The Secret Life of Gascoigne Quilt', 6th April 1965.

Round the Horne. BBC Radio. Series 1: 7th March – 20 June 1965. 16 episodes. Written by Barry Took and Marty. Starring Kenneth Horne, Kenneth Williams, Hugh Paddick, Betty Marsden, Bill Pertwee, Douglas Smith.

Scott On...Money BBC2. Saturday 15th May 1965, 9.30-10.15pm. *Scott On...Food* BBC2. Saturday 5th June 1965, 9.50-10.40pm. Written by Marty and Barry Took. Producer Dennis Main Wilson.

Comedy Playhouse: 'Barnaby Spoot and the Exploding Whoopee Cushion'. BBC1. Friday 28th May 1965, 8-8.25pm. Written by Marty and Barry Took. Exceutive Producer Graeme Muir. Producer Dick Clement. Barnaby Spoot: John Bird. Mr Bostock: John le Mesurier. Justin Fribble: Ronald Lacey. Marcissus Font: Sheila Steafel.

Comedy Playhouse: 'Here I Come Whoever I Am'. BBC1. Friday 11th June 1965, 8-8.25pm. Written by Marty. Executive Producer Graeme Muir. Producer Dennis Main Wilson. Ambrose Twombly: Bernard Cribbins. Mousy Bird (Greta Spavin): Helen Fraser.

Comedy Playhouse: 'Memoirs of a Chaise Longue'. BBC1. Friday 2nd July 1965, 8-8.30pm. Written by Marty and Barry Took. Producer Graeme Muir Voice of the Chaise Longue: Alan Melville. 'Mixed Doubles' with Fenella Fielding and Jack Watling. 'Creature of Habit' with Betty Marsden and John le Mesurier. 'A Warm Reception' with J.G. Devlin and Shay Gorman.

The New London Palladium Show: 'Val Parnell's Sunday Night at the London Palladium'. Performance and script. ITV Sunday 26th September 1965.

The Eamonn Andrews Show: with Marty, Barry Took, Lance Percival, Miriam Karlin and Shepherd Mead. 1965.

Barney is my Darling. BBC1. Friday 17th December 1965 – 21st January 1966, mostly 7.30-8pm. Written by Marty and Barry Took. Producer James Gilbert. Barney Pank: Bill Fraser. Ramona Pank: Irene Handl. Cissie: Angela Crow. Miss Hobbitt: Pat Coombs.

Line Up/Review BBC Television: 7th January 1966. Discussion on TV Comedy. Producer J. Smith.

The Frost Report. Series 1. BBC1. 13, 25 minute episodes. Thursday 10th March – 9th June 1966, mostly 9-9.25pm. Script editor and writer Marty. Producer James Gilbert Starring David Frost, John Cleese, Ronnie Barker, Ronnie Corbett, Sheila Steafel and Nicky Henson.

Round the Horne Series 2 BBC Radio. 13 epsiodes. Sunday 13th March – 5th June 1966.

Frost Over England: BBC1 Sunday 26th March 1967, 7.25-8pm.

The Frost Report. Series 2. BBC1. 13, 25 minute episodes. Thursday 6th April – 29th June 1967, mostly 9.9.25pm.

Frost Over Christmas: BBC1. Tuesday 26th December 1967, 7.30-8.10pm.

Show of the Week: Roy Hudd: BBC2. Tuesday 17th May 1966, 9-9.50pm. Written by Eric Davidson and Dick Vosburgh. Additional material by Bill Solly, Marty and Barry Took. Producer Michael Hurll. Starring Roy Hudd, Barbara Young and Doug Fisher.

Comedy Playhouse: 'Judgement Day for Elijah Jones'. BBC1. Tuesday 7th June 1966, 7.30-8pm. Written by Marty. Director John Street. Producer Dennis Main Wilson. Elijah Jones: Clive Dunn. Arnold: Bernard Cribbins. Elijah's Wife: Priscilla Morgan.

Round the Horne: BBC Radio. 22nd July 1966. Transcription Service recording remake of Series 1, episode 12.

Round the Horne: BBC Radio. 25th December 1966.

Round the Horne: BBC Radio. Series 3. 20 episodes. Sunday 12th February – 25th June 1967, 1.30-2pm.

At Last the 1948 Show. Rediffusion Television. Series 1. Wednesday 15th February – 22nd March 1967, around 10-10.30pm. Starring Tim Brooke-Taylor, Graham Chapman, John Cleese, Marty and Aimi MacDonald.

Dee Time: ITV 13th July 1967, 6.35-7.05pm. Guests Tim Brooke-Taylor, John Cleese, Graham Chapman, Marty and Salena Jones. Music by Bernard Herrmann and the Northern Dance Orchestra. Designer Peter Mavius. Producer Terry Henebery. Director Sydney Lotterby.

At Last the 1948 Show. Rediffusion. Series 2. Tuesdays, 26th September – 7th November 1967, 8.30-9pm (except episode 3 8.45-9.15pm and episode 4 9.30-10pm).

At Last the 1948 Show. Pye Records limited. 1967. 1. 'Book Shop', 'Sheepdog Trials', 'Where Were You?', 'The Wonderful World of the Ant', 'Gentleman Farmer', 'Witch', 'Top of the Form', 'Someone Has Stolen the News', 'One-Man Battalion'. 2. 'Doctor and Man with Skinny Legs', 'Minsterial Breakdown', 'Job Description', 'Engine Driver', 'The Four Sydney Lotterbys', 'Bee-Keeping', 'The Ferret Shop', 'Vox Pop'.

No – That's Me Over Here! Rediffusion. Episodes 1-5, Tuesday 14th November – 12th December 1967, 8.30-9pm. Episode 6, Tuesday 19th December 8.45-9.15pm. Written by Barry Cryer, Graham Chapman and Eric Idle. Music by Mike Vicers. Played by the Cyril Stapleton Orchestra. Designed by Bernard Goodwin (episodes 1-2) and Frank Gillman (episodes 3-6). Producers Bill Hitchcock and Marty. Executive Producer David Frost.

What's So Funny About Our Food: BBC Radio 4. 8th August 1968. Three minute sketch written by Marty and Barry Took.

Broaden Your Mind: BBC2. Monday 28th October 1968. Included 30 second quickie sketch written by Marty and Barry Took. Producer Sydney Lotterby. Cast: Tim Brooke-Taylor, Graeme Garden, Jo Kendall and Nick McArdle.

How to Irritate People. David Paradine Productions Limited, 1968. Written by Graham Chapman and John Cleese. Additional material by Tim Brooke-Taylor and Marty. Executive Producer David Frost Cast: John Cleese, Tim Brooke-Taylor, Graham Chapman, Michael Palin, Connie Booth and Gillian Lind.

Marty: BBC2. Series 1, 6 episodes. Monday 29th April – 3rd June 1968, 8-8.30pm. Director Roger Race. Producer Dennis Main Wilson. Written by Marty Feldman & Barry Took, with John Cleese & Graham Chapman, Terry Jones & Michael Palin, John Junkin, Denis King, Donald Webster, Tim Brooke-Taylor & Graeme Garden, William Lynn, Frank Muir & Denis Morden, George Evans & Derek Collyer, Terry Nation.

Line Up. BBC Television: 29th April 1968. Producer Mike Appleton. Interviewee about 'The Marty Feldman Show' [sic].

Marty Feldman: Now and Then. BBC: 5th June 1968.

Horne A'Plenty. ABC. 29th June 1968. Script editor Barry Took. Additional material by Marty. Producer Pat Johns.

Dee Time: 31st August/14th September 1968. Producer Colin Chapman. With guests Lord Arran, Rod Taylor, Zsa Zsa Gabor, Richard Harris and Marty.

According to Dora: Creature Comforts. BBC1. 3rd September 1968. Script editor David Climie. Written by David Cumming, Marty, Willis Hall, Arthur Macrae and Keith Waterhouse.

Points of View: BBC Television. 19th September 1968. Producer Iain Johnstone. Short piece to camera.

Desert Island Discs: 23rd September 1968. Presented by Roy Plomley. Marty's castaway choice of records: 'The Bridge' Sonny Rollins. Concerto in D Minor for oboe, strings and continuo (opus 9, no. 2) by Tomaso Giovanni Albinoni, performed by the Musici Orchestra with soloist Evert van Tright. 'Parker's Mood' Charlie Parker. Symphonie Fantastique by Hector Berlioz, performed by the London Symphony Orchestra conducted by Pierre Boulez. 'God Bless the Child' Billie Holiday. 'Oh Mr. Porter' Mammoth Gavioli Fair Organ. 'Wednesday Night Prayer Meeting' Charles Mingus. Le Roi David performed by the French National Radio Orchestra with soloist Janine Micheau, composed and conducted by Arthur Honegger. Book: *The Little Prince* by Antoine de Saint-Exupéry. Luxury item: a piano.

Marty. Pye Records Limited 1968. Tracks: 1. 'Irritation', 'Weighing Machine', 'Ticket Agency', 'Father & Son', 'Police Notice', 'God', 'Woodworm', 'Headmaster', 'Lady Chatterly'. 2. 'Weather Forecast', 'Funny He Never Married', 'Eye-O-Fry', 'Travel Agency', 'Parliamentary Report', 'Eat Your Prunes', 'Bishop', 'Ballet', 'Salome'. Tape editing by David Hunt. Producer Monty Presky. Cast: Marty, John Junkin, Tim Brooke-Taylor, Roland MacLeod, Patricia Denys, Mary Miller, Diana Quiseekay and Sonia Dresdel.

Marty. BBC2. Series 2, 7 episodes. Monday 9th December 1968 – 13th January 1969, 8.50-9.20pm. Written by Marty & Barry Took, with John Cleese & Graham Chapman, Terry Jones & Michael Palin, John Junkin, Denis King, Roland MacLeod, Paul McDowell & Robin Grove-White, Jim Franklin, Michael Seddon.

Christmas Night with the Stars: *Marty* segment 'Marty Sings A Song of Christmas'. BBC1. Wednesday 25th December 1968, 6.40-8.45pm.

'Joyous Time of the Year' & 'The B Side'. Decca Records single. 1968.

The Val Doonican Show: 28th December 1968. Producer John Ammonds. From the Golders Green Hippodrome with guests Marty, the Gojos, the Adam Singers, Herman's Hermits and Dev Shawn.

Bradens Week: 28th December 1968. Producer John Lloyd.

Line Up: BBC Television. 31st December 1968. Producer Betty White.

It's Marty: Montreux Promotion. BBC2 4th March 1969. Producer Richard Drewett.

It's Marty: Montreux Compilation. BBC1 17th March 1969.

Comedy Playhouse: 'Tooth and Claw'. BBC1. Monday 28th April 1969, 7.30-8pm. Written by Marty & Barry Took. Director Roger Race. Producer Barry Lupino. Reuben Tooth: Warren Mitchell. Sydney Claw: Marty Feldman. Clanders: Richard Caldicot. Silt: Anthony Dawes. Waiter: Norman Chappell. Narrated by Ronald Fletcher.

Dee Time: BBC Television 3rd May 1969. Producer Roger Ordish. With guests Marty, Ben Gazzara and Sandie Shaw.

Comedy Playhouse: 'The Making of Peregrine'. BBC1. Monday 19th May 1969, 7.30-8pm. Written by Marty and Barry Took. Producer Barry Lupino. Stanley Mold: Dick Emery. Minerva Mold: Pat Coombs. Peregrine Mold: Andrew Ray. Rory: Sam Kydd.

Marty Feldman: One Pair of Eyes BBC Television. 7th June 1969. Producer Francis Megahy.

The Question Why: Recorded 7th September 1969. Producer Peter Chafer.

London Aktuell. BBC Television. 9th November 1969. Documentary contribution.

The Wednesday Play: 'Double Bill' (comprising 'Compartment' and 'Playmates'). BBC1 26th November 1969 Original Music by Carl Davis. Written by Johnny Speight. Script Edited by Shaun MacLoughlin. Produced by Graeme MacDonald. Bill: Marty. The Woman: Eileen Atkins. The Man: Joby Blanshard. The Wife: Diane Aubrey. The Husband: Donald Gee.

I Feel a Song Going Off: The Decca Record Company, 1969. Songs written by Denis King and John Junkin. Musical Director Denis King. Additional Arrangements Ivor Raymonde. Recording Engineers Bill Price and Roy Baker. Assistant Engineer Peter Rynston. Producer Ray Richardson. Tracks: 1. 'Waltzing with You', 'District Nurse Hargreaves', 'The World's in Rhyme', 'The Elephant Song', 'Eurovision Song', 'Ilford Town Hall', 'Kensington High Street', 'La Sauce', 'There's a Little Part of Me', 'Psychedelic Rubbish', 'The Five to Eleven Waltz'. 2. 'Mavis Wavertree', 'You without Me', 'The Great Bell', 'Death', 'The Back of Your Neck', 'My Father's Shirt', 'Please Let Me Love You', 'Bayswater Road', 'Cautious Love Song', 'French Folk Song', 'No Nuts', 'Loo', 'Eternity'.

The Harry Secombe Show BBC Television: 1969-1973. One episode written by Marty and Barry Took.

Christmas Night with the Stars. BBC1. 25th December 1969. 'It's Marty' segment.

The Bed Sitting Room. 1969. Screenplay by John Antrobus. Adapted by Charles Wood from the play by John Antrobus and Spike Millgan. Music Ken Thorne. Photography David Watkin. Production Designer Assheton Gorton. Produced by Oscar Lewenstein and Richard Lester. Director Richard Lester. Cast in order of height Rita Tushingham, Dudley Moore, Harry Secombe, Arthur Lowe, Roy Kinnear, Spike Milligan, Ronald Fraser, Jimmy Edwards, Michael Hordern, Peter Cook and Ralph Richardson, with Ronnie Brody, Dandy Nichols, Jack Shepherd, Frank Thornton, Mona Washbourne, Henry Woolf and introducing Marty as Nurse Arthur.

Jumbo – Ein Elefantenlenben. West Germany, French and Austria co-production, 1970. Director Michael Pfleghar. Jumbo-Kapitan: Eddie Constantine. Orville Wright: Marty, with Jean-Pierre Cassel and Mario Adorf.

Nationwide. 4th March 1970. Producer Derrick Amoore. Interviewee.

Every Home Should Have One. UK release 5th March 1970. Screenplay by Marty, Barry Took and Denis Norden. Story by Herbert Kretzmer and Milton Shulman. Music John Cameron. Photography Ken Hodges. Art director Roy Stannard. Titles Richard Williams Studios. Associate producer Terry Glinwood. Produced by Ned Sherrin. Director Jim Clark. Teddy Brown: Marty. Liz Brown: Judy Cornwell. Wallace Trufitt: Patrick Cargill. Nat Kaplan: Shelley Berman. Inga Giltenburg: Julie Ege. Geoffrey Mellish: Dinsdale Landen. Chandler: Moray Watson. Secretary: Annabel Leventon. Colonel Belper: John McKelvey. McLaughlin: Jack Watson. Mrs. Monty Levin: Patience Collier. Lotte von Gelbstein: Penelope Keith. Joanna Snow: Sarah Badel. Magistrate: Michael Bates. Defence Solicitor: Alan Bennett. Maud Crape: Frances de la Tour. Wednesday Play Star: Dave Dee. Mrs. Kaplan: Hy Hazell. Dracula's victim: Judy Huxtable. Jimpson: Harold Innocent. Tolworth: John Wells. T.V. Production Assistant: Marianne Stone.

Frost at the London Palladium for the British Film and Television Awards: British Academy Film Awards. 8th March 1970. Marty presented award.

Marty Amok. BBC1. Monday 30th March 1970. 8-8.45pm. Written by Marty, Barry Took, Michael Palin, Terry Jones, Johnnie Mortimer and Brian Cooke. Director Roger Race. Producer Michael Mills. Cast: Marty, Tim Brooke-Taylor, John Junkin, Vivian Stanshall, Mary Miller and Robert Dhery.

The Dean Martin Show: 8th October 1970, 11th February 1971, 4th March 1971, 25th March 1971.

Dean Martin Presents Golddiggers in London. 14th November 1970. Guests Marty, Julian Chagrin, Charles Nelson Reilly and Tommy Tune.

The Royal Variety Show: BBC1. 15th November 1970.

Marty Abroad: BBC2. Friday 1st January 1971. 9.20-10pm. Written by Johnnie Mortimer and Brian Cooke. Producer Gordon Flemyng. Cast: Marty and John Junkin.

Frankie Howerd: The Laughing Stock of Television. Thames Television. Wednesday 14th April 1971, 8-9pm. Written by Marty and Barry Took ('Dr. Inlay's Bookcase' sketch), Ray Galton and Alan Simpson, Talbot Rothwell. Directed and produced by John Robins.

One Man's Week: Barry Took. BBC Radio. 1st May 1971. Featured 'Serial Addiction' a previously unused three minute long sketch written by Marty and Barry Took.

The Magnificent Seven Deadly Sins: Tigon Pictures, UK release November 1971. 'Lust' written by Graham Stark, based on a story by Marty. Ambrose: Harry H. Corbett. 'Sloth' written by and starring Spike Milligan. David Lodge, Graham Stark. Guest appearances Ronnie Barker, Peter Butterworth, Marty, Cardew Robinson, Madeline Smith. Director Graham Stark.

Flip Flip Wilson variety show. Series 2, episode 14. 23rd December 1971.

The Marty Feldman Comedy Machine: ATV. 14, 60 minute episodes. Fridays 1st October 1971 – 14th January 1972, mostly 10.35-11.35pm Executive producer Colin Clews. Producer Larry Gelbart. Director John Robins. Written by Marty, Spike Milligan, Barry Levinson, Larry Gelbart, Rudy DeLuca. Regular cast: Marty, Spike Milligan, Hugh Paddick, Bob Todd, Alan Price, Clovissa Newcombe, Patricia Hayes, Valentine Dyall, Roland MacLeod, Jack Parnell and His Orchestra, the Irving Davies Dancers. Guest stars included Orson Welles, Groucho Marx, Roger Moore, Dusty Springfield, Marsha Hunt, Art Carney, Randy Newman, Beryl Reid, Barbara Feldon, Jackie Vernon, Thelma Houston, Godfrey Cambridge, Tom Paxton, Gilbert O'Sullivan.

The Best of the Comedy Machine: Montreux Compilation. 15th February 1972.

The Marty Feldman Comedy Machine: ABC. 14, 30 minute edited episodes. 12th April – 23rd August 1972.

The Marty Feldman Show. Australian TV, 1972. Original music by Geoff Harvey. Cinematography Russell Boyd. Editor Stephen Priest. Director Brian Trenchard-Smith. Produced by David Hannay and Bill Hughes. Cast: Marty and Willie Fennell.

Today Mexico, Tomorrow the World. 1972

Sommer-Sprossen. 1972. Hosted by Elke Sommer. Director Michael Pfleghar.

The Johnny Carson Show: 17th August 1972.

Hollywood Squares: 9th October 1972.

The Sandy Duncan Show: 'The Importance of Being Ernestine'. 15th October 1972. Ben Hampton: Eric Christmas. Sandy Stockton: Sandy Duncan. Kay Fox: Marian Mercer. Alex Lembeck: M. Emmet Walsh. Hilary: Pam Zarit. With Marty.

Hallmark Hall of Fame: 'The Man Who Came to Dinner'. 29th November 1972. Adapted by Sam Denoff from the Moss Hart play. Sheridan Whiteside: Orson Welles. Maggie Cutler: Lee Remick. Lorraine Sheldon: Joan Collins. Banjo: Marty. Beverly Carlton: Michael Gough. Dr Bradley: Don Knotts. Nurse Preen: Mary Wickes.

Flip. Series 3, episode 15. 18th January 1973.

It's Lulu. Series 3, episode 4. BBC1. 6th October 1973. Performer and script. Producer John Ammonds. Director Vic Meredith.

What's My Line? BBC1 13th December 1973. Mystery guest. Chairman David Jacobs. Panel Isobel Barnett, Kenneth Williams, William Franklyn and Nanette Newman. Producer Ernest Maxin.

The Two Ronnies Series 3, episode 2. 1973. Writer.

Pebble Mill at One: 28th January 1974. Interviewee. Producer Roy Ronnie.

Marty Back Together Again: BBC1 4, 30 minute episodes, Wednesday 20th February – 27th March 1974, around 9.30-10pm. Written by Johnny Speight, Marty and Barry Took, Ken Hoare. Additional material by Barry Cryer and Graham Chapman. Songs by Tom Lehrer. Producer Dennis Main Wilson. Cast: Marty, James Villiers, Derek Griffiths, George Claydon, Cheryl Hall.

Hollywood Squares. 24th March 1974.

Round the Horne. Script book by Barry Took and Marty, published by the Woburn Press, 1974. Marty contributed new foreword. 1975 paperback edition published by Futura.

The Johnny Carson Show. 19th August 1974.

Marty Feldman: What Do I Spy With My Little Eye. West Germany Television. 3rd November 1974. Director Jochen Wolf.

Young Frankenstein. A Mel Brooks Film, US release 15th December 1974. Written by Gene Wilder and Mel Brooks. Producer Michael Gruskoff. Original music by John Morris. Cinematography Gerald Hirschfield. Editor John C. Howard. Director Mel Brooks. Dr. Frederick Frankenstein: Gene Wilder. The Monster: Peter Boyle. Igor: Marty. Elizabeth: Madeline Kahn. Frau Blucher: Cloris Leachman. Inga: Teri Garr. Inspector Kemp: Kenneth Mars. Herr Falkstein: Richard Haydn. Mr. Hilltop: Liam Dunn. Gravediggers: Monte Landis and Rusty Blitz. Little Girl: Anne Beesley. Blind Man: Gene Hackman.

Karen: 'Them'. 6th February 1975. Director Hy Averbeck. Writer Simon Munter. Karen Angelo: Karen Valentine. Mr. X: Marty. Dale Busch: Charles Lane.

Lights, Camera, Monty! 24th April 1975. Director Bob Wynn. Monty Hall with The Carl Jablonski Dancers, Michele Lee, Steve Lawrence, Dianne, Janet & Kathy Lennon and appearances by Universal contract players including Marty.

Closed Up-Tight. Film, 1975. Marty as a cat burglar.

When Things Were Rotten: 'Those Wedding Bell Blues'. American Television: 1st October 1975. Created by Mel Brooks. Directed by Marty. Robin Hood: Richard Gautier. Maid Marian: Misty Rowe. Friar Tuck: Dick Van Patten. Alan-a-Dale: Bernie Kopell. With Dudley Moore as Sheik Achmed.

The Adventure of Sherlock Holmes' Smarter Brother. A Gene Wilder Film, US release 14th December 1975. Written by Gene Wilder. Producer Charles Orme. Original music by John Morris. Cinematography Gerry Fisher. Editor Jim Clark. Director Gene Wilder. Sigerson Holmes: Gene Wilder. Jenny Hill: Madeline Kahn. Sergeant Orville Stanley Sacker: Marty. Eduardo Gambetti: Dom DeLuise. Moriarty: Leo McKern. Moriarty's assistant: Roy Kinnear. Lord Redcliff: John Le Mesurier. Sherlock Holmes: Douglas Wilmer. Dr. Watson: Thorley Walters. Bruner: George Silver. Hunkston: Nicholas Smith. Coach driver: Aubrey Morris. Fred: Tommy Godfrey. Queen Victoria: Susan Field. Russian bidder: Joseph Behrmannis. French bidder: Wolfe Morris. With Julian Orchard, Tony Sympson and Albert Finney.

Film '76. 30th January 1976. Interviewee.

Flannery and Quilt. American television pilot, 1st February 1976. Written and created by Marty. Written and produced by Carl Reiner. Luke Flannery: Red Buttons. Sam Quilt: Harold Gould. Milt Lesser: Richard Benedict. Rose Flannery Caselli: Pat Finley. Quilt's Grandson: Michael Lembeck. Kevin Caselli: Howard Storm.

40 Gradi all'ombra del Lenzuolo [Sex With a Smile]. Medusa Produzono, European release April 1976. Written by Torino Guerra. Director Sergio Martino. Producer Luciano Martino. 'La Guardia del Corpo' [The Bodyguard] segment Alex: Marty. Marina: Dayle Haddon. Francois: Mimmo Craig.

Silent Movie. A Mel Brooks Film, US release 16th June 1976. Written by Mel Brooks, Ron Clark, Rudy de Luca and Barry Levison. Producer Michael Hertzberg. Original music by John Morris. Director of Photography Paul Lohmann Editors Stanford C. Allen and John C. Howard. Director Mel Brooks. Mel Funn: Mel Brooks. Marty Eggs: Marty. Dom Bell: Dom DeLuise. Studio Chief: Sid Caesar. Engulf: Harold Gould. Devour: Ron Carey. Vilma Kaplan: Bernadette Peters. Newsvendor: Liam Dunn. With Burt Reynolds, James Caan, Liza Minnelli, Anne Bancroft, Marcel Marceau and Paul Newman.

The Bona Album of Julian & Sandy. D.J.M. Records Limited/This Record Co. Ltd, 1976. Newly recorded *Round the Horne* sketches by Marty and Barry Took. Kenneth Williams and Hugh Paddick recreated their original roles with Barry Took replacing the late Kenneth Horne.

The Bona Book of Julian and Sandy. Robson Books, 1976. Script book by Marty and Barry Took. Extracts were included in *Laughing Matter: The Best of British Humour in One Book*, Topaz, 1976.

The Last Remake of Beau Geste. A Marty Feldman Film, US release 15th July 1977. Written by Marty & Chris Allen. Story by Marty & Sam Bobrick. Producer William S. Gilmore Executive producers George Shapiro & Howard West. Original music by John Morris. Director of Photography Gerry Fisher. Editor Jim Clark. Director Marty. Dagobert 'Digby' Geste: Marty. Beau Geste: Michael York. Flavia Geste: Ann-Margret. Markov: Peter Ustinov. Sheikh: James Earl Jones. Sir Hector: Trevor Howard. General Pecheur: Henry Gibson. Governor: Terry-Thomas. Boldini: Roy Kinnear. Crumble: Spike Milligan. Judge: Hugh Griffith. Miss Wormwood: Irene Handl. Isabel Geste: Sinead Cusack. Captain Merdmanger: Henry Polic II. Blindman: Ted Cassidy. Father Shapiro: Burt Kwouk. Dr. Crippen: Roland MacLeod. Henshaw: Stephen Lewis. Young Beau: Nicholas Bridge. Young Digby: Michael McConkey.

Film '77. 20th November 1977. Interviewee.

Parkinson. 26th November 1977. Producer John Fisher. Guests Marty, George Melly, Roger McGough and Joe Pass.

Nationwide. 19th December 1977. Producer John Gau. Interviewee.

The 49th Annual Academy Awards. For 1976, ceremony 28th March 1977. Marty presented the Best Live Action Short award.

Hollywood Squares. 25th July 1977.

US Against the World. American Television, 1977.

Lordags Hjornet. Dutch Television. 10th December 1977. Interviewee.

The Muppet Show. Series 5, episode 18. ATV. 14th July 1980. Guest.

In God We Tru$t. A Marty Feldman Film, US release 26th September 1980. Written by Marty & Chris Allen. Producers George Shapiro & Howard West. Associate producer Lauretta Feldman. Executive producer Norman T. Herman. Original music by John Morris. Director of photography Charles Correll. Editor David Blewitt. Director Marty. Brother Ambrose: Marty. Dr. Sebastian Melmoth: Peter Boyle. Mary: Louise Lasser. G.O.D.: Richard Pryor. Armageddon T. Thunderbird: Andy Kaufman. Abbot Thelonious: Wilfrid Hyde-White.

The Johnny Carson Show. 30th September 1980.

Fridays. Series 3 episode 5. A.B.C. 30th October 1981. Creator: Bill Lee. Head Writer: Steve Adams. Directors: Paul Miller & Tom Kramer. Guest star: Marty.

Bonjour Monsieur Lewis. Documentary for French Television [making of *Slapstick*], 1981.

Insight: 'The Sixth Day'. American Television 1st November 1981. Writer Lan O'Kun. Director Richard C. Bennett. Hosted by Ellwood Kieser. Gray: James Callahan. Angel: Marty. God: Keenan Wynn. Adam: Randolph Mantooth.

Monty Python and the Hollywood Bowl. US release 25th June 1982. Includes the 'Four Yorkshiremen' sketch written by Graham Chapman, John Cleese, Tim Brooke-Taylor and Marty.

Slapstick of Another Kind. European release December 1982. Re-edited for US release in March 1984. Cinematography Tony Richmond. Editor Doug Jackson. Written, produced & directed by Steven Paul. Based on the novel *Slapstick* by Kurt Vonnegut. Wilbur & Caleb Swain: Jerry Lewis. Eliza & Lutetia Swain: Madeline Kahn. Sylvester: Marty. Dr. Frankenstein: John Abbott. President of the USA: Jim Backus. Colonel Sharp: Samuel Fuller. Anchorman: Merv Griffin. Ah Fong: Pat Morita. Lum Fung: Eugene Choy. Chinese Astronaut: Peter Kwong. Gossip Specialist: Virginia Graham. Quentin the Handyman: Ben Frank. Maria the Maid: Cherie Harris. With Orson Welles as the voice of the alien.

Group Madness. A Michael Mileham Film, 1983. The making of *Yellowbeard*, "the rare" Marty is tracked down and interviewed.

Yellowbeard. US release 24th June 1983. Cinematography Gerry Fisher. Editor William Reynolds. Written by Graham Chapman, Peter Cook and Bernard McKenna. Producer Carter De Haven. Executive Producer John Daley. Director Mel Damski. Captain Yellowbeard: Graham Chapman. Moon: Peter Boyle. El Segundo: "Cheech" Marin. El Nebuloso: Tommy Chong. Lord Percy Lambourn: Peter Cook. Gilbert: Marty. Dan: Martin Hewitt. Dr. Gilpin: Michael Hordern. Commander Clement: Eric Idle. Betty: Madeline Kahn. Captain Hughes: James Mason. Blind Pew: John Cleese. Mr. Crisp & Verdugo: Kenneth Mars. Flunkie: Spike Milligan. Triola: Stacey Nelkin. Mansell: Nigel Planer. Lady Churchill: Susannah York. Lady Lambourn: Beryl Reid. Queen Anne: Peter Bull. Tarbuck: Bernard Fox. Man with Parrot: Ronald Lacey. Mr Prostitute: Greta Blackburn. Admiral: Nigel Stock. Rosie: Gillian Eaton. The Shark: David Bowie.

Digital Marty

"In my case obsession is the norm. Writing, for me, is a pathological condition. I don't even think of it as a talent. It's what I have to do. The fact that somebody is paying me to do it is a constant source of amazement to me, because I would do it for nothing."

Much of Marty's work is sadly 'missing believed wiped' and much of that which remains is neglected (though typing 'Marty Feldman' into YouTube will reveal a surprising amount of rare and otherwise hard to find material). However, some of his very best work has been re-mastered and resurrected on perfect shiny discs. The true Marty devotee would not be without any of these…

The Adventure of Sherlock Holmes' Smarter Brother (20th Century Fox B000GL18K4, 2006.)

The Army Game Volume 2 (Network 7952481, 2006.)

At Last the 1948 Show [Includes 5 compilation episodes]: (Boulevard Entertainment Limited BLVDD0041, 2005.)

At Last the 1948 Show [The Album]: (Cherry Red Records/E.L. Records, 2007.)

The Best of Marty Feldman [An essential *Marty* compilation] (2entertain B0009WL8PK, 2005.)

Bootsie and Snudge – The Complete First Series (Network 7953178, 2009.)

Frost On Sunday [Includes the British Academy Film Awards 1970] (Network B001QXZ816, 2009.)

The Frost Report Is Back (Network B001QXZ80W, 2009.)

Golden Years of British Comedy: The Swinging Sixties [Includes clips from *The Frost Report* and *Marty*.] (White Star B0000A5FBQ, 2003.)

I Feel A Song Going Off [Includes the Christmas single as bonus tracks.] (Decca Records 9846092, 2007.)

In God We Tru$t (Odeon B004P131H4, 2011.)

The Last Remake of Beau Geste (Second Sight 2NDVD3191, 2011.)

The Magnificent Seven Deadly Sins (Slam Dunk Media B000W2221Q, 2007.)

The Mel Brooks Collection [Includes *Young Frankenstein* and *Silent Movie*.] (20th Century Fox blu-ray B002PHI2N8, 2009.)

Round the Horne: The Complete Radio Archive [Pricey completists' box set. More affordable 'best of' collections are also available.] (BBC 0563527498, 2005.)

Slapstick of Another Kind (Cinema Club B0000C24GO, 2004.)

Yellowbeard (Optimum B002BC9YDY, 2009.)

Notes

Prologue

1. This, and all subsequent Bill Oddie quotes, interview with the author, 30th January 2011.

2. 'Too Old to Die Young, Too Old to Grow Up' by David Lewin, the *Daily Mail*, 4th December 1982.

3. Scottish International winger Cooke enjoyed two successful stints with Marty's team, Chelsea, from 1966-1972 and 1974-1978. In 1970 he had been in the squad that beat Leeds in the FA Cup Final.

4. 'It's Marty Frankenstein', the *Daily Express*, 24th January 1975.

5. When the Best Supporting Actor was announced on 8th April 1975, all the candidates were American with octogenarian George Burns winning for *The Sunshine Boys*. He beat Chris Sarandon in *Dog Day Afternoon*, Burgress Meredith in *The Day of the Locusts*, Jack Warden in *Shampoo* and Brad Dourif in *One Flew Over the Cuckoo's Nest*.

6. This, and all subsequent Tim Brooke-Taylor quotes, interview with the author, 19th January 2011.

7. This, and all subsequent Michael Palin quotes, interview with the author, 18th November 2010.

8. *Penthouse* interview by Richard Kleiner, October 1980.

Chapter I

1. "We advertised all over Europe and in America," he told Dutch television in 1977. "Either there weren't many people who looked like me or if there were they didn't want to publicise it. Not many people answered. This kid answered...I suppose I should have looked like that when I was 11 if there was any kind of justice. This kid was living about a quarter of a mile away from the studio where we shot the picture. So it was coincidence. It was also very cheap for Universal because they only had to pay very little bus fare each day. Hollywood economics on a six million-dollar picture. If they could save tuppence a day on bus fare, I think that's the way they cast pictures."

2. 'Off the Screen' by Barbara Wilkins, *People Weekly*, 29th August 1977.

3. *Lordags Hjornet*, Dutch TV interview, December 1977.

4. 'Marty Goes Back to the Silents' by Michael Owen, the *Evening Standard*, 15th August 1970.

5. 'There's More to Marty Than Meets the Eye' by Diane Blackwell, *The Australian Women's Weekly*, January 26th 1972. His paternal grandparents, Barett and Rose, had sixteen children of whom twelve survived. In actual fact Marty's father, Myer, had been born on Christmas Day 1911, making him 22 at the time of his son's birth. Marty's mother, Cecilia Crook, was born on 18th July 1913, and thus was a few weeks shy of her 21st birthday at the time of Marty's birth. "Nobody called them Myer and Cecilia, though," says Marty's sister Pamela Franklin. "They were always known as Mossy and Cissy."

6. 'Religious Mania' by Colin Dangaard in Hollywood, the *Daily Express*, 28th August 1980.

7. This and all subsequent Pamela Franklin quotes, interview with the author, 15th July 2011. Pamela had ambitions to be a hairdresser but at the age of fourteen went to business school to learn secretarial skills. Leaving at sixteen she worked for six months before marrying Norman Galland in 1958. Marty's neice, Suzannah Galland, was born in London in May 1962. Now a successful Life Strategist, she has been described by Fox Entertainment as an expert in pop culture and human behaviour. She lives in Los Angeles. Pamela's second daughter Sue developed diabetes at the age of eleven and died after a long illness. This tragedy split the marriage. Pamela met Los

Angeles-based Stanley Franklin during his business trip to London and the couple married in September 1986. She is now based in America.

8. 'Marty Goes Back to the Silents...' by Michael Owen, the *Evening Standard*, 15th August 1970.

9. *Penthouse* interview by Richard Kleiner, October 1980.

10. 'Off the Screen' by Barbara Wilkins, *People Weekly*, 29th August 1977.

11. *Took's Eye View* by Barry Took, Robson Books, 1983. To be fair, Barry Took only met Marty when the family *was* "moderately well-to-do". As Marty's friend Alan Spencer says: "Marty did not exaggerate about anything. He didn't need to."

12. *Lordags Hjornet*, Dutch TV interview, December 1977. In the same interview Marty explained that: "I don't eat dead bodies [but] I have no objection to cannibalism. Truthfully, I've never understood the Christian objection to cannibalism because I think the Christian belief is that the soul departs the body. I don't think anyone believes in the physical fact of the resurrection like a Stanley Spencer painting, we're all going to come out of our graves in the way that we are put in to them. I won't eat a cow, but if you can eat a cow you can eat a human being. Don't kill him but if I'm dead then I would sooner my friends ate me than the worms ate me. I think that would be a marvellous way for me to go. If your friends really loved you I think that would be rather nice. They would eat you. Cut away the diseased parts and there's 140 pounds of reasonably good meat."

13. Writer Ronnie Wolfe remembers that when they were working together in the late 1950s: "Every place to eat in and around Soho soon got used to Marty. They were always very careful about preparing his food."

14. *Took's Eye View* by Barry Took, Robson Books, 1983. Barry's reference to Dotheboys Hall relates to the dreaded boarding school presided over by Wackford Squeers in Charles Dickens' *Nicholas Nickleby*. A very Marty reference.

15. 'There's More to Marty Than Meets the Eye' by Diane Blackwell, *The Australian Women's Weekly*, 26th January 1972.

16. 'All About Marty', *The Observer*, 13th April 1969.

17. *Penthouse* interview by Richard Kleiner, October 1980.

18. The *Daily Mirror* obituary, 4th December 1982.

19. 'Religious Mania' by Colin Dangaard in Hollywood, the *Daily Express*, 28th August 1980.

20. 'Too Old to Die Young, Too Old to Grow Up' by David Lewin, the *Daily Mail*, 4th December 1982.

21. *Penthouse* interview by Richard Kleiner, October 1980.

22. *Penthouse* interview by Richard Kleiner, October 1980.

23. 'American Dreams' by John Hall on US TV's Latest Find, 19th August 1970.

24. *Penthouse* interview by Richard Kleiner, October 1980.

25. *Took's Eye View* by Barry Took, Robson Books 1983. According to Suzannah Galland however: "the family were certainly called Feldman long before my uncle was born. His grandparents were called Feldman. My mother seems to think prior to that there were several family names, hence the confusion. Their great-grandparents went by the name of Bondel, which means tailor, but Marty was a born Feldman."

26. *Penthouse* interview by Richard Kleiner, October 1980.

27. This, and all other Suzannah Galland quotes, interview with the author, 13th June 2011. "It was very telling that years later Marty bought himself a yellow Bentley – the same model as his father had had," says Galland. "Marty worked for his father for a time but would never tell people that." Pamela Franklin explains that: "My brother worked as a salesman for my father. He was very good with people and he had an eye for design. He didn't work for him very long but he certainly wasn't sacked. He just wanted to move on." "His father never saw his huge success," says Galland, "but he had reached a plateau of security and contentment in his life. He embraced his father. The person who might have dwarfed him emotionally became his role model and ideal." Galland explains that: "Marty's parents were very charitable. They were Monastic people and Marty was involved in that. He was often reluctant but that love for his fellow man certainly rubbed off. Later, not only was he generous with his time with writers, he was also very generous with his money. During his days in Hollywood there were people in the deep South of America who he would send money to." Pamela Franklin says that "our parents were very generous as well. I remember my father invested some money into Marty's *Saucy Girls* show when it appeared in London for a week. We were all very proud of him." Suzannah Galland

continues: "My uncle didn't care about politics and he didn't care about religion but he cared passionately about the world and about people. He deeply wanted to make the pilgrimage to Israel just to be with the people."

28. 'Marty Goes Back to the Silents...' by Michael Owen, the *Evening Standard,* 15th August 1970.

29. F. Scott Fitzgerald was a passion of Marty's, particularly his Pat Hobby stories of a Hollywood hack writer in the late thirties and early forties. He had met Ernest Hemingway in Paris shortly after the publication of *The Great Gatsby* in 1925. Marty identified with F. Scott Fitzgerald throughout his life: "I know he wrote out of a desperate need for money. The fact that out of a desperate need for money he may have written *The Great Gatsby* and I may merely have written *The Army Game* is a difference in our talents, not a difference in our approach." Paris had become a magnet to the world's brightest people and gained a reputation for aiding a writer's imagination and success. It was of the past and of the future: a quality that appealed to Marty. Henry Miller, who would map the obscure alleyways and cafés of Paris, wrote to his New York based friend, Emil Schnellock, in 1930 that: "When I walk down the most wonderful street in the world (St. Denis!) – and also the oldest in Paris – I know that I am taking the road of the Roman legion, the road of the Knights Templar, the road that the fearsome Saint Denis himself trod, head in hand."

30. *Penthouse* interview by Richard Kleiner, October 1980.

Chapter 2

1. 'Marty Makes A Movie' by David Hunn, *Photoplay*, November 1969.

2. As Marty explained in the early 1970s: "I saw Ray about a year ago. His teeth have all gone but the rest of him seems to be intact – apart from his foreskin which we know isn't!" Marty reflected on the "little roving community of bums who all knew each other. I still know some of them now. There's an ex-brass I know who works as a barmaid in a club in the West End and we reminisce about the good old days. The good old days are only good when they're old!"

3. *Penthouse* interview by Richard Kleiner, October 1980. Perelman also contributed to the scripts for Marty's beloved Marx Brothers films *Monkey Business* and *Horse Feathers.* Lardner's first novel *You Know Me Al* was the earliest sign of Marty's interest in baseball. A close friend of F. Scott Fitzgerald and synonymous with the Jazz Age of the 1920s, it is little wonder that Marty read his work so keenly.

4. Benchley, another contributor to *The New Yorker*, subsequently won an Academy Award for his short film *How to Sleep*. He had met Parker, another *New Yorker* scribe, when both were working at *Vanity Fair*. She found later fame as a poet and co-writer of *A Star is Born*. Ogden Stewart joined both of them at the Algonquin Round Table, a regular New York gathering of writers and wits throughout the 1920s. He too went to Hollywood to write the sophisticated comedy *The Philadelphia Story*. Stephen Leacock was a Canadian born humourist who also idolised Benchley and, by virtue of a lengthy correspondence, got a publishing deal. Evergreen and ever thirty-nine comedian Jack Benny would cite him as the funniest writer he had ever known. Leacock also inspired that generation of comedians immediately prior to Marty. Harry Secombe name-checked him as an influence on The Goons in the radio documentary *At Last the Go On Show*.

5. Campbell was an Irish humourist whose greatest pieces were published in the journal *Lilliput*; a publication he was assistant editor on from 1947-1953. Waugh's great satires of the bright, young things and British class system such as *Vile Bodies* and *A Handful of Dust* appealed to Marty's distrust of decadence.

6. Huckleberry Finn and Tom Sawyer creator Twain was, according to his 1910 *New York Times* obituary, the "greatest American humourist of his age" while Sullivan and Guthrie were both steeped in *The New Yorker* style. Marty's crack about Jane Austen writing for Laurence Olivier is a reference to the 1940 MGM production of *Pride and Prejudice*. Despite starring Olivier as Mr. Darcy and a crop of British stars such as Greer Garson, E.E. Clive, Melville Cooper and Edmund Gwenn, it was extremely Hollywood in its retelling of the classic novel.

7. 'There's More to Marty Than Meets the Eye' by Diane Blackwell, *The Australian Women's Weekly*, 26th January 1972.

8. Both Kops and Norman were very much of the East End. Kops, who had had a barrow in Soho, was at the forefront of the "new wave" with his play *The Hamlet of Stepney Green* while Norman's book of *Fings Ain't Wot They Used to Be* was staged by Joan Littlewood's Theatre Workshop. On his trips to London, Thomas was known to broadcast on the BBC, drink in Soho and sleep it off in a caravan. He made his final journey to New York in 1953 and died there at the age of thirty-nine. Minton was a jazz musician and pioneering pop artist whose work *The Death of James Dean* was hung in the Royal Academy. He was dead from a drugs overdose in 1957 at the age of thirty-nine.

9. 'All About Marty', *The Observer*, 13th April 1969.

10. Hayes subsequently joined Ronnie Scott in the Jazz Couriers. After playing in New York and Los Angeles he returned to England in the sixties; forming his own band and guesting with the Duke Ellington Orchestra.

11. *Penthouse* interview by Richard Kleiner, October 1980.

12. In the early 1970s, Marty told Jack Hobbs that: "It's funny. I told Bill Cosby about this recently in America and he told me his fantasy was to be a white musician! He thought the same way. If he kept earning his letters in college he would be white."

13. 'Off the Screen' by Barbara Wilkins, *People Weekly*, 29th August 1977.

14. *A Liar's Autobiography Volume VI* by Graham Chapman, Eyre Methuen Limited, 1980.

Chapter 3

1. The definitive Hollywood biopic of the 1940s cast Larry Parks as the great entertainer. Al Jolson himself provided the vocals, Parks just mimed, but mimed wonderfully. The story was largely fictionalised but sums up the "born in a trunk" myth of vaudeville. 1947 saw a flippant but fun sequel, *Jolson Sings Again*.

2. This, and all subsequent David Weddle quotes, interview with the author, 1st June 2011.

3. Olsen and Johnson made a virtue of their corniness and after years of mugging their way through vaudeville came up trumps with the smash Broadway comedy *Hellzapoppin'* in 1938. The film version is arguably the craziest and funniest film ever to come out of Hollywood. In the early 1940s they made three more films at Universal, the fun factory that Marty would be given the run of almost forty years later.

4. *Lordags Hjornet*, Dutch TV interview, December 1977.

5. 'American Dream', John Hall on US TV's Latest Find, 19th August 1970. The Ritz Brothers had been performing since the mid 1920s and kept going as a group for forty years, although they were at their peak in the late 1930s making big budget films at Fox. They co-starred with Don Ameche in *The Three Musketeers* and Bela Lugosi in *The Gorilla*. The wild-haired, moustachioed Dr. Crock toured the British variety circuit with His Crackpots during the 1940s. It was a very Marty mix of manic comedy and off-key music.

6. 'Marty Goes Back to the Silents' by Michael Owen, the *Evening Standard*, 15th August 1970.

7. This, and all subsequent Denis King quotes, interview with the author, 8th February 2011.

8. *Penthouse* interview by Richard Kleiner, October 1980.

9. Obituary by Lindsay Mackee, the *Glasgow Herald*, 4th December 1982. Logan was the pride of Scotland and had made the Alhambra Theatre, Glasgow and the radio show, *It's All Yours!*, his own in the 1950s. Eric Sykes would write his big break into television for ATV in 1956.

10. 'My Fight to Save Marty by Spike' by Bob Graham, the *Evening Standard*, 6th December 1982.

11. Spike and His City Slickers inflicted manslaughter on most of the popular tunes of the day. Their renditions of 'Cocktails for Two', 'My Old Flame' and 'Laura' were stuffed with gunshot, clinking glasses and Peter Lorre impersonations. Recording on the RCA Victor label into the 1950s and spreading musical decay on American television into the 1960s, Spike died at the age of fifty-three in 1965. Like Marty he couldn't function on a workday without a continuous supply of coffee and cigarettes.

12. Maxin would go on to produce arguably the BBC's finest comedy variety series, *The Morecambe and Wise Show* with his 1977 Christmas special famously achieving viewing figures of over eighteen million people.

13. Tommy Trinder, Cotton and Wheeler were all of the opinion that a great catchphrase was worth a million laughs and "You Lucky People!", "Wakey, Wakey!" and "Aye Aye, That's Your Lot!" worked for them for decades. By 1955 Trinder was the pioneering host of ITV's flagship variety show *Sunday Night at the London Palladium*. Billy Cotton had been hosting his Sunday lunchtime *Band Show* on BBC radio since the late 1940s. His raucous cockney charm, even more prominent on television, made him a national treasure. Wheeler's violin antics and cockney take on opera, "Hopra for the Higgerant", suited Marty's twin passions of music and mirth.

14. With the end of the halls, Randle faced problems with bar bills and taxes and was declared bankrupt in 1955. He died two years later. Miller, the "Pure Gold of Music Hall", played his last West End appearance in 1959. He died in 1963. Max Wall soldiered on through decline and scandal to find fame as an actor; notably playing Archie Rice in *The Entertainer*. While Sandy Powell remained true to his

"Can You Hear Me, Mother?" roots by performing on nostalgic variety bills for the next twenty-five years.

Chapter 4

1. With Marty gone and dropping an "R", the depleted team of Moris and Mitch soldiered on through the fading variety theatres and a handful of television appearances before calling it a day in 1958. Ten years later, with Marty the country's biggest comedy star, Morris and Mitch (with the second 'r' reinstated) had a late additional blooming with a single release on the Saga Trend label. 'The Magical Musherishi Tourists' backed by 'Mister D.J. Man' didn't wobble the hit parade but it was an interesting, timely curio. Mitch Revely wrote the songs. Earlier he had written Wilfrid Brambell's 'Second Hand' and 'Ragtime Ragabone Man' for Parlophone. Revely completed the *Steptoe and Son* set by writing and producing 'Flower Power Fred' and 'I'm Saving All My Love' for Harry H. Corbett over at Decca Records.

2. Law and Craig were writing the situation comedy *Joan and Leslie* which starred real-life couple Joan Reynolds and Leslie Randall in intimate tales of domestic disarray. Having been based in Henley, Marty even moved into Craig's London abode for a short time to be closer to the work. Marty's other early London residences included an apartment in the block of flats in Marble Arch, an apartment in Fitzroy Square and The Logs, 18 Well Road, NW.

3. Haynes was the king of comedy on commercial television. His Oscar Pennyweather character, created for him by Ronald Wolfe and Sid Colin, proved such a hit in *Strike a New Note* in 1956 that the following year he got his own show. The ten-year run at the top was only curtailed by Haynes' untimely death at the age of fifty-two.

4. Obituary by Richard Last, the *Daily Telegraph*, 4th December 1982.

5. *Three "Tough" Guys* cast the American vaudevillian Harry Green, who was resident in England at the time. Peter Welch and Warren Mitchell were in support. Mitchell remembers that: "I was allowed to rewrite some dialogue because I wanted that feeling of *Guys and Dolls*. That over-flowery way of talking instead of the standard Jewish cockney it was written for." Six episodes were broadcast from June 1957 under producers Cecil Petty and Hugh Rennie.

6. The Mandrake was originally a basement chess and drinking club on Meard Street, between Wardour Street and Dean Street in London's Soho. It became a favourite haunt for writers in the 1950s particularly because the restaurant was reasonably priced and the bar stayed open late. Indeed, it was one of Dylan Thomas' haunts.

The resident jazz group comprised double bassist Wally Wrightman and pianist Cab Kaye. Ronnie Scott was a frequent visitor: his girlfriend, Sue, served behind the bar. It became well known as a haven for public figures to escape the public with its frugal decor; dark wood panelling, simple chairs and tables sans tablecloths.

7. *Took's Eye View* by Barry Took, Robson Books, 1983.

8. 'There's More to Marty Than Meets the Eye' by Diane Blackwell, *The Australian Women's Weekly*, 26th January 1972. By the time international stardom was his, Marty had come to terms with the fact that every journalist who interviewed him assumed that he had been born looking like he looked. For the majority of the time he didn't bother correcting them and, when asked how anyone could have fallen for those looks, simply went along with the perceived "beauty and the beast" notion and made a joke out of it.

9. *Took's Eye View* by Barry Took, Robson Books, 1983.

10. In the first episode of *Round the Horne*, broadcast in March 1965, Marty took his own revenge on the dummy when BBC cuts saw Peter Brough forced to chop him up and sell him as matches.

11. They would create classics like *Meet the Wife*, *The Rag Trade* and *On the Buses*. Chesney had, in fact, been a featured musical performer on the show as early as 1952, his Magic Talking Mouth Organ breaking up the comedy shenanigans of tutor Harry Secombe.

12. This, and all subsequent Ronnie Wolfe quotes, interview with the author, 1st February 2011.

13. *Took's Eye View* by Barry Took, Robson Books, 1983.

14. This, and all other Rose Wolfe quotes, interview with the author, 1st February 2011.

15. 'American Dreams', John Hall on US TV's Latest Find, 19th August 1970.

16. *What Do I Spy With My Little Eye*, West Germany Television, November 1974

Chapter 5

1. So much so that hit records, a Hammer Film Productions big screen version and even a board game resulted. Bernard Bresslaw's Private "Popeye" Popplewell character

became the star of the show with his mournful "I Only Arsked!" catchphrase and although he left for pastures new – though hardly different – in the summer of 1958, *The Army Game* soldiered on. Ironically, at the very time Bresslaw was starting in *The Army Game* he could have been starring opposite Marty for ATV. He had been in the original line-up for *Three "Tough" Guys*.

2. Interview with the author, 4th February 2010. Lune's character cast a similar shadow to that of Charles Hawtrey who had been ousted since the first series. Both William Hartnell and Norman Rossington had been original cast members and all three would immediately go on to add television star clout to the 1958 film *Carry On Sergeant*.

3. William Hartnell was clearly delighted to be back when he told the *TV Times* (23rd September, volume 20 no. 256) that: "I think we're going to be a happy family. We'll certainly have a jolly good go at it."

4. Thanks to the Network DVD releases of the first series of *Bootsie and Snudge* and what's left of *The Army Game* the discerning comedy buff can recreate this enjoyable experience. I know I have!

5. *Took's Eye View* by Barry Took, Robson Books, 1983.

6. This, and all subsequent Ian La Frenais quotes, interview with the author, 15th November 2010. Clement and La Frenais later became famous for *The Likely Lads*, *Porridge* and *Auf Wiedersehen, Pet*, not to mention script-doctoring films like *The Rock*.

7. *Perfect Day* is a classic Stan and Ollie short from 1929 and relates the mayhem of preparing for a picnic in the country. The *Perfect Day* of the title is ironic. Director James Parrott had originally intended to include the actual day as the second reel but so much comic mileage resulted from the departure that he chose to end the fun with the boys' car sinking in to a puddle. Ray Galton and Alan Simpson had already established the character-based comedy of Hancock on radio from 1954. The television series had begun in 1956. Both embraced the ordinary to maximise the star's brand of comic pomposity. Boredom had become an art form in the classic 1958 radio episode 'A Sunday Afternoon at Home'.

8. "I am very fond of Old Johnson," the thirty-eight-year-old Clive Dunn told Frank Duesbury of the *TV Times* (October 28th 1960, volume 21 no. 261). "I have played all sorts of parts in my time, characters based on life, though slightly exaggerated. It is a combination of making fun of someone and oneself." As the actor was called to the set he adopted the mannerisms of Old Johnson: "'Coming, sonny, coming,' he croaked, moving with a slip-one-purl-one gait of a very old man. His head was

shaking as he came to a doddering halt to pick up his wig. Frankly, he did not need it. He seemed to have aged forty-five years just by thinking about the part."

9. This, and all subsequent Warren Mitchell quotes, interview with the author, 25th February 2011.

10. In fact, Marty and Barry are credited on thirty-three episodes in that first series, mostly together, sometimes apart and occasionally with other writers. Ray Whyberd would make a large contribution. For Marty it was something of a flashback to his *Educating Archie* days for it was the pseudonym of ventriloquist Ray Alan, best known for his work with Lord Charles. John Antrobus, Stanley Myers, Tom Espie, Hugh Woodhouse and Ray Rigby were the other writers to pick up the scraps from the Granada Television table.

11. The *TV Times* credits John Antrobus as the third writer on the first ten episodes although he doesn't get a mention on the credits of the actual programmes.

12. Comedy was a passion, certainly, but more importantly it was a living. As he told Ken Bailey of the *People* in 1971: "Look at the money being funny makes for me. You could say I'm fatalistic about it. I'd be a charlatan if I said I didn't want it. Because, in a capitalistic society, it's what comics get. This doesn't mean I don't want to change society to give more equal shares. But to insist on being a pauper in our world is suicide. I'd prefer for us all not to need money, if it could be done without anybody being a pauper."

13. Also known as hyperthyroidism, it made the thyroid gland, the master gland of metabolism, over active. This would make the eyeballs not only protrude but also weaken the muscles thus resulting in a lack of movement of the eyeballs.

14. As he frustratedly told Dutch television in 1977, "I read reviews saying: 'Why does he pop his eyes?' I don't pop my eyes. My eyes pop. There they are."

15. 'Marty Goes Back to the Silents...' by Michael Owen, the *Evening Standard*, 15th August 1970.

Chapter 6

1. 'That Marty Face – I Never Noticed It' by Barry Took, *Radio Times*, 5th June 1969. During Marty's illness Barry Took wrote another series for Granada, *Colonel Trumper's Private War*. Starring Dennis Price and Warren Mitchell, it was scripted alongside Hugh Woodhouse, Bill Craig and Dick Vosburgh. Peter Eton produced and

it was broadcast just before the second series of *Bootsie and Snudge*. Although Marty's influence must have touched the show by the very virtue of the people working on it, he is not credited as a writer. Still, this series is often erroneously credited to him.

2. *Took's Eye View* by Barry Took, Robson Books, 1983.

3. The second series was edited by Barry Took and Marty Feldman. Other writers assigned scripts were Ray Whyberd, David Cumming and Derek Collyer, Peter Lambdoe, John Smith and Doug Eden.

4. *Took's Eye View* by Barry Took, Robson Books, 1983.

5. "He asked me three or four weeks ago," Marty joked with Jack Hobbs in the wake of *The Marty Feldman Comedy Machine*. "It's become a reflex with him!"

6. *Took's Eye View* by Barry Took, Robson Books, 1983.

7. In actual fact there were ninety-eight episodes of *Bootsie and Snudge* in the original 1960s run. In January 1964 Granada resurrected the characters for *Foreign Affairs* and stuck them in service at the British Embassy in Bosnik. Only eight episodes resulted, five written by Took. Milo Lewis and Peter Eton kept further continuity as director and producer. In 1974 a further series of six *Bootsie and Snudge* episodes were broadcast, in colour for the first time. David Climie, Ronnie Cass and *The Army Game* veteran Lew Schwarz wrote the scripts with, this time, Bootsie as a millionaire pools winner and Snudge as his financial adviser. Bill Podmore produced and directed.

8. Marty had certainly had experience of this during his teenage days in Soho. Later Marty lent his support to Release, a voluntary organisation which gave advice to drug-takers. "I'm interested in postulating alternatives," he told William Hall in 1969, "and I take the proposition that there are alternatives to the way we live now."

9. *Terry-Thomas Tells Tales: An Autobiography*, Robson Books, 1991. The character of "Mossy" was clearly named in honour of Marty's father. Pamela Franklin remembers: "That made us laugh. I also remember seeing one of his television skits and there was a Jewish mother wearing bejewelled glasses and talking about her son who never telephoned home. That was Marty including our mother in a sketch because she was a typical Jewish mother. She didn't recognise herself though. Marty would take great delight in doing that sort of thing. He could be quite naughty like that, but then we all were!"

10. From Holland Bennett, issued on 7th November 1963, BBC Written Archives.

11. George Cole was best known at the BBC for the situation comedy *Life of Bliss* in which he starred as the bumbling bachelor from 1960-1961. As a cockney he was most celebrated as the eternal wide-boy Flash Harry in the *St. Trinian's* films, the latest instalment, *The Pure Hell of St. Trinian's*, having been released in 1960. Alfred Marks had starred in the last batch of his Associated-Rediffusion sketch show *Alfred Marks Time* in 1961 and was certainly at home with East End Jewishness. Leonard Sachs was a familiar jobbing actor as likely to appear in *Hancock's Half Hour*: 'Twelve Angry Men' as *Maigret*: 'High Politics', while Sydney Tafler had come off the back of his partnership with Sid James in the BBC situation comedy *Citizen James*. A joint photograph in *Spotlight* could have been labelled "Spivs Are Us".

12. A friend and colleague of the Goons and *The Goon Show*, Stark had already swum in Marty's ken by playing a down-on-his-luck pancake pan salesman in a John Antrobus-scripted *Bootsie and Snudge* broadcast on 14th April 1961. Stark had also starred in the third series episode 'The Rescue', written by Barry Took and broadcast on 15th November 1962.

13. Dated 1st May 1964, BBC Written Archives.

14. Soon after this time Granada closed their studio in Chelsea and moved production completely to Manchester, thus allowing Took to re-join the BBC on a permanent basis.

15. From E. Caffery, Assistant Head of Copyright, to Marty's agent, Kenneth Ewing, dated 12th June 1964.

16. A seventh script was also commissioned: "although only six out of these seven will probably be transmitted," it is noted. "One of existing six will not be used although they have all been accepted."

17. In an internal BBC memo from John Law, dated as late as 3rd September 1964, the show is still being referred to as *You're Only Old Once*. *The Walrus and the Carpenter* had first appeared in Lewis Carroll's *Through the Looking Glass* in 1871 and featured the two devious friends on the cynical trail of an oyster lunch. Their friendship was rich in conversation and subterfuge, as the most oft-quoted lines of the poem reveal: "'The time has come,' the Walrus said, 'to talk of many things: Of shoes and ships and sealing-wax. Of cabbages and kings.'" After much debate, Alice dismisses them as "both very unpleasant characters."

18. This, and all subsequent Nicholas Young quotes, interview with the author, 7th January 2011. Felix Aylmer was indeed old, nearly seventy-five when the pilot was recorded. He had been acting since 1911, notching up treasured eccentrics in *The*

Ghost of St. Michael's with Will Hay, Hammer's *The Mummy* and *The Road to Hong Kong*. And Hugh Griffith was indeed a pickled, fiery Welshman who specialised in larger-than-life performances. He was nurtured through Ealing comedies such as *The Titfield Thunderbolt* and won an Oscar for *Ben Hur*. In 1963 he was nominated again for *Tom Jones*.

19. The Audience Research Department report, 22nd March 1965, BBC Written Archives.

20. Terence Alexander was a familiar face to television viewers with a co-starring role as co-pilot Bill Dodds in *Garry Halliday*. His recent films had included *The League of Gentlemen*, *Carry On Regardless* and *The Intelligence Men* with Morecambe and Wise.

21. This, and all subsequent Dick Clement quotes, interview with the author, 15th November 2010. In 1976 Marty tried to resurrect *The Walrus and the Carpenter* for American television. Claiming a "creator and writer" credit with Carl Reiner, who also produced, the thirty-minute pilot episode of *Flannery and Quilt* starred Red Buttons as Luke Flannery and Harold Gould as Sam Quilt. It didn't prove successful.

22. *Penthouse* interview by Richard Kleiner, October 1980.

23. Interview with the author, 17th November 2010.

24. 'Marty Goes Back to the Silents...' by Michael Owen, the *Evening Standard*, 15th August 1970.

25. 'American Dreams', John Hall on US TV's Latest Find, 19th August 1970.

26. This was dated 6th October 1964, BBC Written Archives. Marty signed the contract on the 17th October 1964, pp-ing for Barry Took. Times would change for as Marty's status grew it would be Barry Took who would usually attend to the mundane paperwork.

27. Terry Scott clearly liked birds. His comedy single, suitably entitled 'I Like Birds', was released on the Pye label in 1966.

28. Letter to Heather Dean to Kenneth Ewing, 2nd February 1965, BBC Written Archives.

29. Letter from Kenneth Ewing to Heather Dean, 8th February 1965, BBC Written Archives.

Chapter 7

1. Internal memo dated 24th November 1964, BBC Written Archives.

2. This, and all subsequent Sheila Steafel quotes, interview with the author, 15th December 2010.

3. BBC Audience Research Department report, 21st June 1965, BBC Written Archives.

4. BBC Audience Research Department report, 19th July 1965, BBC Written Archives.

5. *The Kenneth Williams Diaries*, edited by Russell Davies, Harper Collins, 1993.

6. Although the guinea had been replaced by the pound in the early 19th century, the term was still used in such transactions as land, horses, fine tailoring and art. It gave the contract an aristocratic air that suited the BBC's image of gentlemen broadcasters. The value of the guinea reflected the rises in the price of gold, thus, while there were twenty shillings in the pound there were twenty-one shillings in the guinea.

7. One such television assignment was "Ned Sherrin's new Saturday programme" which Marty and Barry were due to write in the August of 1965. It had been discussed in correspondence between Heather Dean at the BBC, agent Kenneth Ewing and Sherrin himself that the writers would pen the pilot show and eleven further programmes for an autumn slot. But, as Ewing wrote on 3rd August 1965, "I am afraid, however, that this is a little premature as the two writers, at this stage, are not prepared to commit themselves to the programme for such a long time. I think there will probably be some further direct contact between them and Ned, and out of this an arrangement may come to pass, but at this stage at any rate, we are not in a position to accept the engagement you suggest." Many comedians asked for the writing services of Marty and Barry. In the end they resorted to a joke book, the 1966 edition of *The Joke Teller's Handbook*. They never used it themselves. "It was awful!" remembered Took, "we would just hand it to the comedian and say: 'Here you go, work them out yourself.'"

8. *The Kenneth Williams Diaries* edited by Russell Davies, Harper Collins 1993.

9. *Round the Horne* introduction by Barry Took, the Woburn Press 1974.

10. 'American Dreams', John Hall on US TV's Latest Find, 19th August 1970.

11. *Took's Eye View* by Barry Took, Robson Books, 1983. *ITMA*: the shortened version

of *It's That Man Again* was the hit radio comedy of the 1940s. Full of jokes designed to "win the war", the actual title was taken from the phrase wry announcers would use when charting the European dominance of Adolf Hitler. Handley was surrounded by a cast including Jack Train, Maurice Denham, Molly Weir and latterly Hattie Jacques, the show only coming to an end in 1949 upon the death of the star. The Rowton Houses were safe lodgings for the working classes of the 1890s and 1900s, the brainchild of the wealthy philanthropist Lord Rowton. Marty had had first hand experience of the Rowton Houses during his teenage years, although he didn't stay at them "so much because you had to pay two nights in advance!"

12. Memo from Miss D.L. Ross to agent Kenneth Ewing, 29th April 1965, hoping for "confirmation that the scriptwriters are prepared to write these three additional programmes on the terms and conditions to which they have already agreed for the series". BBC Written Archives.

13. *Took's Eye View* by Barry Took, Robson Books, 1993.

14. Ewing knew his clients lacked interest in this radio series. Producer John Browell realised as much on 11th May 1965, writing that it was "extremely unlikely that Barry Took and Marty Feldman will be able to write *Wilkie* this year, in view of their commitments and probably not for six months of next year. Personally I feel that they are not terribly anxious to undertake this commitment, and have no intention of putting themselves out to fulfil it."

15. Naturally, at this time all the tele-recordings survived in the BBC archives. Alas, now the entire series and the *Comedy Playhouse* pilot are on the "missing believed wiped" list.

16. The *Scott On...* series failing to return until September 1968 when the special, devoted to 'Marriage' was written by Bryan Blackburn.

17. Letter dated 4th March 1965, BBC Written Archives.

18. Letter dated 16th March 1965, BBC Written Archive.

19. This, and all subsequent Bernard Cribbins quotes, interview with the author, 24th February 2011. Johnny Speight's *Till Death Us Do Part* would be the hit of the run and be the most notable series to emerge.

20. The BBC Written Archives hold a belatedly signed contract from 26th April 1966; just three weeks before transmission. The concept of the show was a mock

documentary of Roy Hudd's life with revealing interviews with his "family and friends" telling the true, sordid story of his rise to fame.

21. *Took's Eye View* by Barry Took, Robson Books, 1983.

22. *Round the Horne*, introduction by Barry Took, the Woburn Press, 1973.

Chapter 8

1. Mindfully hell-bent on poking fun at the news and those who made it, *TW3* had been subjected to tight control by the BBC when it emerged with machete in hand in 1962. Indeed, it was not re-commissioned for a third series in the election year of 1964 for fear of influencing the vote.

2. Interview with the author, 3rd March 2011.

3. This, and all subsequent Terry Jones quotes, interview with the author, 18th November 2010.

4. *The Frost Report is Back*, broadcast 24th March 2008, would showcase some of Marty's best sketches for the series and reunited some of the team, including Sir David Frost himself, Ronnie Corbett, Sheila Steafel, Nicky Henson, Barry Cryer and Julie Felix. John Cleese, Terry Jones and Michael Palin would contribute interview soundbites.

5. This missive had been signed on Frost's behalf by Mr. L.D. Constable and stipulated that: "The contract with Hartwest will allow for their exclusive distribution in the USA and its territorial possessions through Hartwest and Kenneth Horne has given me an assurance that he will not record the same or similar material for broadcasting or any other purpose without our consent for the next four years from the date of the payment of the transcription fees. You may recall that in years gone by, Horne and Murdoch took their series to Harry Allen [sic] Towers." The Kenneth Horne and Richard Murdoch radio show, *Much-Binding-in-the-Marsh* would seem slightly out of Towers' comfort zone. A notorious and charming hustler, his biggest successes included a series of *Fu Manchu* films in the 1960s and a couple of *Sherlock Holmes* romps in the 1980s; both starring Christopher Lee. The *Round the Horne* contract detailed that Marty and Barry Took "should be offered...the fees normally payable for world permanent rights for commissioned material."

6. For readers not from countries where this fact is hardwired into the national consciousness, England won, 4-2. Arranging the tickets was also one of Mossy's final

acts of kindness. As Pamela Franklin says: "My dear father passed away August 15th 1966." He was 64 years of age.

7. This letter from the Head of Light Entertainment was dated 31st May 1966, BBC Written Archives.

8. On 26th July 1966 Marty and Barry were also commissioned to write six half hours for Kenneth Williams. The series, intended to feature Hugh Paddick in regular support, was discussed as a revue-type programme of sketches and general comedy in the *Round the Horne* style. This was for John Law to oversee, but when the series, *The Kenneth Williams Show*, finally arrived in 1970, Marty and Barry did not contribute any material.

9. 'Off the Screen' by Barbara Wilkins, *People Weekly*, 29th August 1977. Indeed, in November 1967 Frost would put Marty back behind the camera to co-produce the first series of *No – That's Me Over Here!* A vehicle for Ronnie Corbett, Marty told the *TV Times*: "I honestly feel that now he will shoot right into the star ratings. His technique is tremendous. It's so good it's almost imperceptible."

10. Have we mentioned he went to the 1966 World Cup Final with Marty Feldman?!

11. *TV Times*, 23rd-29th September 1967.

12. Jazz singer Annie Ross was also the sister of Jimmy Logan; the first comedian to buy one of Marty's jokes, so there was an awful lot of love in the room.

13. Tim has vague memories of singing silly songs on the show but not the current single. Marty would swallow his pride and guest on *Dee Time* several times during the height of his own series on the BBC.

14. 'Off the Screen' by Barbara Wilkins, *People Weekly*, 29th August 1977.

15. Marty would be able to charm most female journalists. Joan Levine, interviewing him for the *Los Angeles Times* in 1976, found him "just as charmingly unpredictable as he is on screen. He is quick witted, often saying outrageous things while keeping the straightest face. One has to listen carefully to keep up with his soft-spoken, glib commentaries. He has a compact but very muscular frame, which he accentuates with tight T-shirts...topped with a newsboy cap. He is always accompanied by a lit cigarette. A European hipster." Despite Marty claiming to be "smaller than life", Levine concluded that "the total effect is surprisingly sexy."

16. Tim married Christine Weadon in 1968 and had two sons, Ben and Edward.

17. *Group Madness* interview, 1983.

Chapter 9

1. *The Kenneth Williams Diaries* edited by Russell Davies, Harper Collins 1993.

2. 11c Albert Hall Mansions, SW7. The letter was reproduced in *Round the Horne*, the Woburn Press, 1973.

3. *The Kenneth Williams Diaries* edited by Russell Davies, Harper Collins 1993.

4. The Duty Engineer's report for *Marty*: BBC2 2000 – VT Ex. Television Centre 6, of 3rd June 1968 recorded that the pioneering use of colour was "generally satisfactory though some faces a little pink. Slight streaking and occasional 'Hanover bars' also. Film was a good match with studio material."

5. Barry Took would keep an eye on all *Round the Horne* programmes, even those farmed out to the fresh writing team of Johnnie Mortimer and Brian Cooke, who caught the spirit of the show immediately. The series, broadcast in the spring of 1968, was a major success although it would finally see the departure of Betty Marsden. Joan Sims was lined up to replace her for the fifth series, set for recording in the early part of 1969.

6. The report, dated 5th June 1968, records the reaction index of sixty-six, which was a very good one. BBC Written Archives.

7. *Took's Eye View* by Barry Took, Robson Books, 1983.

8. A BBC memo headed "Marty no. 5 Muir/Norden" and copied to John Law.

9. A letter penned on 21st May 1968 from Eric Sykes' London offices, 9 Orme Court.

10. 'Marty Goes Back to the Silents...' by Michael Owen, the *Evening Standard*, 15th August 1970.

11. *From Fringe to Flying Circus: Celebrating a Unique Generation of Comedy 1960-1980* by Roger Wilmut, Eyre Methuen Ltd, 1981

12. Both Brooke-Taylor and Junkin were singled out by Dennis Main Wilson for renewed contract options "immediately". He went on to: "recommend that Roland MacLeod should also be contracted for the series. I recommend further that Mary Miller should be put under contract as well." 28th May 1968, BBC Written Archives.

13. Although Nation had written the script that would make his name and fortune when he pitted Doctor Who against the Daleks in 1963, his comedy pedigree was a good one. He had penned several episodes of Tony Hancock's excellent 1963 series for ATV and would go on to work on the Frankie Howerd comedy chiller *The House in Nightmare Park*.

14. The impersonation sees Fraser tackling Bass's celebrated performance as Tevye in *Fiddler on the Roof* which had taken the West End by storm. Although the two had last appeared as Bootsie and Snudge in *Foreign Affairs* in 1964 they had remained linked in the public eye. Not least of all because they had appeared together in the 1967 ABC comedy series *Vacant Lot*. Dick Clement and Ian La Frenais wrote the pilot with Jeremy Lloyd, Jimmy Grafton, Fred Robinson and *Marty* contributor David Climie scripting the rest. *Bootsie and Snudge* veteran Milo Lewis produced the series. Climie later had a hand in the short-lived revival of *Bootsie and Snudge* in 1974.

15. *Marty* would allow the star to indulge in both the fantasy of playing at the top level and his anger at certain aspects of the game. "That sketch I did on a sports commentator (the one that goes progressively madder as England loses the match) was really a personal attack written out of revenge," he explained. "I'm a football fan and I get annoyed by biased commentators."

16. In 1970 Orson Welles and Dom DeLuise performed the sketch, re-named 'The Bachelor', on *The Dean Martin Show*, replacing the gossipy performances of Marty and Tim with ponderous theatricality and gravitas within a gentleman's club.

17. The nation need not have worried for, rather atypically for the time, the BBC retained prints of all thirteen episodes of *Marty*. The only segment currently missing believed wiped is Marty's brief contribution to the 1968 *Christmas Night with the Stars*. This insert was filmed, on location, with the Ealing Grammar School's boy choir on 14th December 1968.

Chapter 10

1. England really was the most happening place on the planet. But it was a handful of years between the mop-top Beatles picking up MBEs at Buckingham Palace and John Lennon sending his medal back in his Rolls Royce; between England winning the World Cup at home and West Germany winning in Mexico. 1969 was the last hurrah. Paul McCartney could sing about "Her Majesty" and hordes of English football fans could proudly wander through the streets of Turin. It was the last stand of England's hipness.

2. 'Marty Goes Back to the Silents...' by Michael Owen, the *Evening Standard*, 15th August 1970.

3. Horne's untimely death at the age of sixty-one curtailed advanced plans for the fifth series of *Round the Horne*. Barry Took almost immediately oversaw another BBC radio show, *Stop Messin' About!*, which, unsurprisingly, starred Kenneth Williams and plugged the *Round the Horne* gap. Hugh Paddick and Douglas Smith were in support. Joan Sims, who was set to star in the aborted *Round the Horne* series, was also included, as often as not warbling songs written by her familiar colleague Myles Rudge. Johnnie Mortimer and Brian Cooke wrote most of the scripts and even Julian and Sandy-alikes continually made an appearance. Williams and Paddick would resurrect them one last time in 1987 when Terry Wogan stood in for Kenneth Horne in *Wogan's Radio Fun*.

4. Letter dated 2nd October 1968, BBC Written Archives, and one that contradicts the letter from Dennis Main Wilson that kick-started *Scott On...* in 1964, a letter that does include call for a "format" from Marty and Barry. Writers as diverse and talented as Dick Vosburgh, Dave Freeman and John Kane wrote the subsequent *Scott On...* programmes, mainly under the production eye of Peter Whitmore. Strangely enough there is no record of Marty and Barry approaching the BBC with regards *Dad's Army* which, from July 1968, had seen Clive Dunn and writers Jimmy Perry and David Croft unashamedly presenting (in the opinion of this writer at least) Old Johnson from *Bootsie and Snudge* under the name of Corporal Jones.

5. Even so, Marty wasn't involved in Spike Milligan's belated return to the BBC for the first of his Q series in the March of 1969. Spike, the godfather of alternative comedy, was a one-man force although it is safe to assume that without *Marty*, Spike would not have been given the call for Q.

6. Letter dated 20th February 1969, BBC Written Archives.

7. The report, dated 25th April 1969, gave the show a Reaction Index of eighty-two, which was astronomically high. BBC Written Archives.

8. 'Marty Makes A Movie' by David Hunn, *Photoplay*, November 1969.

9. Songs like 'The Elephant Song' and 'Mavis Wavertree' were amongst those previously heard in *Marty*. John Junkin and Denis King had also written the song for Marty's contribution to *Christmas Night With the Stars*: "It was called 'A Joyous Time of the Year' and had a joke at the expense of Don Partridge simply because it was like a Partridge in a Pear Tree," chuckles Denis King. The song was released as a Decca Records single with, helpfully, 'The B Side' as the B side track. Both numbers

were included as bonus tracks on the 2007 compact disc release of *I Feel A Song Going Off*. In 1973 Junkin, King and Tim Brooke-Taylor teamed up with Barry Cryer for the radio show *Hello Cheeky*: a showcase of non-stop silliness in song and prose. In 1976 Yorkshire Television presented it with pictures.

10. Decca Records reissued the recording in their popular *The World of...* series; a collection that re-packaged everyone from Paddy Roberts to the Goodies. Marty's album had an additional prefix: *The Crazy World of Marty Feldman*. Only a handful of artistes got more than the "world" including *The Romantic World of Anthony Newley* and *The Big Band World of Ted Heath*.

11. Letter dated 16th April 1969, BBC Written Archives.

12. Interview with the author, 12th December 2010.

13. Audience Research Department report dated 28th May 1969, BBC Written Archives. The show received a disappointing Reaction Index of fifty.

14. 'Battling for Laughs' by James Thomas, the *Daily Express*, 29th April 1969. As predicted 'Tooth and Claw' didn't result in a series commission. Of the batch of *Comedy Playhouse* programmes in question the most endearing series to emerge was *The Liver Birds*.

15. Mitchell starred in seven series of the original run of *Till Death Us Do Part* from 1966 to 1975, and the character was still being revived for series and specials well into the 1990s. In America, Alf was re-invented as Archie Bunker in *All in the Family*. Carroll O'Connor starred in the show throughout the 1970s.

16. 'All About Marty', *The Observer*, 13th April 1969.

17. *Rent-a-Dick* being a notably ramshackle romp packed to the gills with the cream of British comedy and, as directed by Jim Clark, often resembling the Feldman vehicle, as well as the film version of *Up Pompeii* and its two historical sequels for star Frankie Howerd.

18. 'Marty Makes A Movie' by David Hunn, *Photoplay*, November 1969.

19. 'Success Goes to Marty's Stomach' by William Hall, *The Show*, 4th November 1969.

20. 'Marty Makes A Movie' by David Hunn, *Photoplay*, November 1969.

21. 'Success Goes to Marty's Stomach' by William Hall, *The Show*, 4th November 1969.

22. 'Marty Makes A Movie' by David Hunn, *Photoplay*, November 1969.

23. Julie Ege first came to prominence in Britain as a James Bond Girl in *On Her Majesty's Secret Service*. Her star career was brief but students of her work are recommended to study her in Hammer Films' *Creatures the World Forgot* and *The Legend of the 7 Golden Vampires*. She tries to seduce Leslie Phillips in *The Magnificent Seven Deadly Sins* and succeeds with Jack Palance, much to her ill-fate, in *Craze*. She is turned into one of *The Mutations* by Donald Pleasence and raises temperatures as Vincent Price's nurse in *Percy's Progress*. After she retired from acting she actually became a qualified nurse back in Norway. She died from breast cancer in 2008 at the age of sixty-four.

24. In fact he only went on to direct fun nonsense like the frantic all-star comedy *Rent-a-Dick* and the knowing Vincent Price/Peter Cushing horror *Madhouse*. As an editor he remained at the top, winning an Academy Award for *The Killing Fields* in 1984. Tellingly, Marty himself clung to him in Hollywood and signed him up as his editor on his directorial debut *The Last Remake of Beau Geste*. The animations for *Every Home Should Have One* were by Richard Williams, himself a later Oscar-winner for his work on *Who Framed Roger Rabbit?*

25. *Monthly Film Bulletin* review by John Gillett, April 1970.

26. Michael Fish, whose boutique was on Clifford Street, catered for the likes of David Bowie and the Rolling Stones as well as providing the hip style of Peter Sellers in *There's A Girl in My Soup* and the distinctive frilly shirts for Jon Pertwee in *Doctor Who*.

27. 'Last Words of the Pop-Eyed Star' by Baz Bamigboye in New York, *The Sun*, 4th December 1982.

Chapter 11

1. 'That Marty Face – I Never Noticed It' by Barry Took, the *Radio Times*, 5th June 1969.

2. *Took's Eye View* by Barry Took, Robson Books, 1983.

3. *Points of View* afforded the viewing and listening public the opportunity to write

to the BBC and have their opinions aired on television. The arch introductions linked the reading out of the letters – said missives in vision with a voice-over from a suitably disgruntled or elated actor. The show started in 1961 and is still going strong. Barry Took wasn't the first host and he certainly wasn't the last but he left an indelible mark on the programme. His tenure from 1979 to 1986 covered a shifting Golden Age of television. As a result an entire generation remembers Took as a wry pundit rather than anything else.

4. Contractual letter dated 1st June 1968, BBC Written Archives.

5. 'That Marty Face – I Never Noticed It' by Barry Took, the *Radio Times*, 5th June 1969

6. Memo from Jack Beale of the copyright department dated 6th February 1970, BBC Written Archives.

7. 'More in Marty Than Meets the Eye', the *Daily Mirror*, 31st March 1970.

8. Letter dated 13th May 1969, BBC Written Archives.

9. Second letter, dated 20th May 1969, BBC Written Archives.

10. 'That Marty Face – I Never Noticed It' by Barry Took, the *Radio Times*, 5th June 1969

11. Vintage Marty material was included in the 1981 special *Dean Martin's Comedy Classics*.

12. 'Marty Goes Back to the Silents...' by Michael Owen, the *Evening Standard*, 15th August 1970.

13. Interview with the author, 26th January 2011.

14. 'American Dreams', John Hall on US TV's latest find, 19th August 1970. Marty had never suffered Hollywood fools gladly. The Kenneth Williams diary entry for Sunday 10th September 1967 records a journey "to Talk of the Town for the show. The tops was Tony Martin & Cyd Charisse and they were absolutely terrible. Lost the house halfway. Marty Feldman came round with Lauretta and was very sweet about it all. He actually said, 'The show was going fine till Burke and Hare came on...' which is really true." The show was never transmitted.

15. 'Marty Goes Back to the Silents...' by Michael Owen, the *Evening Standard*, 15th August 1970.

16. Letter from Jack Beale to Michael Mills, 20th August 1970, BBC Written Archives.

17. Michael Mills had made it clear internally at the BBC that he wanted to pay as little as possible for the programme. On 25th August Jack Beale had offered Kenneth Ewing a "joint fee of £750". Secretary Jill Foster had added a hand-written note to this correspondence recording that Ewing wanted more money. Finally, the agreed fee stood at £850 with fares included, plus £3.10 expenses per day.

18. Letter from Jill Foster to Jack Beale, dated 1st October 1970, BBC Written Archives. The director in question was Gordon Flemyng who, a decade earlier, had helmed several episodes of *The Army Game*.

19. One of the key *Marty* players who had become a regular in the second series of *Broaden Your Mind* and made his first appearance in *The Goodies* as a corrupt police constable in the fourth episode. Marty would appear in *The Goodies* by proxy when director Jim Franklin included a clip of the *Marty* sketch 'Jungle Florist' in the 1975 episode 'Scatty Safari'.

20. *Lordags Hjornet*, Dutch TV interview, December 1977.

21. A discovery of the TV talent show *Opportunity Knocks*, Liverpool-born Freddie Starr dominated 1970s variety with his frantic comedy and energetic impersonations – notably as an ape-like Mick Jagger. Although he has been an infrequent television performer since the late 1990s he has continued to tour the country with his unique brand of humour. His immortality is undoubtedly assured thanks to a headline in an edition of *The Sun* newspaper from 1986 which screamed: "Freddie Starr Ate My Hamster". The article alleged that Starr had returned to a friend's house after a nightclub performance in Manchester and demanded a sandwich. When the friend's girlfriend refused because of the lateness of the hour, Starr put her pet hamster between two pieces of bread and ate it! In his 2001 autobiography, *Unwrapped*, Starr denies the story stating: "I have never eaten or even nibbled a live hamster, gerbil, guinea pig, mouse, shrew, vole or any other small mammal."

22. Interview with the author, 8th April 2008.

23. Bernard Cribbins had played the part previously and the 'Pride' segment resurrected another of his old *Comedy Playhouse* successes, 'Impasses', as written by Ray Galton and Alan Simpson. Cribbins' role here was played by *Bootsie and Snudge*

star Alfie Bass. Harry H. Corbett's chief adversary in the 'Lust' sequence is played by *Round the Horne* star Bill Pertwee.

24. Indeed, it had been the fact that Groucho Marx was going to appear in the show that tempted Spike Milligan to join the writing team. The mackerel that got the mackerel, in fact. Spike would stop at nothing to write some material especially for Groucho, his boyhood hero and inspiration. Marty however was disappointed: "You want your heroes to be marvellous people," he said. "I met Groucho and all he did was talk about his bowels. You could not talk to him as a comic or a wit. You were talking to an old man."

25. These writers included Rudy de Luca and Barry Levinson who had contributed to *The Tim Conway Show* for CBS, veteran scribe Sheldon Keller who had written for Danny Kaye and Dick Van Dyke, and Larry Gelbart himself whose book for *A Funny Thing Happened on the Way to the Forum* had been filmed in England by Richard Lester.

Chapter 12

1. 'Marty Goes Back to the Silents...' by Michael Owen, the *Evening Standard*, 15th August 1970.

2. 'Your Laughs are Killing Me' by Ken Bailey, the *People*, 3rd October 1971.

3. *Oz* had first appeared in Australia in 1963. The London-based publication first appeared in 1967 and become a vital part of swinging sixties culture. The other high profile witnesses during the 1971 decency trial were disc jockey John Peel, artist Felix Topolski, activist Caroline Coon and lateral thinker Edward de Bono. Brian Leary was the prosecuting counsel. The three accused publishers were found guilty but acquitted on appeal. In November 1991 the BBC screened *The Trials of Oz*, Tony Palmer's dramatization of the trial. Lee Cornes played Marty.

4. 'There's More to Marty Than Meets the Eye' by Diane Blackwell, *The Australian Women's Weekly*, 26th January 1972.

5. Interview with the author, 29th May 2011. Brian Trenchard-Smith continues to enjoy a successful career directing for both television and the cinema. His cult favourite hits include *BMX Bandits, Night of the Demons 2, Leprechaun 3, Leprechaun 4: In Space, Britannic* and *Tyrannosaurus Azteca*.

6. Marty would mock Lew Grade for years afterwards. His appearance on the Dutch

TV chat show *Lordags Hjornet* was recorded on Grade's birthday: "Does Lew Grade mean anything in Denmark?" he asked wickedly. "Who's Lew Grade?" said the interviewer. "Precisely!"

7. 'There's More to Marty Than Meets the Eye' by Diane Blackwell, *The Australian Women's Weekly*, 26th January 1972. Years before Barry Took witnessed Marty's mortal fear of pigeons: "We would be strolling around central London and I would often have to walk one or two feet in front of him just to scare the pigeons out of his path."

8. Letter from Duncan Wood to John Moore and David Gower, dated 6th June 1972, BBC Written Archives.

9. The *Evening Standard*, 21st July 1972.

10. *The Two Ronnies* would resurrect vintage *At Last the 1948 Show* material while minor league *Marty* material was picked up by Howerd for his 1971 Thames special *The Laughing Stock of Television*. Marty Feldman Scripts Limited had been established to keep tabs on his written work, usually the re-cycling or repeating of vintage material.

11. Contract dated 27th September 1973, BBC Written Archives.

12. *The Kenneth Williams Diaries* edited by Russell Davies, Harper Collins, 1993. A decade after this particular *What's My Line?* recording, when Kenneth Williams was still whoring away his talents on television panel games, he returned to Manchester for *Whose Baby?* on Saturday 5th May 1984. George Best — a momentary picture of sobriety — was also on the panel.

13. This, and all subsequent Derek Griffiths quotes, interview with the author, 30th November 2010.

14. Letter from Brian Spiby, Assistant Head of Artists' Contracts, TV, dated 17th July 1973.

15. Letter from Dennis Main Wilson to Jill Foster, dated 17th October 1973, BBC Written Archives.

16. The *New York Times* obituary by Carol Lawson, 4th December 1982. Still, even in Hollywood the sheer amount of what he was earning never really registered. "I've always been a fool with money," he said.

17. *The Adventure of Sherlock Holmes' Smarter Brother* publicity, 1975. It had also been mentioned in the classic Holmes adventure *The Hound of the Baskervilles*. It was the house that the Goons built in a way. Anne Levy's second husband, Ted Levy, was a respected architect and found this, the perfect house for Marty. The painting and decorating provided one of the first jobs for the firm that Spike Milligan's son, Sean, had set up with Peter Sellers' son, Michael.

Chapter 13

1. *Making FrankenSense of Young Frankenstein*, 2000.

2. Dwight Frye had played Fritz in *Frankenstein* (1931). Bela Lugosi had created the role of Igor in *Son of Frankenstein* in 1939. Rondo Hatton had already set out his stall as the monster movie star without make-up. Deformed as a result of acromegaly; his startling features saw him cast as *The Brute Man* and the Creeper in the Sherlock Holmes classic *The Pearl of Death*. These were popular on late night TV at the time of Marty's first Hollywood experience.

3. *Making FrankenSense of Young Frankenstein*, 2000.

4. Kahn had originally been cast as the flighty Inga but turned it down. Mars played the Lionel Atwill memorial role from *Son of Frankenstein,* complete with hilarious twist on his darts match with Basil Rathbone.

5. *Making FrankenSense of Young Frankenstein*, 2000.

6. *Young Frankenstein*, audio commentary, 2000.

7. *Young Frankenstein: Building the Perfect Beast*, Wholly Cow Productions for Fox, 1999.

8. Interview for Mexican television, 1974.

9. Interview for Mexican television, 1974. Hammer Films had just produced *Frankenstein and the Monster From Hell* and *Young Frankenstein* was clearly not a Hammer parody but a Universal one. Indeed, there was a very tangible link with the past forged by the casting of John Carradine. He had played one of the hunters who encounters the blind hermit in *The Bride of Frankenstein* and, playing Count Dracula, he appeared with Glenn Strange as the Frankenstein Monster in both *House of Frankenstein* and *House of Dracula*. Carradine recorded a voice-over for *Young Frankenstein* in the role of Beaufort Frankenstein but, rather annoyingly, this scene was deleted from the finished film.

10. *Young Frankenstein* audio commentary, 2000.

11. *Making FrankenSense of Young Frankenstein*, 2000.

12. 'It's Marty Frankenstein' by Ivor Davis in Hollywood, the *Daily Express*, 24th January 1975.

13. *Young Frankenstein* audio commentary, 2000.

14. An enchanting still image of the scene survives, however, and graced the back cover of the 20th Century Fox Home Video DVD release of the film in 2000.

15. *Making FrankenSense of Young Frankenstein*, 2000.

16. *Lordags Hjornet*, Dutch TV interview, December 1977.

17. *Making FrankenSense of Young Frankenstein*, 2000.

18. The 1983 remake of the classic wartime comedy starring Jack Benny and Carole Lombard. Brooks starred opposite his wife Anne Bancroft.

19. This, and all subsequent Alan Spencer quotes, interview with the author, 1st June 2011.

20. *Young Frankenstein* audio commentary, 2000.

21. The film got only one major nomination; for Best Adapted Screenplay. Gene Wilder and Mel Brooks lost out to Francis Ford Coppola and Mario Puzo for *The Godfather: Part II*. Gene S. Cantamessa and Richard Portman were nominated for Best Sound while Madeline Kahn received a Best Supporting Actress nomination for *Blazing Saddles*.

22. The outside of the theatre screening the preview of Mel Funn's *Silent Movie* at the end of the film is littered with posters for *Young Frankenstein*.

23. 'Marty Goes Back to the Silents...' by Michael Owen, the *Evening Standard*, 15th August 1970.

24. The *Sunday Express*, 16th May 1976.

25. David Weddle also remembers Marty being in awe of, but at ease with the great

American comedians: "Marty did meet Red Skelton and Dick Van Dyke, and had great admiration for both of them." Indeed, Van Dyke had starred in *The Comedian*, a fictionalised and unofficial account of the life of Marty's biggest idol, Buster Keaton. "He never met Buster," says Weddle, "but he did meet his wife, Eleanor. We talked about this and I know he would have loved to meet him. I believe Eleanor gave Marty a porkpie hat," Buster's iconic trademark. Keaton's last completed work was *A Funny Thing Happened on the Way to the Forum*, which he shot in Britain. It was directed by Richard Lester and: "I know Marty did talk to Richard Lester about the making of *Forum* while he was working on *The Bed Sitting Room*," says Weddle. "He said that Lester regretted he did not make better use of Keaton in *Forum*. But obviously the script and Keaton's health would have made that difficult to do."

26. *Penthouse* interview by Richard Kleiner, October 1980.

27. *Lordags Hjornet*, Dutch TV interview, December 1977. Marty had become somewhat disillusioned by Tati at this stage: "Tati fascinates me," he continued. "I'd love to make movies in the way Tati makes them. I hope now to be able to do that. Tati works in a very Keatonesque kind of way. He works much the way Keaton used to work... There was a time when Tati made the M. Hulot pictures... he was more subjective. I loved him then. I like him now but I do not love him anymore... There was a time when Tati was observing people under a microscope but he was also the creature under the microscope. He's totally become the scientist and he used to be the bacteria as well and that's when I loved him."

28. *Monthly Film Bulletin* review by Geoff Brown, Volume 43 no. 515, December 1976.

29. The *Morning Star*, 4th December 1982.

30. *Young Frankenstein* audio commentary, 2000.

31. *Penthouse* interview by Richard Kleiner, October 1980.

32. *Lordags Hjornet*, Dutch TV interview, December 1977. In fact the closest translation for tummler is a noisy mischief-maker or prankster which just about sums up Mel Brooks. *Silent Movie* got a clutch of Golden Globe nominations in 1976. Mel Brooks was nominated as Best Actor in a Musical or Comedy and the film was nominated as Best Picture Musical/Comedy. Bernadette Peters was nominated as Best Supporting Actress, Marty as Best Supporting Actor. When the winners were announced on 29th January 1977, he lost out to Laurence Olivier in *Marathon Man*.

Chapter 14

1. *Lordags Hjornet*, Dutch TV interview, December 1977.

2. Marty's character name was only a slight deviation from Ormond Sacker, as featured in Sir Arthur Conan Doyle's first draft of *A Study in Scarlet*. Holmes himself uses the name Sigerson as an alias in *The Adventure of the Empty House*.

3. *Monthly Film Bulletin* review by John Pym, Volume 43 number 505, February 1976.

4. Wilmer had chalked up thirteen episodes as Sherlock Holmes for BBC television in the sixties while Walters had made a fine Doctor Watson opposite Christopher Lee's great detective in *Sherlock Holmes and the Deadly Necklace* (1962). Walters had also joined Peter Jeffrey for a gag appearance as Watson and Holmes in *The Best House in London* (1969). Gene Wilder, nervous at directing his own film, had asked Mel Brooks to take on the duties. Brooks declined but did offer advice and a brief vocal cameo as the lion tamer. Tonally, the film leans toward the 1939 Basil Rathbone classic *The Adventures of Sherlock Holmes*, complete with Wilder in top hat and indulging his love of music hall.

5. 'Success Goes to Marty's Stomach' by William Hall, the *Show*, 4th November 1969.

6. The *Sunday Express*, 16th May 1976.

7. "Marty Goes Back to the Silents... " by Michael Owen, the *Evening Standard*, 15th August 1970.

8. Ironically, Marty brought Hollywood clout to European comedy. *40 Gradi all'ombra del Lenzuolo* or *Sex With A Smile* as it became for English-speaking audiences, saw him as a tight-suited, carrot-chomping Chicago bodyguard who stayed fully clothed and close to his ward whether she was in a swimming pool, a romantic clinch or a shower. He had played American aviator Orville Wright in the West German, French and Austrian co-production *Jumbo – Ein Elefantenlenben*. Slapstick comedy and his bizarre appearance were always to the fore in these ventures.

9. *Spike – An Intimate Memoir* by Norma Farnes, Fourth Estate 2003.

10. *Took's Eye View* by Barry Took, Robson Books, 1983.

11. Marty himself was the proud owner of three cars: a prized dune buggy, a dark blue Rolls Royce and a Chevy runaround. He had also, unsuccessfully, tried to re-

launch an old British hit, *The Walrus and the Carpenter*, on American television as *Flannery and Quilt*. The misadventures of a ham-fisted longshoreman and a mild-mannered calligrapher had more of *The Odd Couple* about it.

12. Although Marty would enjoy these jam sessions it would remind him of his limitations: "I can never remember to get out of the way of the other instruments. I especially offend the bass player – my bass drum is getting in his way all the time. I play bop drums. I grew up in a bop era, and I'm dropping bombs in my bass drum." He had already played his last solo trumpet voluntarily: "There's a tremendous gap between your head and the bell of your trumpet," he said. "I was playing trumpet by myself in the corner at a party in America with a blissful expression on my face. For two hours! Lauretta looked at me and said she thought I had really flipped. I was drunk enough to think that I was playing marvellous things. Someone was sober enough to record them. When they played it back to me I realised I had been talking musical gibberish. That's the last time I played the trumpet." Subsequently, Marty's list of hobbies would include: "Digging baroque Italian composers, writing poetry and enjoying jazz. He plays drums, trumpet, sousaphone and value trombone to himself – no one else will listen."

13. *Penthouse* interview by Richard Kleiner, October 1980.

14. "With a different set of equipment I might have been a footballer," he told David Hunn of *Photoplay* in 1969. Marty's list of hobbies would invariably list: "Full-time soccer fanatic (playing and watching)."

15. 'Off the Screen' by Barbara Wilkins, *People Weekly*, 29th August 1977. As he told *Penthouse* in 1980, the English are "still a little bit suspicious of anaesthetics. If you're a man, you take a swig of rum and they cut your leg off. They think having something like chloroform is rather effete. The English think of hypnotists, psychiatrists, and all fringe religions as the same thing. On the other hand, maybe it's gone too far the other way in America. The mind doctors become the shamans and replace the priests." Marty had distrusted psychiatrists since the *Educating Archie* days, of course. "Pay me first or else I'll let you go mad!" He saw them as housekeepers. "They're headkeepers. They look after the place when you go out of your head! But I'm very particular about who I let in my house. How much more particular should I be about who I let in my head!"

16. He had already travelled to Canada at the end of January 1975 to direct a cat food commercial for television and Mel Brooks had given him an episode of his Robin Hood spoof television series *When Things Were Rotten* to cut his directorial teeth on. He had also claimed direction of several plays on the London fringe in the 1960s.

17. The *Sunday Express*, 16th May 1976. Grant had, himself, contributed to the essence of *Boy's Own* adventure via Hollywood in his 1939 classic *Gunga Din*, made over at RKO. Marty was put next to the bungalow of that other East End boy, Alfred Hitchcock, and he had a full set of drums set up just in case he got writer's block and wanted to bash away his frustration.

18. Interview by Bart Mills, *The Guardian*, 15th September 1976.

19. *Lordags Hjornet*, Dutch TV interview, December 1977.

20. Interview by Bart Mills, *The Guardian*, 15th September 1976.

21. *Penthouse* interview by Richard Kleiner, October 1980.

22. *Lordags Hjornet*, Dutch TV interview, December 1977.

23. The *Sunday Express*, 16th May 1976.

24. 'Last Words of the Pop-Eyed Star' by Baz Bamigboye in New York, *The Sun*, 4th December 1982.

25. *Lordags Hjornet*, Dutch TV interview, December 1977.

26. *Young Frankenstein: Building the Perfect Beast*, Wholly Cow Productions for Fox, 1999.

27. Interview by Bart Mills, *The Guardian*, 15th September 1976.

28. *Lordags Hjornet*, Dutch TV interview, December 1977. When Marty guested on *The Muppet Show* in 1980 he performed a sketch with a camel whom he named Lauretta. It was perhaps his affectionate nod of gratitude for his wife's assistance on *The Last Remake of Beau Geste*.

29. Marty's widowed mother was now living in Spain. "It's where Jews go when they can't go to Miami," he explained, "it's Miami with garlic." Cissy would outlive her son. She died on 12th June 1986, a month before her 73rd birthday.

30. Interview by Bart Mills, *The Guardian*, 15th September 1976.

31. *Terry-Thomas Tells Tall Tales: An Autobiography*, Robson Books, 1991.

32. *Lordags Hjornet*, Dutch TV interview, December 1977.

33. *Penthouse* interview by Richard Kleiner, October 1980.

34. *The Hollywood Interview*, 13th February 2008.

35. 'Off the Screen' by Barbara Wilkins, *People Weekly*, 29th August 1977.

36. *Monthly Film Bulletin* review by Tom Milne, Volume 44 no. 526, November 1977.

37. *Lordags Hjornet*, Dutch TV interview, December 1977.

38. *Monthly Film Bulletin* review by Tom Milne, Volume 44 no. 526, November 1977.

39. Letter from David Gower to Jane Annakin, 9th June 1976, BBC Written Archives.

40. Marty finally signed the contract on 14th June 1976 and his contribution to forty years of BBC television was duly included. Marty finally put Howard West in charge of all these dealings and put cheques through his suitably named America-based corporation, Wanka Productions Limited. The fact that America didn't get the disrespectful joke delighted Marty. The BBC's John Dyas noted on the 24th January 1978 that "Howard West is not going to be an easy person to deal with." While West wrote to Barry Took's wife, Lyn on 21st November 1978 saying: "As I'm sure you are aware, the BBC is not the most efficient organization."

41. *Took's Eye View* by Barry Took, Robson Books, 1983. Barry was finding great success on radio with shows *The Impressionists* and *Kaleidoscope* while his television appearances included *On the Move* and Yorkshire TV's sketch show *N.U.T.S.* which he also devised. Roy Kinnear, fresh from Marty's Sherlock Holmes romp and set to appear in *Beau Geste*, also starred. Perhaps for Barry those memories of warming up for *Marty* were still raw. He was his own man again. In a smaller pond, but his own man nonetheless.

42. *In God We Tru$t* publicity, 15th August 1980.

Chapter 15

1. *Lordags Hjornet*, Dutch TV interview, December 1977.

2. 'Off the Screen' by Barbara Wilkins, *People Weekly*, 29th August 1977.

3. *Penthouse* interview by Richard Kleiner, October 1980.

4. 'Last Words of the Pop-Eyed Star' by Baz Bamigboye in New York, *The Sun*, 4th December 1982.

5. 'Last Words of the Pop-Eyed Star' by Baz Bamigboye in New York, *The Sun*, 4th December 1982.

6. The *LA Times* obituary by Charles Champlin, 9th December 1982.

7. 'Religious Mania' by Colin Dangaard in Hollywood, the *Daily Express*, 28th August 1980. As he said in 1977: "I worked on a film once with a producer who said to me his main fear was that I would fall on my face and figure it!"

8. Interviewed by Thomson Prentice, the *Daily Mail*, 30th December 1977.

9. 'Marty Goes Back to the Silents...' by Michael Owen, the *Evening Standard*, 15th August 1970.

10. 'Too Old to Die Young, Too Old to Grow Up' by David Lewin, the *Daily Mail*, 4th December 1982.

11. 'Off the Screen' by Barbara Wilkins, *People Weekly*, 29th August 1977.

12. In September 1977 he represented the United Kingdom in NBC's celebrity charity sports special *Us Against the World*.

13. 'Off the Screen' by Barbara Wilkins, *People Weekly*, 29th August 1977. Anita Bryant was a former beauty queen and pop singer who, in 1977, was a political activist in favour of prohibiting adoption for gay couples in Florida. She was famously hit in the face by a gay rights protester's fruit pie.

14. *The New York Times* obituary by Carol Lawson, 4th December 1982.

15. *Penthouse* interview by Richard Kleiner, October 1980.

16. *Lordags Hjornet*, Dutch TV interview, December 1977.

17. *Penthouse* interview by Richard Kleiner, October 1980. Marty was a humanist. He detested the liberal gun culture of America. He couldn't stand dishonesty. He said that: "Limited free speech is worse than no free speech. It gives the illusion of

freedom." But, as his religious belief had been fractured, so had his political. He referred to himself as "apolitical, not a communist or an anarchist, though. I'm interested in protest. I'd simply like to see freedom of choice everywhere. I insulted a Cabinet Minister who came up to me and said, 'Of course you vote Labour,' and I said, 'No I don't because I'm a socialist!'"

18. Interview by Thomson Prentice, the *Daily Mail*, 30th December 1977.

19. Marty could find his rhythm of life within baseball as well. But it always came back to music. As he told *Penthouse* in 1980: "You know, this collaboration idea is true of any relationship in life. It's true for a shortstop – knowing that second base will be covered: he just turns and spins and throws the ball to second, and second base will throw it to first base, knowing the man is going to be up, going to be keeping his foot on the base. It's faith in each other, knowing that nobody is going to drop the ball. And yet it happens. With Billy Russell it happens all the time. And yet the [Los Angeles] Dodgers pull off double play after double play, because they have a kind of trust in each other as professionals, because they play together all the time. Like jazz musicians. You've got to play together a long while to be good."

20. *Group Madness* interview, 1983. The culture of celebrity didn't impress him. "Being a celebrity simply means being a known face," he said. "It doesn't matter whether the face belongs to a mass murderer or a saint; if it's known, you get the celebrity treatment."

21. Bruckman was a gag writer for some of Marty's greatest comedy heroes, including Laurel and Hardy, W.C. Fields, Harold Lloyd and, most notably of all, Buster Keaton. He worked on such films as *Our Hospitality*, *Sherlock Jr.* and *The General*. He committed suicide after work dried up for him in the 1950s. In 1996 *Young Frankenstein* star Peter Boyle won an Emmy for his performance as a psychic in *The X Files* episode 'Clyde Bruckman's Final Repose' (writer Darin Morgan 'borrowed' the name).

22. Weddle remembers having an office "about a mile across from Marty's old bungalow on the Universal lot. It is still there. Every month or so I walk down there and stop for a moment's reflection. Once I saw Vince Vaughn inside so I guess it's his bungalow now."

23. *Lordags Hjornet*, Dutch TV interview, December 1977.

24. *In God We Tru$t* publicity brochure, 15th August 1980.

25. Sellers failed to win the Oscar and it has been suggested the sheer disappointment

hastened his death from a heart attack in July 1980, just a few weeks before Marty's film was released.

26. *In God We Tru$t* publicity brochure, 15th August 1980.

27. He had lapel badges of all three of his comedy heroes and would often wear them out in and around Hollywood and was forever happy to explain that they were his Holy Trinity. It was Marty's equivalent of rosary beads.

28. *Lordags Hjornet*, Dutch TV interview, December 1977.

29. *Penthouse* interview by Richard Kleiner, October 1980.

30. 'Religious Mania' by Colin Dangaard in Hollywood, the *Daily Express*, 28th August 1980.

31. *Penthouse* interview by Richard Kleiner, October 1980.

32. Altman's hits of the decade included his two unquestioned masterpieces, *M.A.S.H.* and *Nashville*.

33. Blewitt had previously worked largely in documentary, including the first two *That's Entertainment* films. He had also edited the successful rock 'n' roll biopic *The Buddy Holly Story*.

34. *Penthouse* interview by Richard Kleiner, October 1980.

35. Kaufman, riding high in popularity at the time thanks to both *Saturday Night Live* and *Taxi*, brought an eccentric flair to his supporting role. His flamboyant performance contrasted with Marty's subtle innocence perfectly. The very fact that Kaufman was cast at all highlights Marty's clout as a comedy filmmaker.

36. 'Too Old to Die Young, Too Old to Grow Up' by David Lewin, the *Daily Mail*, 4th December 1982.

37. *Took's Eye View* by Barry Took, Robson Books, 1983.

38. *The New York Times* obituary by Carol Lawson, 4th December 1982.

Chapter 16

1. *Penthouse* interview by Richard Kleiner, October 1980.

2. In 1986 Spencer created the cult TV detective spoof *Sledge Hammer!* He subsequently co-wrote and created *The Nutt House* with Mel Brooks. *Young Frankenstein* actress Cloris Leachman starred. "Mark Blankfield was also in that show," says Spencer. "I told him that he was like a surrogate Marty because he was a devotee of Buster Keaton and could do wonderful physical comedy. Marty was unique but Mark has that same quality. He was tremendously flattered." Spencer's current project is *Bullet in the Face* for the Independent Film Channel.

3. *Penthouse* interview by Richard Kleiner, October 1980.

4. For Muppet nerds – and who isn't? – Marty's episode is especially poignant for the *Sesame Street* cross-over. The Ali Baba scene features "Open Sesame", you see, and out pour the Count, Bert and Ernie and the gang. Marty is particularly taken with the Cookie Monster. There is something about those eyes! So much so, that during the finale all the Muppets have Marty eyes. Marty's appearance is testament to his star standing at the time. The eclectic list of notable guest stars that season included Roger Moore, Johnny Cash, Gene Kelly and Debbie Harry!

5. Granted a limited release in 1982 with a musical score by Michael Legrand, the film was subsequently re-edited and given a more science-fiction friendly score by Morton Stevens. It was released in March 1984, nearly eighteen months after Marty's death.

6. 1981 also saw the release of Bruce "Baby Man" Baum's single 'Marty Feldman Eyes' on the Boot label: a timely parody of 'Bette Davis Eyes' by Kim Carnes.

7. 'Too Old to Die Young, Too Old to Grow Up' by David Lewin, the *Daily Mail*, 4th December 1982.

8. 'Last Words of the Pop-Eyed Star' by Baz Bamigboye in New York, *The Sun*, 4th December 1982.

9. After Marty's death David Weddle became a successful producer and writer for American television. He helped re-launch both *The Twilight Zone* and *Battlestar Galactica* as well as writing episodes of *Star Trek: Deep Space Nine*, *Ghost Stories* and *The Fearing Mind*. He worked for three years as a writer and co-executive producer on *CSI: Crime Scene Investigation* for CBS and has recently signed up to write and co-executive produce the second season of Steven Spielberg's *Falling Skies*. "Writing for

a TV show, you end up sitting in a room with five or six other writers brainstorming episodes," says Weddle. "These sessions of bouncing ideas around and re-writing your scripts are not unlike the fun times Marty and I spent together thirty years ago. If it hadn't had been for his encouragement, I would never have become a writer. I am forever in his debt."

10. 'My Fight to Save Marty by Spike' by Bob Graham, the *Evening Standard*, 6th December 1982.

11. *Penthouse* interview by Richard Kleiner, October 1980.

12. 'Last Words of the Pop-Eyed Star' by Baz Bamigboye in New York, *The Sun*, 4th December 1982.

13. WitzEnd Productions did ultimately make thirteen episodes of *Mog* for Central Television in 1985 and 1986; largely adapted and scripted by Dick Clement and Ian La Frenais. Allen McKeown, a mainstay of WitzEnd in Los Angeles and newly married to Tracey Ullman, would act as executive producer. Enn Reitel played Marty's intended role.

14. 'Too Old to Die Young, Too Old to Grow Up' by David Lewin, the *Daily Mail*, 4th December 1982.

15. 'My Fight to Save Marty by Spike' by Bob Graham, the *Evening Standard*, 6th December 1982. Speaking in 1977 Marty explained, "Satire in America is possible. It's not that likely because apart from Public Broadcasting America is... commercial television, so there are all sorts of pressures which are put on the people who make programmes. They do do a show called *Saturday Night* [*Live*] which is not unlike *That Was the Week That Was*. It doesn't have the bite but when you see it in context of all the other commercial television shows which have no teeth at all, then it's a pretty courageous show. But that's the only one. If it doesn't sting, if it doesn't hurt anybody, if there's no pain, then the satire hasn't worked. If somebody doesn't yell, you haven't hit your target. So if they don't yell, I feel I've failed."

16. Boyle was cast as a character called Moon in tribute to the Who drummer Keith Moon who was originally to have appeared in the film. Suitably, his boyish good looks had swollen to Robert Newton-like features through alcohol. He had died in 1978 at the age of thirty-two.

17. Marty had strong opinions of where the different groups sat at the comedy table. "[*Beyond the*] *Fringe* was more politically pertinent because it had something to

say about how we chose our leaders and how we allow our leaders to lead us," he was quoted as saying in the *Daily Mail* obituary. "Monty Python is about silliness of behaviour and anarchy. Its general attitude is that life is absurd. The *Fringe* people wanted to try to change things. Monty Python did not."

18. *Group Madness* interview, 1983.

19. Interview with Mike Walsh, Australian Television, 1983.

20. *Lordags Hjornet*, Dutch TV interview, December 1977.

21. 'Last Words of the Pop-Eyed Star' by Baz Bamigboye in New York, *The Sun*, 4th December 1982.

22. 'Too Old to Die Young, Too Old to Grow Up' by David Lewin, the *Daily Mail*, 4th December 1982.

23. *Young Frankenstein* audio commentary, 2000.

24. 'Too Old to Die Young, Too Old to Grow Up' by David Lewin, the *Daily Mail*, 4th December 1982.

25. He even related the whole story in a rather tasteless DC comic strip for *Solo* magazine.

26. YouTube blog, 2007.

27. *The Guardian* report by Penny Chorlton, 4th December 1982.

28. 'Star Marty drugs death riddle' by Alan Watkins, *The Sun*, 4th December 1982.

29. *Mail on Sunday*, 5th December 1982.

30. 'Blunder killed Marty' by Bob Smith in New York, the *News of the World*, 5th December 1982.

31. *Young Frankenstein: Building the Perfect Beast*, Wholly Cow Productions for Fox, 1999.

32. 'Star Marty drugs death riddle' by Alan Watkins, *The Sun*, 4th December 1982.

33. *Mail On Sunday*, 5th December 1982.

34. *The Daily Telegraph* report by Henry Miller in New York, 4th December 1982. On 8th December 1982, *Variety* reported: "He had worked that day and was due to appear only incidentally in final shots to be done."

35. *The Scotsman* obituary, 4th December 1982.

36. 'Last Words of the Pop-Eyed Star' by Baz Bamigboye in New York, *The Sun*, 4th December 1982.

37. *The Scotsman* obituary, 4th December 1982.

38. Interview by Stafford Hildred, the *Daily Star*, 4th December 1982.

39. The actor had played Captain Merdmanger in *The Last Remake of Beau Geste* and the Sheriff of Nottingham in *When Things Were Rotten*.

40. 'Farewell Marty...and he has last laugh' by Philip Finn, *the Daily Express*, 7th December 1982.

Epilogue

1. Interview by Bart Mills, *The Guardian*, 15th September 1976.

2. Interview with Mike Walsh, Australian Television, 1983.

3. 'Lest we forget you, Marty', the *Daily Express*, 10th December 1982.

4. *The Marty Feldman Comedy Machine* Montreaux compilation was screened as part of a Channel 4 salute to ATV on 30th December 1987 while Jonathan Ross hosted *It's Marty Resurrected: Some of the Best of Marty Feldman* on BBC2, 4th July 1995 ahead of the release of a BBC Video compilation.

5. She was interviewed for *Angels Don't Swear: Marty Feldman Revisited*; a BBC Radio 4 celebration hosted by Gene Wilder and broadcast on 22nd March 2007, and she gave her blessing to Jeff Simpson's BBC4 documentary *Marty Feldman: Six Degrees of Separation*, first transmitted on 31st March 2008.

6. Interview by Terry Willows, the *Daily Star*, 11th January 1983.

7. As a result a subsequent staging of *Round the Horne... Revisited* used only Brian Cooke and Johnnie Mortimer material from the fourth series. In 2008 Lyn Took returned to the wealth of work her late husband and Marty had written for a new touring stage production *Round the Horne – Unseen and Uncut*. Jonathan Rigby, Robin Sebastian and Nigel Harrison returned as Kenneth Horne, Kenneth Williams and Hugh Paddick respectively.

8. *Took's Eye View* by Barry Took, Robson Books, 1983.

Photo section

Photos on pages 1, 2, 3 (top), 14 (top and bottom right) and 15 © Pamela Franklin and Suzannah Galland.
Photo on page 14 (bottom left) © Alan Spencer.
Other photos from the author's own collection, and used for the purpose of publicity, criticism and review. Acknowledgment is made to the BBC, Universal, 20th Century Fox, and David Paradine Productions.
Any omissions will be corrected in future editions where possible.

Index